Teaching for
Lifetime Physical Activity
through Quality High School
Physical Education

Publisher: Daryl Fox
Acquisitions Editor: Deirdre McGill
Project Editor: Susan Teahan
Publishing Assistant: Michelle Cadden
Managing Editor: Wendy Earl
Production Editor: Leslie Austin
Copy Editor: Sally Peyrefitte
Proofreader: Martha Ghent
Compositor: Marian Hartsough Associates
Cover Designer: Yvo Riezebos
Cover Artist: Roy Shultz
Manufacturing Buyer: Stacey Weinberger
Marketing Manager: Sandra Lindelof

Library of Congress Cataloging-in-Publication Data

Hastie, Peter A., 1959-
  Teaching for lifetime physical activity through quality high school physical education /
Peter A. Hastie.
    p. cm.
  Includes bibliographical references and index.
  ISBN 0-205-34354-6
    1. Physical education and training—study and teaching (Secondary)—United States.
  I. Title

GV365.H39 2003
613.7'071'173—dc21   2002067454

Benjamin
Cummings

ISBN 0-205-34354-6
1 2 3 4 5 6 7 8 9 10—MAL—06 05 04 03 02
www.aw.com/bc

This book is dedicated to Mr. Randel Robertson,
of Craigslea High School in Australia—
clearly the most outstanding secondary school
physical educator I have seen in action.

P. H.

BRIEF CONTENTS

CONTENTS

If you are a student about to launch yourself into the 15 chapters that follow, you are going to be surprised by what you find. There will be some things here that you have never heard of before—and much more that you might never imagined to be an important part of preparing to become a physical education teacher. If you are a teacher educator, perhaps about to riffle through the pages to see whether the book might be useful for one of the classes in your preservice program, you too will find some unexpected content. To borrow a succinct phrase from the automotive hucksters of Detroit—nobody is going to confuse this with your parents' PE textbook!

Of course, new recruits to teaching and their mentors will be surprised for very different reasons. If you are a novice, there is so much to learn that nearly anything going much beyond your own prior experience in physical education classes may seem new, and sometimes even startling. In addition, previous experience with bland educational materials may have left you quite unprepared for Peter Hastie's brand of straight talk—and his distinctly edgy notions about what ought to be happening in the gymnasia of our public schools.

In contrast, most professors of education will find little here that they have not previously encountered in one form or another. Nevertheless, it will not take much browsing for them to get the sense that this book does not fit the template of expectations for a typical curriculum and instruction guide that purports to nurture future educators. The author has framed the entire discussion of what matters in the physical education curriculum from a perspective that is dramatically different from the norm, but that also is perfectly clear to any reader (and that indeed is a surprise).

For teacher educators, that conceptual frame will give new meaning to didactic content concerning methods and materials—and a startling sense of importance and urgency about the need to get them right for the next generation of physical education practitioners. Many of us in teacher education are quite unused to finding a textbook author who betrays unsettling passions and genuinely divergent opinions. But here he is, and those of you (whether professor or student trainee) who can listen with an open mind are in for an exciting ride.

A single proposition undergirds the entire book. If physical education classes do not make a demonstrable difference in how students subsequently behave as adults, then they were not worth the valuable time and resources devoted to them in public schools. Any of us might say that (and no doubt many have), but I doubt that many of us truly are willing to have our profession—or our careers— live or die by the sharp sword of that standard. The author of this book presumes that we ought to.

The book's next sustaining proposition is that unless the content taught in the name of physical education (cognitive, motor, or affective) connects to the lives of students in ways that make sense to them, and unless they find it affirming, interesting, and desirable, required study in physical education will not make any positive difference in their subsequent lives. In short, if they don't like what they are taught, the whole enterprise of physical education will fail.

Indeed, all of Hastie's own experience, as well as his reading of the research evidence, leads him to assert that negative consequences are the more likely case. Physical activities that don't make sense to students, that yield no pleasure, or that are experienced in class environments full of aversive and disrespectful messages will produce adults who are *less likely* to make vigorous physical activity a regular part of their lives.

Some activities taught in physical education classes may be difficult to master, or even involve uncomfortable levels of effort. But if they connect with the lives that students actually live and can imagine themselves living in the future, then, the author asserts, those activities will be accepted and valued—and make a lifelong difference. This book is a guide for shaping a physical education curriculum that can connect with students in exactly that way.

Given that prelude, if you anticipate that the book devotes substantial space to bemoaning the state of physical education in public schools (and blaming everyone and everything in sight—teachers, teacher educators, school administrators, taxpayers, and the values espoused in American culture), you are in for another surprise. Although he certainly does believe that we ought to start over from scratch with regard to the physical education curriculum, Hastie makes short work of all that and moves on promptly to an analysis of the problem (a four-chapter section dealing with adolescents, their worlds, and their bodies) and then to the appropriate content for helping secondary school students include moderate to vigorous physical activity as a regular part of their lifestyle (another four-chapter section on aerobics, weight training, sport education, and adventure education).

If you suspect that something so ambiguous could never be accomplished in the format presently used for most secondary level physical education, you are absolutely right. The section with chapters on block scheduling, project-based learning, fitness and sports clubs, and technology present Hastie's vision of something other than 50-minute blocks on M,W,F, or 75-minute classes on Tu and Th.

And further, if you suspect that even with a major overhaul of structure and content, the implacable problem of motivating students still would haunt the gym—again you are right. The surprise is that Hastie is perfectly aware of that problem and in the penultimate chapter offers an honest appraisal—but no panaceas. For each chapter, his advice about strategy and tactics for making physical activity attractive to students may or may not constitute a significant resource. What I can assert, however, is that in that chapter he has moved the whole professional dialogue about motivation to a new and more fruitful level than we have sustained in the past.

Finally, if you have followed this overview with care, you will already be hearing a chorus of teachers' voices chanting the familiar, old refrain, "Swell, but it never could happen in my school!" And again, many of them would be correct in that assessment. That is exactly why Hastie closes with a chapter that, as far as I am aware, has never before been attempted in a physical education textbook: "Understanding and Working with the Micropolitics of Physical Education." For my money, a more accurate title would have been, "How Good Teachers Survive and Get What They Want While Living in the Intensely Political Culture of a Public School." We all will be hearing more about micropolitics in physical education, and it is my hope that in four years, when Hastie revises this text for a second edition, he will write an even longer and more detailed chapter on the subject.

You will note that I have not said you will find this book an "easy read" or a comfortable fit with what you already know and believe. To the contrary, I suspect that the author fully intended to push us outside our personal comfort zone. In each case, however, he does his best to explain what justifies the temporary discomfort and offers a helping hand in the form of a rich array of resources beyond the book itself. (I found the web sites listed at the end of each chapter truly astonishing in number, variety, and relevance.)

The only guarantee I can offer prospective readers is that they are unlikely (very unlikely) to find themselves bored by yet another textbook. Surprised, uncomfortable, irritated, or even a little frightened, perhaps, but bored? No way. This is a lively and useful book written by a veteran physical educator—one who has been there, done the work, and learned hard lessons from the experience. If you read closely, perhaps you will see the outlines of your own future—a vision of the physical education you really want to give your students.

Lawrence F. Locke
Emeritus Professor of Education and Physical Education
University of Massachusetts/Amherst

Every student is influenced by his or her experiences in physical education. Those students who are not skillful often find themselves placed in embarrassing situations, while those who are skillful get bored by the content presented in many classes. If we were to take a poll of high school students concerning their participation in physical education and physical activity, we would obtain some thought-provoking and potentially disturbing results. First, only about one-half of young people in the United States regularly participate in vigorous physical activity, and one in four reports no vigorous activity. Second, fewer than 25% of all high school students participate in daily physical education, and of these, only 19% report being physically active for 20 minutes or more in those classes. Third, and perhaps most disturbing of all, few physical education programs provide students with interesting, meaningful, and intrinsically rewarding opportunities to participate skillfully. Ennis (1996) commented, these programs are "discriminatory and limit access not only to the joys of participation, but also to many personally and socially rewarding and satisfying ways to gain health-related benefits of physical activity."

It is the aim of this book to address these three responses. Nonetheless, as Tinning, Macdonald, Wright, and Hickey (2001) remind us, "You are—by your actions, your choices, your sensitivities, your understanding, your knowledge, and your attitude—responsible for what goes on in your classes." Reading this text, completing the in-school tasks, and reflecting on the end-of-chapter challenges is just the beginning. I hope that this book will provide you with a stimulus to go beyond being an ordinary teacher to be one whom students remember as a significant figure in helping them adopt physical activity as part of their lifestyle. You have my best wishes.

Organization of the Book

This book is divided into four parts. Part One (Chapter 1) sets the scene by focusing on the current status of high school physical education. It takes a potentially controversial stance that current practice is bankrupt and needs replacing—a stance not picked as a whim because of my own negative experiences with high school physical education, but from the consistently repeated calls by respected authors for transformation. Indeed, entire editions of both *Quest* (44/3, 1992) and the *Journal of Physical Education, Recreation, & Dance* (JOPERD) (58/2, 1987 and 63/7, 1992) have been allocated to this conversation. Terms such as *endangered species* and *crisis* have been common in these discussions. Parts Two, Three, and Four of this book provide practicing and prospective secondary school physical educators with ways to provide students with an engaging and relevant pedagogy. With specific reference to making physical education meaningful for students, Chen (1998) notes that we need to "help students transform the purpose of an activity into a personal desire, turn their interest in an activity into a personal striving, and bridge their knowledge and skill into a willingness so that they will continuously pursue a physically active lifestyle."

Part Two (Chapters 2–5) focuses on high school students themselves. Tinning and Fitzclarence (1992) comment that today's youth are "engaging with radically new cultural conditions and bring with them new sensibilities, needs, and expectations." It makes sense, then, that before we can identify an engaging and relevant pedagogy, we need to understand the youth culture associated with those we teach. The four chapters in Part Two address that concern. Chapter 2 examines adolescent development not from a biological or psychological perspective, but from a cultural one, particularly in the sense of a world that is significantly different from the one any of us experienced while we were growing up.

Notwithstanding, physical education is a practice of public display, and we are currently experiencing a cultural obsession with physicality. Given that the slim, muscular body is the dominant icon of desirability, we also know that many students in our classes feel that they don't match up to this ideal. Our task is to help students become critical consumers of the myriad of messages bombarding them from the popular media such as magazines, television, and the Internet. Chapter 3 examines the intricate interplay between physical activity, the body, and physicality. Chapter 4 focuses on youth physical activity and provides a strong message that we need to shift our thinking from the conception of *fitness* to one of *activity*.

Important in educating students for lifetime activity is providing opportunities for them to contribute to their own activity programs. Chapter 5 presents strategies to promote student empowerment. Students are given voice and choice within physical education.

Part Three (Chapters 6–9) provides the content suitable for inclusion in a high school curriculum. Chapter 6 presents ways in which students can develop aerobic fitness by engaging in content that is fun, challenging, and individualized. Chapter 7 takes a similar format but focuses on the development of strength fitness.

Chapter 8 focuses on the inclusion of sport within physical education. Many teachers conduct sports units that permit dominant, aggressive male players to control the game, marginalizing and alienating low-skilled girls and boys. Chapter 8 provides a curriculum model aimed specifically at addressing such exclusionary practices.

Chapter 9 provides examples of many outdoor adventure activities that can be included within physical education programs. The activities provide a number of learning experiences valued by educators but not always available within the mainstream fitness and sport content areas.

Part Four (Chapters 10–13) focuses on current issues that are facing physical educators. Chapter 10 examines the organizational structure of block scheduling, a movement that is gaining popularity throughout many secondary schools nationwide. This chapter provides a number of templates for organizing physical education instruction under the block system and allocates significant discussion to the potential of project-based learning.

Chapter 11 addresses the reality that many schools now require only a one-semester commitment to physical education for student graduation. As a direct attempt to counter this prelude to extinction, this chapter presents the concept of abandoning the common idea of formalized physical education as we see it and replacing it with a school fitness and sports club.

Chapter 12 examines the biggest change in education in the past decade: technology. The purpose of this chapter is to provide some ideas about how technology can become part of the arsenal of tools available to the physical education teacher. A further change in American education has been the increasing diversity in schools. Chapter 13 outlines the prospects for, and challenges associated with, presenting an engaging and relevant physical education to students in school settings with predominately minority students.

Part Five (Chapters 14–15) examines change. In particular, it examines changing students' attitudes toward activity and changing teachers' attitudes toward reform. Chapter 14 presents strategies a teacher can implement to help students become self-motivated, whereas Chapter 15 examines the micropolitics that operate in all school settings. The purpose of Chapter 15 is to provide you with strategies to gain acceptance and status within the workplace without having to compromise many of the wonderful and innovative ideas you have for physical education.

Specific Chapter Features

It is not uncommon for many textbooks to begin each chapter with chapter objectives. In this book, however, I begin each chapter with a scenario for approaching upcoming material as problematic, rather than information to be learned, studied, reproduced in a test, and then forgotten. To this end, the conclusion of each chapter includes a section for self-reflection. Rather than listing a series of statements about what you *should* know (which is the function of chapter objectives), these reflective statements ask you to consider how confident you feel in carrying out the applications from the chapter into the work setting. In many cases, your response will be "not that confident at all." Fear not, for this is the role of professional development. Your education as a teacher does not end upon graduation. Come back to these reflection sections as you develop as a teacher, and constantly ask yourself the same questions. The answers you give will tell a lot about your sincerity as a professional.

Also included in each chapter is a series of in-school tasks and suggestions for portfolio artifacts. Most quality teacher preparation programs will have extensive field experiences in which you visit schools and observe or teach young people. The tasks presented in each chapter serve as stimuli for your observations during these school visits. Likewise, many teacher education programs now require their students to produce portfolios as evidence of their learning and professional growth. You will notice that each of the suggested portfolio artifacts is cross-referenced with notation. The notation represents the specific National Association for Sport and Physical Education (NASPE) Beginning Teacher Standard that would be achieved through successful completion of a task. Any student who completes all the artifacts in this book would have a magnificent résumé.

Chapters 6–9 have an additional chapter-concluding element. For each of these four chapters, there is a series of samples for each of the seven NASPE content standards. Each content standard is described, followed by one or two techniques appropriate for assessing student achievement of the specific content standard.

Acknowledgments

The author would like to thank the following, who gave freely of their time:

- The reviewers of the original book proposal as well as those who read the chapter drafts. Their contributions certainly enhanced this text:

  Arthur Miller, University of Montana

  Elaine Gregory, Ed.D., Syracuse University

  Don McBrayer, University of North Alabama

  Gay Timken, Ph.D., University of Rhode Island

  Christine Sims, Ph.D., University of Southern Colorado

  Jacalyn Lund, Ph.D., Ball State University

  Victor Mancini, Ed.D., Ithaca College

  Susan Tarr, Ph.D., University of Wisconsin at River Falls

- Paul Smith, of Allyn and Bacon, who provided the original approval for this project and showed great confidence in its potential;

- All those at Benjamin Cummings, who made the transition particularly easy and who adopted the challenge to make this text the best it could be;
- Leslie Austin and her production staff, particularly Sally Peyrefitte, who is now eligible for entry into the *Guinness Book of World Records* for wearing out the most pencils on a single manuscript—their efforts have been outstanding.

The author would also like to thank those who posed for and contributed to the photographs and artwork for this book.

Lastly, I would like to thank the faculty and students within the Department of Health and Human Performance for their continued encouragement and support. It is most appreciated.

Peter Hastie
Auburn University

References

Chen, A. (1998). Meaningfulness in physical education: A description of high school students' conceptions. *Journal of Teaching in Physical Education, 17,* 285–306.

Ennis, C. D. (1996). Students' experience in sport-based physical education: [More than] apologies are necessary. *Quest, 48,* 453–456.

Tinning, R., & Fitzclarence, L. (1992). Postmodern youth culture and the crisis in Australian secondary school physical education. *Quest, 44,* 287–303.

Tinning R., Macdonald, D., Wright, J., & Hickey, C. (2001). *Becoming a physical education teacher: Contemporary and enduring issues*. Sydney: Pearson Education Australia.

CHAPTER 1

Contemporary High School Physical Education— Moving Out of the Box

Scenario

It is the second lesson of the day. Seventy students amble into the gymnasium. Some are dressed for activity; others are not. Small groups of students find their way into various levels of the bleachers and begin to chat about last night's party, tomorrow's football game, or what song has been taking the charts by storm.

When the teacher arrives, he struggles to gain the attention of the group, for the students know that his first task will be to call roll. After roll call eventually comes to an end, the teacher produces three basketballs, which he gives to three of the more physically skillful boys in the class because he knows they are the ones who will take the opportunity to play. Many of the students remain in the bleachers, seizing their opportunity to prolong their conversation, while some students straggle onto the floor. Still others take two Frisbees and begin to pass the disks among themselves in a corner of the gym, making sure that they do not invade the territory of the boys playing basketball.

Meanwhile . . .

In another high school, five students enter their physical education class and immediately begin to set up the step aerobics benches, for today they will present their group routine to the rest of the class. Following this presentation, they will share with the group the two new moves they have choreographed.

At the same time, three other students are logging their weight-lifting data from the previous lesson into a computer near the teacher's office. The teacher at that moment is interviewing three other students about their experience in Ms. Brown's new spin class, which they are taking at the local health club. These students are participating in out-of-school activities that count toward their credit for physical education, and they are here to report to their teacher, Ms. Smithers, that they will be keeping a log of their attendance, their heart rates, and their self-tested one-mile run scores.

These two scenarios are both possible within the realm of high school physical education in the United States. You may guess, however, that one is more prevalent than the other. A general picture of secondary school physical education would reveal that the majority of teachers are essentially presenting physical education classes in a manner that is particularly "casual." A casual climate comes at a cost of a lower level of expectation for performance in the subject matter requirements, particularly for instructional tasks. In such a climate, students are held accountable only for participating and making minimal effort, not for trying to achieve high levels of performance. Siedentop, Doutis, Tsangaridou, Ward, and Rauschenbach (1994) call such classes "no sweat" physical education: The act of teaching is no sweat, because the teacher asks only that the students behave themselves—and for the students, the act of learning involves "less than sweaty" levels of exertion.

Beyond these negative consequences of laxness in secondary physical education, other authors have been more condemning of current practice. In particular, numerous authors report cases of student alienation and disengagement (e.g., Carlson, 1995; Ennis, 2000), demoralization (Robinson, 1990), gender inequity (e.g., Napper-Owen, Kovar, Ermler & Mehrhof, 1999), and negative student attitudes (e.g., Ennis et al., 1999). As Tinning (1994) has noted, physical education can be an oppressive practice, doing violence to the developing self-identity of some, perhaps many, adolescents.

An Endangered Species

High school physical education in the United States has been declared an endangered species. Many states require no formal component of physical education toward graduation, while many others require only one semester. Furthermore, in many cases, this one-semester requirement can be satisfied by participation on a school athletic team, in the school band, or even—in the extreme—in the choir! *What is most regrettable is that the states have allowed this to happen* (Table 1.1).

High school physical education has reached so great a crisis that numerous forums have been undertaken to investigate ways in which it can be rescued or salvaged. Various arguments have been made at these forums, and two of the field's most distinguished leaders paint a very gloomy picture of the prospects for secondary school physical education.

Table 1.1   National Physical Education Requirements for Secondary Schools

Daily for grades 8–12

Illinois * (various substitutions are available
    for credit)

2 years/units

California *
Nebraska (includes health)
Nevada
New York *
Virginia
Washington *

1½ units

Louisiana *
Texas *
Utah *
Vermont (can substitute only for ¼ credit)
Wisconsin

1 unit

Alabama *
Connecticut
Delaware *
Hawaii
Indiana
Iowa *
Kansas
Missouri
Maine
Montana
New Hampshire *
New Mexico *
North Dakota *

Oregon *
South Carolina *

1 unit of Health & Physical Education

Alaska *
North Carolina

½ unit

Arkansas
Florida *
Georgia
Kentucky
Maryland *
Ohio

Local school district determination

Arizona *
Colorado
Massachusetts
Michigan *
Minnesota
New Jersey *
Pennsylvania
Rhode Island
Wyoming *

No requirement

Idaho
Mississippi *
Oklahoma
Tennessee (students can take a course in
    "Lifetime Wellness")

* Indicates substitution possible (e.g. athletics, band, or other activity).

Both Larry Locke and Daryl Siedentop present the drastic claim that high school physical education is essentially bankrupt. Locke (1992, p. 363) contends that "we have a programmatic lemon." Both these scholars suggest that the current system of instruction does not work and has very little potential to work in the future. Siedentop argues that high school programs in physical education fail to perform in the areas that are valued by their main consumers: students in secondary schools (1992, p. 70). For them, the subject is devoid of any real meaning.

Locke (1992) also presents the following two caustic comments:

- "In current programs, there are so many design flaws, the limitations placed on teachers by workplace conditions, changes in youth culture and the inexorable forces of history, trying to make lemonade with what we have is beyond most of us, and it probably won't yield the product we want in any case." (p.363)

- "If PE is to have a significant presence in the secondary schools of the 21st century, *it is better to chuck the dominant model and thereby most school programs and start over from scratch.*" (p. 362)

The dominant model that Locke refers to is a curriculum of multi-activity programs emphasizing team and lifetime sports, particularly competitive, male-oriented team activities.

Physical education class

Starting from Scratch

Locke and Siedentop believe we need to completely reconceptualize the way in which physical education is delivered to students. This means producing something substantially different from the dominant model of short units of instruction in team sports, which marginalize many students. In particular, Siedentop (1992) identifies the following challenges in developing a new physical education:

- We must think differently about school time—the traditional 50-minute class period within a seven-period schoolday that ends at 3 P.M. is dysfunctional.

- We must develop programs and experiences that focus on long-term mastery of skills rather than cover a "smorgasbord" curriculum.

- We can no longer be satisfied with compliance as the optimal operating relationship between students and teachers.

- We must continue to be aware that sport and fitness are sought and valued in our culture partially because of social outcomes.

In developing high school physical education programs, educators often begin with a question: What should the students learn, or what is the essential knowledge? The National Association for Sport and Physical Education (NASPE) has developed the ideal of the physically educated person as one who *has* developed skill, *does* regularly participate in exercise, *knows* the benefits of an active lifestyle, *is* physically fit, and finally, *values* the role of physical activity. Following this model, NASPE has developed several standards for students of physical education at various grade levels.

A Major Departure

Instead of asking what should students *learn* or *become* as a result of their participation in high school physical education, perhaps a more appropriate question should be, *Who* are the students we are attempting to teach in high school physical education, and how do *they* see the need for activity? This question is particularly relevant given the findings of Cothran and Ennis (1998), who suggest that teachers and students frequently hold potentially conflicting values about the educational and noneducational aspects of physical education.

We could examine the typical physical and social changes of adolescence from a developmental psychology perspective, but perhaps it would be more helpful to examine the world in which these students live. What is the youth culture of the 21st century? How do students view activity in their personal worlds?

Given that these students have distinct tasks in youth, to what extent can physical education contribute not only to their knowledge and understanding of the world and of themselves, but also to their daily lives? If the our goal for high school physical education is to help students embrace physical activity for a lifetime, we need to identify the factors that will lead them to adopt that ideal. The fundamental challenge, then, is to find the answer to this question: How can we develop a curriculum that is both relevant and engaging for youth?

When we examine current practice in physical education in light of this proposed ideal, it becomes clear that drastic change from current practice is needed in many schools. In too many instances, students participate in short units of games and sports in which they develop little if any skill beyond that which they already have, receive no expert instruction, and derive little pleasure because they feel the activity has very little relevance to their current or future worlds.

Placing students in situations in which their bodies are under scrutiny or "on display" and they are made to feel inadequate, either by their peers or by their teachers, is hardly the recipe for encouraging students to become active beyond the classroom. Some states in the United States[1] offer alternative curricula that aim to enhance students' participation in physical activity by helping them establish their own exercise patterns. These programs recognize that the limited time available for physical education in schools will not lead students to embrace the ideal of lifetime physical activity. We need to expand students' scope of opportunity, alert them to the possibilities for participating in activities outside physical education class, and count those activities toward physical education credit. We need to consider partnerships between the school and the private sector or the community in the delivery of physical activity for students. We need

Surfing can be a lifetime activity

---

[1] Alabama, for example, has a course titled LIFE: Lifelong Individualized Fitness Education.

to recast the role of the teacher from activity director to activity facilitator, that is, a knowledgeable resource and an expert in physical activity. This teacher must also be an expert manager who can help students manage their time and the resources they have available to them in and out of school. The physical education teacher essentially becomes an owner/manger of a school-based health club. To this end, we need to hold students accountable for the work they produce. We cannot expect students to take on new roles and take them seriously if we do not reward them or hold them responsible for carrying out these roles. We need to challenge them by introducing new and exciting ways in which they can include activities in their lives.

The role of the physical education teacher is not diminished with this change. If students were expected to take more required and elective courses, the possibilities for physical education could be quite extensive, particularly if the teacher were prepared to engage school-community links as part of the physical education process. Block scheduling could allow more time for single lessons and provide students considerable opportunities in substantive project-based learning. Remember that the goal is to help students develop the skills and knowledge that will lead them to embrace physical activity as part of their lifestyle. As Tinning and Fitzclarence have commented, it is an irony that so "many of the adolescents bored with school physical education see physical activity as significant to their lifestyles outside the school context" (1992, p. 287).

A Challenge Directly to *You!*

It is clear that we are living in a time when physical activity is valued, and lifetime involvement in physical activity is both desirable and possible. However, Siedentop has commented that "the mechanisms for educating and socializing this generation towards lifespan involvement are still weak and notoriously uneven" (1992, p. 72). Significantly, Siedentop notes that school physical education is still the only process that has the potential for education and socializing all children—and you—toward this ideal of lifetime involvement.

As a forewarning, however, Locke maintains that the possibilities for significant change in secondary school physical education will be determined in large measure by the kinds of people who have been attracted to careers there. Particularly, he notes that two variables will be critical in this challenge: "those peoples'

> Do you see yourself as a potential change agent in presenting a physical education that is supportive, nurturing, and accepting: one that is so dynamic and challenging that it produces enthusiastic and intense engagement?

professional interpersonal skills" and, perhaps even more significantly, "what they believe about themselves, adolescents, the subject matter, and education" (1992, p. 369). However, Locke also notes that many teachers find it particularly difficult to "let go" of what they currently do. Locke sees this strong desire among many teachers to "hang on to what is familiar in a daily routine" as the major handicap in organizing any effort to restructure physical education (1992, p. 370).

So, how committed are you to challenging the status quo that dominates secondary school physical education: the "no sweat" curriculum and resistance to change?

What Does This Book Provide?

By the time you have read this book, have mastered some of the skills it describes, and have reflected upon your experiences with the in-school tasks and the portfolio assignments, you will be better able to answer yes to the question posed above.

To that end, it is the purpose of this book to help you see different options for teaching American teens and to help you design learning experiences that are both engaging and relevant. Included are chapters on empowering students, on giving them a voice and choice in their physical activity participation. Also included are chapters concerning the development of programs that extend beyond the tradi-

Are you a teacher first, or a coach?

Off-campus experiences

tional 40-minute lesson and are aimed at creating exciting student-driven projects and off-campus experiences. These are presented with extensive chapters on the core content of contemporary physical education programs.

Unfortunately, within the United States schools differ in their ability to present various curricula to students. Whereas some schools have at their service indoor swimming pools, well-furnished and well-equipped gymnasia, and inviting changing rooms, other schools operate in a context of violence, poverty, and noncertified teachers. Therefore, a chapter is included that discusses teaching in diverse settings and presents lessons learned from teachers who have focused on this particular challenge and attained some positive outcomes.

Finally, this book aims to give you tools to help both students and teachers change. Students need help if they are to look on physical education as a meaningful and engaging option both within and beyond their high school education. You also have to face the reality that many students will always see physical education as "no sweat" and will be threatened by demands for increased accountability and expectations.

You also need to become aware of the micropolitics that exists in schools and to develop strategies that will allow you to be successful, not only in surviving the school year, but also in initiating some of the innovations that may be stimulated from reading this text.

IN-SCHOOL TASKS

Program Sophistication

Arrange to visit a nearby high school and speak with the head of the physical education department. The purpose of this exercise is to examine the extent to which this program is demonstrating practices that would suggest whether physical education has a high or low status within the school.

Consider in your discussion the following four issues: program goals, assessment, school-home links, and advocacy. The answers you will get should provide you with deep insight into the role and place of physical education within the school.

1. "Could you show me your overall curriculum plan?"
   - Can they?
   - Does the document look up to date?
   - Are the *specific* dates listed in the document for testing, reporting, reviewing?
   - Does the document look as though it has been recently reviewed?
   - Could the teacher instantly *locate* the document?

2. "How do you assess students, and can you show me some examples of student work?"
   - How *do* they grade? By dressing and attendance? By attitude and effort? Where does fitness testing fit in? Are skills assessed, and how?
   - Can they show you any samples of student work—such as workbooks, computer printouts of exercise programs, photographs of projects, videos of skillful performance, or student portfolios?
   - How accessible are the artifacts? Does the teacher have to search for them, or are they readily filed and retrieved?

3. "Could you show me any communications you make between school and home, such as newsletters, a PE web page, or other notices?"
   - Can they?
   - What format do these take?
   - Does the physical education teacher make any contribution to school newsletters?
   - How does this teacher feel about school-community links?

4. "What relations do you have with the rest of the school? How do you market physical education to the faculty and students?"
   - Are there ever any public displays of physical education student work— such as field days or open house days, or presentation of projects?
   - Do you involve teachers from other disciplines (e.g., science or computing) in any PE programs?

- How accessible is the physical education facility to students and teachers not involved directly in physical education? For example, is the weight room open before or after class hours?

- Do you run an intramural program?

Reflection

- To what extent do you think this program is complying or resisting current practices of "the same old–same old" physical education? What evidence did you see or hear to support your assertions?

- Does this program act, look, or feel "tired"? Is there an air of dynamic excitement, in which vigorous attempts are being made to provide a relevant and engaging pedagogy to students—or does the program seem to be one that maintains the status quo?

- Which of the four answers surprised you the most? Which were the most predictable?

- Would you like to work in this school? Why or why not?

PORTFOLIO SUGGESTIONS AND ARTIFACTS

The notation following each task is derived from the *National Standards for Beginning Physical Education Teachers* developed by NASPE. These standards are based on a national consensus of the profession for what beginning teachers of physical education should know and be able to do.

The notation indicates, first, the relevant standard (e.g., S8 = reflection), and second, the specific disposition (D), process (P), or skill (S) that would be demonstrated by completion of this task. The standards range from 1 to 9:

1. Content knowledge
2. Growth and development
3. Diverse learners
4. Management and motivation
5. Communication
6. Planning and instruction
7. Learner assessment
8. Reflection
9. Collaboration

Your Physical Education History (S8–P4)

As part of understanding how you see physical education, it is worthwhile to examine your past history with the subject. Examine some of the following stimulus questions to provide a beginning set of reflections.

Programming

- What activities dominated your school PE program?
- Did you have any choice about content? On what basis was that choice available?

Organization

- Did you participate in single-sex or mixed classes? (or were their choices?)
- What were the expectations and protocols regarding dress?
- How were your classes managed? Were they essentially teacher centered, or did students have a voice in some class decisions?
- Did you notice any differences between the teachers' interactions with girls and boys?

Assessment

- How were your grades determined?
- How public was testing (especially fitness testing)?
- What was the consequence of testing within physical education? That is, were there any examples of formative assessment?
- What beliefs about physical education did these procedures reflect?

Your Professional Beliefs (S6–K1,2)

In this section of your portfolio, you begin to describe your philosophy about teaching physical education at the secondary school level. Begin by answering the following global question: What is an ideal physical education program for the American high school student in the 21st century? In answering this question, you may address the following areas: curriculum, instruction, management, and assessment.

You will revisit this portfolio item as you complete your teacher education program and perhaps even as you continue reading this book. However, this preliminary exercise will at least provide a template for you to revisit.

REFLECTION TIME

Now that you have read this chapter, how confident do you feel in

- being able to envision a program of physical education that is substantially different from current practice?

- your preparedness to critically examine your own physical education backgrounds and your beliefs about the purposes for physical education?

- your training in the skills required for sustaining change in the rough-and-tumble political environment of a public school?[2]

REFERENCES

Carlson, T. B. (1995). We hate gym: Student alienation from physical education. *Journal of Teaching in Physical Education, 14,* 467–477.

Cothran, D. J., & Ennis, C. D. (1998). Curricula of mutual worth: Comparisons of students' and teachers' curricular goals. *Journal of Teaching in Physical Education 17,* 307–326.

Ennis, C. D. (2000). Canaries in the coal mine: Responding to disengaged students using theme-based curricula. *Quest, 52,* 119–130.

Ennis, C. D., Solmon, M. A., Satina, B., Loftus, S. J., Mensch, J., & McCauley, M. T. (1999). Creating a sense of community in urban schools using the "Sport for Peace" Curriculum. *Research Quarterly for Exercise and Sport, 70,* 273–285.

Locke, L. F. (1992). Changing secondary school physical education. *Quest, 44,* 361–372.

Napper-Owen, G. E., Kovar, S. K., Ermler, K. L., & Mehrhof, J. H. (1999). Curricula equity in required ninth-grade physical education. *Journal of Teaching in Physical Education, 19,* 2–21.

Robinson, D. W. (1990). An attributional analysis of student demoralization in physical education settings. *Quest, 42,* 27–39.

Siedentop, D. (1992). Thinking differently about secondary physical education. *Journal of Physical Education, Recreation and Dance, 63* (7), 69–72;77.

Siedentop, D., Doutis, P., Tsangaridou, N. Ward, P., & Rauschebach, J. (1994). Don't sweat gym: An analysis of curriculum and instruction. *Journal of Teaching in Physical Education, 13,* 375–394.

Tinning, R. (1994). Baggy T shirts, Reeboks, schooling, popular culture and young bodies. In J. Kenway & J. Collier (Eds.), *Schooling what future?* Geelong, Australia: Deakin Centre for Education and Change.

---

[2] These questions are based on observations presented by Locke (1992).

WEB RESOURCES

The following web link list was generated upon publication of the text; however, over time, the sites may become obsolete if an organization dissolves, discontinues online services, or relocates to a different URL. If a link listed below does not connect, please search for the organization by name.

http://www.pelinks4u.org/

PE Links is a web site devoted to "developing skillful and healthy movers." With sections devoted to elementary, secondary, and adapted physical education, as well as coaching, technology, and interdisciplinary studies, the site also includes details of workshops and conferences.

http://www.pecentral.org/

PE Central is a specialist site for health and physical education teachers, parents, and students. Their goal is to provide the latest information about developmentally appropriate physical education programs for children and youth. The web site encourages submissions from teachers and students and also has a job search database.

http://www.aahperd.org/naspe/

The National Association for Sport and Physical Education seeks to enhance knowledge and professional practice in sport and physical activity through scientific study and dissemination of research-based and experiential knowledge to members and the public.

http://www.cahperd.ca/

Home page of the Canadian Association for Health, Physical Education, Recreation and Dance (CAHPERD).

CHAPTER 2

American Adolescent Development and Youth Culture

Scenario

The sun is setting at the mall, and swarms of new customers are being drawn by the soft light of 91-foot advertising totems.

Boys looking for girls and girls looking for boys. Yellow hair, green hair, pink hair, spiked hair and no hair. Pierced eyebrows, tongues, and chins. Shorts below the knees and miniskirts well above them.

Boys posing as men, self-consciously puffing on cheap sweet cigars. Girls practicing to be women with their masks of makeup and their midriffs exposed.

Sullen-looking boys with poor posture and knit caps pulled down to their eyes. Tough boys with tattoos bulging out of their "wife beater" tank tops.

"Come on, guys, off the table, keep moving," a security guard tells a group of kids acting as if this were their backyard.

It's a typical Friday night at the Block at Orange—ground zero of the retail industry's most concerted attempt to court the lucrative youth market (Anton and Earnest, 2000).

Introduction

The scenario presented above, while perhaps a little overstated, does portray a legitimate picture of youth in the 21st century. It presents teens as tough, independent, image-conscious, and threatening. Although these descriptions might sound particularly "new millennium," throughout history young people, by virtue of their youth, have *always* been a source of envy, nostalgia and lust to their elders. Even Socrates was critical of the youth of his day. More noteworthy perhaps is the assertion made by every generation of adults that the young people are enjoying a hedonism that the adults were too respectable or myopic to pursue during their own youth (see Brake, 1980). Giroux (1998, p. 2) argues, "American society increasingly produces and spreads through the media a hyped-up rhetoric of moral panic about the state of youth culture."

It has been stated as a truism that "kids don't change, but the world in which they live does"—and the differences that we see across generations are those attempts by the youth of the day to come to grips with and find an identity. In this new millennium, however, we find that youth in particular are living in a world *vastly* different from the one inhabited by youth in the past. There has been such a radical change that a new concept has been developed to describe this massive social change: postmodernism.

Postmodern youth

The purpose of this chapter is to outline and examine this postmodern world as it exists for American youth and, through the examination of youth culture(s), to explore the serious implications for physical education in schools. In essence, it is hoped that this chapter will provide you, the prospective physical education teacher, a deeper and more tolerant understanding of the students who make up our secondary schools and to provide a basis on which you will feel more confident in your ability to connect and interact with *all* the students in your classes.

So Who Are America's Youth?

In our discussion of youth, youth culture, and the world in which young people live, it is perhaps most important first to examine who these young people actually are. How many of them are there? Where do they live? Who do they live with? Data gathered from various sources dating from the end of the 1990s provide the following snapshot profile of teens in the new century:

- 23.4 million American youth are between the ages of 12 and 17—this represents just less than 10% of the total population.
- 65% of these youth are white, 15% African American, 16% Hispanic, 4% Asian, and 1% Native American or Native Alaskan.
- 68% live with two parents, 23% with the mother only, 4% with the father only, and 4% with none—more than 50% of African American children live with their mothers only.
- 18% of children live in poverty, though this figure is nearly 35% for African American and Hispanic children.
- 81% of children are in good health.
- 31% of American teenagers volunteer their free time toward community service.

Although these statistics provide some interesting demographic data, it is perhaps more useful for the prospective teacher to understand some of the significant changes that are occurring in the adolescent world of the high-schooler.

Many secondary education books describe the biological and physiological, learning and cognitive, and social and personality transitions at various stages of adolescent development. These texts typically describe how these changes interact with the family, peer group, educational/school, and work contexts of adolescent life. Describing adolescence as the beginning of the transition from childhood to adulthood, these books give attention to the phenomenon of puberty, the development of hypothetical reasoning and problem solving, and the establishment of an independence of self.

Focusing on the rapid growth and increase in body consciousness among adolescents, many authors describe specific differences between boys and girls. Boys are described as outstripping girls in height and weight, talking more about sex than girls, and spending more time out of the house. Girls are described as vague and diffuse, interested in romantic love, giggly, and prone to having crushes on older men.

As teenagers get older, their striving for independence and autonomy increases, accompanied by increasing parental conflict. As teenagers become rebellious and moody, privacy becomes a great issue. Older teens are described as typically fearful of adults asking questions and becoming overly involved in their teen's decisions. It is also suggested that in the later years of adolescence, students begin to explore their vocational options, and use their current work opportunities to begin making tentative career choices.

This developmental approach to understanding adolescence does provide some clues about certain developmental markers, but as Tinning, Macdonald,

Most adolescent developmental literature does not consider minorities

Wright, and Hickey (2001, p. 95) comment, a major criticism of this approach is "that it takes the characteristics and tasks of adolescents to be the same for all people across all cultures and socioeconomic groups." This description of adolescent development might even be considered particularly "white" and, indeed, racist. For example, what empirical data exist to suggest that African American girls living in poverty are indeed vague and diffuse, interested in romantic love, giggly, and prone to having crushes on older men? Indeed, Lerner and Galambos (1998) state that there is a major limitation in the contemporary scientific literature about adolescent development. These authors lament that most studies have been limited to examination of European American, middle-class samples.

Adopting the example from Tinning et al. (2001, p. 95), we may suggest that the adolescent experience of a young man recently arrived in Los Angeles from rural Vietnam will be vastly different from that of an affluent young woman from a private school in New England, and the experiences of a young mother trying to complete high school graduation requirements will be different from those of a young Native American living with his traditional community in New Mexico.

Thus, given the number of contextual features that are part of the teenager's world, it may be more appropriate to suggest that many of the changes that are typically seen as "biological and psychologically determined" are often largely produced by the context in which young people live. Tinning et al. (2001) again provide an eloquent argument supporting this case:

> . . . for one girl menstruation may mean little more than the inconvenience of wearing a pad, for another it may be seen as a significant move to adulthood and preparation for motherhood, while for yet another it may be a traumatic experi-

ence marked by pain and embarrassment. In traditional indigenous cultures, the transition from child to adult may be clearly marked and celebrated; in other cultures there are more ambiguities about a young female or male person's developing sexuality. (p. 96)[1]

The developmental perspective of youth, then, is a simplistic notion of what the concept of youth entails, particularly as it ignores so many cultural and significant features. We may be better served to examine the notion of youth *culture* as a heuristic for understanding the students who enter our school and, ultimately, our physical education classes.

Adolescent Youth Culture(s)— The Tasks of the American Teen

Adolescence has been described as a phase of life beginning in biology and ending in society (Petersen, 1988). To gain more insight into adolescence, it is perhaps more useful to examine that society in general and youth culture in particular. Youth culture is not, as Rollin (1999) reminds us, just music, fashion, and vulgar language. Culture serves as the fabric of one's being and includes language, beliefs, attitudes, and patterns of communication and behavior (Tiedt & Tiedt, 1990). An examination of youth culture needs to include the personal, the aesthetic, the educational, the medical, the economic, the political, and the technological elements of American life.

"Generation Y"

If we were to provide a label to the current generation of young people (as has been done in the past), the most used term is "Generation Y." In comparing them to Generation X, many social commentators see this particular group of teens as more optimistic. Jane Buckingham of the marketing firm Youth Intelligence suggests that the youth of Generation Y "embrace things that are more lighthearted, from Britney Spears and the Spice Girls to Buffy [the Vampire Slayer]. It doesn't have to be all angst" (Span, 1999). Whereas Gen X'ers grew up in a time of recession, rampant divorce, the AIDS epidemic, and predictions of environmental disaster and lower living standards than those of their parents, their successors have grown up seeing economic prosperity, a flattening divorce rate, noticeable medical progress, and movements such as recycling and saving the rainforest. Generation Y'ers are seen as practical, clear-eyed survivors who

---

[1]Reproduced from Tinning, R., Macdonald, D., Wright, J., & Hickey, C. *Becoming a Physical Education Teacher: Contemporary and Enduring Issues,* with the permission of Pearson Education Australia Pty Limited. Copyright © 2001 Pearson Education Australia Pty Limited.

know "how that world really works" (Rollin, 1999, p. 312). Other authors have suggested that this generation, also called Millennials (born between 1982 and 2000), will also be better educated and more affluent, but also actually harder workers and better community builders (Howe & Strauss, 2000).

It is also recognized that today's American youth are the most racially and ethnically diverse generation in American history. That modern youth borrow tastes and styles from everyone, and indeed everywhere, has not gone unnoticed by the many marketing companies who show significant interest in youth (and the youth market). "You're seeing more cultural mixing," says Michael Wood of Teen Research Unlimited. "Where there were clear lines between Caucasian and Asian American and African American, those lines are becoming very blurred. Think Tiger Woods" (Span, 1999). Perhaps because of these factors, the teens of 2001 are optimistic about race relations in America, believing that race relations will get better (Farley, 1997).

However, there are other observers who take another perspective. School practitioners seem to concur with Giroux's contention that racism is rampant in modern America. For example, one particular school counselor from an ethnically and financially diverse school district suggests the optimism many speak of appears to break down along class lines (Lazar, 2001). For example, teens who grow up with generous opportunities for after-school activities and high expectations from their parents appear to be quite upbeat about the future. Those who are from working-class and low-income families (and have not been on the receiving end of the economic boom of the late 1990s), don't appear to be as optimistic.

Note here that the issue is one of class, not race. Howe and Strauss (2000) remark that *money* will be one of the great millennial divides. Class and money, they believe, will rise above gender or race as a flashpoint for student political argument.

Generation Y and Their Schooling

There is little doubt that the nature of schooling has changed even within the decade of the 1990s. The most obvious indicator of this change is the extent to which technology has become commonplace in many education settings. Moreover, savvy teens are now probably more computer literate than many of their teachers and are certainly the computer experts in their homes.

Other changes in schooling include the increase in the use of block scheduling as an organizing format for the curriculum, as well as more long-term projects, often involving work outside of school. Schools are also becoming more ethnically diverse.

With over 98% of American teenagers actually attending school, they do in the main seem to have reasonably positive opinions of it. Rollin (1999) provides data on what 10th graders enjoy about school (Table 2.1).

Table 2.1   Reasons Why 10th Graders Enjoy School

	White %	African American %	Hispanic %
Think subjects are interesting	68.8	79.1	74.5
Get a feeling of satisfaction	74.8	85.8	81.3
Have nothing else to do	30.1	29.0	31.1
Need education to get a job	96.5	96.7	96.8
Go to meet friends	85.5	66.1	80.1
Play on a team or belong to a club	55.3	49.3	45.3
Have teachers who care and expect students to succeed	72.4	81.6	76.0

Source: Data from Rollin (1999, p. 327). Reproduced with permission of Greenwood Publishing Group, Inc., Westport, CT.

While acknowledging the increase of cultural mixing in certain locales of American youth, we must avoid the trap of generalizing to all teenagers and trying to depict the "representative" youth. To do so would not only be naive, but also perhaps racist. As Rollin comments, economically disadvantaged teens are excluded from many elements of what we think of as teen culture. Such generalizations are also often accompanied by unpleasant stereotypes of minority teens (for example, perceptions of greater sexuality among African American girls and more widespread presence of drug pushers in African American communities).

With this in mind, let us try to get a more accurate perspective on the youth of the new millennium. Table 2.2 provides just one summary of the teenagers who will be your prospective students.

Teen Cultures

Although many authorities refer to teen culture, it is perhaps more appropriate to use the plural, *cultures.* Indeed, one could argue that there are indeed too many differences among various teen groups to make a definitive account of one single way of life. Giroux (1998, p. 4) notes that "the category of youth is constituted across diverse languages and cultural representations as well as racial and class-based experiences"—meaning that young people experience vastly disparate political, cultural, and economic conditions.

The following list provides a sample of contemporary youth subcultures. Subcultures "arise as attempts to resolve collectively experienced problems aris-

Table 2.2   A Compendium of Characteristics of Adolescents

Dimension	Characteristics
At home	• Fascination with electronic gadgets: CDs, pagers, cell phones, video games
Audio entertainment	• Private listening: headphones, but also sometimes very loud and public, as with boom boxes
	• FM radio a major source of listening, but MP3s a newer source, downloadable from the Internet
Television	• Almost daily television viewing, reaching up to 7 hours per day in some cases
	• MTV, Fox, and BET the major networks watched
	• Teen-based comedies, dramas, and soap operas the main fare
	• Significant increase in viewership of talk shows
The car	• Cruising is still a significant leisure activity
	• Alternate vehicles now more popular (pickup trucks, SUVs, and off-road vehicles)
Fashion	• Jeans and T-shirt still rule, but with numerous iterations (e.g., denim overalls popular with many girls)
	• Older teens are becoming more conservative in their dress
	• White teens becoming more hip-hop, African American teens are becoming more preppie
Hair and hats	• More simple hair styles for white girls
	• Significant attention to hair in boys, with multiple styles, colors, and levels of shaving
	• Braids, weaves, and cornrows increasingly popular
	• "The baseball cap has become the icon of the nineties" (Rollin, 1999)
Tattoos and body piercing	• Body piercing becoming popular (navels, eyebrows, and, for some, noses and lips)
	• Ankle and shoulder tattoos, particularly in white middle-class girls
Music	• Impossible to identify one particular sound or group that is dominant
	• Rap is still significant to many (but still mostly male)
	• Christian rock is also making inroads

ing from contradictions in the social structure, and that they generate a form of collective identity from which an individual identity can be achieved outside that ascribed by class, education and occupation" (Brake, 1980, p. vii). How many of the following subcultures can you even identify? Can you describe their common characteristics?

- Altos
- Hip Hoppers
- Kakkers
- Hardcores
- Hardrockers
- Mass Rabbits
- Gabbers
- Straight Edgers
- Punks

Common Tasks of Teens

Although it may not be possible to describe the "typical" teen, there are nonetheless certain challenges facing youth of all circumstances. Whether we call these tasks or responsibilities, they are trials that all teens must somehow pass through. These include the development of a set of identities, the development of some form of autonomy, and the creation of a personal biography.

Development of Adolescent Identity

Identity can be described as a "dynamic set of meanings about how we see ourselves and how others see us" (Tinning et al., 2001, p. 97). *Meanings* (plural) is used deliberately here, because teenagers will have a number of identities, depending on the contexts in which they find themselves. For example, they may have one identity for home, and another for their peer group. The "sullen-looking boys with poor posture and knit caps pulled down to their eyes" described in the scenario at the beginning of this chapter may indeed only dress and act this way for the purpose of going to the mall and hanging out with friends. In other situations, they may be just like the kid next door.

As such, researchers are now suggesting that if we are to fully understand the social experience of young people, it is essential to take into account the various social spaces that constitute their daily life. Indeed, five "fields of practice" or "sites" can be identified in which identity is constructed: family, peer group, school, media, and physical culture. Even so, these fields do not include the "back regions" that some kids use—the "hang-out" places such as the mall and the street—except indirectly, because most of those spaces are peer related.

The notion of *dynamic* is also used purposefully. As Giroux comments, "Identities are always in transit: they mutate, change and often become more complicated as a result of chance encounters, traumatic events, or unexpected collisions" (1998, p. 9).

In developing identities, many students will associate with themselves specific gender and ethnic identities. Indeed, in some cases, white males are co-opting African American culture. As actor Danny Hoch explains, "This identity crisis manifests itself culturally. You see rich white kids wearing baggy pants and rolling up their pant legs because it will make them look poor. Then you've got young poor kids in the ghetto donning Tommy Hilfiger sailing gear and Timberland camping gear and Nautica hiking gear when none of them have ever sailed or camped or hiked" (see Munoz, 1999). The following excerpt expands on this issue:

> *Danny Hoch felt a surge of mind-whirling confusion as he listened to the young boys standing before him. He was in a small town in the middle of the Iowa cornfields—the heart of Apple Pie and American Dream country, right? So, why were these blond teenage boys in his face, telling him, "Yo man, I'm black, and if you don't believe me I'm gonna get my posse and show you. . . ."Why were they spraying graffiti on farm houses and listening to Fat Joe, Snoop Dogg and Trick Daddy instead of Garth Brooks and the Dixie Chicks?*
>
> *Hoch realized he had bumped into a new American cultural phenomenon. "These were the blondest kids I'd ever met," said Hoch, a Brooklyn native whose 1997 theatrical show "Jails, Hospitals and Hip-Hop" earned him critical acclaim. "But hip-hop had permeated them. We saw these kids throughout the country. America likes to think of itself as strip malls and apple pie and everybody eats at Denny's. And here are these kids completely attracted to hip-hop."* (Munoz, 1999)

Development of Autonomy

One of the tasks of youth lies in the movement away from total dependence on the family to some level of independence. Adolescent teens are therefore in the process of developing some autonomy. Douvin and Adelson (1966) put forward the idea that there are three forms of autonomy: (1) emotional autonomy ("Ok, now I am less dependent on my parents/family"), (2) behavioral autonomy ("What can I do on my own?"), and (3) value autonomy (exploring and accepting values that run counter to those of parents and the local community). Most teens achieve emotional and behavioral autonomy, but very few achieve value autonomy. In many cases emotional and behavioral autonomy are supported and encouraged by the family, whereas value autonomy is often resisted.

In achieving emotional autonomy, most adolescents will develop strong peer relationships. Although some observers believe that this indicates emotional

Many adolescents search for autonomy

disengagement from the family, it is more likely that youth are *extending* their emotional bonds to others outside the family. Indeed, pollsters at Teen Research Unlimited report that when teens are asked whom they admire the most, their primary answer is always their parents. In the teen lexicon, "Friendships may come and go, but parents are always there for you."

Behavioral autonomy is that area in which teens achieve their highest levels of autonomy. It can also be the most challenging. First, they may wish to engage in many features of the youth culture that their parents consider inappropriate. At the same time, while school is a particularly social setting, most adolescents make significant efforts to become integrated into the peer culture. Further, as Fasick maintains, they must learn this by themselves: ". . . being unfamiliar with the shifting foci of adolescent cultural patterns, parents are of little help to their children in their efforts to find a place among their peers" (1984, p. 150). Do the words "You just don't get it, Mom!" bring back memories?

Creation of a Personal Biography

A third task of modern youth is one that was not a task of their parents. Previous generations followed in their parents' footsteps, being socialized mainly through family and school into many adult roles (either in career path or home duties). Brettschneider (1990) refers to contemporary adolescents as being called on to produce their *own* biography (i.e., lifestyle and career path). With the rapid expansion of occupational structures and changes in the world of work, most families have a significantly reduced ability to play a direct role in their children's future occupations. Moreover, modern youth also have access to many more socializing agents, namely television, the Internet, and other forms of popular media. All of these filter the influence of family and school.

Having access also means having choice, something not commonly associated with schooling. Thus, Brettschneider comments that "the motor of individualization runs on high revs in leisure time" (1990, p. 8). It is in this leisure time that youth will interact with movies, television, music, and the Internet, as well as their peers, who are also being bombarded with multiple images. The natural extension of this almost self-socialization is that adolescents are essentially free to compose their own lifestyle biographies.

There is a catch, however. As Tinning and Fitzclarence (1992, p. 297) note, "In a world of greater variety and options, paradoxically there are fewer real options available from which adolescents can produce their own biographies." The rationale for this statement is twofold. First, work-related status continues to determine the adult social structure and individual opportunity involved with adulthood. Second, the high school system still maintains its emphasis on continued dependence (or homogeneity); that is, school personnel are oriented to the belief that adolescents are *not yet* ready to take on productive roles on society (Fasick, 1984). High school, then, does little to promote autonomy in youth.

The emphasis on work-related status and the dependence ethic of schools both serve to actually *limit* the options available to teens as they attempt to construct their life projects. So, while adolescents are bombarded with choices from the media, the nature of future work and the conforming nature of schooling significantly limit the real possibilities.

Postmodern American Society

This chapter has repeatedly referred to the *new* world that occupies today's youth. Described as existing in a period of "postmodernism," this world has seen rapid social, economic, and cultural changes—in particular, significant economic restructuring and the development of a global economy. The postmodern era coincides particularly with the rise of consumer capitalism, as well as a shift from industrial production to electronic, managed, service-and-information economies. Deindustrialization and economic restructuring have led to the pronouncement that we are living in an "information society." Consider the number of information technologies that are now commonplace: electronic banking, cellular phones, compact CD players, and the Internet, to name but a few.

As noted, the changes at the end of the last century were not simply economic ones. There have also been significant changes in social expectations, in the nature of work, in education, and, in many cases, in family formations. Jobs that once existed no longer exist, as automation and technology offer more profitable substitutes. More and more parents are working two or more jobs, and more of these jobs are part-time without accompanying benefits. Teens are being required to take responsibility at home, both for themselves and for family tasks. Indeed, the notion of family itself has undergone considerable change, with many teens now living with relatives other than their mother or father.

From a political perspective, the new millennium has seen a rebirth in political conservatism. Giroux (1998) suggests that this conservatism serves to privilege market values over human values, an ideology that he believes subordinates human needs to the laws of the free market. From the context of youth, the policy issues of this conservatism have "shifted from social investment in youth to legislation primarily designed to contain and discipline them" (Giroux, 1998, p. 2). See, for example, the debate on curfews at the end of this chapter.

One of the major accompaniments of consumer capitalism is the notion of globalization. According to the International Labour Organization, globalization is defined as a process of growing interdependence among all people of this planet, in which people are linked together economically and socially by trade, investment, and governance. These links are spurred by market liberalization and information, communication, and transportation technologies. As part of this globalization process, many corporations have mobilized their financial resources, manufacturing and distribution facilities, and products to parts of the world offering cheaper labor and raw materials—and governments that tend to be lax in enforcing laws that protect labor, consumers, and the environment. As Viviano (2001) reports, even the Mafia has gone global!

As working life in cities across the world becomes increasingly connected, so too does daily living. Consider the following description of one group of youth:

Rapper Puff Daddy pulses from the speakers. Young men and women bathed in the hazy glow of black lights hunch over small tables, occasionally touching hands. (Moore, 2000)

No, this is not a description of a group of teens from urban Los Angeles, but of boys and girls gathered in Iranian coffeehouses. Such a description clearly identifies how Islamic youth have become influenced by the global accessibility to youth culture as it becomes available on satellite television and the Internet—notably, in this case, unbound by economic sanctions or religious codes. To borrow from Tinning and Fitzclarence (1992), postmodern adolescent life in Los Angeles is increasingly linked to life in Tokyo, Berlin, and Sydney, Australia.

Youth Culture and Media

Rollin (1999) has commented that nothing has changed teen life as much as the Internet. Savvy adolescents can now design their own web pages, play MUDs (multi-user games), and talk in chat rooms using either their real name or a fictitious one. The topics of these cyber conversations can be as diverse as teen interests themselves, and without restriction. Concurrent with the multitude of sites for gaining information, be it encyclopedic or even criminal, there are also many web sites that are designed by and for youth to have a voice.

The "literacies of the postmodern age [then], are electronic, aural, and image–based" (Giroux, 1998, p. 32). According to Aronowitz and Giroux (1992), learning in this age is located "elsewhere." By this they mean that apart from schooling, young people develop their identities through forms of knowledge from popular spheres such as rap music, daytime television, fanzines, Hollywood films, sprawling shopping malls, and the computer hacker culture.

Although faced with this image bombardment, adolescents still have the power of choice over how they use and view these images. Indeed, the fact that teens have greater control over their media choices than over other of their socializing agents (e.g., school and family) leads to greater self-socialization. Giroux (1998) comments that youth

> live in an electronically mediated culture for which channel surfing, moving quickly from one mode of communication to another, becomes the primary methods through which they are educated. (p. 5)

Youth Culture and Consumerism

Giroux's quote underscores the sense of "choice" as central to much of what is valued in postmodern society. He laments, however, that this accompanying focus on "hyperindividualism" has created a setting in which citizenship has everything to do with creating consuming subjects.

That youth are part of this increasing focus on consumerism in postmodern society has not been ignored by merchandisers. Indeed, in 1999 teenagers contributed $153 billion in retail sales in the United States. The growth in teenage spending has been so great—a 25% increase over the previous three years, and a market expected to continue to grow—that many marketing companies are now targeting American youth for their opinions about what's cool and, in particular, what's "in." Rollin (1999) suggests that teenagers in the 90s were the most polled, questioned, evaluated, scrutinized, and speculated-about group in the nation. One particular example of this attention to youth opinion is presented below:

Teens are significant consumers

Jane Rinzler Buckingham, looking not much older than a high school kid herself in cargo pants and boots, steers the focus group with practiced ease. Her firm, Youth Intelligence, has recruited this cadre to help a client, a major cosmetics manufacturer, figure out how to develop a perfume that will appeal to teenagers—attracting teenagers being a mission that currently preoccupies much of American business. The girls will each receive 50 bucks for their hour of disgorging opinions. Youth Intelligence—this cool town house in Greenwich Village is the company's carefully teenager-attuned headquarters—will, at the end of this two-month, three-city project, pocket a fee in the mid-five figures. (Span, 1999)

What Does This Mean for Physical Education?

Given our understanding of the postmodern world and youth culture as part of that world, it would be foolhardy for any physical education teachers to expect their students to look, act, and think the same way they do. Teens' developing identities may result in specific tensions not only between their desires and their parents' expectations, but also between their desires and their teachers and curricula. So much of what is presented to students is viewed by them as irrelevant and boring, yet is seen by teachers as subject matter worth learning. Tinning and Fitzclarence (1992) offer a number of scenarios describing the apparent disjunction between school physical education and the lives of young people that mirror these different agendas. These scenarios show that many teens are serious about their engagement with physical activity outside of school but find their in-school experiences particularly unattractive.

A second implication of postmodernism and youth culture for physical education is that the world of the 21st-century teenager is particularly rich in choice.

PE activities don't always match youth interests

Moreover, much of what teenagers see in the world is couched in the context of entertainment. For example, channel surfing allows numerous viewing choices, and if a particular show is not entertaining, then it is simply a matter of using the remote to find one that is. This promotes the demand for instant gratification, which extends to other parts of the teenager's world. In physical education, activities that students consider unentertaining or that require delayed gratification may be particularly problematic.

Finally, another aspect of consumerism is the commodification of the body. This and the idea of physical activity as a marketable commodity have significant import for physical education. The following chapter addresses this particular issue.

IN-SCHOOL TASKS

1. Interview four adolescents about things in their life that are important to them. Consider particularly in your questioning the reasons why these things are important. Try to get some idea of how the adolescents construct their personal biographies. Get these teenagers' perceptions about

   - television shows (what they watch, what they like)
   - dress (what they wear, what they like)
   - friends (what makes a good friend, who do they hang out with)

   What are these students' opinions/views about physical activity?

   - How important is it to them?
   - Do they participate in activity?
   - What sort, in what context, who with?

   What implications do the answers to the above questions have for the teaching of physical education in schools?

2. From your interviews above, find out which television shows are most popular among your sample. Watch two episodes of one of these shows, and analyze how the characters are depicted:

   ▪ What is their age range?

   ▪ What do their wear?

   ▪ What are their social agendas?

   ▪ How commercialized are their lifestyles?

   ▪ How central are their peers to their roles?

   As a physical education teacher, how does this aspect of youth culture fit into *your* objectives for the subject?

IN-CLASS DEBATES

You may find participating in one or both of the following debates a fruitful exercise in examining certain aspects of youth culture.

1. Are teenage curfews a legitimate way of addressing the "problems" of modern youth culture?

   ▪ Read the following student's response to the issue of teenage curfews.

   ▪ Prepare a case either for or against the legitimacy of curfews.

   Well, of course to start with, our town has a set 10:00 curfew for those under age 16. But the cops around here drive the "strip" (the place where everyone drives around and just talks to each other or hangs out) and they're just looking for someone to pull over. When they do, they hit them up for everything they can find! Sometimes we'd go sit at the bowling alley, but now they started a $5.00 cover charge just to get in if you're not 21!!! They pull you over for in-line skating after 10 just to see if you're 16 (same if you're walking), and the city voted to put up NO TRESPASSING signs up and down the "strip" so they have another reason to arrest us!!! We live in a small town with nothing else to do. The adults and city say that the under-age drinking and smoking are getting worse than they've ever been. And it's not just the normal stoners and drinkers, even preps and jocks and anyone who can't find anything else to do have been partying. Each class that passes through our high school is getting heavier into the drinking and stuff. . . . Parties are being busted every day. And they wonder why. . . . No one tries to think of something for us to do; they just keep taking more and more privileges away from US. My friends and I are getting really sick of it. [Adapted from www.libertarianrock.com, a web site protesting what its contributors believe to be unjust laws and political harassment.]

2. How effective is midnight basketball as a way of offsetting the rise of gang violence and youth crime?

- Read the following article about midnight basketball.
- Prepare a case either for or against the following proposition: "A detrimental aspect of midnight basketball programs is that they may provide a false sense of hope, especially when African American youth have the potential of developing a belief that sport is their only way of succeeding in this society."

In 1986, Mr. G. Van Standifer, town manager in Glenarden, Maryland, determined that the temptation for young adults for crime and drug activity was greatest between 10:00 P.M. and 2:00 A.M. His thoughts turned to an alternative to idle time crime and substance abuse was an intervention effort he named the Midnight Basketball League (MBL). With the support of businesses, law enforcement, political, and community leaders, the first Midnight Basketball League program took place during the summer of 1986. It was reported that the program contributed to a reduction in the incidence of reported crimes by almost 60% in Glenarden. As a result, a number of different communities have adopted midnight basketball as a crime reduction strategy, and its effectiveness in reaching at-risk young adults.

PORTFOLIO SUGGESTIONS AND ARTIFACTS

Your Autobiography (S1–D1,2: S8–D1)

Creating an autobiography helps you increase your awareness of beliefs and practices about teaching and learning. In writing your autobiography, you might consider the following questions:

- What role did your family play in your decision to teach?
- What are some early experiences that affected your decision to teach?
- When did you decide to become a teacher?
- What did your decision mean to you at the time?
- What about teaching interested or attracted you?
- What were some of the qualities of your most outstanding teachers when you were a student?
- How have teachers influenced your decisions to teach?
- What are some early experiences that continue to influence what and how you plan to teach?

- What are some central teaching ideas that guide you?
- What do you imagine you will be doing in five years?

REFLECTION TIME

Now that you have read this chapter, how confident do you feel in

- your ability to look beyond the initial appearance of a youth in your class that looks out of the mainstream?
- your ability to be introspective about the values and attitudes that you bring to your physical education classes?
- your ability to attend to all students in your classes, even those whose agendas might seem unlike yours?
- your ability to ask questions of teens and respect the perspective of their answers?

REFERENCES

Anton, M., & Earnest, L. (2000). Courting teenagers at the mall. *Los Angeles Times*, October 27, Section PA, A-1.

Aronowitz, S., & Giroux, H. A. (1992). *Postmodern education*. Minneapolis: University of Minnesota Press.

Brake, M. (1980). *The sociology of youth culture and youth subcultures: Sex and drugs and rock 'n' roll?* London: Routledge & Kegan Paul.

Brettschneider W. (1990). Adolescent's leisure, sport and lifestyle. In T. Williams, L. Almond, & A. Sparkes (Eds.), *Sport and physical activity: Moving towards excellence* (pp. 536–551). London: E&FN Spon.

Douvin, E., & Adelson, J. (1966). *The adolescent experience*. New York: Wiley.

Farley, C. J. (1997). Kids and race. *Time*, November 24, 88–91.

Fasick, F. A. (1984). Parents, peers, youth culture and autonomy in adolescence. *Adolescence, 19*, 143–157.

Giroux, H. A. (1998). *Channel surfing: Racism, the media, and the destruction of today's youth*. New York: St. Martin's Griffin.

Howe, N., & Strauss, W. (2000). *Millennials rising: The next American generation*. New York: Vintage Books.

Lazar, K. (2001). Study finds new generation on right path: Authors say Millennials get bad rap. *Boston Herald*, May 27.

Lerner, R. M., & Galambos, N. L. (1998). Adolescent development: Challenges and opportunities for research, programs, and policies. *Annual Review of Psychology, 49*, 413–446.

Moore, M. (2000). Slowly, Iran is loosening its cultural restraints: Tolerance being tested on dating, dress codes. *Washington Post*, November 26, p. A20.

Munoz, L. (1999). Where black and white youth meet. *Los Angeles Times*, October 9, p. F-1.

Petersen, A. C. (1988). Adolescent development. *Annual Review of Psychology, 39*, 583–607.

Rollin, L. (1999). *Twentieth-century teen culture by the decades*. Westport, CT: Greenwood Press.

Span, P. (1999). Teens are, like, so next week. *Washington Post*, June 17, p. C1.

Tiedt, A. L., & Tiedt, I. M. (1990). *Multicultural teaching: A handbook of activities*. Boston: Allyn & Bacon.

Tinning, R., & Fitzclarence, L. (1992). Postmodern youth culture and the crisis in Australian secondary school physical education. *Quest, 44*, 287–303.

Tinning, R., Macdonald, D., Wright, J., & Hickey C. (2001). *Becoming a physical education teacher: Contemporary and enduring issues*. Sydney: Pearson Education Australia.

Viviano, F. (2001). New face of mafia in Sicily: High-tech transformation—with global tentacles. *San Francisco Chronicle*, January 8, p. A1.

WEB RESOURCES

The following web link list was generated upon publication of the text; however, over time, the sites may become obsolete if an organization dissolves, discontinues online surfaces, or relocates to a different URL. If a link listed below does not connect, please search for the organization by name.

http://www.brat.org/

BRAT is a youth and young adult activist electronic magazine and organization located in Louisville, Kentucky, whose goal is to promote social awareness about and among youth, encourage community-based activism, and support independent, progressive cultures.

http://www.youthculture.com/

Based in Toronto, Canada, Youth Culture is a research and strategy company devoted exclusively to the youth market. Youth Culture has a North American client base and invests most of its resources in understanding the Canadian teen experience.

http://library.thinkquest.org/12426/index.html

Culture Shock—an exploration of modern day youth cultures.

CHAPTER 3

Physical Activity, the Body, and Physicality

Scenario

Janet and Rusty, teen sister and brother, are completing a number of after-school tasks. At the supermarket, while passing the checkout, each glances at covers of the magazines. After leaving the store, Janet heads to a hair appointment, Rusty to the dentist. In their respective waiting areas, they spend time glossing through the magazines. On arrival home, both teens devour the magazines they receive on subscription. Janet and Rusty look at the models in the magazines. Janet and Rusty look in their mirrors. Both feel they don't measure up.

Introduction

As was discussed in Chapter 2, adolescence is a time of significant physical and social change. These changes are also accompanied by a developing ability to think abstractly and, with this, an increasing capacity for self-reflection. This self-reflection and the ability to critique mark the beginning of a period of extreme physical and psychological self-consciousness (Kearny-Cooke & Steichen-Asch, 1990).

We also noted in Chapter 2 that teenagers are now becoming socialized through different agents. Whereas parents were once the predominant source of knowledge and wisdom, teens now have a more sophisticated peer group, as well as access to the ever-burgeoning media to influence them. You will recall how television, the Internet, and other forms of popular media filter the influence of family and school, leading to significant self-socialization.

The socializing effects of the media and the predominance of social relationships work together to form a new consciousness about the adolescent body—namely, "it matters." What "matters" is that the body is now an object of commodification—that is, the body is a marketable commodity. Physical appearance (read: fit, hard muscles and cut abs for boys, and Kate Moss-thin for girls) is becoming significantly more important in providing status. As teens are bombarded with media images of the desired body (and what it can get you), they also learn that others read bodies in a particular way. As a result, adolescence is a time when teens are particularly concerned and interested in images of the body—what is considered desirable, what is considered worthy.

The Commodification of the Body

Anyone doubting the potential of the popular media to socialize teens toward a particular view of the desirable body need go no further than speaking to teens themselves. Consider the findings of in-depth discussions with one group of adolescent girls:

> *Fifty-nine percent of the girls stated dissatisfaction with their bodies, and although only 29% of them fit the standard medical definition of overweight, 66% wanted to lose weight. Most disturbing of all was the fact that 47% of the girls surveyed said looking at pictures in fashion magazines made them want to lose weight now, and 69% claimed those pictures influenced what they consider to be their ideal body. (Field et al., 1999)*

Teens are concerned about their bodies

Thirty years ago, the average fashion model weighed about 8% less than the average American woman. Now she weighs 23% less.

To explain this impact, we turn to the notion of the commodification of the body. The body can be thought of as a product, an article of trade—something of value in the market. If you believe this to be overstating or perhaps overanalyzing the situation, consider the following brand names: Coke, Calvin Klein, Budweiser, and Levi Strauss. While none of their products have a direct concern with health and fitness, all of their advertisements present bodies that fit the ideal of "slim, hard, and beautiful." Ed Bark, television critic of the *Dallas Morning News*, writes of the 30-second fantasy—a.k.a. "Wouldn't it be great if your life were just like a beer commercial?"

> *Have a beer and be the proud owner of a washboard belly. Or choose the right brew and enter a fantasy world full of luscious, libidinous women. Beer advertising has evolved from beechwood-aged to beach volleyball. (1991, p. 1C)*

The images of the body as a commodity are not just projected at men. Indeed, a plethora of magazines, television advertisements, and other images directed at both men and women present the body as profitable merchandise. Consider the launch of a new product for women: the "Ultrabra Airotics," a bra that features a crescent-shaped airbag in each cup. A small rubber pump allows the wearer to inflate and deflate the bra as circumstance requires.

The advent of such gadgets leads some to question whether women are selling themselves or merely selling out. As Libby Brooks writes,

> *Sometimes it feels as though women's bodies exist only to tell lies with. A slick of gloss, a layer of elastic, an injection of collagen—femininity is constructed to the extent that nothing need be natural any more, least of all the "natural look." Who do you want to be today? (Brooks, 2001)*

Brooks continues to reinforce the commodification aspect: "Lingerie designers see cash, magazine publishers see cash, advertising agencies see cash, global business sees cash. In the breast-obsessed West, you can sell almost anything you want to with a nice pair . . . including yourself."

Giroux (1998) comments that this form of popular culture "increasingly teaches kids to gaze inwardly at the body as a fashionscape, a stylized athletic spectacle" (p. 32). In this spectacle, the body has become a metaphor for health, well-being, discipline, and success—"work that body!"

Tinning (1994), too, suggests that the body has become increasingly important as an indicator of an individual's worth. In Tinning's interpretation, the body provides evidence of personal values such as self-discipline (through evidence of work on the body), and of status and wealth (through clothing, cosmetic use, comportment, and grooming).

Commodification of Physical Activity

It is not just the body that has taken on the pernicious influence of the market. Physical activity itself has become commodified. Bark (1991) notes that "sexual prowess, group-bonding and instant athleticism also are prime selling points" of beer commercials. Indeed, of the 33 spots shown during one Sunday's and Monday's five televised pro football games in Dallas, 12 sold beer in tandem with intense physical activity. Sports included softball, basketball, roller-skating, scuba diving, wheelchair racing and beach volleyball." Exercise, then, is seen as something that can be used to create the ideal body, which then provides significant market value.

The Concept of Hegemonic Masculinity

One particular way of examining the concept of the body as a commodity is to examine the concept of hegemonic masculinity. Hegemony can be thought of as a subtle way of maintaining a particular dominant authority. Introduced by Italian socialist Antonio Gramsci in the early 1900s, hegemony is the name given to the process through which the elite maintain their dominant status through a subtle imposition of ideology on the masses (see Schell & Rodriguez, 2000). Hegemonic masculinity, then, is the description given to the forms of masculinity that are prescribed as normal and highly valued. In Western societies, hegemonic masculinity is the masculinity of wealth and power. As it relates to physical activity, the highly valued form of masculinity is one characterized by physical prowess at sport and, increasingly, a physical appearance of cut abdominals and fit, hard muscles (see Tinning et al., 2001). A certain status is placed on those who achieve these masculine attributes. Men without these attributes (that is, men with subordinated masculinities) are, in contrast, devalued and even stigmatized. As Davison (2000) notes, "You can excel in the classroom as a male student but if you don't excel in the gym then you don't have the same status."

A logical extension from the notion of hegemonic masculinity is that self-worth is increasingly tied to body image. Wienke (1998) claims that most men feel bodily dissatisfied in comparison to the ideal type because it is believed that those men closest to the ideal reap certain cultural and social benefits not available to those further away.

As Gillett and White (1992) comment, in a contemporary visually oriented consumer culture, men are spending more time than ever on the management, discipline, and display of their bodies. The latest data would seem to corroborate their claims. In 1999, American men paid more than $2 million for gym memberships and another $2 billion for home exercise equipment. The magazine *Men's Health* now has a subscription of over 1.6 million. *Time* magazine also reports that in 1996, men underwent 700,000 cosmetic procedures (Cloud, 2000). Finally, a psychological disorder known as reverse anorexia, or bigarexia, has been identified—a condition in which men see themselves as scrawny when they are really quite big and muscular, leading to compulsive exercising.

Hegemonic masculinity not only reinforces a particular ideal for men's bodies, but also serves to subjugate women's bodies. Tinning et al. (2001) comment that, "where wealth, power and sporting prowess are markers of hegemonic

Women's sports can be aggressive

forms of masculinity, ideal notions of what it means to be female are also constructed in relation to these" (p. 100). Popular culture provides numerous messages about what it means to be feminine, namely, a heterosexual woman who fits a particularly narrow definition of physical attractiveness.

In the world of sport (and for us, physical education), hegemonic masculinity serves to limit the opportunities for girls to participate in the physical culture. Davison claims that whereas boys who do not excel in the gym are perceived as lower in status, girls who do excel in the gym, or those who portray masculine traits, are also subordinate. Consider the following example:

I like to be first to get to the puck. If the other person gets the puck, I want to make sure I get them off the puck. And sometimes that's physically aggressive but it's always within the rules. Well, usually [laughs]. I will never let another person physically overpower me. (from Theberge, 1997)

On reading this quote, one would assume that it was from a male hockey player. Indeed, no: Theberge's study centered on physicality and gender issues among *women* hockey players. The point here is that aggression and physicality are seen as acceptable, even desirable, in men's sports, but that in women's sports the same traits often lead to homophobic attitudes and stigma. Pallotta-Chiarolli (1998) presents the classic stereotype: "Oh, you're a (female) weightlifter, you must be gay."

What Does This Mean for Physical Education?

As we have discussed, adolescents live in an information society that constantly barrages them with information that confirms, reinforces,and reproduces a particular bodily stereotype. However, no matter how we look at it, physical education involves putting adolescent bodies on display in a very public forum. There are clear connections, then, between school physical education and the development of self-identity, particularly through the body and physicality. As Tinning (1994) notes, this has considerable potential for undermining the developing self-identities of students, particularly for those who perceive that their body does not "measure up." Is it any wonder then, that so many students arrive dressed for physical education wearing baggy T-shirts or, worse, choose not to participate at all?

A second problem for physical education is the potential lack of connection between the commercialized form of physical activity and the curriculum within schools. Tinning and Fitzclarence (1992) suggest that "the constant use of physical activity in the media as a major focus for commercial development and exploitation creates unrealistic expectations of the nature of school physical education" (p. 288). That is, physical education is projected into a world in which

Teachers are expected to entertain

physical activity is associated (unproblematically) with desirable bodies and a lifestyle of consumption, fun, and entertainment. Activity as it is presented to students in the school setting does not match their vision of physical activity in their out-of-school lives. Indeed, activity in youth culture often embraces values such as spontaneity, nonconformity, sociability, and creativity in pursuits such as in-line skating, skateboarding, and street basketball. Where physical education fails particularly to entertain, students may perceive it as boring and irrelevant (Tinning & Fitzclarence, 1992).

Of more damaging consequence, however, is the practice of many physical education classes that leave little room for alternative bodies. Many practices in physical education can sort and categorize bodies and reinforce the hegemonic ideal of the masculine body and the demand to be athletic and measure up to a masculine standard. Picking teams in which the most skillful take the powerful roles of captains and the lesser athletes are chosen last is but one example of a practice that has no place in schools

Boys and girls can participate together in team sports

if we are to present a supportive and accepting physical education. Moreover, splitting classes into, for example, "football for boys and aerobics for girls" serves only to reinforce the narrow stereotypes of masculinity and femininity. Many girls would enjoy participating in a flag football unit, while some boys are indeed very skillful at dance and gymnastics.

Physical Education Teachers as Part of the Problem

For most physical education teachers, sport and physical activity are in the center rather than in the periphery of their life histories (Tinning, 1994). Indeed, nearly 100 percent of physical educators played competitive sports during high school. While this in itself is not a negative finding, it does pose the question as to (a) whether these teachers are able to be critical consumers of the presentation of the "body" as central to their biographies and, perhaps of more significance, (b) whether these teachers can identify practices within physical education that reinforce traditional and narrow conceptions of masculinity.

A second feature of physical educators is that they have most likely been trained in institutions that present a functionalist, medical science–based view of the body. Tinning et al. (2001) comment:

> *All this serves to consolidate the view that physical education is about the function of the body as a machine that moves, runs, jumps, throws, catches, strikes and so on. It is worth pondering the extent to which this form of knowledge actually equips physical education teachers to deal with the complex practices and relations associated with teaching and learning in schools. We can ask how such scientific knowledge actually helps teachers to understand and reconcile the bodily experiences of pleasure, of rejection, of pain, of nurture, of empathy, of gender and of alienation that are so deeply embedded in the movement cultures associated with sport and physical education. (p. 173)*

How Can We Respond?

It should be clear from reading this chapter that physical education has the significant potential to be a particularly oppressive practice. Nevertheless, physical education classes can be positioned within a teen's social, physical, and educational sphere in such a manner as to broaden the ways boys and girls think about their bodies and to offset the contradictions and oppressive concepts of masculinity that the media bombard them with. Speaking from the perspective of men's gender identity, Davison (2000, p. 64) suggests that "the creation of a discursive space where young men can speak of possible contradictions inherent to masculine performances may allow for a better understanding of body health and may encourage more respect for their bodies and other boys' bodies and offer students the possibility to enjoy physical education class to a greater extent." So, too, may we as physical educators present a subject that helps students understand the socially constructed nature of their bodies. To achieve this objective, we must actively seek to incorporate specific practices within physical education.

Specific Practices to Include in Physical Education

Our first challenge is to recognize that the "exercise–body beautiful complex" is covertly disempowering. As we have read, popular culture (especially youth culture) foregrounds physicality, bodies, physical activity, and youth in ways that are seldom challenged within physical education (Tinning, 1994). Hence, we must begin to challenge those messages of popular culture that reinforce the narrow view of the body. Tinning and Fitzclarence (1992) suggest we help students become critical consumers of media messages. Being critical means "being able to recognize how language use and choices of visual images help to create particular sets of meanings which connect with values and beliefs that are important to the consumer" (Tinning et al., 2001, p. 149).

This process is not simply a case of debunking current magazine articles. For example, we are well aware of the substantial health risks associated with overweight. Thus, it is not prudent to suggest that overweight girls should simply accept their body shape and not be encouraged to lose weight. We need to carefully construct a teaching and learning setting where students perceive the climate as *caring, encouraging, and accepting*. This is particularly important when we recognize that many adolescent girls do not value exercise as a health-promoting activity. For many, *thinness*, not fitness, is the goal when they try to lose weight. Varnum (1998) reports that girls say they are more likely to diet, often with the help of appetite suppressants, than to exercise. Described as "less effort and quicker results," dieting is most often the weight loss mechanism of choice. To quote one girl from Varnum's report, "Exercise doesn't necessarily help you lose weight. It may, but a lot of your weight from exercising comes from muscle. Even though that's a good thing, it doesn't matter. You're still putting on weight and you want to look skinny—you don't want to be muscular. . . . It makes you bigger."

A caring, encouraging and accepting environment is also necessary to engage all boys within physical education. Often vilified as nerdy or gay, boys who do not possess the stereotyped attributes of masculinity are at potential risk not only of embarrassment, but also of alienation and humiliation. In some cases, this can lead to an unhealthy and self-disempowering indulgence in self-blame. These are hardly attributes that are likely to lead to a lifelong engagement and enjoyment of physical activity. It is particularly important to note that self-efficacy in physical activity is predictive of participation in physical activity (see Allison, Dwyer & Makin, 1999).

IN-SCHOOL TASKS

Perceptions of Ideal Body Shape

Ask a group of high school students to examine the silhouettes shown in Figure 3.1.

One set is of males, the other of females. Have each student identify which of the silhouettes represents (a) the most attractive/desirable body shape for their own gender and (b) their perception of their own body shape. In addition, ask students to identify the most attractive/desirable body shape for the opposite gender.

Analyze the data, and derive answers to the following:

1. What is the perceived ideal body shape for girls by girls, and for girls by boys?

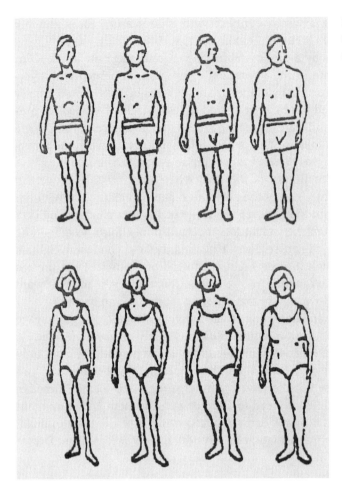

Figure 3.1   Male and female body-type silhouettes

2. What is the perceived ideal body shape for boys by boys, and for boys by girls?

In your college class, or with the group of students who completed the exercise, discuss these results in terms of the influence of peers and the media in dictating personal perceptions about self-image.

Countering Media Messages

In this exercise, you will have your students examine magazine advertisements from the perspective of their message(s) concerning "desirable bodies." Ask your students to bring to class copies of advertisements from magazines that specifically use exercise or a svelte body to promote a product unassociated with health and fitness.

First, have students describe the subtle messages about the body and exercise from a commodification perspective. Second, have the students create alternative messages, those that debunk the dominant ideal. For example:

Picture: Of a super-slim model in a silky dress that is being blown in the wind.

Alternative text: "I try to stay in on windy days. You can see why. There's really not much to me. And I'm not just talking about my vacant expression."

IN-CLASS DEBATES

Read the following excerpt from Memphis' *Commercial Appeal* newspaper ("Thick or Thin," 1995). It presents a different perspective of desired body image. It also presents us with a dilemma.

Model Cindy Crawford's slim silhouette looks OK to Christina Wicks, 17, a senior at White Station High School. "But that's not how I prefer to look. I'm my own

Many teens prefer to be thin

kind of person," said the black teenager, who was wearing big earrings and sporting a fashionably cropped hairdo one day recently.

"Most girls I know want to have shape," she said. "They want big hips and butts because, I guess, that's what black men prefer. I know some people like the slender look. But I don't understand it myself."

To calorie-counters who measure beauty in inches, those must seem like strange words. In fact, they reflect what may be a typical attitude among young black women. A new study, produced by researchers at the University of Arizona, points to a sharp difference in the way black and white girls view their bodies.

While 90 percent of the white junior high and high school girls in the study reported dissatisfaction with their weight, 70 percent of black teenagers were satisfied with their bodies.

Black girls described the perfect size as full hips and thick thighs. And even significantly overweight black teenagers called themselves happy.

White girls, on the other hand, defined perfection as 5-foot-7 and 100 to 110 lbs., about the same measurements as paper-thin model Kate Moss.

[Copyright 1995, the *Commercial Appeal*, Memphis, TN]

Given that African American women are at greater risk for hypertension and diabetes, diseases that seem to be exacerbated by excess weight, what implications do these findings have for us as physical educators? How do we create a climate in physical education that both caters to the development of a positive self-image and a debunking of body-image stereotypes and also promotes positive health behaviors?

PORTFOLIO SUGGESTIONS AND ARTIFACTS

An "All bodies Are Welcome Here" Poster (S3–D1,2,3: S4–P2)

Design a poster that presents the message that everyone is welcome in your physical education classes. Structure the poster so that three major points are developed:

1. "Subordinated" bodies deserve equal access to the joys of physical activity.
2. Teasing, bullying, and other forms of harassment will not be tolerated.
3. Your classes operate in a context of care and encouragement.

REFLECTION TIME

Now that you have read this chapter, how confident do you feel in

- your ability to examine the role and importance of physical activity as it contributes to your own personal identity?

- your ability to protect all students in your classes from potential harassment concerning their skillfulness and their physique?

- your commitment to provide a caring and supporting class climate where all students feel valued and safe?

- your ability to help students to be critical of media images that portray narrow definitions of the acceptable body?

REFERENCES

Allison, K. R., Dwyer, J. J., & Makin, S. (1999). Self-efficacy and participation in physical activity in high school students. *Health Behavior, 26* (1), 12–24.

Bark, E. (1991). 30-second fantasies: Wouldn't it be great if your life were just like a beer commercial? *Dallas Morning News*, December 1, 1991, p. C1.

Brooks, L. (2001, March 21). You can sell almost anything with a nice pair. *Sydney Morning Herald*. Retrieved Wednesday, March 21, 2001, from http://www.smh.com.au/news/0103/21/features/features5.html

Cloud, J. (2000). Never too buff: A new book reveals a troubling obsession: How male self-worth is increasingly tied to body image. *Time*, April 24, 2000, 155 (16), 64–68.

Davison, K. G. (2000). Boys' bodies in school: Physical education. *The Journal of Men's Studies, 6* (2), 255–266.

Field, A. E., Cheung, L., Wolf, A. M., Herzog, D. B., Gortmaker, S. L., & Colditz, G. A. (1999). Exposure to the mass media and weight concerns among girls. *Pediatrics, 103* (3): e36. Retrieved from *Pediatrics* electronic pages: www.pediatrics.org/cgi/content/full/103/3/e36

Gillett, J., & White, P. G. (1992). Male bodybuilding and the reassertion of hegemonic masculinity: A critical feminist perspective. *Play and Culture, 5*, 358–369.

Giroux, H. A. (1998). *Channel surfing: Racism, the media, and the destruction of today's youth*. New York: St. Martin's Griffin.

Kearny-Cooke, A., & Steichen-Asch, P. (1990). Men, body image and eating disorders. In A. E. Andersen (Ed.), *Males with eating disorders* (pp. 54–74). New York: Brunner/Mazel.

Pallotta-Chiarolli, M. (1998). *Girls' talk: Young women sport from their hearts and minds*. Sydney: Finch Publishing.

Schell, L. A., & Rodriguez, S. (2000). Our sporting sisters: How male hegemony stratifies women in sport. *Women in Sport and Physical Activity Journal, 9* (1), 15–34.

Theberge. N. (1997). "It's part of the game": Physicality and the production of gender in women's hockey. *Gender and Society, 11,* 69–88.

Tinning, R. (1994). Baggy T shirts, Reeboks, schooling, popular culture and young bodies. In J. Kenway & J. Collier (Eds.), *Schooling what future?* Geelong, Australia: Deakin Centre for Education and Change.

Tinning, R., & Fitzclarence, L. (1992). Postmodern youth culture and the crisis in Australian secondary school physical education. *Quest, 44,* 287–303.

Tinning, R. Macdonald, D., Wright, J., & Hickey C. (2001). *Becoming a physical education teacher: Contemporary and enduring issues.* Sydney: Pearson Education Australia.

Varnum, S. (1998). In search of approval, girls attack themselves. *Concord Monitor,* June 7, 1998.

Wienke, C. (1998). Negotiating the male body: Men, masculinity and cultural ideals. *The Journal of Men's Studies, 62* (2), 255–282.

WEB RESOURCES

The following web link list was generated upon publication of the text; however, over time, the sites may become obsolete if an organization dissolves, discontinues online surfaces, or relocates to a different URL. If a link listed below does not connect, please search for the organization by name.

http://www.about-face.org

A site dedicated to combating negative and distorted images of women and promoting alternatives through education, action, and humor.

http://webmd.lycos.com/content/article/1728.59692

Discusses the Adonis complex—where men fight stereotypes of "desirable" body image as do many women.

http://www.mtholyoke.edu/~nware/

Examines women's body image and the media. Check out particularly the link to the image gallery, where "alternate" captions to media posters are humorously and very thoughtfully written.

http://www.mirror-mirror.org/edtest.htm

An eating behavior test—perhaps useful for students who you might feel are at risk of an eating disorder.

CHAPTER 4

Current Fitness Status of American Youth

Scenario

A television blares in a darkened room.
A child lies sprawled on a couch, eyes glazed.
There is no movement and barely a hint of breath.
Then a hand reaches out, slowly, to a bowl on the coffee table. It scoops up potato chips, moves upward to the mouth.
There is crunching. Some crumbs.
Then the child becomes still again—entranced.　　　　　(Melvin, 1993)[1]

Meanwhile . . .

Over at south Riverdale's Jimmie Simpson Recreation Centre, Ann Truong, 13, is zooming around the gym on roller skates.
　　"When I stay at home I get so bored," says Truong, who was out with a group of friends one recent Sunday afternoon. "Here you can meet people and have fun."
　　All it costs is 50 cents to rent a pair of skates. No one here is wearing designer duds or sports logos. Among this casual crowd—both guys and gals moving to thundering reggae tunes—anything goes.　　　　　(Turner, 1994)

Introduction

When you read these scenarios, you may wonder which of them is more common. The answer seems to be both. There are many adolescents in the United States who are physically active. Likewise, there is a large number of American youth who fall in the overweight to obese categories. Indeed, the latest figures suggest that 11% of American youth fall above the sex- and age-specific 95th percentile of body mass index (U.S. Department of Health and Human Services [USDHHS], 2000a).

---

[1] Reprinted with permission of the *St. Petersburg Times*.

In this chapter, we will examine five key questions related to the fitness status of American youth. The first is, simply, how fit *should* these youngsters be—what are the standards? That question prompts the second: How fit *are* they—how do these teenagers match up to the fitness standards that have been set? The third question asks, What are the barriers to teenagers becoming and staying active? Once we have an understanding of the level of youth activity and the factors that mitigate against activity, the fourth question arises: What is the role of physical education in the promotion of youth fitness? The final question is, What are the purposes of fitness testing, and how is it conducted?

How Fit Should Teenagers Be?

The issue of how fit adolescents should be is not a new one. Throughout the last century, concerns have been periodically raised about the fitness status of American youth. During the First World War, for example, there were concerns about the levels of fitness of military recruits. Many claimed that U.S. soldiers were unprepared for the tasks of war and that the physical education of the time was too "soft." This physical education was essentially a curriculum of game play and dance.

A major controversy arose in 1954, when tests by Kraus and Hirschland found that 60% of American students failed a fitness test that only 9% of European youth were unable to pass. Indeed, the data from this report was a catalyst for the development of the President's Council on Youth Fitness. It was during this time that *Time* magazine awarded American children an "F," for flabby.

More Recent Focus on Health-Related Fitness

In more recent times, fitness standards have been designed to reflect more health-based issues. The original fitness tests of the 1950s included items such as the standing long jump and the 50-yard dash. While these items give an indication of a student's explosive power and running speed, they provide little evidence of that student's health status. To this end, the American Alliance for Health, Physical Education, Recreation and Dance (AAHPERD) developed a series of tests that measure "health-related fitness." Health-related fitness test items were developed to provide a measure of one's status regarding the factors that are associated with increased risk of mortality from cardiovascular disease.

The items that relate to these dimensions are endurance runs (to measure cardiovascular fitness), skinfold testing (to measure body composition), sit-up and push-up tests (to measure musculoskeletal endurance, and flexibility tests (to measure low back and hamstring function).

Activity can be incorporated into the lifestyle

A Move to Criterion-Referenced Scoring

The earliest fitness tests, including the National Children and Youth Fitness Study I (NCYFS I), reported their results as percentiles; that is, they were norm-referenced scores. For example, the 50th percentile for the one-mile run for a 14-year-old boy was 7:51. This 50th percentile was regarded as the standard for "passing" a particular test item. By its very nature, then, half of the children who take this test must fail it.

The fitness tests of today, such as the Fitnessgram and the President's Challenge, represent a major change in the way fitness testing data are interpreted. These tests use criterion-referenced standards, which examine scores against a particular health criterion. As a result of this change in focus, it may be possible that students from a quality physical education program can *all* reach a particular health standard on a test. Likewise, it may also be the case that where opportunities for activity are limited, very few students may reach the health standard.

Health-Related Standards

Tables 4.1 and 4.2 provide benchmarks indicating the *minimum* health standards for the Fitnessgram and President's Challenge test items. In the case of Fitnessgram, a range is provided that indicates the lowest level for health to an upper, more desired level. The President's Challenge offers scores at a number of levels. These are named the "awards." The scores presented here are those that qualify students for the Health Fitness Award.

Table 4.1 Upper and Lower Limits of Heath Fitness Zones for the Fitnessgram

Boys' scores

Age	1-mile run (mins:secs)	Percentage of fat	Curl-ups (number)	Trunk lift (inches)	Push-ups (number)
12	10:30–8:00	25–10	18–36	9–12	10–20
13	10:00–7:30	25–10	21–40	9–12	12–25
14	9:30–7:00	25–10	24–45	9–12	14–30
15	9:00–7:00	25–10	24–47	9–12	16–35
16	8:30–7:00	25–10	24–47	9–12	18–35
17	8:30–7:00	25–10	24–47	9–12	18–35
17+	8:30–7:00	25–10	24–47	9–12	18–35

Girls' scores

Age	1-mile run (mins:secs)	Percentage of fat	Curl-ups (number)	Trunk lift (inches)	Push-ups (number)
12	12:00–9:00	32–17	18–32	9–12	7–15
13	11:30–9:00	32–17	18–32	9–12	7–15
14	11:00–8:30	32–17	18–32	9–12	7–15
15	10:30–8:00	32–17	18–35	9–12	7–15
16	10:00–8:00	32–17	18–35	9–12	7–15
17	10:00–8:00	32–17	18–35	9–12	7–15
17+	10:00–8:00	32–17	18–35	9–12	7–15

Source: FITNESSGRAM® data reproduced with permission, The Cooper Institute, Dallas, TX.

A Move to Focus on Activity Rather Than Fitness

Whereas fitness testing measures a number of components such as flexibility and muscular endurance, the study of Blair (1992) resulted in a major shift in the notion of "fitness." The essential message from Blair was that measurements of *activity* in youth are indeed more valid estimates of fitness than the tests themselves.

The key to this new focus was the accumulation of epidemiological data on exercise showing that significant health benefits could be gained from simply engaging in moderate exercise. Furthermore, as is demonstrated in Figure 4.1, the gains are particularly striking when one moves from being totally sedentary to participating in even limited amounts of moderate exercise. Such was the magnitude of these findings that Freedson and Rowland (1992) argued that it would be better to focus on teenagers' activity levels even more than their fitness levels.

The term "moderate to vigorous physical activity" (MVPA) has been coined to take into account the broader range of physical activities that help develop fitness, and a number of authors provide suggested levels of minimum energy

Table 4.2   President's Challenge Standards
(Criteria for a Healthy Level pf Fitness)

Boys' scores

Age	1-mile run (mins:secs)	BMI	Curl-ups (number)	Sit and reach (centimeters)	Push-ups (number)	Pull-ups (number)
12	9:00	14.8–24.1	20	21	9	2
13	8:00	15.4–24.7	25	21	10	2
14	8:00	16.1–25.4	25	21	12	3
15	7:30	16.6–26.4	30	21	14	4
16	7:30	17.2–26.8	30	21	16	5
17	7:30	17.7–27.5	30	21	18	6

Girls' scores

Age	1-mile run (mins:secs)	BMI	Curl-ups (number)	Sit and reach (centimeters)	Push-ups (number)	Pull-ups (number)
12	10:00	14.7–24.2	20	23	8	1
13	10:30	15.5–25.3	25	25	7	1
14	10:30	16.2–25.4	25	25	7	1
15	10:00	16.6–26.5	30	25	7	1
16	10:00	16.8–26.5	30	25	7	1
17	10:00	17.1–26.9	30	25	7	1

Source: Reprinted with permission from the *President's Challenge Physical Activity and Fitness Awards Program Manual,* 2001, Bloomington, IN: The Presidents Challenge.

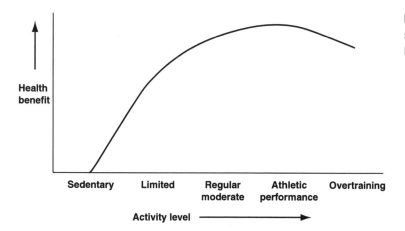

Figure 4.1   Relationship between activity and health benefits.

expenditure. For example, Jackson, Morrow, Hill, and Dishman (1999) recommend 150 kcal of energy expenditure in activity per day, while Blair (1992) advises a figure of 3–4 kcal/kg/day. In the case of children, however, Corbin, Pangrazi, and Welk (1999) encourage activity expenditure of 6–8 kcal/kg/day.

Regarding the amount of daily activity that is needed, one particular point has been established: *Activity can be accumulated*. To be exact, although 30 minutes of activity per day at the pace equivalent of brisk walking is indeed sufficient to derive health benefits, this 30 minutes can be accumulated in blocks of as short as 10 minutes.

At this point, it is useful to clarify the notions of activity, exercise, and fitness. The USDHHS (1996) uses the following definitions.

- *Physical activity*—any bodily movement produced by skeletal muscles that results in an expenditure of energy; includes occupational, leisure time, and routine daily activities; activities requiring light to moderate or vigorous effort

- *Exercise*—physical activity consisting of planned, structured, and repetitive bodily movement that is done to improve or maintain one or more components of health-related fitness

- *Health-related physical fitness*—a measure of a person's ability to perform physical activities that require endurance, strength, or flexibility; achieved through a combination of regular exercise and inherent ability

Active youth

Following these definitions, we see that fitness is a product of leading an active lifestyle. It can also be achieved through the more purposeful activity known as exercise. As we begin the new millennium, the thinking is that we need to center our attention more on the process of helping youth become more *active*. In particular, we need to help them find ways to incorporate activity into their lifestyle so that it will encourage continued participation in exercise. This should be our objective, not the product or outcome of fitness. Given sufficient levels of activity, the outcome will take care of itself.

As mentioned earlier, an energy expenditure of 3–4 kcal/kg/day and the accumulation of 30 minutes per day of MVPA have been cited as sufficient levels of activity. The *Healthy People 2010* document (USDHHS, 2000a) also lists a number of specific goals relating to participation in physical activity. These are included in Table 4.3.

The *Healthy People 2010* report provides the guideline of 30 minutes of daily moderate activity, as well as three 20-minute sessions per week of vigorous activity. However, the National Association for Sports and Physical Education (NASPE), the Year 2000 Dietary Guidelines for Americans, and a consensus group from the United Kingdom (see Biddle, Sallis & Cavill, 1998) all recommend a more substantial amount: at least 60 minutes per day of moderate to vigorous activity. This amount was considered more appropriate given the rapid increase in youth obesity, combined with the findings that young people rarely do continuous vigorous exercise (see Sallis, 2000).

Body Composition

In addition to activity, another standard is relevant when we examine the fitness status of American youth: body composition. According to the Centers for Disease Control and Prevention (CDC), a teenager with a BMI in the 85th to 95th percentile is considered at risk for being overweight. Those in the 95th percentile or higher are considered overweight. Figures 4.2 and 4.3 provide the CDC growth charts, which can be used to determine BMI and thereby status of overweight.

Table 4.3   *Healthy People 2010* Physical Activity and Fitness
                 Objectives Relevant for Children and Adolescents

---

- Increase the proportion of adolescents who engage in moderate physical activity for at least 30 minutes on 5 or more of the previous 7 days.
- Increase the proportion of adolescents who engage in vigorous physical activity that promotes cardiorespiratory fitness 3 or more days per week for 20 or more minutes per occasion.
- Increase the proportion of children and adolescents who view television 2 or fewer hours per day.
- Increase the proportion of trips made by walking.
- Increase the proportion of trips made by bicycling.
- Increase the proportion of the nation's public and private schools that require daily physical education for all students.
- Increase the proportion of adolescents who participate in daily physical education.
- Increase the proportion of adolescents who spend at least 50% of school physical education class time being physically active.
- Increase the proportion of the nation's public and private schools that provide access to their physical activity spaces and facilities for all persons outside of normal school hours (that is, before and after the school day, on weekends, and during summer and other vacations).

Source: U.S. Department of Health and Human Services. *Healthy People 2010, Understanding and Improving Health,* 2000, Washington, DC: Author.

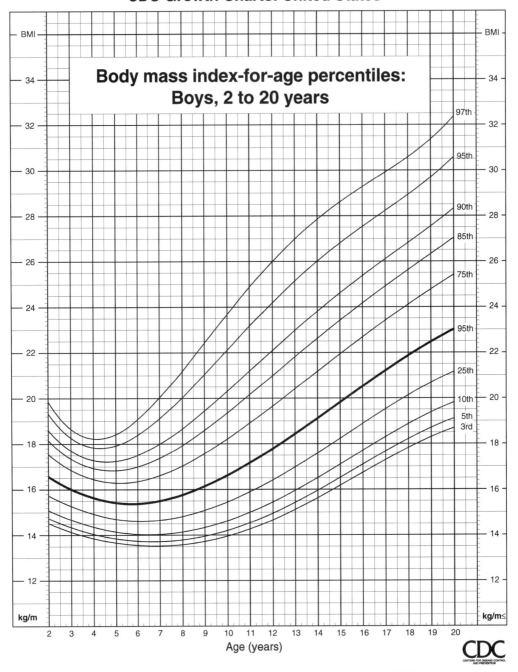

Figure 4.2   CDC growth charts, body mass index-for-age percentiles: boys 2–20 years.

Source: Developed by the National Center of Health Statistics in collaboration with the National Center for Chronic Disease Prevention and Health Promotion (2000).

CDC Growth Charts: United States

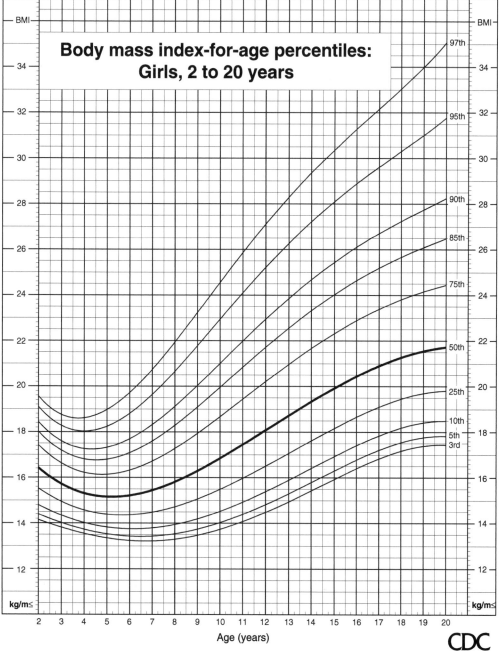

Figure 4.3   CDC growth charts, body mass index-for-age percentiles: girls 2–20 years.

Source: Developed by the National Center of Health Statistics in collaboration with the National Center for Chronic Disease Prevention and Health Promotion (2000).

How Fit and Active Are Teenagers?

Once we have determined the standards of fitness and activity that teenagers should be reaching, the next challenge is to measure those levels. Most of you reading this book will have participated in fitness testing in the schools at some time, and, indeed, Fitnessgram and the President's Challenge provide very clear protocols for the way in which the data are to be collected.

Participation in physical activity is more difficult to assess, because most of the information is typically obtained from diaries and recall questionnaires, as well as reports from parents. As such, there are legitimate questions about the reliability of some of these data, particularly where students have to recall over an extended period. Indeed, considerable attention has been placed in the last few years on the development of reliable and accurate tools for quantifying physical activity behavior in children and youth.

The two most common methods for deriving objective measures of activity are heart rate monitors and motion sensors (otherwise known as activity monitors). Heart rate monitors provide ongoing counts of heart rates. From these, the percentage of time spent at certain levels above resting heart rate can be determined. This information, in turn, can be used as estimates of moderate and vigorous activity.

Activity monitors (which are worn on the hip) are designed to detect vertical acceleration, such as that which occurs during walking or jogging. This accel-

Activity monitors worn on the hip

eration signal is summed over a user-specified time interval, at the end of which the summed value or activity "count" is stored in memory. Researchers have developed age-specific count ranges corresponding to MVPA and VPA.

Pedometers have also been used to measure activity levels. Cheaper than heart rate and activity monitors, pedometers provide a count of footsteps and distance, thereby providing an estimation of energy expenditure. Pedometers are useful tools in measuring the health target of 10,000 steps per day.

Youth Fitness

The last nationally representative study of youth *fitness* was the NCYFS I, which was presented in January 1985 (see JOPERD, 1985). Scores are presented as averages for ages 10–18 for the following tests: sum of triceps and subscapular skinfolds, sit and reach, bent-knee sit-ups, chin-ups and mile walk/run. However, this study did not classify students based on whether or not they met health-related fitness standards. Nevertheless, fitness tests administered throughout California in 1999 found that only about one in five students in the 7th and 9th grades met the standards for all health-related fitness components Further, more than 40% did not meet the minimum fitness standard for cardiorespiratory endurance (California Department of Education, Standards and Assessment Division, 1999).

One of the problems of relying on fitness tests is that some students can pass these tests because of advanced levels of physical maturity for their age or other positive hereditary dispositions, but nevertheless, fail to reach an adequate level of daily activity. Conversely, other children who are active may not pass fitness tests because of their own developmental characteristics.

Perhaps the best summary of the state of youth fitness comes from Corbin and Pangrazi (1992), who respond to the naysayers and prophets of doom about the levels of youth fitness. When these authors studied test scores using norm and criterion-referenced standards, they found the following results:

- More children and youth meet criterion-referenced health standards than norm-referenced standards (50th percentile).

- The majority of American children and youth meet criterion-related standards for individual test items.

- The majority of American children and youth could not meet the criterion-related health standards for a battery of items for either of the two test batteries studied.

Corbin, Pangrazi, and Welk (1999) continued to provide counterarguments to those who claimed youth fitness levels had become alarmingly low. These comparisons are found in Table 4.4.

Table 4.4   Comparison of Conventional and
Alternative Wisdoms Regarding Youth Fitness

Conventional Wisdom	Alternative Wisdom
Most American youth are inactive and unfit.	Youth are more active than adults as a group. Still, many are less active than they should be.
The level of youth fitness is considerably lower now than in previous years.	With the exception of having more body fat, youth are probably no less fit now than 30 years ago. Fit children may be more fit, and unfit children less fit, than in previous decades.
The best way to improve youth fitness is to create programs that require youth to exercise at levels know to produce fitness.	The best way to improve youth fitness is to convince children that exercise is something they can enjoy and to educate them to be informed exercise and fitness consumers.

Source: From "Toward an Understanding of Appropriate Physical Activity Levels for Youth," by C. B. Corbin, R. P. Pangrazi, and G. J. Welk, in *Toward a Better Understanding of Physical Fitness and Activity* by C. B. Corbin and R. P. Pangrazi, 1999, Scottsdale, AZ: Holcomb Hathaway.

Youth Activity Levels

As noted previously, we should perhaps be spending more time examining the extent to which teenagers are engaging in appropriate levels of physical activity, rather than being too occupied with their fitness scores. Several reports and studies have been conducted using extensive databases to collect data on this very topic.

The report of the U.S. Surgeon General (USDHHS, 1996) provides one summary:

- Only about one-half of U.S. young people (aged 12–21) regularly participate in vigorous physical activity—one-fourth report no vigorous physical activity.

- Approximately one-fourth of young people walk or bicycle nearly every day.

- About 14% of young people report no recent vigorous or light to moderate physical activity. This indicator of physical activity is higher among females than males and among African American females than white females.

- Males are more likely than females to participate in vigorous physical activity, strengthening activities, and walking or bicycling.

- Participation in all types of physical activity declines strikingly as age or grade in school increases.

- Among high school students, enrollment in physical education remained unchanged during the first half of the 1990s. However, daily attendance in physical education declined from approximately 42% to 25%.

- The percentage of high school students who were enrolled in physical education and who reported being physically active for at least 20 minutes in physical education classes declined from approximately 81% to 70% during the first half of the 1990s.
- Only 19% of all high school students report being physically active for 20 minutes or more in daily physical education classes.

Responses from the media to these findings were quick. Reuters issued a news story proclaiming, "Physical activity by U.S. teens plummets," and a *Washington Post* columnist suggested that American youth were indeed "The young and the *rested.*"

Data from the 1997 Youth Risk Behavior Surveillance (see Kann et al., 1998) provide similar findings, most notably the following:

- 63.8% engaged in vigorous activity for at least 20 minutes three or more times in the past seven days.
- Only half reported any stretching or strengthening activities on three or more days in the past seven days.
- Girls were less likely to be vigorous than boys.
- African American girls were less active than white girls.
- Students in grades 11 and 12 were less active than those in grade 9.

YRBS data for 1999 show the following among U.S. high school students:

- More than one in three (35%) did not participate regularly in vigorous physical activity.
- Regular participation in vigorous physical activity dropped from 73% of 9th grade students to 61% of 12th grade students.
- Nearly half (45%) did not play on any sports teams during the year.
- Nearly half (44%) were not even enrolled in a physical education class; enrollment in physical education dropped from 79% in 9th grade to 37% in 12th grade.
- Only 29% attended daily physical education classes, a dramatic decline from 1991, when 42% of high school students did so.

Of all these data, two pieces of information stand out most prominently: First, the decline in physical activity is already well under way as students enter their high school years; second, opportunities for students to become active within the setting of the school diminishes as they get older. In essence, participation in vigorous physical activity and physical education class time devoted to physical activity are substantially below the goals set in *Healthy People 2010.*

PE enrollments are declining

Apart from the major reports on activity, data are available from subsidiary sources. For example, national transportation surveys have found that walking and bicycling by children aged 5–15 dropped 40% between 1977 and 1995. In addition, more than one-third (37%) of all trips to school are made from one mile away or less, but only 31% of these trips are made by walking.

As a response to the accumulation of scores indicating insufficient levels of physical activity by significant numbers of American youth, on June 23, 2000, then President Clinton issued a directive to the secretary of health and human services and the secretary of education to work together to identify and report on "strategies to promote better health for our nation's youth through physical activity and fitness." In its executive summary, those secretaries provided the following lead statement:

> Our nation's young people are, in large measure, inactive, unfit, and increasingly overweight. In the long run, this physical inactivity threatens to reverse the decades-long progress we have made in reducing death from cardiovascular diseases and to devastate our national health care budget. In the short run, physical inactivity has contributed to an unprecedented epidemic of childhood obesity that is currently plaguing the United States. (USDHHS, 2000)

Few students walk to school

Obesity Levels

Data on obesity has also provided some indication of the extent of student activity. For example, the National Health and Nutrition Examination Survey (NHANES) reports that between 1976–1980 and 1988–1994, the percentage of U.S. adolescents (aged 12–19) who were overweight increased from 5.4% to 9.7% of girls and 4.5% to 11.3% of boys (Figure 4.4).

Physical inactivity seems to be a major factor in the increase in obesity. Nonetheless, many health advocates have also pointed out other sources that contribute to the problem—in particular, the fast-food industry and its advertisers, who promote the often irresistible combination of larger portions plus lower cost. Indeed, how many of us have been asked whether we would like to "super-size" our meal at the fast-food drive-through?

Who Is Most at Risk?

Despite the consensus that many American teenagers are not engaging in sufficient levels of physical activity to achieve health-related standards, some adolescents are particularly at risk. For the overall youth population (aged 12–18), girls are less active than boys, and older students are less active than their younger counterparts.

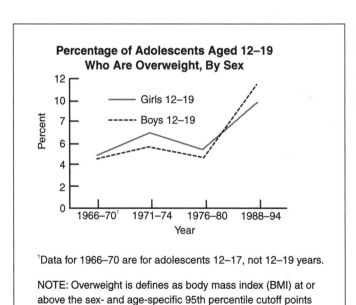

Figure 4.4   Youth obesity.

Source: Centers for Disease Control and Prevention, National Center for Health Statistics, Division of Health Examination Statistics. Unpublished data.

There are also differences in activity and inactivity patterns by ethnicity, with teenagers in minority groups engaging in less physical activity and more inactivity than their non-Hispanic white counterparts (see Gordon-Larsen, McMurray & Popkin, 1999). The exception was Asian females, who have low levels of physical activity and overweight.

As noted, the current recommendation is that adolescents and youth engage in at least three bouts of continuous moderate to vigorous physical activity per week and accumulate at least 30 minutes of daily moderate level physical activity. Whereas 31.2% of non-Hispanic whites fail to reach this standard, for non-Hispanic African Americans this figure reaches 36.7%. Furthermore, a substantial proportion of non-Hispanic African American females (49.5%), Asian females (44.1%), and Hispanic females (41.6%) report zero to two sessions of moderate to vigorous activity per week (Gordon-Larsen et al., 1999). Pivarnik, Fulton, Taylor, and Snider (1993) report that the aerobic capacity of African American female adolescents averaged 14% less than those of non-African American females, the difference being primarily a function of body weight.

Sport and Youth Activity

Aside from school physical education, participation in sports programs provides opportunities for teenagers to be active. The data on these are interesting and have implications for the structure of high school physical education. Given that school sport is particularly exclusionary in the United States (typically there are only one or two teams in each sport per school), one would hope or expect that a number of students have the opportunity to participate in sport competition in the intramural setting. However, only about 10% of American youth participate in intramural sports. Add to this that attrition in youth sport reaches a maximum at ages 14 to 15, and we can see that access to sport as an avenue for activity seems to be limited.

Pate, Trost, Levin, and Dowda (2000), however, do report that 70% of male students and 53% of female students participate on one or more sports teams in school and/or nonschool settings. Nevertheless, these authors also report that

Youth sports contribute to activity

these rates varied substantially by age, sex, and ethnicity; that sport participants are more likely to be younger than older; and that participants are more likely to be white students than African American or Hispanic. Furthermore, these authors report only small numbers of females (31%), and even lower numbers of minority females (23% Hispanic and 24% African American) participating in nonschool sports settings.

What Are the Barriers to Youth Activity?

Given there are some areas of concern for the activity levels of teenagers, the next challenge is to examine the barriers to being active: those features that either increase the potential to be active or increase the likelihood of inactivity.

Sallis (2000) notes that activity levels can be influenced by personal or environmental factors. Personal factors include biological factors and psychological factors. The biological factors that tend to influence activity participation include gender (boys are more active than girls), age (younger are more active than older) and obesity (overweight are less likely to be active than nonoverweight). The psychological features that relate to a likelihood of increased activity include knowledge of activity (that is, knowledge of *how* to exercise; knowledge *of* health benefits does not correlate with increased activity), cues to be active, intention to be active, and self-efficacy.

Factors in the teenager's environment also provide potential barriers to participation in activity. These can be divided into two categories. The first relates to the teenager's social world, peers, parents, and teachers. Of these, peer influence is the strongest. At this stage, there is little research or evidence on the effect of teachers on adolescent activity patterns. For parents, the influence seems to be greater for younger children rather than youth. However, maternal education has been shown to be inversely associated with high inactivity patterns. For example, an adolescent youth with a mother who possesses a graduate or professional degree is less likely to be inactive (see Gordon-Larsen et al., 1999). Furthermore, high family income is also associated with increased moderate to vigorous physical activity and decreased inactivity.

The second environmental factor influencing activity engagement is the young person's physical world. Indeed, one interesting report from a study using objective measures of youth activity is that adolescents exhibit lower levels of MVPA on the weekends compared with school days (Trost, Pate, Freedson, Sallis & Taylor, 2000). The explanation for this finding is that adolescents seem to spend more of their weekend time either sleeping or indoors.

With regard to time spent indoors, one factor may be the many hours that teens spend doing sedentary activities, most notably using electronic media. A 1999 national survey found that young people aged 2–18 spend, on average,

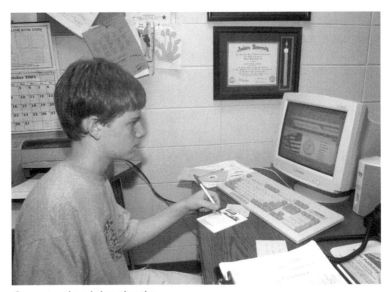

Computer time is inactive time

over four hours a day watching television, watching videotapes, playing video games, or using a computer (Kaiser Family Foundation, 1999). This significant time in inactivity has led to a new twist on the metaphor of the couch potato, namely, the *tech potato*.

The attraction of the electronic world is not the only factor that keeps teens indoors. High serious crime in the neighborhood, for example, is also a significant barrier to achieving higher levels of moderate to vigorous physical activity (see Gordon-Larsen et al., 1999). Furthermore, as Siedentop (1998, p. 212) notes, "The Carnegie Council on Adolescent Development (1992) in their landmark study of discretionary time among youths concluded that young adolescents who live in low-income neighborhoods are most likely to benefit from supportive youth development services; yet they are the very youth who have least access to such programs and organizations."

The Role and Place of Physical Education in Youth Fitness

The evidence presented so far in this chapter suggests that increasingly fewer teens are participating in physical education. This is a serious issue given the finding of Gordon-Larsen et al. (1999) that participation in *daily* school physical education classes was associated with an increased likelihood of engaging in high levels of moderate to vigorous physical activity. Moreover, the CDC and other authors have suggested that school-based programs are the *preferred* model for promoting lifelong activity patterns (e.g., Sallis & McKenzie, 1991). Indeed, program writers for AAHPERD's *Physical Best Teacher's Guide* note that "teens may lack the knowledge they need to be physically active in safe and interesting ways. In other words, they may not know how to set up a personal physical activity program that meets their individual needs, set goals, monitor their own progress, or reward themselves appropriately and effectively" (AAHPERD 1999, p. 28).

Although quality physical education programs have the potential to achieve this goal, it will be difficult to reach all students in a time of decreased enrollment in the subject. As Siedentop (1998) notes, *nowhere* in the United States has there been an increase in the time allocated to physical education. What has been more prevalent is a continued pattern of state departments of education decreasing requirements for physical education. This reduction is further complicated by the fact that many states allow students to substitute other classes for physical education.

Fitness Tests Urged in Non-PE Schools

Any Illinois school district that wants to let students skip physical education should have to prove its students are fit by giving them a fitness test, an Illinois Board of Education member insisted Thursday.

Marilyn McConachie stunned some observers at the board's monthly meeting by suggesting her own solution to the growing number of requests to waive Illinois' requirements for daily physical education instruction.

McConachie, a Northbrook resident, proposed that districts be required to test their students for fitness before receiving a PE waiver, and then prove student fitness had improved if they wanted a waiver extended a second year.

"I regard the debate over these waivers as trivial and a waste of time. We're dealing with the wrong game," McConachie said. Her proposal, she said, "deals more directly with the problem, rather than rearranging the deck chairs."

State Education Supt. Glenn "Max" McGee, himself a marathon runner and triathlete, quickly hailed McConachie's idea as "terrific" and told staff to explore it.

McConachie's motion stopped dead in its tracks a proposal by state board staff that districts be allowed to drop from PE any freshmen or sophomores who participate in interscholastic athletics.

Source: From "Fitness Tests Urged in Non-PE Schools," by R. Rossi, January 19, 2001, *Chicago Sun-Times*, p. 16.

Is Physical Education Missing the Boat?

Siedentop (1998) has commented that the fitness boom among adults in middle and upper income brackets is one of the major social phenomena in recent American history (p. 159), and indeed, those 35 and older have shown substantial increases in regular exercise. This is at the same time when the percentage of teenagers engaging in regular activity is decreasing. Perhaps this extract best summarizes the current trend:

> *By 10 A.M. on a recent Sunday, Adria Bated-Dowling had swum a half-mile in Lake Michigan, ridden her bike 12 miles and run 3 miles in the Danskin Women's Triathlon.*
>
> *Her 11-year-old daughter watched.*
>
> *Like many in her generation, Bated-Dowling, a 40-year-old Wauwatosa homemaker, has embraced the fitness movement with gusto. She competes often in marathons and triathlons.*
>
> *And like many in her generation, Bated-Dowling's 11-year-old daughter, Maeve, would rather read a book than ride a bike. She played soccer for a while, but is quitting that sport, her mother said.* (Fauber, 1995. Reprinted with permission of the *Milwaukee Journal Sentinel*.)

Given that this scenario is not altogether a rarity, many authors have suggested that we might rethink the fitness objective for physical education. Instead of setting objectives solely focused on getting students to reach specific standards, a more important objective is to help students establish regular exercise patterns that can be continued into adulthood. That is, the goal in physical education needs to be more oriented to the *process* of maintaining lifetime activity and exercise rather than the product of short-term fitness improvement.

Siedentop (1998) has extended this view beyond just physical education. He suggests that we need to develop activity as a *social norm* in schools. However, he also notes that this can be done only if the entire school believes in and supports attractive programs that include all children and youth. Specific strategies for working toward this objective are presented in Chapter 11 of this book.

Contemporary Fitness Education Programs

Corbin and Lindsay (2002) have presented a model that serves as a template by which we need to conceptualize the teaching of fitness in schools. The key point is that we must move beyond "doing fitness to kids" by presenting them with ways in which they can become active for a lifetime. Corbin and Lindsay's model presents a stairway to fitness achievement, and they note that the most critical stage is helping students to move from step 2 to step 3 (Figure 4.5).

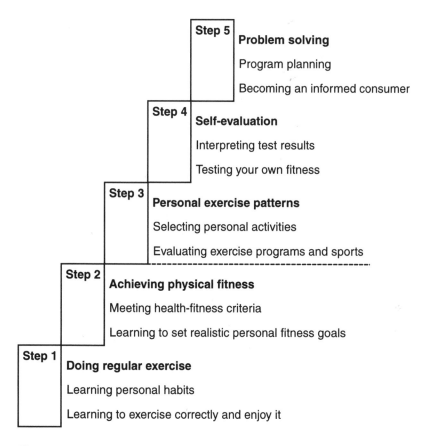

Figure 4.5 Stairway to lifetime fitness.

Several states have adopted this model as fundamental to courses in personal wellness or fitness, and these courses have come to represent the physical education requirement for high school graduation. Studies of programs that incorporate this lifetime fitness focus have shown that in the years following the class, significantly fewer students reported sedentary behaviors in comparison with students who had taken a more traditional physical education program (Dale & Corbin, 2000).

Enhancing Activity in Non-Fitness-Related Physical Education

Many school physical education programs still choose to include a significant component of sport, games, and leisure pursuits into their curricula. Although a number of games, and sports will indeed produce energy expenditures of greater than 3 METS (the criterion for moderate-to-vigorous physical activity), most secondary school physical education programs seem to be conducted in a climate best described as "no sweat." You will recall that these classes take place in a particularly casual climate, where expectation for performance in the subject matter requirements is low, and where students are held accountable for participating and making a minimal level of effort, rather than for achieving high levels of quality performance (see Siedentop, Doutis, Tsangaridou, Ward & Rauschenbach, 1994).

Certainly, most of these sport-based programs are not even close to achieving the *Healthy People 2010* objective of having students spend greater than 50% of lesson time in MVPA. In a study of middle school students, McKenzie, Marshall, Sallis, and Conway (2000) observed figures close to this 50% criterion, but it must be noted that the lessons in which these figures were reached were those with a fitness focus. What is needed to reach lesson percentages closer to 50% are settings in which students participate in small-sided teams, in games that are meaningful and purposeful, and where the context of sport is both engaging and rewarding. Chapter 8 of this book provides a particular curriculum model that can work toward achieving these goals.

System for Observing Fitness Instruction Time (SOFIT)

In terms of monitoring activity levels within physical education, McKenzie, Sallis, and Nader (1992) have developed an observation instrument that allows for

Step aerobics is noncompetitive

calculating the amount of lesson time that is spent in MVPA. With the acronym SOFIT (System for Observing Fitness Instruction Time), an observer records the level of physical activity of a number of preselected students. Each 20 seconds, a student is coded as either lying down, sitting, standing, walking, or very active (using more energy than he or she would during ordinary walking). Adding the "walking" and "very active" scores and dividing these over the total of all scores compute the percentage of MVPA.

The Whole Concept of Fitness Testing Revisited

It should be clear by this point in the chapter that the focus on fitness in teenagers' lives should now be directed toward the place and extent of their physical activity. This has significant implication for the whole concept of fitness testing, because we have come to see activity as a process, whereas fitness is viewed as more of a product. However, this change in focus does not relegate fitness testing to a scrap heap of obsolescence in physical education. It simply changes the focus of the purpose of fitness testing.

Pate and Hohn note that the primary purpose of testing should be for diagnosing, providing feedback, setting goals, and charting improvements (Pate & Hohn, 1994). Let us examine some of these individually.

Diagnosis

The purpose of a fitness diagnosis is to determine the current status of one's fitness. Unfortunately, in many physical education programs, results of these tests have been used for awarding grades, for the public exaltation of students who achieve the best scores, or even for reporting the data to a state department of education. This is in contrast to (or even violation of) the fundamental ethic of the tests themselves—to provide a score for an individual student that may then be used to change activity behavior.

Given our focus on activity, perhaps the first diagnosis a student receives should come from self-examination of his or her own activity levels. Indeed, this diagnosis could be the content of a very first class in a required high school physical education course. Here, the concepts of energy expenditures in kcal/kg/day or of accumulated activity could be introduced as a lead-up to the more formal testing that follows.

The fitness tests that follow this calculation of activity status provide a diagnosis of more specific areas of a student's physical biography. While one student may have excellent levels of cardiorespiratory fitness, his flexibility may be below the age-related recommendation. Another student may be able to reach healthy standards for muscular strength and endurance but still be over a recommended level for body fat. In all cases, data offer a different profile for different students.

When the teacher conducts these diagnostic tests, however, it is critical to avoid the possibility of humiliating a student by making him or her perform in front of the entire class. Indeed, once students have been taught the appropriate protocols for the various fitness tests, self-testing should be encouraged. Indeed, most tests only require a stopwatch and the help of a partner.

Feedback

Because the modern fitness tests provide health-related criterion scores, students can get clear and immediate feedback about their fitness profiles. The data that are generated from fitness tests provide feedback to students about those areas in which they need to improve. Likewise, regular testing provides students with feedback concerning their progress toward specific fitness goals.

Setting Goals

One of the most likely guarantees of someone dropping out of an exercise program is to set unrealistic expectations. A person who sets goals that are unreasonable and unreachable is likely to give up. Students need to be given assistance in setting rational and achievable goals. Improvement increments should be small, sufficient time should be allocated for the necessary activity to take place, and, at times, a reward system included.

Charting Improvements

As mentioned, the achievement of some fitness goals takes time. In cases like these, it is valuable to have ongoing feedback concerning progress. Charting improvements is an important component of working toward a goal. Even small improvements in test scores can provide enough incentive for one to continue toward the long-term target. For a more lengthy discussion about changing activity behavior, be sure to read Chapter 14.

IN-SCHOOL TASKS

Assessing Influences on Physical Activity

Visit a nearby high school, and arrange to conduct a survey with one physical education class. Have all students complete the questionnaire presented in

Table 4.5. Collate the data for both boys and girls. Examine the complied scores from this class, and reflect on the key influences on their activity levels.

Determining Student Activity Levels

Visit a nearby high school and arrange to complete a SOFIT analysis for two physical education classes. Upon gathering your data, consider those factors that either promoted and/or inhibited activity levels (e.g., class management, the nature of the tasks, teacher prompts, and enthusiasm).

Table 4.5   Influences on Physical Activity

Make a check in the box for each of these that apply.

Biological and demographic influences
- ❏ Age: Two checks if you are less than 18
- ❏ Male sex
- ❏ No (or minor) history of activity-related injuries
- ❏ One parent who graduated from college
- ❏ Both parents lead an active lifestyle
- ❏ Parents are in professional (white-collar) occupations

Psychological influences
- ❏ High level of confidence in your ability to do regular physical activity
- ❏ Enjoy physical activity
- ❏ Believe that you can find time in your day for doing physical activity
- ❏ Believe there are very few barriers to doing regular physical activity
- ❏ Strong intentions to be physically active
- ❏ Belief that the personal benefits of physical activity outweigh the costs

Social influences
- ❏ Friends or family are active role models
- ❏ Friends or family encourage physical activity
- ❏ Friends or family participate in regular physical activity
- ❏ Friends or family directly help you be physically active

Physical environment
- ❏ Weather or climate is favorable for preferred activities
- ❏ Feel safe being active outdoors near home
- ❏ Attractive outdoor space is convenient
- ❏ Exercise equipment or supplies in the home

IN-CLASS DEBATES

You may find participation in one or both of these debates a fruitful exercise in examining the whole notion of activity and fitness.

1. Should physical education majors have their fitness levels assessed?
   - Locate and read the article "Should Physical Education Majors Have Their Fitness Levels Assessed?" by D. S. Melville and D. James, 1990, *Journal of Physical Education, Recreation & Dance, 61* (1), 30–32.
   - Prepare a case either for or against the statement that physical education majors should be assessed on their fitness.
2. Should physical education teachers be fit?
   - Read the accompanying article "Should Physical Education Teachers Be Fit?"
   - Prepare a case either for or against the statement that teachers should be fit.

Should Physical Education Teachers Be Fit?

Should PE teachers be fit? It seems like a reasonable question. I would guess that most people would naturally respond, "Yes!" After all, it makes sense. You teach others about physical skills and movement. You promote exercise and activity. You encourage healthy living through positive lifestyle choices. Of course you should be fit. It would be hypocritical not to be. Fitness should be an integral part of your life. You should be a walking, talking advertisement for fitness and healthy living.

Unfortunately, that's not reality. Regardless of its accuracy, the average person judges another person's level of fitness by observing such qualities as body composition and daily habits. It is likely to be assumed, therefore, that some members of the physical education program are not fit and do not convey a fitness lifestyle. In fact, there may be more physical educators like that than we're willing to admit. It's a touchy subject. Many physical education professionals are offended by questions regarding their level of fitness or commitment to a healthy lifestyle, but a quick look around at any large convention or workshop makes you wonder. It appears that some people are talking the talk but not actually walking the walk. Is it fair to assume that people are unfit because of the habits they have or don't have? Can we judge healthy living by the way a person looks?

An article titled, "The Worlds Fittest Fat Man," in the March issue of *Men's Health* magazine, profiles a very unusual individual. Dave Alexander, a 52-year-old oil distribution company resident from Arizona, who stands 5'8" tall and weights 250 pounds, proves that fitness isn't always about looks. During a typical week, Alexander rides his bike 200 miles, runs 30 miles, and swims 5 miles. Think about that for a moment. That's 40 miles per day on the bike for 5 days per week, and 5 miles per day of running for 6 days per week, and 1 mile per day of swimming for 5 days per week.

That's impressive.

This guy even has finished 30 triathlons in 30 weeks! What's mind-boggling about all of this isn't the amount of exercise that Alexander does; it's the fact that he appears to be 100 pounds overweight. Would you consider this guy fit? It would be difficult to accomplish what he does without being fit. But his body screams heart disease, high blood pressure, high fat diet, and inactivity. At least from the outside.

Although body composition is a component of health-related fitness, vanity is not. Fitness is a pursuit, a process, a lifestyle. It's about making the right choices for living a higher quality life. It's not about looking good in your Speedo or bikini. Unfortunately, society has a tendency to judge fitness from the outside. Which brings me to the role of the teacher.

As teachers we have an enormous responsibility to be role models for youngsters. Because our profession deals with healthy, active living, it is imperative that we convey such a lifestyle to our students. We can't reach them in today's society by telling them: Do as we say, not as we do. We have to lead by example. If we want to create healthy, active,

self-responsible adults, then we have to be healthy, active, self-responsible adults. At times, that may mean our physical appearance is more important than psychological fitness. Think of it this way. You wouldn't ask a bald person how to grow hair, and you wouldn't ask a poor person how to make money. So why would you expect your students to ask an overweight, out-of-shape, inactive person to help them become fit? As unfair as it may be, how a person looks still remains the most popular way to assess an individual's level of fitness and lifestyle choices. As physical educators we have to practice what we preach and pursue it with a passion. If we're not passionate about it, how can we expect to excite our students?

Whether you entered this profession because of your love for sports or fitness or physical activity, your commitment to healthy living will be the most influential factor on the children you teach and the lifestyle decisions they make. Although it shouldn't matter if you have bulging biceps or if your abdomen looks like a washboard, you're going to be judged at times by those standards of appearance. Deep down, what really matters is the example you set for healthy living. Not everyone is going to have the perfect body, no matter how much they exercise. But everyone can live active, healthy lifestyles that in most cases deliver a physique we can all be proud to possess.

It's never too late to start living a healthy lifestyle. And it's never too late to become a positive role model. And that's what being a physical educator is all about.

Source: Reprinted, by permission, from C. Hinson, 1998, "Should PE teachers be fit?," *Teaching Elementary Physical Education, 9* (3), 23.

PORTFOLIO SUGGESTIONS AND ARTIFACTS

Personal Fitness Profile (S1–D1)

Present your own activity and fitness profile. How much activity *do* you do weekly? What *is* your status on a number of fitness test items? What *have* you done recently to reach health-related fitness standards for your age? *Note*: School-based fitness tests provide scores only to age 18. A good resource for adult standards is Morrow, Jackson, Disch, and Mood, *Measurement and Evaluation in Human Performance*, Champaign, IL: Human Kinetics Publishers, 1995.

REFLECTION TIME

Now that you have read this chapter, how confident do you feel in

- convincing your local education authorities that physical education can contribute to the accumulation of healthy levels of physical activity in youth?
- convincing teenagers that activity is for everyone, not just those involved in sport?
- becoming a schoolwide advocate for activity, not just within the context of physical education?
- being able to administer fitness tests and interpret health-related results?
- assisting at-risk youth in finding safe, enjoyable, and plausible ways for them to become more active?

What is your fitness status?

REFERENCES

American Alliance for Health Physical Education, Recreation and Dance (AAHPERD). (1999). *Physical education for lifelong fitness: The Physical Best teacher's guide.* Champaign, IL: Human Kinetics.

Biddle, S., Sallis J. F., & Cavill, N. A. (1998). *Young and active? Young people and health-enhancing physical activity: Evidence and implications.* London: Health Education Authority.

Blair, S. (1992). Are American children and youth fit? The need for better data. *Research Quarterly for Exercise and Sport, 63,* 120–123.

California Department of Education, Standards and Assessment Division. (1999). *California physical fitness test 1999: Report to the governor and legislature.* Sacramento, CA: California Department of Education.

Corbin, C., & Lindsay, R. (2002). *Fitness for life.* Champaign, IL: Human Kinetics.

Corbin, C. B., & Pangrazi, R. P. (1992). Are American children and youth fit? *Research Quarterly for Exercise and Sport, 63,* 96–106.

Corbin, C, B., Pangrazi, R. P., & Welk, G. J. (1999). Toward an understanding of appropriate physical activity levels for youth. In C. B. Corbin & R. P. Pangrazi (Eds.), *Toward a better understanding of physical fitness and activity.* Scottsdale, AZ: Holcomb Hathaway.

Dale, D., & Corbin, C. B. (2000). Physical activity participation of high school graduates following exposure to conceptual or traditional physical education. *Research Quarterly for Exercise and Sport, 71,* 61–68.

Fauber, J. (1995, August 14). Kids losing interest in fitness: Trend shows adults are staying more active than young people. *Milwaukee Journal Sentinel,* p. 8.

Freedson, P., & Rowland, T. (1992). Youth activity versus youth fitness: Let's redirect our efforts. *Research Quarterly for Exercise and Sport, 63,* 133–136.

Gordon-Larsen, P., McMurray, R. G., & Popkin, B. M. (1999). Adolescent physical activity and inactivity vary by ethnicity: The National Longitudinal Study of Adolescent Health. *Journal of Pediatrics, 135,* 301–306.

Jackson, A. W., Morrow, J. R., Hill, D. W., & Dishman, R. K. (1999). *Physical activity for health and fitness.* Champaign, IL: Human Kinetics.

JOPERD (1985). The national children and youth fitness study. *Journal of Physical Education, Recreation, and Dance, 56* (1), 44–90.

Kaiser Family Foundation (1999). *Kids & media @ the new millennium* [Monograph]. Menlo Park, CA: Author.

Kann, L., Kinchen, S. A., Williams, B. I., Ross, J. G., Lowry, R., Hill, C. V., et al. (1998). Youth risk behavior surveillance—United States, 1997. In CDC Surveillance Summaries, August 14, 1998. *Morbidity and Mortality Weekly Report, 47,* (SS–3), 1–89.

Kraus, R., & Hirschland, R. (1954). Minimum muscular fitness tests in school children. *Research Quarterly, 25,* 178–185.

McKenzie, T. L., Marshall, S. J., Sallis, J. F., & Conway, T. L. (2000). Student activity levels, lesson context, and teacher behavior during middle school physical education. *Research Quarterly for Exercise and Sport, 71,* 249–259.

McKenzie, T. L., Sallis, J. F., & Nader, P. R. (1992). SOFIT: System for observing fitness instruction time. *Journal of Teaching in Physical Education, 11*, 195–205.

Melvin, J. (1993, September 14). Unsound of mind and round of body. *St. Petersburg Times*, p. 6.

National Center for Chronic Disease Prevention and Health Promotion. (2000). *Promoting better health for young people through physical activity and sports: A report to the president from the secretary of health and human services and the secretary of education.* Washington, DC: Author,

National Center for Health Statistics (2000). *Health, United States, 2000.* With adolescent health chartbook. Retrieved from http://www.cdc.gov/nchs/products/pubs/pubd/hus/tables/2000/updated/00hus69.pdf

Pate, R. R., & Hohn, R. C. (1994). *Health and fitness through physical education.* Champaign, IL: Human Kinetics.

Pate, R. R., Trost, S. G., Levin, S., & Dowda, M. (2000). Sports participation and health-related behaviors among U.S. youth. *Archives of Pediatric Medicine, 154*, 904–911.

Pivarnik, J. M., Fulton. J. E., Taylor, W. C., & Snider, S. A. (1993). Aerobic capacity in black adolescent girls. *Research Quarterly for Exercise and Sport, 64*, 202–207.

Rossi, R. (2001, January 19). Fitness tests urged in non-PE schools. *Chicago Sun-Times*, p. 16.

Russell, C. (1994, November 8). The young and the rested: CDC study shows teens get little exercise. *Washington Post*, p. A1.

Sallis, J. F. (2000). Overcoming inactivity in young people. *The Physician and Sportsmedicine, 28* (10), 31–32.

Sallis, J. F., & McKenzie. T. (1991). Physical education's role in public health. *Research Quarterly for Exercise and Sport, 62*, 124–137.

Siedentop, D. (1998). *Introduction to physical education, fitness, and sport.* Mountain View, CA: Mayfield.

Siedentop, D., Doutis, P., Tsangaridou, N., Ward, P., & Rauschenbach, J. (1994). Don't sweat gym: An analysis of curriculum and instruction. *Journal of Teaching in Physical Education, 13*, 375–394.

Trost, S. G., Pate, R. R., Freedson, P. S., Sallis, J. F., & Taylor., W. C. (2000). Using objective physical activity measures with youth: How many days of monitoring are needed? *Medicine and Science in Sports and Exercise, 32*, 426–431.

Turner, J. (1994, December 13). Just do it: Whether it's badminton, roller skating or dancing, being active is important—and fun—for young people. *Toronto Star*, p. B4.

U.S. Department of Health and Human Services. (1996). *Physical activity and health: A report of the surgeon general.* Atlanta: U.S. Department of Health and Human Services, Centers for Disease Control and Prevention, National Center for Chronic Disease Prevention and Health Promotion.

U.S. Department of Health and Human Services. (2000a). *Healthy People 2010.* (Conference edition, two volumes). Washington, DC: Author.

U.S. Department of Health and Human Services. (2000b). *Promoting better health for young people through physical activity and sports: A report to the president.* Washington, DC: Author.

U.S. Department of Transportation, Federal Highway Administration, Research and Technical Support Center. (1997). *Nationwide personal transportation survey.* Lantham, MD: Federal Highway Administration.

WEB RESOURCES

The following web link list was generated upon publication of the text; however, over time, the sites may become obsolete if an organization dissolves, discontinues online services, or relocates to a different URL. If a link listed below does not connect, please search for the organization by name.

http://www.just move.org/

Introduces "Fitness Center," an initiative of the American Heart Association providing a personal exercise diary and fitness news.

http://www.fitnessforyouth.umich.edu/

The Fitness for Youth web site serves as a resource for information about the health and fitness of America's youth. Included are innovative and exciting programs to increase children's fitness levels; ways to successfully promote physical education, activity, and sport in your community; helpful tips on running your programs; cutting-edge research and statistics on children's health; links to other healthy-related web sites.

http://www.americanheart.org/

Contains links to a number of exercise/physical activity position statements and recommendations. Also links to American Heart Association scientific statements about specific topics (e.g., "Benefits and Recommendations for Physical Activity Programs for All Americans" and "Understanding Obesity in Youth").

http://www.aahperd.org/naspe/template.cfm

Web site of National Association for Sports and Physical Education.

http://www.foundation.sdsu.edu/projects/spark/index.html

Web site of the SPARK physical education program.

http://www.fitness.gov/

Web site of the President's Council on Physical Fitness and Sports.

http://www.indiana.edu/~preschal/

Web site of the President's Challenge.

http://www.youthsport.net/

Web site of the Youth Sport Centre, a source of sport and fitness information for teachers, sport development officers, coaches, and players for sports.

http://www.activeliving.ca/

Web site of the Coalition for Active Living, a group of organizations and individuals working together to promote healthy, active living among all Canadians, enhance quality of life, and reduce the risk of illness associated with sedentary lifestyle; features links to over 30 organizations.

http://www.lin.ca/resource/html/impact.htm

Describes the impact and benefits of physical activity and recreation on Canadian youth-at-risk (by Canadian Parks/Recreation Association).

CHAPTER 5

Giving Youth Voice and Choice: Strategies for Empowerment

Scenario

It is the third lesson of a 9th grade unit on Frisbee. Four students are gathered in one corner of the gym, discussing the rule issue of the day, namely, how many steps a player can take with the disk before passing. Meanwhile, four other students are busy allocating students to the six teams that will participate during the unit. These students are members of the selection panel. Finally, six students who are members of the sport board for this unit are discussing the awards that will be given at the completion of the season. Ms. Franks, the teacher, is at that moment monitoring the warm-up stations that the students on the "exercise and fitness committee" have developed to get students ready for the Frisbee activity.

Meanwhile, at another school . . .

Coach Brown is leading his class in a series of structured calisthenics. Aligned in formal rows, these students are engaging in an orchestrated exercise program in preparation for their flag football unit. In Coach Brown's class (where the message is "Do as you're told, and don't make trouble"), the students participate in preset activities each day before taking part in regimented skills drills.

Introduction

"While racial boundaries among contemporary youth are more fluid, young people today inhabit a society that is largely indifferent to their needs and makes them scapegoats for many of the problems caused by deindustrialization, economic restructuring, and the collapse of the welfare state" (Giroux, 1998, p. 13). Part of this indifference is exemplified in what Hellison (1991, p. 308) refers to as a "guidance gap." Hellison asserts that because of escalating social problems, youngsters in America are getting less and less guidance to function in a society that provided them with a widening range of choices.

As a result of this indifference and accompanied lack of guidance, educators and others need to recognize the importance of providing not only opportunities for youth to voice their concerns, but also, and equally, the conditions—institutional, economic, spiritual, and cultural—that will allow them to "reconceptualize themselves as citizens and develop a sense of what it means to fight for important social and political issues that affect their lives, bodies, and society" (Giroux, 1998, p. 31). Citizenship in the traditional sense involves a range of roles that individuals can play in forming, maintaining, and changing their communities. However, according to Giroux (1998), "In the new world order, citizenship has little to do with social responsibility and everything to do with creating consuming subject" (p. 15).

Students then, should have an input into framing their own futures, rather than being passive recipients of an education created by adults and adult perceptions of students. By perceptions we mean "thoughts, beliefs, and feelings about themselves, other persons, and events" (Schunk, 1992, p. 3). It can be seen from the scenarios presented at the beginning of this chapter that the two teachers have remarkably different perspectives on the role of student voice in physical education.

Sanctioned graffiti walls allow nondestructive expression

There are numerous reasons for refocusing on the role students play in curriculum making, including:

- understanding the students' worlds on which teachers and students can build to enhance learning
- encouraging in students a sense of being proactive, where their opinions are valued
- adopting a community approach within schools to enhance student and teacher experiences
- encouraging and furthering students' responsibility for learning and excitement in learning and exploration
- enhancing the classroom and school climate through understanding what affects it
- increasing student ownership so that they are vested partners in school or/and curriculum reform.

Unfortunately, physical education is often a site where students receive little of the recognition they deserve to be contributing members to their activity programs. This chapter will address three keys issues relating to recognizing students as valuable resources in classroom decisions and providing opportunities for student empowerment: (1) giving students voice, (2) giving students choice, and (3) helping students become personally and socially responsible.

Giving Students Voice

Graham (1995) has noted that it is easy to get caught up in teaching "numbers" and to forget that each student has feelings and opinions about what we teach and how we are teaching it. Essentially, we have undervalued the opportunity to hear from students their opinions concerning the practice of physical education.

Giving students voice involves the concept of negotiating the curriculum between teachers and students. Boomer (1982) suggests that negotiating the curriculum means deliberately planning to invite students to contribute to, and to modify, the educational program, so that they will have a real investment both in the learning journey and in the outcomes. He further notes that this is made possible only through the teacher's change in belief, moving from a teacher-planned curriculum to one that engages student interest: a teacher- and student-planned curriculum. In essence, the teacher is providing students with a form of ownership. Ownership, in this case, is defined as a feeling of possession or a "right."

Holdsworth (1998, p. 15) has presented a continuum of "stages of youth/student voice," which he suggests progresses through the following stages:

1. speaking out
2. being heard
3. being listened to
4. being listened to seriously and with respect (including a willingness to argue with students with logic and evidence)
5. incorporating youth/students' views into action taken by others
6. sharing with young people decisions, implementation of action, and reflection on the action

Recording students' opinions

Holdsworth (1999) does, however, provide a caveat. Giving students a voice involves much more than consulting them. It is much more concerned with making students realize that they have a valued and recognized role within their community—where what they think and say is measured against what they do, how they are appreciated, and what difference they make. To have a "voice" and make no difference is possibly more profoundly alienating than having no voice at all! In a similar way, Mellor (1998) reports an air of cynicism by students who believe their voice is not heard when they become involved in school government.

For most of them there is no point in trying to participate and get involved in influencing decisions. . . . It will get them into trouble with administrators and teachers, have them offside with some of their peers, create havoc within classrooms where they should be doing real school work, distract them from their exams, and it's a waste of their time anyway, because schools don't want students to be part of any real decision making. . . . They are not convinced they will not be listened to by their seniors. (p. 5)

There are several levels within physical education at which students can be provided with a voice. At the highest level, students can be given voice concerning the curriculum itself; that is, students can be involved in the selection of the content that will make up a semester's or year's work. This process may initially present a significant dilemma in that the diversity of student options will be significant. The teacher then must find a way to get a representative voice from the students that will be agreed upon by the whole class. In these cases, the students will need to be given a voice as to which members of their class are provided the opportunity of gathering student opinions, and making a rational and mutually agreeable set of suggestions to the teacher. Such an introduction to this democratic process will require a period of training by the teacher.

Giving students choices as to curriculum content does not necessitate that all students in the class participate in the same task. At the most basic instructional level, teaching by invitation and intra-task variation provides ways in which students can match content for their own challenge level. However, in the context of this chapter, we are concerned with a more significant curriculum challenge. Consider, for example, project-based learning. In project-based learning, students design their own work projects, as well as assess their performance and progress. A critical feature of project-based learning is that projects originate from students rather than being assigned by the teacher. This may result, for example, in some students undertaking a series of activities relating to strength and conditioning while other students design and build a climbing wall in the school's gym (see Chapter 10 for more details on project-based learning).

The next level of student voice will involve the capacity to make decisions *within* selected units. For example, students may elect to implement special rules during a unit of floor hockey. Students may choose not to invoke the offside rule during 4-a-side matches, or they may choose to limit the role of the goaltender in moving beyond the crease.

Giving students voice in this context gives the game more meaning and has been found to lead to greater compliance with rules during game play. Students who are provided with some ownership often describe feeling a sense of commitment to a particular unit (or project). Ownership of content leads to taking a protective role for that content's success and well-being. As one boy noted in a hockey unit in which students had considerable voice:

> *You know we weren't going to allow anyone to spoil the season by goofing off or not taking it seriously. We had a responsibility to make it work, since we made it up in the first place.*

Table 5.1 provides a summary of how student voice could be included during physical education.

Table 5.1   Opportunities for Student Voice within Physical Education

Level of Voice	Specific Examples
Highest—students determine curriculum design	• Selection of units to comprise a semester's program (e.g., soccer, badminton, and aerobics—3 weeks each) • Design of individual or group projects for project-based learning (e.g., design and build a climbing wall, or redesign and modernize the weight room) • Selection of activities available at the school fitness and sports club
Intermediate—students have input during particular content areas	• Student committees make decisions about class management rules, game play rules, and competition formats • Students decide whether to achieve aerobic objectives through either aerobic dance, step aerobics, water aerobics, cardio karate, or some combination • Students work in groups to solve problems during adventure education programs
Lower level—students have voice within individual lessons	• Students determine how many players will be on a team during end-of-class scrimmages • Students determine the format of the warm-down

Providing Students with Choices

In addition to giving students voice, another powerful option teachers can provide is to give them choice. Self-determination theory proposes that students may become more motivated when three basic needs are met: competence, relatedness, and autonomy (or choice). The more self-determined a person is, the more likely he or she will also be intrinsically motivated. Further, when behaviors are self-determined, a person is more likely to initiate and persist in a behavior than when behaviors are determined from sources external to self. For example, Kushman (1997) found that 150 students out of 200 expressed the belief that they learned better outside school. Moreover, this learning outside was seen as empowering because they could learn at their own pace, they had selected what to learn, and the learning was considered to have more personal meaning.

A second factor involved in giving students the opportunities to make choices lies in their often-limited experience in considering options. For many students, parents and teachers have directed their every move. Giving students choices and providing them with activities that require problem solving can lead to better decision making in contexts outside physical education, in other school activities, at home, and in their communities.

The key in this equation is autonomy—giving students choice. What is important here is that choice is indeed offered, more than the extent of that choice. Even either/or choices are seen as steps toward autonomy. Take for example, a study by Prusak (2000), in which adolescent girls in the 7th and 8th grade were placed into two walking groups: choice and no choice. The choice group classes could choose to participate in one of three of nine walking activities each day, while the no-choice group classes participated in all the same activities but did so in order. Prusak found that after only nine days of choice/no choice, significant differences in situational motivation were found indicating that the choice group (1) was more intrinsically motivated, (2) had higher sense of identified regulation, and (3) had a lesser sense of external control. These students felt more in control of their exercise and, hence, were more motivated to participate and to continue participation.

As with giving students voice, giving students choice also will operate at a number of levels (Figure 5.1). For example, three teachers may offer concurrent units on basketball, hockey, and tennis, and students may sign up for any one of

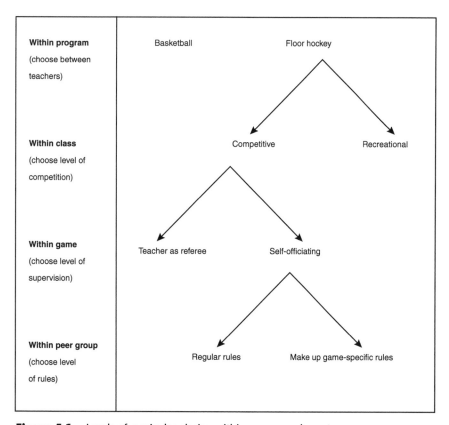

Figure 5.1 Levels of curricular choice within games and sports.

these. This is perhaps the most common form of choice within schools. However, within the hockey unit, the teacher may offer students the choice of participating in a competitive league or a social league. In the competitive league, students will form persisting teams and play in formal competition with the objective of determining the best team. In the social league, students may form different teams each day and play pick-up games against another ad hoc group of students.

Choice can also operate at a more micro, or peer group, level. Take, for example, teams within a unit of sport education. During the early stages of a sea-

Setting the pace on a walking track

son of flag football, one team may choose to work on passing plays during a particular lesson. A second team may spend its time having a quarterback try-out, while a third may be practicing its kicking game (see Chapter 8 for full details of sport education).

To give students choice, then, is a form of empowerment. Jewett, Bain, and Ennis (1995, p. 81) refer to empowerment as "the capacity to take effective action on one's own behalf." Note here the importance of "effective action." In all the football

cases described above, the students were empowered to work on problems of their own determining and, as a result, to develop a certain level of autonomy.

Giving students choice does not apply only to participation in team sports. Fitness activities offer significant potential for allowing students to make decisions about their participation (Figure 5.2). First, students may be given a choice at the global level; that is, during a particular lesson they may be able to complete circuits of the schools walking track, or they may prefer to participate in a formal aerobic dance class conducted by the teacher. In the weight room, students may choose to work on their own self-designed program or follow a prescribed circuit designed by the teacher.

Fitness activities also allow for students to regulate their own level of intensity. When walking on the track, they can set the pace anywhere from pedestrian to vigorous. Similarly, most aerobic dance exercises allow for individual modification to the intensity of the exercise. These are all choices that should improve student motivation and enhance engagement.

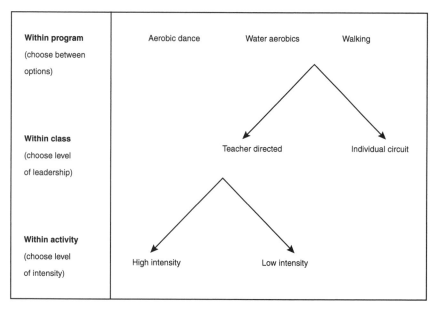

Figure 5.2   Levels of curricular choice within fitness programs.

The ultimate form of choice within physical education lies in situations where instead of formal classes, the school activity program is conducted as a form of fitness and sports club. In these cases, students are provided with a full choice of (1) activity, (2) time, (3) venue, and often (4) instructor. Indeed, under this organization, some students may gain physical education credit for participating in classes at a local health club or local rock-climbing club. For full details of this arrangement, see Chapter 11.

Helping Students Develop Personal and Social Responsibility

When students are given opportunities to have a voice and choice, they are also being asked to demonstrate a degree of personal responsibility. To help students become responsible, we need first to shift responsibility to them, which means giving power to students. Hellison (1995) has provided a model that helps us teach responsibility through physical activity and has presented a number of key points within it. Hellison suggests that students need to learn to take responsibility for their personal well-being (meaning their effort and self-direction) and for social well-being (meaning respecting the rights and feelings of others and caring about others).

Recreational Frisbee allows students to develop mutual support

The fundamental ethic of Hellison's program, "Taking Personal and Social Responsibility" (TPSR), is perhaps best summarized by the following quote: "Helping students take personal and social responsibility, in part means sharing power with students and shifting decision making to them. TPSR does not mean 'getting inside kids' heads' but getting them inside their own heads" (Hellison, 1995, p. 7).

TPSR, then, provides a series of learning experiences in which the challenge is to move through a series of *goal levels*. From the lowest level, irresponsible behavior, the levels progress to caring, giving support, showing support, and helping others (i.e., ultimately demonstrating maximum sensitivity and responsiveness to the well-being of others). An ultimate goal of TPSR is for the students to extend such caring for others beyond the gym into their lives outside school. A brief description of the levels follows (Hellman, 1995):

Level 5: Outside the gym

Attempts to enact these levels outside the gym, in the home, the neighborhood, and other social contexts

Level 4: Helping

Extend the sense of responsibility beyond the self to encourage, support, and help others

Level 3: Self-Direction

Able to work without supervision on personal plans

Level 2: Effort

Willing to participate and accept challenges while under the teacher's supervision

Level 1: Respect for others rights and feelings

While not participating, students are under control to the extent that they are not interfering with others' (students' and teachers') rights to learn and teach

Level 0: Irresponsibility

Not under control; students make excuses and blame others or deny responsibility for their actions

Hellison provides a number of strategies we can use to help students in relation to issues of respect, participation, self-direction, and helping. These strategies include awareness talks, time for reflection, group meetings, opportunities for individual decision making, and counseling time. An individual lesson could include one or all of these strategies, whose roles and purposes are presented in Table 5.2.

It should be noted that all of these strategies are bound up in the specific qualities of the teacher; that is, we can't on one hand give students the opportu-

Table 5.2 Strategies for Promoting Student Responsibility and Decision Making

Strategy	Process
Awareness talks	• Help students understand the levels, their meaning, and their purpose
Time for reflection	• Students are asked to evaluate the extent to which they achieved a particular level and were able to work toward a particular goal • Can be as simple as a thumbs-up or -down response, or more detailed such as writing in a journal
Group meetings	• Students share ideas, opinions, and feelings • Can lead to the development of rules • Can be used as a form of program evaluation and improvement
Opportunities for individual decision making	• Designed to build negotiation and choice into each of the levels • Involves choosing personal goals and activities but may also involve choosing a teacher-directed option
Counseling time	• The teacher and students meet one-to-one • Often involves sharing perspectives or co-evaluating a student's level of responsibility • Not just for interaction with those in trouble, but with all students

nities to make decisions but then on the other hand override that decision once it has been made. Hellison provides a number of specific instructor qualities he believes are critical for promoting students' progression through the levels. Focusing on an inclusive and student-centered approach rather than an authoritative style, these qualities include the following:

- strength of purpose—you can't develop TPRS unless you believe in its principles
- respect for students as unique individuals—to care about and treat students with dignity
- listening—critical for helping students develop individual decision-making skills
- being genuine—being yourself rather than being cool
- being vulnerable—admitting that you don't get it right every time or that you don't know everything
- intuition—recognizing and acting upon cues
- perseverance—you have to outlast the students!
- having a sense of humor and a playful spirit

The foundation of TPSR emphasizes the individual learner's well-being. Although caring and social responsibility are important goals (the latter is, after all, the SR in TPSR), self-awareness and personal well-being are central to the model. Hellison clearly places the individual at the center of his model and directs

TPSR promotes caring and social responsibility

Table 5.3   Summary of Key Issues of TPSR

1. Putting kids first

Caring about kids as whole people

Importance of the instructor-student relationship

Respecting their struggles, individuality, voices, and capacity for decision making

2. Purpose

Taking responsibility for one's well-being and for being sensitive and responsive to the well-being of others

Taking Responsibility Levels	Teacher Values	Class Values
I. Respect for others rights and feelings		
Control temper and mouth	Respect for students	Self-control
Right to be included	Empowerment	
Peaceful conflict resolution	Equity	
II. Effort		
Explore effort and new tasks	Self-paced task mastery	Teamwork and coachability
Self-motivation	Task variation	
Courage to persist when going gets tough	Competitive choices	
III. Self-direction		
Independence	Empowerment	Self-teaching
Goal-setting progression		
Courage to resist peer pressure		
IV. Helping		
Sensitivity and responsiveness	Well-being of others	Teaching/helping others
Leadership and group welfare		
V. Outside the gym		
Trying these ideas outside the gym	Transfer	Outside the gym
Being a role model		

Source: Reproduced with permission, Don Hellison, University of Chicago.

attention to student empowerment, choice, and self-direction. Such empowerment and self-direction are prerequisite to becoming socially responsible, particularly beyond the context of the movement setting. Table 5.3 provides a summary record of how the levels, teaching strategies, teacher qualities, and class climate all work to help empower students and help them become responsible.

If you are particularly interested in practical guidelines for creating physical activity programs that instill a sense of social and personal responsibility, Hellison et al. (2000) present a book that shows the way for university students and faculty to connect with youth in their communities through service learning, internships, and other outreach programs. Included in this text are practical ways to develop a variety of proven youth physical activity programs—from adventure experiences and coaching clubs to mentoring and teen parent programs.

IN-SCHOOL TASKS

Curriculum Choices

Visit a local high school and inquire about the structure of their program, with particular focus on the degree of student choice at the curriculum level. For instance, do students get a choice of content at any stage during the year (and/or do they have a voice about this content)?

Instructional Choices

Visit a local high school and watch two lessons, one with a skill focus and a second with a fitness focus. Using Figures 5.1 and 5.2, determine the level of choice (extensive to none) provided to students during these lessons. Further, take particular note of the conditions of these choices. To what extent are these choices limited or open, and how does the teacher respond to student choices?

Reflect on the extent to which these particular lessons are providing opportunities for self-determination and empowerment. In addition, identify situations in this lesson where you believe voice or choice could have been offered to students but was not.

PORTFOLIO SUGGESTIONS AND ARTIFACTS

A Levels Chart (S4–D1,2: K2,3)

Design a chart that outlines the different levels of TPSR that you could post in your classroom or gym. Include on your chart not only the levels and definitions, but also pictorial examples of the levels in action.

A Personal Goals Form (S4–D4, K5)

Design a form that students could use as a template for designing a personal activity/fitness/skill plan. Include in the form areas for content goals, level goals, and reflection about the achievement of these goals.

Your Philosophy of Student Choice (S4–D4, S8–D3)

Add a section to your philosophy statement that deals with student choice within physical education. What is your position regarding giving students some control over their curriculum?

REFLECTION TIME

Now that you have read this chapter, how confident do you feel in

- providing students with opportunities to have a voice in the conduct of their physical education classes?

- allowing students to have legitimate input into their choice of participation in physical education?

- managing the balancing act between your own curricular goals and cases where students present alternatives that follow a different path?

- designing a series of lessons that help students learn and move through Hellison's series of goal-levels?

REFERENCES

Boomer, G. (1982). *Negotiating the curriculum: A teacher-student partnership.* Sydney: Ashton Scholastic.

Giroux, H. A. (1998). *Channel surfing: Racism, the media, and the destruction of today's youth.* New York: St. Martin's Griffin.

Graham, G. (1995). Physical education through students' eyes and in students' voices: Implications for teachers and researchers. *Journal of Teaching in Physical Education, 14,* 478–482.

Hellison. D. (1991). The whole person in physical education scholarship: Toward integration. *Quest, 43,* 307–318.

Hellison, D. R. (1995). *Teaching responsibility through physical activity.* Champaign, IL: Human Kinetics.

Hellison, D., Cutforth, N., Kallusky, J., Martinek, T., Parker, M., & Stiehl, J. (2000). *Youth development and physical activity: Linking universities and communities.* Champaign, IL: Human Kinetics.

Holdsworth, R. (1998). Two challenges. *Connect, 110,* 15–17.

Holdsworth, R. (1999). *Authentic student participation in action: Some observations on contagious institutional deafness, selective hearing and acquired laryngitis syndrome.* Presented at the annual meeting of the Australian Association of Research in Education. Melbourne, Australia.

Jewett, A., Bain, L., & Ennis, C. (1995). *The curriculum process in physical education.* Dubuque, IA: Brown & Benchmark.

Kushman, J. W. (1997). *Look who's talking now: Student views of learning in restructuring schools*. Portland, OR: Northwest Regional Educational Laboratory

Mellor, S. (1998). Student cynicism about political participation: "What's the point?" *Connect, 11*, 3–7.

Prusak, K. A. (2000). The effect of choice on the motivation of adolescent females in physical education. *Dissertations Abstracts International, A61* (2), 484.

Schunk, D. (1992). Theory and research on student perceptions in the classroom. In D. H. Schunk and J. L. Meece (Eds.), *Student perceptions in the classroom* (pp. 3–23). Hillsdale, NJ: Lawrence Erlbaum Associates.

WEB RESOURCES

The following web link list was generated upon publication of the text; however, over time, the sites may become obsolete if an organization dissolves, discontinues online services, or relocates to a different URL. If a link listed below does not connect, please search for the organization by name.

http://www.hellison.com

Contains three video presentations relating to teaching personal and social responsibility: "Teaching Social Responsibility," "Principles in Real Life Schools," and "Solutions or Band-Aids."

http://www.vcsf.org/youth/yepwelcome.html

The Volunteer Center's Youth Empowerment Program is an award-winning program that promotes youth service and service learning. It is based on exploding the misconception that adolescents are not capable of being responsible, making appropriate decisions, having a serious thought or conversation, or handling any type of independence. Has a number of useful, practical links.

CHAPTER 6

Designing a Quality Aerobic Fitness Program

Scenario

"Quick, sign my mom's name here!"
"What for?"
"I found out—just sign. It's today, so I typed this up in computing."
"Today! So, did you do one for me?"
"Sure, I've already signed yours."

Meanwhile . . .

"I ain't doin' it, no way."
"C'mon, man, it's not that bad."
"Maybe not for you, but it's hot and I hate it. I might jog a bit, but I'm not busting a gut just for this."
"Well, OK, I'll just go slow with you."

Introduction

You guessed it: Today is the one-mile run test for this class. Jackie and Rebecca have invented their scheme for getting out of the test, while Brian and Desmond have their own strategy to avoid the dreaded activity. Ms. Thurston is equally frustrated. The state requires that all scores for fitness tests be reported annually in May, and she knows that the students don't like to do it and that many will attempt to finagle ways to avoid taking the test—but that's just too bad.

Unfortunately, this scenario is perhaps one of the most common pictures in all of physical education. Students are required to take tests for which they are not prepared, for which they see no purpose, and which are essentially aversive. Yet, the practice continues, to the benefit of few and the frustration of many.

The situation, however, need not be the norm. There are many ways in which students can engage in aerobic activity that is fun and that they see as purposeful. Fitness testing under these circumstances simply becomes a useful way of monitoring progress. The likelihood of avoidance is strongly reduced when students have first learned in the classroom or the gym the benefits of aerobic fitness and, even more important, enjoyable ways to develop aerobic endurance. Recall that knowledge of health effects is only weakly related to engagement in physical activity, but that knowledge of *how* to exercise is strongly related. This chapter presents ways in which students can develop aerobic fitness through engagement in content that is fun, challenging, and individualized toward personal goals.

Essential Knowledge for Students

At the completion of any high school program on developing aerobic fitness, all students should know the following:

- some basic physiology of aerobic exercise
- some of the health benefits gained from aerobic exercise
- the relationship between aerobic exercise and weight loss
- the notions of resting and training heart rates and the concept of training zones
- exercises programs that will result in improved aerobic fitness
- how to design a program so that when they leave school, they feel confident and comfortable in their participation

Basic Physiology of Aerobic Exercise

Many university students in physical education will complete entire courses in exercise physiology and during the process of these courses will gain understanding of a large number of terms, concepts, and principles concerning exercise. Although students in secondary schools may not require as extensive a knowledge of exercise physiology, it is important that they have some understanding of how the cardiovascular system works and, particularly, how it responds to exercise.

In order to develop cardiovascular fitness, one needs a strong and healthy heart. We could simply describe the physiology of cardiovascular exercise as pump, circulate, and uptake; that is, blood is pumped from the heart, it is circulated throughout the body, and the working muscles take up the oxygen in the blood. Students need to understand that the major factor that determines cardiovascular fitness is the heart's ability to supply oxygen to the working muscles and that this oxygen helps the cells produce the energy necessary to exercise.

Pump

At rest, the heart will pump about 5 liters of blood every minute. At exercise, this amount can increase to 20 liters. However, the heart itself is a muscle and will respond to training. The first key point is cardiac output. Cardiac output is the amount of blood sent out by the heart in a one-minute period. This output is a function of the heart rate (the number of beats per minute) and the stroke volume (the amount of blood pushed out with each beat).

One effect of training is that the heart becomes stronger and can beat with greater force. As a result, stroke volume will increase, and the heart has to beat less to send the same amount of blood throughout the system. Moreover, during exercise, the heart can pump more blood to the muscles, allowing for a greater level of work by those muscles.

Circulate

The blood vessels themselves are important to cardiovascular fitness. Hemoglobin is an iron-rich compound in the blood that helps transport oxygen. With training, hemoglobin levels can increase. Therefore, more oxygen can be circulated with the same heart rate and stroke volume.

A second factor in transport is blood pressure. Blood pressure is defined as the force by which blood is pushed against the walls of the arteries. When the heart contracts, the pressure exerted is the systolic blood pressure. The pressure on the arteries when the heart relaxes is known as diastolic blood pressure. Blood pressure is typically reported as a fractional score, such as 120/80 (read 120 over 80), with the systolic reading being the top score. Normal blood pressure should fall below values of 140/90. Exercising can help reduce blood pressure, even by as much as 10 units (e.g., from 160/100 to 150/90).

Uptake

The third factor that affects cardiovascular efficiency is the ability of the cells to take up oxygen. With training, blood vessels develop a greater number of capillaries, and hence more blood is available at the site of the cell. Second, cells themselves can produce more mitochondria, which are the keys to accessing oxygen.

Health Benefits Gained from Aerobic Exercise

The health benefits of aerobic exercise can be divided into two categories: (1) disease prevention and (2) personal enhancement. For adults, cardiovascular diseases continue to be the leading cause of death in the United States (and most other Western countries as well). Indeed, the American Heart Association suggests that one in every five Americans has evidence of some cardiovascular disease. In terms of *prevention*, regular cardiovascular exercise can help reduce this mortality in the following ways:

- raises HDL cholesterol levels, which helps reduce the risk of atherosclerosis (the buildup of fatty deposits on the walls of arteries)
- reduces the risk of having a heart attack
- reduces the risk of dying from a heart attack if one occurs
- reduces the risk of stroke (blockage of an artery supplying the brain)
- reduces the risk of high blood pressure
- helps in managing high blood pressure.

In youth, some more specific benefits are accrued, including potential reductions in body fat, a reduction in blood pressure for hypertensive adolescents, and higher levels of HDL cholesterol (see Bar-Or, 1999).

The second benefit of increased aerobic fitness relates to more immediate outcomes, those that result in various aspects of *personal enhancement*. These can include improvements in physical appearance (e.g., better muscle tone and reduced levels of body fat), an enhancement in self-esteem (exercisers can feel a sense of accomplishment), reductions in stress, and, in many cases, improvements in academic and physical performance. Students may not be fully aware of these advantages because we often focus entirely on the role of aerobic fitness in preventing disease.

The Relationship between Aerobic Exercise and Weight Loss

There is a simple formula for the relationship between aerobic exercise and weight loss: The longer you engage in physical activity, the more calories you will burn. Furthermore, during aerobic exercise the body derives its energy from its fat stores. However, this is not the only advantage of exercise in losing weight. Active exercise can change certain enzymes in the muscle system so that the body becomes more efficient in burning fat—a form of double whammy.

It takes 3,500 calories to burn one pound of fat. An exercise program consisting of 30 minutes of moderate activity (about 250–300 calories) and a reduction of 250 calories in the diet (a McDonald's cheeseburger has 320 calories, one slice of pizza almost 250) can provide a 500-calorie deficit in just one day. Over a one-week period, a consistent exercise program and some extra dietary discipline can work wonders for promoting fat loss. Furthermore, the maximum recommended fat loss is one to two pounds per week.

Resting and Training Heart Rates

The measurement of heart rate before, during, and after activity is perhaps the best (and most practical) way to monitor aerobic fitness. Moreover, one's heart rate during exercise is an excellent indicator of the intensity of that exercise.

Probably many students are already able to take their own heart rate (that is, their pulse), but it may be necessary to revise the methods or to teach them the carotid and wrist methods. Furthermore, counting should start with a zero count and be measured for either 6 or 10 seconds.

Students should also be encouraged to monitor their resting heart rate. With training, the heart becomes more efficient not only during activity, but also at rest. As a result, resting heart rate is regarded as a good indicator of fitness. Resting heart rate is best calculated first thing each morning on waking. However, resting heart rate can also be determined after a person has been sitting or lying down, relaxed, after a period of 5–15 minutes.

As noted, exercise intensity is effectively measured according to one's heart rate. As a result, working at different heart rates will result in different outcomes, and this leads to the concept of *target heart rate zone*. Target heart rate zones are calculated as a percentage of one's maximum heart rate (MHR). Although maximum heart rate is best measured in a physiology lab during an exercise stress test, according to the American College of Sports Medicine, most people can estimate their maximum heart rates from a simple formula: 220 – age = maximum heart rate. Thus, a 14-year-old will have an estimated MHR of 206; a 45-year-old member of the school's teaching staff will have a MHR of 165.

There are four typically outlined target heart rate zones. These are provided in Table 6.1.

A graphic representation of how this table relates to high school students is presented in Figure 6.1.

Table 6.1   Training Heart Rate Levels

Intensity Level	Percentage of MHR	Purpose
Heavy intensity	85–100% MHR	Training for competition
Moderate intensity	70–85% MHR	Often called the "cardio zone"
Light to moderate intensity	60–70% MHR	Often called the "fat-burning zone"
Light intensity	50–60% MHR	Recommended for beginner, sedentary, or overweight exercisers

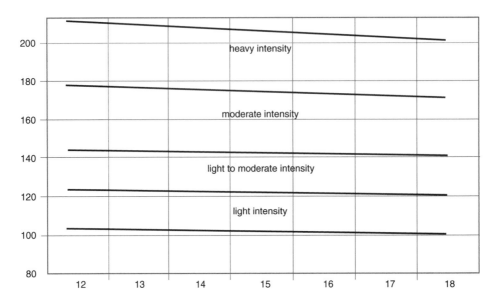

Figure 6.1   Target Heart Rate Zones

Exercises That Will Result in Improved Aerobic Fitness

There is an almost endless list of physical activities that students can undertake to help improve aerobic fitness. All that is necessary is for students to complete these activities at a pace that will elevate the heart rate into the appropriate target zone. Furthermore, many of these activities require little skill. Walking, jogging, and running are natural actions that can elevate the heart, while swimming, in-line skating, and cycling require initial learning but are certainly activities that can be pursued for a lifetime. Further, there has been a huge increase in the number of cardiovascular exercise machines available in many settings. These range from expensive computer-driven treadmills and stair steppers to less sophisticated exercise cycles. Some sports also involve a high aerobic energy demand. These include aquatic sports, such as water polo; winter sports, such as ice hockey; many of the court games, such as basketball and badminton; and some field-based games, such as Frisbee. In any case, to improve aerobic fitness, the activity must follow three key principles: (1) the exercises must involve large muscle groups, (2) the activity must be rhythmic or sustained, and (3) at least 10 minutes of continuous activity must be achieved in any one session.

In addition to the activities listed above, there has been a recent explosion in the popularity of aerobic fitness classes. Originally, the only format was aerobic dance itself; from this basic form many hybrids have evolved, including step aerobics, cardio funk (aerobics done to modern dance music using club-type dance steps), cardio karate, water aerobics, and spin cycling classes. The following sections of this chapter describe some beginning skills in all these activities.

Helping Students Design Their Own Programs

One of the positive features of cardiovascular exercise is that a person does not need a personal trainer or great knowledge to devise an enjoyable, engaging training program. All a person needs is to maintain an elevated heart rate for a period as long as 10 minutes. Indeed, in helping students learn about maintaining and improving their aerobic fitness, we might be better served to help them understand the things they do *not* have to do. An analysis of four major myths about aerobic training may help students better under the key concepts.

- *Myth 1: You have to exercise for long periods.*

  Rebuttal: Exercise benefits are cumulative—10-minute bouts three times a day can lead to health benefits. Longer periods of sustained aerobic exercise offer greater benefits; the key is total time in the appropriate heart rate zone.

- *Myth 2: Heart rates have to be greatly accelerated to yield a benefit.*

  Rebuttal: The training heart rate zone for a 15-year-old can be as low as 123 to yield a health benefit.

- *Myth 3: You have to participate in structured exercise.*

  Rebuttal: Any activity that involves some moderate intensity can be beneficial. Playing with the dog, shoveling snow, dancing, or even brisk walking all contribute to putting some stress on the heart and hence produce health benefits. The key is to find an activity that is fun and to be consistent.

- *Myth 4: You have to be fatigued at the end of the exercise for it to be worthwhile.*

  Rebuttal: No. You do not have to be exhausted at the end of any exercise for it to be beneficial. Yes, you may have to breathe more heavily, and you have to accelerate your heart rate—but not to exhaustion.

Putting Together a Floor Aerobics Routine

A quality aerobics workout will include a number of components. When we think of the term "aerobic dance," we mostly identify with the peak aerobic phase of high-intensity exercise. We visualize lots of high-impact movements, jumping, swinging of the arms, and of course, elevated heart rates. However, this is only one component of the entire package. Like any sport performance, it is only when we enter the playing field that we have 100% intense physical involvement. People do not arrive at a basketball arena, dress, and then go onto the court ready to play. They spend time warming up, limbering up, practicing their shots, rebounding, and jogging. So it is with an aerobics workout. The components of a workout include the general warm-up, the aerobic warm-up, the peak aerobic phase, the toning and conditioning phase (in some programs), and finally the flexibility and cool-down phase.

General Warm-Up

The warm-up gets the body ready to perform. It allows the body to move gradually from an inactive to an active state. There is a gradual increase in heart rate and blood flow to the muscles, and the beginning of an increase in core body temperature. The warm-up also allows the person to become mentally prepared for the activity to follow.

The time required for a warm-up is a very individual one and depends on age and fitness level. A minimum warm-up time of 5 to 10 minutes is generally considered adequate, but it is not uncommon for teachers to allocate individual warm-up opportunities to students. However, in many cases, this time becomes a sort of mini social hour, with lots of standing around and talking among friends. This is often masked by the skill of looking busy stretching. The warm-up needs to be active, although it is certainly done at a slow pace with an incremental increase in intensity. The teacher needs to be vigilant that the students are indeed beginning to move, by jogging and walking as the warm-up develops.

Aerobic Warm-Up

The aerobic warm-up is the first part of the overall routine and consists of low- to moderate-intensity movements on the floor. The emphasis is on using the large muscle groups, but with minimal jumping or hopping (the high-impact exercises). Activities can include walking, lunging, and any other activities that move the participants around the workout area. As the warm-up continues, moderate arm movement may be incorporated.

The aim of the warm-up is to move the participants into the target heart rate or exercise heart rate zones. This should be achieved within a 5- or 10-minute period.

Peak Aerobic Phase

The peak aerobic phase is that part of the workout when the more strenuous activities occur. This part of the routine will involve movements of higher impact and higher-level arm patterns. The main objective is to keep the heart rate within the target zone, with continuous movement being the key. This is the major component of the exercise routine and can last between 20 and 30 minutes.

Aerobics class

Aerobic Cool-Down

The aerobic cool-down aims to slowly decrease the heart rate, but to continue exercise in a manner that allows blood in the working muscles to return to the heart rather than pool in the lower extremities.

The cool-down also serves to help reduce the potential of muscle soreness and also to assist in removing metabolic waste. The cool-down should be long enough (at least 5 minutes) to provide for an overall recovery. The cool-down simply involves a gradual slowing of the movements (particularly the arms), until the pace and range of motion reach a level similar to the warm-up period.

Flexibility and Cool-Down

The flexibility and cool-down phase of the routine will involve slow and sustained stretching of the muscles used during the workout. Stretches should be held between 15 and 30 seconds and, in particular, the quadriceps, hamstrings, and lower leg muscles need specific attention.

Sample Movements for Floor-Based Aerobic Dance Routines

Tables 6.2 through 6.4 provide details of the many and varied movements available for designing an aerobic workout routine. These tables list the movements

Table 6.2   Locomotor Movements Suitable for an Aerobic Dance Routine

Locomotor Movements	Variations
Walking (one foot will always be on the ground)	In place Forward Backward Diagonally On the toes

Step–tap
    Walk forward
    Step together
    Walk backward
    Step together	

Grapevine
    Step left with left foot
    Cross behind with right foot
    Step left with left foot
    Cross in front with right foot
	Can begin on either side

Running (at some point, both feet are off the ground)	Running in place Running forward Running backward Running diagonally High knee runs

Jumping	Jumping in place
	Jumping forward
	Jumping backward
	Jumping sideways
	Quarter, half, and whole turns
	Split jumps (one foot goes forward, one back)
	Straddle jumps
	Heel jacks
	    Jump with feet together
	    Jump, but extend one leg to the side and
	    touch the heel to the floor
	    Jump to return feet together
	    Repeat to the opposite side

Hopping	In place
	Forward
	Backward
	Hop and kick
	Flea hop
	    Hop on one leg
	    Lift opposite knee to hip height
	    Step onto raised leg
	    Hop with opposite knee bending
	Pendulum hop
	    Hop on one leg
	    Extend the other to the side
	    Repeat and alternate

Table 6.3   Nonlocomotor Movements Suitable for an Aerobic Dance Routine

Nonlocomotor Movements	Variations
Knee lifts	To the front To the side
Kicks	To the front To the side
Heel lifts	

Squats
   Step to the side
   Squat as though sitting
   Close to the starting position	

Table 6.4   Arm Movements Suitable for an Aerobic Dance Routine

Arm Movements	Description
Arm Reaches	Reach up, to the side, or down
Arm Scissors	Cross the arms across the body (alternate arms)
Bow and Arrow	One arm extends to the side, the other is pulled back at the elbow
Punches	Punching straight or across the body
Uppercuts	Punching from low to high position
Pectoral Presses	Arms are out to the side in an L-position, hands face upward, bring the forearms together at face level
Upper Back Flies	Lean forward and bring arms upward to the sides (fists are usually clenched)

in a number of categories, including locomotor movements, nonlocomotor movements, and associated arm movements. Variations within these categories are also provided.

Tables 6.5 through 6.7 show three sample routines that might be used for the different components of the workout. Although each is limited to 32 counts, they provide a sample of the types of activities that are appropriate for inclusion in each phase.

Table 6.5   Sample Active-Warm-Up Routine

Movement	Repetitions	Counts
March in place	8	1 each (total = 8)
Step—tap	4	2 each (total = 8)
Grapevine	4—to the right and left	4 each (total = 8)
Knee lift	4—to the right and left	4 each (total = 8)

Table 6.6   Sample Warm-Up Aerobics Routine

Movement	Repetitions	Counts
Lunge	4—to right and left	2 each (total = 8)
3 runs forward, knee lift and then back	1	1 each (total = 8)
Grapevine and clap	4—to right and left	4 each (total = 8)
Squats	4	4 each (total = 8)

Table 6.7   Sample Peak Aerobics Routine

Movement	Repetitions	Counts
Flea hops	8	1 each (total = 8)
Jumping jacks	4	2 each (total = 8)
Pendulum hops	8	1 each (total = 8)
Skipping forward	8	1 each (total = 8)

Advantages and Disadvantages of *Step* Aerobics

The original use of the step in aerobic fitness was as a tool in fitness testing. It was only in the 1980s that it became an attractive addition to floor aerobics. The step adds a number of choreographic possibilities to a routine, allowing for movement on and off the step, as well as across and along it. In addition, there is an increased energy cost, because the step provides added emphasis on the lower body.

Step classes follow a pattern similar to that of floor aerobics classes in that they contain a general warm-up, an aerobic warm-up, and a peak aerobic phase. It is valuable to include some step movements during the warm-up phases, and new moves can also be introduced here. These new moves, however, should be introduced at half pace. A further use of the step is as a prop for stretching.

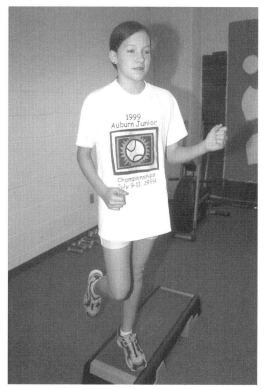

Steps add intensity

The intensity of a step class will depend first on the height of the bench, while further stress can be achieved by adding propulsive movements or small jumps. This is, of course, in addition to the use of the arms and the intensity of the floor-based exercises.

Although step aerobics offers a number of advantages, it also poses some challenges. First, and most obvious, is the initial cost of purchasing the steps. Although some programs have been creative and constructed their own timber versions, in all cases the steps must be slip- and skid-proof. Second, students with knee problems should probably not perform these workouts or at least should use lower steps. Pryor and Kraines (2000) also make a number of recommendations regarding the techniques of stepping:

- placing the whole foot on the step
- stepping to the center of the platform
- keeping the step in one's line of vision at all times
- slightly bending the knees when stepping
- never stepping up or down with one's back to the step

Step Exercises

Table 6.8 outlines many of the moves that can be used in step aerobics. These tables list the movements in a number of categories, including locomotor movements, nonlocomotor movements, and associated arm movements. Variations within these categories are also provided.

Tables 6.9 through 6.10 show two sample routines that might be used for the different components of the workout. Although each is limited to 64 counts, they provide a sample of the types of activities that are appropriate for inclusion in each phase.

Table 6.8   Sample Step Aerobics Movements

Name	Footwork	Picture
Basic step	R up—L up—R down—L down	1
Tap up	R up—L tap—L down—R down	2
Knee up	R up—L knee lift—L down—R down	3
V step	R up wide—L up wide—R down—L down	4
A step	L up —R up together —L down—R tap	5
Turn step	R up—L up—R down—L tap	6
U turn	R up—L up—R down—L tap	7
Over the top	R up—L up—R down—L tap	8
Across the top	L up (wide)—R up (together)—L down—R tap	9
Diagonal over	R up (long)—L up (together)—R down—L tap	10
L step	L up—R tap—R down—L tap	11
Straddle up	R up—L up—R straddle down—L straddle down	12
Straddle down	L straddle down—R straddle down—L up—R up	13
Lunge down	R Tap down—R up (*this is a 2 count*)	14

Table 6.9   Sample Step Routine—Warm-Up Phase

Movement	Repetitions	Counts
Basic step	2 on each leg	4 each (total = 16)
L step	One to right, one to left	8 each (total = 16)
Knee up	4—to the right and left	4 each (total = 16)
V step	One to right, one to left	4 each (total = 8)
Basic step	On right leg	4 each (total = 8)

Table 6.10 Sample Step Routine—Peak Phase

Movement	Repetitions	Counts
Over the top	Right—left—right—left	8 each (total = 16)
Repeater	Right and left	4 each (total = 16)
Straddle up	Right foot lead	4 each (total = 16)
Lunge down	Right side then left	4 each (total = 16)

Selecting Music and Steps

The music that is used for aerobic workout routines needs to have a steady beat, one that is simple enough for all students to follow. Some modern music has an underlying beat that the trained ear can pick up, but for aerobics classes, where people need to keep up with the music and their movement at the same time, we need a clearly identified rhythm.

The different phases of an aerobics workout have a different tempo, or speed of music. The warm-up and stretching, the low-impact and cool-down sections of the routine need music that is moderate or at walking pace, in the range of 110 to 140 beats per minute (BPM). Peak aerobic routine speeds lie in the range of 140 to 160 BPM, which is considered jogging pace (Pryor & Kraines, 2000).

Professionally produced aerobics tapes can be purchased through specialist catalogues that provide premade sequences, but it is also fun to make your own or have students bring in music. When students provide music, they first must have tested it to make sure it fits the tempo and, of course, is socially acceptable (while most rap music has a definite beat, some lyrics are not appropriate in the school setting).

In step aerobics, the beat is different. The ideal speed for a step class, according to Pryor and Kraines, is between 122 and 127 beats per minute, with a suggested maximum speed of 135 BPM. With step aerobics, the intensity of the routine is increased not by increasing the tempo of the music, but by either increasing the height of the platform or moving around the step, increasing the use of the arms, or increasing the impact movements (e.g., jog and hop versus walk and slide). As with floor aerobics, prepared tapes for step classes are also available.

Aerobic Dance Videotapes— What They Offer, Cautions to Take

One only has to look through the catalogues of fitness magazines, publishing companies, and the Internet to find a plethora of aerobic videos—preprogrammed routines that people can purchase, watch, and follow in their own homes. Most of these routines follow the pattern of stretching, warm-up, the aerobic phases, and the cool-downs. They contain music and a dynamic instructor. It is possible to use these videotapes in a number of ways in the physical education setting. One may think it appropriate to put a tape in the VCR and have the students follow the instructor on the tape. However, video television screens are small, and students need enough space to move about—so these videos are not really suitable for whole class instruction. However, they may be used as a station within an aerobics circuit. The challenge there, of course, is that as groups move through the circuit, they will be performing different sections of the videotape. The other option is to rewind the tape to a certain point, but this becomes cumbersome.

Perhaps the major benefit of the extensive array of videos is that they can serve as a resource for the teacher in designing routines. Certainly it may be possible for teachers to collect information about new moves or new sequences that the teacher can incorporate into their own routines. Alternatively, the teacher can blacken the video screen and use only the music from the tape to lead the class.

Alternative Aerobic Training Programs—Reducing Boredom and Providing Challenge

There will be times during any program where students (and teachers) will look for some change. Apart from floor and step aerobics, a number of other derivations on the same theme have come about. All involve using large muscle groups in some rhythmic, consistent exercise, and all aim to elevate the heart rate into a 60–80% of MHR training zone. By having some elemental skills in these programs, you will be able to present a wide variety of options for students.

Aerobic Kickboxing

A marriage of aerobics, boxing, and martial arts, aerobic kickboxing is performed under various names, including Tae Bo, Cardio Karate, Te-Geri, Karbo, Cardio Kickboxing, or Cardio Karate. The National Association of Professional Martial Artists program uses Cardio Karate or Fitness Kickboxing. Unlike conventional martial arts courses, participants wear aerobic outfits, loose-fitting workout clothes, athletic shoes, and, for bagwork, hand-wraps and light gloves. Despite the different names, the activity involves the rhythmic repetition of traditional fighting skills (e.g., punches, blocks, kicks, elbows, and knee strikes), as well as training skills (e.g., jump rope, mimicking hitting,

Students practice kickboxing skills

and air bag). Some kickboxing classes also involve equipment such as heavy bags and pads.

As an activity to develop cardiorespiratory fitness, kickboxing rates as a great calorie burner, with up to an estimated energy expenditure of 800 calories per hour and a high percentage of maximum oxygen uptake. Hence, many students may find it a very intense workout.

One fun component of aerobic kickboxing is that it is suited to high-energy instrumental versions of familiar dance music. In contrast to the more restrained, dancelike movements of traditional aerobics ("grapevine" and "crossovers," for example), devotees of kickboxing extol the high-intensity, pumped-up, stress-busting power and athleticism of their workout.

Indeed, one of the more popular attractions of kickboxing is that it is perceived as a great stress reliever. Add this to the fact that this form of exercise teaches students some self-defense techniques and is particularly eye-catching, especially for those who may not be attracted to aerobic dance. Some basic kickboxing skills are provided in Tables 6.11 and 6.12.

Table 6.11 Some Basic Aerobic Kickboxing Skills: Punches

Skill	Key Technical Points	Avoid
Jab	• Elbows by side, hands up • Extend the arm out • Palm down • Aim for a jab at chin height • Bring the movement straight back to the ready position	• Throwing the arms out • Fully extending the elbows • Allowing the elbows to leave the side
Cross	• Turn hips, and pivot the leg of the punching arm • Extend the arm across the body • Squeeze shoulder blades, and contract back	• Extending the arm fully • Rotating the upper body and not the hips
Uppercut	• Dip the knees to take weight evenly over both legs • Push up toward the jaw • Make a bicep, and bring the punch forcefully upward • Drive up through the punch from the lower body	• Using only the shoulders and not the hips • Dropping the nonpunching arm
Hook	• Step out to a wider base • Pivot on the same heel as the punching arm • Lead arm makes a tight L shape • Foot, hip, and shoulder all pivot toward the target	• Stopping the punch at the target; the hands must be brought back to ready • Turning only the leg—use the whole body
Air bags	• Turn the forearms at 45 degrees • Use fast repetition movements to strike the imaginary speed bag • Hold hands high • Move arms in a circular motion	• Letting arms drop

Table 6.12 Some Basic Kickboxing Skills: Kicks

Skill	Key Technical Points	Avoid
Basic front snap kick	• Bring the knee up • Kick the heel out toward the target • Squeeze the thigh • Flex the ankle • Kick between the elbows	• Kicking with the foot dorsiflexed • Dropping the hands
Basic back snap kick	• Lean forward to bend over • Look over the shoulder of the kicking leg • Pick up the kicking knee, extend behind, and bring back down • Stand back up straight	• Not looking back over the kicking shoulder • Standing too upright
Side kick	• Open up the stance—stand wide • Keep hands in a guard position • Look in the same direction as the kick • Step the back leg up; take 80% of weight on this leg • Bring knee to chest—heel pointed out • Extend kick to the target • Push the heel to the target • Bring back in, and step back down	• Kicking with the foot flat • Attempting to kick too high in the beginning or learning stages
Basic roundhouse kick	• Take 80% of the weight on the nonkicking leg • Place the back hand on the hips and the front hand up to make a guard • Let toes of kicking leg only barely touch the floor • Bring knee up at 45-degree angle (lower for beginners) • Pivot planted foot 180 degrees • Extend kick with ankle flexed • Bring it back and place down	• Placing too much weight on the kicking leg
Front knee raise	• Keep one leg back, with the heel up • Pull the other leg up as the elbows are pulled down • Think of holding an opponent's head and driving it into your knee	• Leaning back • Being passive with the arms
Side knee raise	• Place right leg out to the side, the left to the front • Keep 80% of weight on the right leg • Lean over the right leg • Bring the hands down as the knee raises	• Leaning back • Being passive with the arms

Water Aerobics

Water aerobics is typically performed in a vertical position in shallow and/or deep water. Water's unique properties provide an environment for people of all abilities. An advantage of water aerobics is that the buoyancy creates a reduced-impact exercise alternative that is easy on the joints, while the water's resistance challenges the muscles. Furthermore, advanced swimming ability is *not* required.

Water lends itself to a well-balanced workout that improves all the major components of physical fitness: aerobic training, muscular strength, endurance, flexibility, and body composition. Water aerobics is one area that is growing in popularity, with estimated participants now numbering over 10 million.

As on land, there are several variables that affect the exercise intensity during vertical water exercise:

- the water depth in which the person is exercising
- the speed of movement through the water
- the amount of force applied to movements (how "hard" you work)
- the length of the person's limbs

As a result, an individual can easily manipulate the intensity during a workout and, hence, try to keep the training heart rate within the desired zone. Nevertheless, a water aerobics routine that involves both upper and lower body movements expends somewhere between 400 and 500 calories an hour.

Tables 6.13 through 6.15 provide some sample actions that can be incorporated into a water aerobics routine.

Table 6.13 Water-Based Exercises for the Upper Body

Exercises	Key Teaching Points
Biceps or triceps curls	Pull palms forward toward the surface Reverse the palms to face the pool bottom when pressing down
Canoe arms	Palms down, have both arms waist high to one side Pull both palms past the hip on one side (like using a canoe paddle)
Lateral raises	Lift arms up and away from the body
Deep pulls	Begin in a lunge stance Pull both arms forward from the hips Reverse palms, and pull water back
Figure-eights	Draw figure-eights with each arm on each side

Table 6.14 Water-Based Locomotion Exercises for the Lower Body

Exercises	Key Teaching Points
Marching	Walk in place, but lift the knee to hip weight Keep one foot on the floor at all times
Jogging	Marching action, but with a small flight phase
Water walk	Walk as though on land Remember to use the arms
Two-step	Walk with the one leg leading Right step, with the left foot coming only as far as the right heel Remember to lead with both legs
Pedaling	Like riding a bike—neither foot leaves the floor Lift each heel off the floor to have the weight on the ball of the foot

Table 6.15 Water-Based Jumps and Kicks

Exercises	Key Teaching Points
Jumping jacks	Feet and arms start by the side Move both out to attain a wide stance with the arms on the surface of the water Close and repeat
Leg swings	Lift one leg forward as the opposite arm swings forward Bend the supporting leg
Tuck and extend	Start in the lunge position Bring the knee of the front leg into the chest and then extend Complete the action on the opposite leg
Cross-country ski	Start in a lunge position Jump up and change the position of the legs (front to back and back to front)
Pendulum kick	Raise one leg to the side Hop and swing the legs from side-to-side like a pendulum Try to almost make contact of the legs in the neutral (central) position
Zig-zag jumps	With feet together, jump to the left, but facing slightly to the right Repeat, jumping to the right, but facing left Progress across an imaginary center line
Squats	Beginning with the feet together, take one step to the side Squat down as if sitting in a chair Return to basic stance, then step and squat to the other side

Aerobic Circuits

One way of incorporating a number of different activities from various aerobic disciplines is through the use of circuits. A circuit is simply a series of stations that a student rotates through according to a timed sequence. An advantage of circuits is that students can adjust the activity intensity at each station. Further, as their knowledge of content increases, students can begin to design their own circuits with activities they enjoy.

In designing circuits, there are several features to consider:

- *Total length of the circuit*—how long will the entire circuit take to complete?

- *Number of stations*—how many stations are included in the total circuit?

- *Time at each station*—how long will students spend in activity at each station?

- *Transition time*—how long do students have to move from one station to the next (is there a rest period involved)?

- *Station description*—how long will it take to read? (Clear instructions need to be placed at each station so that students understand the activity.)

- *Provision of equipment*—what equipment is needed at each station?

- *Equipment return*—what are students expected to do with the equipment at a station on completion of that station?

- *Number of students per station*—this has implications for the space that needs to be made available and the amount of equipment required

- *Recording*—are students expected to make a record of their work at a station (e.g., number of repetitions, heart rate, or perceived intensity?)

- *Number of total circuits*—do students complete just one complete circuit, or is the circuit repeated?

- *Choice of activity at a station*—to what extent is the activity at a specific station flexible? (For example, you may provide a step bench with instructions to "step up and down from the bench for one minute," or, if you wish to be more flexible, you may simply say, "Using any step combination you want, work over and back the bench for the 2-minute time allocation.")

- *Content focus*—are all exercises of high intensity, or are there some stretching and/or less demanding stations?

- *Where do students* begin—in circuits where all activities have similar levels of intensity, it will not matter if a student begins at station 2 or 7. However, if you wish to include rest and/or recovery stations that are designed to be reached later in the workout, you need to be aware that some students will reach this point ahead of others.

Jump rope is great for circuits

Although most circuit training involves a rotational format, with groups of students moving around activities in a set order, it is possible to have a written program that students progress through in sequence. In this way, students can work with a partner through a series of tasks cards. Although this has implications for equipment availability (because all students may need the ropes or step benches at the same time), it does allow students to work at their own pace. Some may choose to spend 30 seconds at each station and make four total circuits, while others may choose to spend one minute at each station and make only two total circuits. This circuit organization allows for the allocation of rest and/or drink breaks throughout a circuit, particularly at the point where students will be needing one.

An example of a water aerobics circuit is provided in Table 6.16.

Table 6.16 A Sample Water Aerobics Circuit

Station	Activity	Equipment/Notes
1	Side leg lifts	May choose to wear a flotation device around ankle for extra intensity
2	Jump rope	Hand motion is under the water
3	Abdominal crunches	Use a noodle or water weights for flotation
4	Jumping jacks	Arms either in or out of the water to vary intensity
5	Cross-country skiing	Arms either in or out of the water to vary intensity
6	Climb the ladder	Arms out of the water
7	Side arm raises	Holding a weight
8	Russian kicks	Heels touch to each side
9	Biceps curls	Use either a water weight or resistance bands to vary intensity
10	Front kicks	May choose to wear a flotation device around ankle for extra intensity

Aerobic Sports

The development of aerobic fitness does not have to be limited to individual activities and group exercise classes. A number of dual and team sports have the potential to produce a moderate level of physical activity and provide for continuous play. In this case, moderate activity is determined as an activity that exceeds 3 METs (1 MET is approximately equal to the energy expenditure associated with quiet sitting).

There are many games that meet these two criteria, and 10 minutes of activity in these will help develop some degree of aerobic fitness. Most of these can be included comfortably within a high school physical education program. Indeed, all of these games will exceed a MET level of 3: badminton (4–9), Frisbee (4–8), basketball (5–12), lacrosse (6–12,) floor hockey (5–10), team handball (6–10), and soccer (5–10). A further positive aspect of these games is that they all are easily adapted for play with small-sided teams. Small-sided teams result

Handball provides moderate activity

in more intense playing conditions and more active involvement for all players (see Chapter 8 for designing units of work for sport seasons).

Including Students with Disabilities

Although many students with disabilities will not be able to complete the full body movements that are so fundamental to many aerobic training programs, there are still ways in which these students can improve their aerobic capacity. Students who are ambulatory may be able to participate in many of the activities engaged in by nondisabled students, such as walking, jogging, or swimming, perhaps with minor modifications. Students in wheelchairs can increase their metabolic demand through participation in exercises requiring them to move their chairs, or, in many cases, in seated aerobics.

For designing exercise modifications for a student performing seated aerobics, one of the most helpful planning experiences is to take an aerobics or step class while seated. This will help you see what movements and movement combinations are awkward and which are more intense. Nonetheless, there are some specific principles that need to be followed in presenting seated aerobics. These are listed in Table 6.17.

Table 6.17 Activities for Seated Aerobics

Movements to Avoid	Application to Disabilities
Rotation of the trunk	• The oblique abdominal muscles and the erector spinae group may be unusable or only partly usable in students with spinal cord injuries. • Students with spinal cord injury may also have metal rods or surgical implants to provide support and trunk stability. • Students with impaired balance may lose balance when twisting. • For any student in a chair, twisting movements could lead to abrasion sores.
Asymmetrical arm movements with full extension (e.g., windmill-like movements)	• Students with balance problems will have problems. • This does not mean that you are limited to moving both arms at a time; moving one arm singly is a good example of lowering the intensity level an exercise. In that case, the student may need to use the other arm for balance or support.
Excessive arm movements above the shoulders	• These can lead to excessively elevated heart rates and blood pressure.
Trunk extension and flexion	• Those with spinal cord injuries may not be able to perform these movements due to an absence of muscle control or due to implanted spinal rods. • Those with poor balance control may lose their stability and sway forward.

Movements to Include	Key Technique Points
Marches	• Movement is one of shoulder flexion and extension. • Elbows are bent, and the arms move in opposition. • Increase intensity by straightening out the elbow joint or by lifting the arms to a march in front of the torso. • Decrease intensity by decreasing range of motion.
Presses	• Useful more in the warm-up phase. • Should not go above shoulder level. • You can decrease the intensity by going half time. • Vary location of the press. • Complete one arm at a time, so that the other may be used for balance.
Shoulder flexion/extension and abduction/adduction	• Take care not to overwork the anterior deltoid. • Vary the location. • Vary the intensity by varying the degree of flexion in the elbow joint. • Vary the intensity by varying the speed of the exercise or by double-counting the movement. • Avoid the "one arm flex—one arm extend" combination.
Shoulder rolls and lifts (shoulder shrugs)	• Useful mainly in the warm-up and cool-down phases.
Swimming strokes	• Breaststroke, crawl, and dog paddle strokes are most appropriate. • Avoid the backstroke, because it goes over the head. • Be careful not to include one-arm full extension movements.
Arm curls	• Vary the location (side, front, chest high, shoulder-high, shoulder-high front, etc.). • Vary the intensity with the beat. • Vary the intensity with range of motion. • Avoid asymmetrical movements.

IN-SCHOOL TASKS

Walking Track

Visit a nearby high school, and ask to tour their grounds. Consider the possibility of developing a walking trail. What facilities does this school have beyond the track that could be used to develop a trail? Are there any local facilities near the school that might also encompass this activity?

Opportunity for Teaching Specific Aerobic Exercise

Visit a nearby high school, and ask to interview the teachers about their aerobic fitness program. Does anyone specifically teach aerobics, kickboxing, or any other aerobic training method? Which teachers in particular? What are their backgrounds in this activity? Do these teachers see aerobics as a gender-specific activity—that is, attractive only to girls? What facilities are available for these classes—are there step benches, jump ropes, etc.?

PORTFOLIO SUGGESTIONS AND ARTIFACTS

Aerobics Routine (S1–K1; S6–K3)

Design an aerobics routine of 50 minutes that includes all the relevant sections: the warm-ups, the main aerobics component, and the cool-down. Consider using different floor and arm patterns throughout. Indicate on your routine plan those exercises that students can modify to increase or decrease the intensity of the workout.

Step Aerobics Routine (S1–P1, K7)

Repeat the above task, but incorporate a step. You may videotape this routine (or at least segments of it) to demonstrate your competence in the actual movement forms themselves.

Aerobics Video Critique (S6–K4, P4)

View a commercially available aerobics videotape (step, kickboxing, or aerobic dance). Comment on the suitability of using this tape for a high school physical education class: Are the moves too difficult, is the instructor clear, or is the pace too fast?

Aerobic Music (S6–K4, P4)

Make a music CD or cassette for use in an aerobic dance or step aerobics class. Consider the components of the exercise routine as well as the suggestions for speed.

STUDENT ASSESSMENT OPPORTUNITIES

In 1992, the National Association for Sport and Physical Education (NASPE) appointed the Standards and Assessment Task Force to develop content standards and assessment material based on the question "What should students know and be able to do in physical education?" Seven content standards were developed based on the definition of a physically educated person. These standards provide the key tools for assessing student performance in physical education.

Presented below (and in Chapters 7, 8, and 9) is a series of assessment examples that correspond to each of the seven standards. Each content standard is listed and described, followed by one or two techniques appropriate for assessing student achievement of the specified content standard. The assessment examples provided are not meant to be a complete listing of available assessment techniques, nor are they necessarily the best ones for all situations. Feel free to use these in your classes or develop new ones more suited to your situation.

NASPE Standard 1: Demonstrates Competency in Many Movement Forms, and Proficiency in a Few Movement Forms

1. Student routine: Students compose and perform an aerobics routine of 5 minutes' length. In this routine, the students show some aerobic warm-up and peak aerobics movement.

2. Teacher observation checklist: The teacher may randomly select three or four exercises for the student to demonstrate (from a step class, water aerobics, or other cardio activity). The teacher provides the name of the exercise, so the student must be able first to identify the matching movements and second, to perform these correctly.

NASPE Standard 2: Applies Movement Concepts and Principles to the Learning and Development of Motor Skills

1. Choreographed aerobics routine: The student writes an aerobics routine for an area of their specialty (floor, step, or aerobic kickboxing). The routine will be in column format: column 1 = number of repetitions; column 2 = specific movements; column 3 = number of counts.

2. Video analysis: The student watches a video of a commercially available or televised aerobics class. The student will correctly identify the various segments of this video and will be able to explain the exercises within, and purposes of, each section of the class.

NASPE Standard 3: Exhibits a Physically Active Lifestyle

1. Exercise log: The student keeps a current exercise log of his or her participation in aerobic exercise. This log is submitted to the teacher each week, with an annotated account of improvement, inhibitors of improvement, and motivational facilitators or obstacles. A sample log is shown.

Name _____

Class _____

Date	Activity	Distance	Duration	Heart Rate
3rd March	Aerobics class		50 mins	154 BPM
4th March	Walking	2 miles	30 mins	122 BPM
5th March	Aerobics class		50 mins	148 BPM
6th March	Swim class	500 yards	20 mins	152 BPM

Figure 6.2   Sample exercise log

NASPE Standard 4: Achieves and Maintains a Health-Enhancing Level of Physical Fitness

1. Self-testing data: The student participates in a relevant test of aerobic endurance and muscular strength and meets the criteria for his or her age and gender. (See Tables 6.18 through 6.20 for health–related reference standards.)

2. Personal goals project: The student assesses his or her current fitness level through self-administration of a relevant fitness test. The student then designs a personal program with specific goals over a predetermined period. At the end of the time, the student determines the extent to which those goals have been met.

Table 6.18 Health-Related Reference Standards—1-Mile Run

Age	Fitnessgram		President's Challenge (Health Fitness Award)	
12	Boys	10:30	Boys	9:00
	Girls	12:00	Girls	10:30
13	Boys	10:00	Boys	8:00
	Girls	11:30	Girls	10:30
14	Boys	9:30	Boys	8:00
	Girls	11:00	Girls	10:30
15	Boys	9:00	Boys	7:30
	Girls	10:30	Girls	10:00
16	Boys	8:30	Boys	7:30
	Girls	10:00	Girls	10:00
17	Boys	8:30	Boys	7:30
	Girls	10:00	Girls	10:00
17+	Boys	8:30	Boys	7:30
	Girls	10:00	Girls	10:00

Source: Reprinted with permission from the President's Challenge Physical Activity and Fitness Awards Program Manual, 2001, Bloomington, IN: The Presidents Challenge. *Source:* FITNESSGRAM® data reproduced with permission, The Cooper Institute, Dallas, TX.

Table 6.19 Health-Related Reference Standards—12-Minute Walk/Run

Age	Male (Distance in Yards)		Female (Distance in Yards)	
	Good	Better	Good	Better
13	2500	2650	1800	1900
14	2600	2800	1900	2100
15	2600	2800	1900	2100
16	2600	2800	1900	2100
17	2800	3000	2000	2300
17+	2800	3000	2000	2300

Table 6.20 Health-Related Reference Standards—Walk Evaluations

Walking Time	Males (Miles)		Females (Miles)	
	Good	Better	Good	Better
30 minutes	2.0	2.2 or further	1.85	2.0 or further
35 minutes	2.13	2.25 or further	1.5	2.13 or further
45 minutes	2.23	2.4 or further	2.0	2.23 or further

NASPE Standard 5: Demonstrates Responsible Personal and Social Behavior in Physical Activity Settings

1. Teacher checklist: The teacher observes students as they participate in class activities. Sample positive social behaviors include praising the efforts of others, setting up and packing up equipment without being asked, and accepting the advice and help of others. A rubric of "always," "often," "sometimes," or "rarely" could be used to classify student achievement.

2. Self-report: Students complete a report concerning their development of independent learning. Students are asked to respond to the following statements: (a) "I have begun (or will soon begin) to participate in an out-of-school aerobic training program," and (b) "I have initiated (or soon will initiate) an action plan within my family to help us all reach a target of 210 minutes of moderate activity per week."

NASPE Standard 6: Demonstrates Understanding and Respect for Differences among People in Physical Activity Settings

1. Teacher checklist: The teacher observes students as they participate in class activities. Evidence of inclusive and discriminatory behavior is coded based on whether students demonstrate behaviors that allow their classmates to participate freely with equipment or that exclude some classmates at particular stations.

2. Group project: Students form a small group to design a series of aerobic exercises that could be accessible to students with a specific physical disability.

NASPE Standard 7: Understands That Physical Activity Provides the Opportunity for Enjoyment, Challenge, Self-Expression, and Social Interaction

1. Written report: Students compose a report that requests classroom teachers within the school to join then during their daily walking club. The report will outline the benefits of participation in the activity and their opinions about how this will promote teacher-student collegiality within the school.

2. "Adopt a little brother/sister" portfolio: Students will create a portfolio that journalizes their adoption of a younger friend or neighbor to include in some aerobic exercise. The portfolio may include a log of activities, photographs, and parent and child reactions.

REFLECTION TIME

Now that you have read this chapter, how confident do you feel in

- designing a series of step aerobics lessons for a class that includes a group of boys who have traditionally resisted this activity?
- designing a water aerobics circuit?
- demonstrating the aerobic exercises that are included in floor, step, and cardio karate routines?
- identifying the key principles of an aerobic training workout and being able to incorporate these into a lesson plan?
- identifying key modifications to games such that their major outcome enhances the players' aerobic fitness?
- being able to become an advocate for helping your school to become an "active school"?

REFERENCES

Bar-Or, O. (1999). Health benefits of physical activity during childhood and adolescence. In C. E. Corbin and R. P. Pangrazi (Eds.), *Toward a better understanding of physical fitness and activity*. Scottsdale, AZ: Holcomb Hathaway.

Brick, L. (1996). *Fitness aerobics*. Champaign, IL: Human Kinetics.

Champion, N., & Hurst, G. (2000). *The aerobics instructor's handbook*. New York: Simon & Schuster.

Malkin, M. (1995). *Aerobic walking, the weight-loss exercise*. New York: John Wiley & Sons.

Pappas Gaines, M. (1993). *Fantastic water workouts*. Champaign, IL: Human Kinetics.

Pillarella, D., & Roberts, S. (1996). *Fitness stepping*. Champaign, IL: Human Kinetics.

Pryor, E., & Kraines, M. G. (2000). *Keep moving: Fitness through aerobics and step*. Mountain View, CA: Mayfield.

WEB RESOURCES

The following web link list was generated upon publication of the text; however, over time, the sites may become obsolete if an organization dissolves, discontinues online services, or relocates to a different URL. If a link listed below does not connect, please searech for the organization by name.

http://www.fitnesstutor.com/

An extensive site that provides fitness training information, including details of exercise heart rate, a number of fitness calculators, and an internal search engine.

http://www.aerobicspot.com/choreogr.htm

Choreography web page from Aerobic Spot, London, KY. Dozens of patterns for step, hi-lo, and kickboxing classes.

http://www.afaa.com/

Home page of the Aerobics and Fitness Association of America.

http://www.waterdanceonline.com

Provides a chart that compares deep-water walking/running with land-based activities.

http://www.bodytrends.com/gourley.htm

Provides a good outline of basic aerobic exercise principles for improved health and fitness.

http://www.leanteamrunner.com/Runner/Exercise.html

A good site providing extensive details of the benefits of walking and running, with a strong focus on weight control.

http://www.turnstep.com

Lists a number of routines for all forms of aerobic exercises.

http://www.turnstep.com/Adaptive/index.html

Advice for integrating all people into your aerobics classes, regardless of ability or disability.

CHAPTER 7

Designing a Quality Muscular Strength and Endurance Fitness Program

Scenario

In this scenario, we find ourselves in a collegiate weight-training room, one of the type found in a student activities center. These facilities are free to students who want to go and voluntarily exercise. They are often busy places, and they give us a good idea of the types of activities that seem most attractive to collegians. As we watch the males, we see a preponderance of upper body exercises being completed. Biceps are straining, the bench press machines are all in use, and just about every dumbbell is being pushed or curled. The few women in the gym are completing leg curls and sit-ups.

Introduction

The culture of the development of "beach muscles" is perhaps not a very surprising phenomenon in the collegiate weight room. Students who spend time in these facilities most likely have a strong sense of physical activity as part of their personal identities. Looking good is important, and seeing the payoff on their investment of hard work in the physical domain is very rewarding.

In the high school physical education setting, however, our agenda is significantly different. First, in our classes, we have a heterogeneous group of students, all with various experiences in weight lifting. For students whose personal identity is not reinforced by notions of physicality, this weight room might indeed appear to be quite an irrelevant place and, for some, may even appear intimidating. Second, these students' perceptions about the roles of weight training can be quite misguided. Many high school students believe that "you will get all big and muscley," and for many students this is not a desired objective. You will recall the students described in Chapter 3 who focused on thinness, for example, and rejected exercises as counterproductive to that goal.

Given these potential barriers to students' perceptions of weight training, we as teachers are confronted with the task of motivating and inducting all students into a positive culture of strength training, not with an objective of just improving their physique, but for the health benefits that can accrue from such participation. For those students who have strong conceptions of their own physicality, this will not be too difficult. We can indeed stress the legitimate objectives of improved sport performance and improvements in physique. We do, however, need to involve and invite students into the setting who have previously not seen the weight room as part of their world.

Many students may not understand the health benefits that can be gained from weight training. These include increased bone density, muscular strength, and anaerobic power and capacity (see Nieman, 1999). Of particular value is the role weight training can play in the development of lean body mass, particularly through changes in one's metabolism. Given that obesity is the most prevalent health problem of American adolescents, weight training is one activity that can assist in the development of a healthy body composition. For seriously overweight students, weight training is potentially less aversive and difficult than aerobic training programs. Strength training, thus seen as an aid in the development of *health*, has more of a chance of inviting these students into a weight lifting culture than the notion of developing a more muscled physique. To this end, we need to reinforce and educate students that the work they will be doing within their physical education course will not result in their getting "big." Moreover, the opportunity to get huge muscles will not take place even with intensive training—their bodies are simply not set up that way.

Weight training
achieves many goals

In presenting weight training to students, particularly to those with little or no experience in the weight room, we therefore need to show that it is a place where individual specific goals can be met. In the weight room, comparisons to other people are irrelevant; only those to oneself pre- and post-training are important. The weight room, then, can accommodate multiple goals within a single class. We hope to develop in all students the development of self-efficacy toward weight training, so that this activity can become an enjoyable part of their own movement culture from a "feel good, be good for me" part of their life, not necessarily a "get big, get noticed" agenda.

In designing a high school strength and endurance fitness program, we are also aiming to help these students become independent and self-directed learners. Your tasks as a teacher are numerous. You have to be a source of information, a motivator, an advocate, and—perhaps most of all, given the misconceptions that many students hold about strength training—an evangelist.

Essential Knowledge for Students

At the completion of any educational program on weight training, there are some essential things that students should know as a result of participating in a strength and endurance fitness program. At the very least, students should know

- about the muscles and muscle groups
- some general training principles
- the terminology and vocabulary that they will hear if they join a gym or, in the case of some students, work out with a sports team
- exercises they can do for specific muscles or muscle groups in order to improve or reach their objectives
- how to act and respond safely, not only when they are lifting but also in the weight room itself
- how to design a program so that when they leave school, they feel confident and comfortable in their participation
- how to make good decisions about the use of facilities at sites including health clubs, college weight rooms, or worksite fitness centers

Knowledge of the Muscle Groups

When learning about the muscles and muscle groups, students need to know the major muscle groups. Again, this is not simply an academic exercise. There is a vocabulary of strength training that is used commonly in many contexts outside the physical education class.

The students not only need to know the major muscle groups but also should learn the specific names and their correct spelling. There is, of course, an anatomical hierarchy, and it will be your decision as a teacher to determine the level of sophistication that you want students to reach. For example, some students might learn only the term quadriceps, but others might learn the terms rectus femoris, vastus lateralis, vastus intermedius, and vastus medialis. Likewise, students in one class may learn to associate the muscles at the back of the leg as the hamstrings, while other students may know these as the biceps femoris, semimembranosus, and semitendinosus muscles. This decision is a curriculum one, but in all cases, at whatever level you choose, students should be able to spell, know, and identify these muscles.

In terms of identification, students should at least be able to identify the muscle groups on themselves and a paper chart. For those teachers who are daring and have a class where there is a good level of camaraderie, surface anatomy lessons can be fun. In these lessons, students use an eyebrow pencil to draw the outline of different muscles on a fellow classmate. In particular, they attempt to follow the specific muscular contour. This is especially helpful in sections where you want students to learn the specific functions of muscles, because muscles will always cross a joint. Having students understand where a muscle inserts on a bone will help them understand muscle function. This understanding of muscle function can also be hierarchical, from bending and straightening the arm in the simplest terms, to the more sophisticated notions of flexion, extension, adduction, abduction, and rotation.

General Training Principles

High school students should know and understand the general training principles applied to strength training. As for aerobic training, the *Frequency Intensity Time Type (FITT)* principle describes the key concepts of overload and progression. In strength training, new terminology is introduced, including "repetitions" and "sets." Table 7.1 provides a good example of how these principles are applied to strength training.

Students should know and understand that training is very specific to the muscle group used. Whereas aerobic training is very general to the whole cardiovascular system because of the circulatory nature of the blood, skeletal muscles are essentially independent. As a result, the training effect is very specific. For example, working the biceps will result in improvement in those muscles only. There will be no carryover to adjacent muscles unless they too are somehow involved in the effort to move the weight.

Students should also understand that training of a muscle is very specific to the workload. Training a muscle one way is going to get different results from training the muscle some other way. Training with sets of three repetitions with

Table 7.1   FITT Principles Applied to Strength Training

	Basic Health-Related Fitness	Intermediate Health-Related Fitness	Athletic Performance
Frequency	2–3 times per week: allow for minimum one-day rest between sessions	3–4 times per week: alternating upper- and lower-body segments will allow for consecutive training days	4–5 times per week: training activities are specific to sport participation
Intensity	Very light, less than 40% of a maximal effort	Light to moderate, 50% to 70% of maximum effort	Specific load adaptation required for sport participation
Time	1–2 sets of 6–12 repetitions	1–3 sets of 6–15 repetitions	3–5 sets of 5–20 repetitions
Type	Body weight, single and multijoint activities involving major muscle groups	Resistance exercises such as leg press, bench press pull-ups, and additional presses and pulls	Advanced sport-specific multijoint lifts (may include Olympic-type lifts)
Overload	Not necessary to bring the student to overload during base-level training	Introduce one of the components of overload: 1–2 times per week	Program design should stress variable intensities and directions to bring student into overload; 2–3 times per week
Progression and specificity	Priority is to have the student develop the correct movement technique; progression is minimal	Introduce program design and incorporate variation	Specific sets, repetitions, and exercises to meet desired outcomes

Source: Adapted, by permission, from *Physical Education for Lifelong Fitness: The Physical Best Teacher's Guide*, by the American Alliance for Health, Physical Education, Recreation and Dance (AAHPERD), 1999, Champaign, IL: Human Kinetics, p. 88.

a high weight will have a vastly different response to sets of 15 repetitions with a low weight. In contrast, cardiovascular training effects from cycling, running, or swimming, regardless of the form of exercise that is selected, still put a stress on the system as a whole.

As students become more sophisticated or your unit becomes more specialized, students can start to learn some specific training principles. In terms of the motion, the lowering and raising actions should be slow and controlled in order to apply the force consistently. However, for those students who are interested in strength training for power sports, some explosive work is also necessary. In learning the skills, however, all students should learn to apply force throughout the entire range of motion.

Avoid creating muscle imbalances

The third training principle is to avoid creating imbalances between paired muscle groups. While the biceps and triceps are not expected to reach similar strength levels, students should learn that both are training, with one being neglected while the other gets all the work.

Finally, all strength-training programs should be accompanied by a good flexibility routine. Students should be encouraged to warm up and stretch at the beginning and end of all training sessions. Further, much of a student's times in a weight room will involve waiting for the partner to complete a set of exercises. Teachers should encourage students to take the opportunity to stretch in these situations, particularly the muscles about to be exercised.

Terminology and Vocabulary

Irrespective of their level of involvement, all students, from freshmen taking their first unit to seniors taking advanced electives in strength and conditioning, need to know some fundamental terms. It is these terms that are the vocabulary of the weight room, and they are universal to all settings. Table 7.2 provides essential terms that are part of the weight-training vocabulary.

Exercises for Specific Muscles or Muscle

Tables 7.3 through 7.10 give an outline of the various exercises that can be used to train the different muscles and muscle groups. Each table has three columns. The first column gives the exercise name, the muscle that is worked, and the various apparatus that can be used to carry out the exercise. Column 2 gives the

Table 7.2   Basic Weight-Training Vocabulary

Term	Definition
Dumbbell	An individual weight that is held in one hand
Barbell	A bar onto which weights are placed and then held in two hands
Exercise machine	A fixed apparatus that allows the lifter to select his or her own level of resistance
Free weight	A dumbbell or barbell that can be moved from place to place within the weight room
Press (or push)	Where the joint is opened during the movement
Curl	Where the joint is closed during the movement
Repetitions	The number of exercises performed in a row
Sets	The number of series that are worked through
Repetition maximum (1RM)	The AAHPERD *Physical Best* (1999) guideline for determining 1RM in a safe manner is as follows: 1. Have the student perform the exercise at a safe weight for no fewer than 6 and no more than 12 repetitions. 2. Multiply the number of repetitions by 0.03, then add 1. 3. Multiply this score by the amount of weight lifted (e.g., 8 reps of 150 pounds → 8 x 0.03 = .24 + 1 → 1.24 × 150 = 186 pounds)

technique cues for performing the lift, while Column 3 outlines the most common errors that occur during lifting. Where an exercise description includes an asterisk, this indicates that the use of a spotter is strongly recommended.

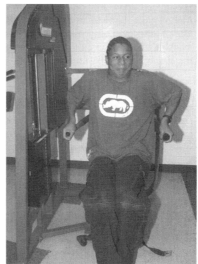

Exercise machines

Table 7.3   Exercises for the Chest

Exercise	Key Techniques	Common Errors
Bench press * Pectoral group ✔ Dumbbells ✔ Barbells ✔ Machines	• Keep back flat on the bench • Keep feet flat on the floor • Grasp the bar at shoulder width • Lower the bar to the chest • Stop at the bottom • Push the bar straight up • Inhale while lowering, exhale while lifting • Varying the width of the grip will emphasize different muscle groups: narrow grip = triceps; wider grip = pectorals	• Lowering the weight too fast and, hence, bouncing off the chest • Locking the elbows • Pushing outward instead of upward
Incline press * Upper pectorals ✔ Dumbbells ✔ Barbells ✔ Machines	• Same beginning position as for the bench press • Raise the bar to a point above the eyes • Maximum weight that can be lifted will be less than for a flat bench press • This lift can be simulated on a machine by placing an incline bench with the shoulder-press machine	• Lowering the bar too far down the chest • Pushing the bar outward, and not toward the top of the head
Flies * Pectoral group ✔ Dumbbells	• Lie on a flat bench with a dumbbell in each hand • Face palms inward, and extend arms above the chest • Keep the elbows slightly bent • Slowly lower the weights to the side, then return to starting position • Can be done on an incline or decline bench • Contraindicated for those with shoulder injury	• Using straight arms • Using too much weight • Lowering the weights too far
Pullovers Triceps ✔ Dumbbells ✔ Barbells ✔ Machines	• Lie on your back on a bench • Grasp the barbell with hands about 6 inches apart • Keep arms slightly bent • Lower the bar behind the head and reach toward the floor • Return to starting position • A single dumbbell can be used instead of a barbell • Can use the low pulley station on an exercise machine using the same technique, except that the starting position is on the floor	
Push-ups Triceps	• Support body with the hands and feet • Keep back straight • Lower the chest to the floor • Maintain the same posture during the entire movement • Varying the hand placement with relation to the shoulders changes the muscle group stressed • A modified push-up is recommended for those who cannot do 8 standard push-ups • The modified push-up begins with the body supported on the hands and knees, with the back straight	• Dropping of the hips • Elevating the hips

*Indicates that the use of a spotter is strongly recommended.

Table 7.4   Exercises for the Shoulders

Exercise	Key Techniques	Common Errors
Overhead press ✔ Dumbbells ✔ Barbells ✔ Machines	• Begin with the weight at the chest • Push the weight to extend the arms • Return to the starting position	• Arching the back • Locking the elbows • Swaying the body under the weight
Raises ✔ Dumbbells	• Begin with a dumbbell in each hand • Arms straight • Lift the weights on both sides until they reach shoulder level • Return to the starting level • Movement can also be to the front	• Raising the weight too high
Upright rowing ✔ Barbells ✔ Machines	• Use a pronated (hands on top of the bar) grip • Hold the hands close together • Start holding the weight at waist level • Pull the weight upward to the chin • Squeeze the shoulder blades together • Return to the starting position	

Table 7.5   Exercises for the Front of the Arm

Exercise	Key Techniques	Common Errors
Standing barbell curls (biceps) ✔ Barbells	• Grip the bar with palms upward • Keep hands shoulder-width apart • Flex the elbows until the bar reaches near the collarbone • Lower the weight slowly to return to the starting position • Bend at the knees • Standing against a wall helps keep the back straight • Can be done using the low pulley station on a machine	• Bending the back • Using the body to swing the weight up • Locking out the elbows on the downward movement
Dumbbell curls (biceps) ✔ Dumbbells	• Begin seated on a flat or incline bench • Use a palms up grip, with arms extended • Bend the arms until the weights reach the shoulder • Return to the starting position	• Bending the back • Using the body to swing the weight up • Locking out the elbows on the downward movement
Reverse curls (brachioradialis) ✔ Dumbbells ✔ Barbells ✔ Curl bar	• Seated or standing position • Use a palms-down grip • Lift the weight by bending the elbows until the bar reaches the collarbone	

continued

Table 7.5   Exercises for the Front of the Arm *(continued)*

Exercise	Key Techniques	Common Errors
Pull-ups ✔ Horizontal bar	• Hang from a bar • Keep hands slightly more than shoulder-width apart • Use a pronated grip • Pull up until the chest reaches the bar • Return to the starting position • Behind-the-neck pull-ups are an advanced option	• Swinging the body
Chin-ups ✔ Horizontal bar	• As for pull-ups, but with a supinated grip • These are easier than pull-ups	• Swinging the body

Table 7.6   Exercises for the Back of the Arm

Exercise	Key Techniques	Common Errors
Triceps extensions on the lat machine ✔ Machine	• Use a narrow palms-down grip on a lat pulldown station • Fully extend the arms, with the elbows held close to the side • Allow the hands to be pulled up to the chest; then push weight down again • Lean in for better isolation of the muscle	• Moving elbows to push the bar down
Bench triceps extensions ✔ Barbells	• Lie on a bench, using a pronated grip and keeping hands 6 inches apart • Push the weight above the chest until the arms are extended • Carefully lower the weight until it touches the forehead • Push the weight back to the starting position	• Using too much weight
Parallel bar dips ✔ Parallel bars	• Begin with the weight supported on the hands between two parallel bars • Lower the body slowly by bending the elbows until the angle reaches 90 degrees • Push up to straighten the arms	• Leaning too far forward during the lowering movement • Locking the elbows

Table 7.7   Exercises for the Forearm

Exercise	Key Techniques	Common Errors
Wrist curls ✔ Dumbbells ✔ Barbells	• Remain in a seated position • Keep forearms resting on the thighs and hands extended over the knees • Lower and raise the weight as a far as possible	
Wrist rollers	• Hold a piece of wood with a roped weight in front of the body • Using a pronated grip, wind the rope around the wood • Unwrap the weight by reversing the direction	

Table 7.8   Exercises for the Upper Back

Exercise	Key Techniques	Common Errors
Shoulder shrugs ✔ Barbells ✔ Machines	• Hold the bar in a palms-down grip • Keep hands shoulder-width apart • Keep arms extended • Lift (shrug) the shoulders, and lift the bar • Return to starting position • For use with a machine, remove the bench from the bench press station, and grasp the handles	• Bending the elbows • Using the arms to lift the weight • Extending the neck at the end of the motion
Bent-over rowing ✔ Dumbbells ✔ Barbells ✔ Machines	• Bend at the waist, with knees bent and the arms holding the weight (trunk at 45-degree angle) • Keep elbows wide • Lift the weight to chest level • Squeeze at the back of the motion • Return to starting position • The shoulder blades should move together as the prime mover • Can be completed using the low pulley station on a machine	• Using the elbows to begin the movement
Pull-ups ✔ Horizontal bar	• Hang from a bar, elbows fully extended • Keep hands slightly more than shoulder-width apart • Use a pronated grip • Pull up until the chin passes the bar • Return to the starting position • Behind the neck pull-ups are an advanced option	• Swinging the legs • Not extending the arms
Chin-ups ✔ Horizontal bar	• As for pull-ups, but with a supinated grip • These are easier than pull-ups	• Swinging the legs • Not extending the arms
Lat pulls ✔ Machine	• Arms hold the handles of the bar outside the shoulder • Pull the bar till it reaches the shoulder blades • Squeeze the shoulder blades together • Return to the starting position • Can be pulled in front to the level of the chest • Wide grip works the lats more; narrow grip works the biceps more	• Leaning forward or back too far during the pulldown

Table 7.9   Multi-Joint Exercises for the Lower Body

Exercise	Key Techniques	Common Errors
Squats ✔ Barbells	• Stand with feet shoulder-width apart • Point toes inward slightly • Squat down until the thighs are almost parallel to the floor • Straighten up toward the starting position • Good squat racks are essential	• Back bending over • Bouncing at the bottom of the squat • Squatting past parallel with the floor
Leg presses ✔ Machines	• Adjust the machine's seat so that the knees are at a 60-degree angle • Push with the legs until the knees are nearly extended • Return slowly to the starting position	
Lunges ✔ Barbells ✔ Dumbbells	• Stand with feet shoulder-width apart • Rest the bar on the back of the shoulders • Step forward with one leg, and bend until the thigh is nearly parallel to the floor • Push back to straighten • Repeat with the other leg • Stationary lunges create less anterior and posterior stress	• Letting the back and the head tilt over in the direction of the lunge • Letting the knee touch the ground • Looking downward • Bending the back

Table 7.10   Auxiliary Exercises for the Lower Body

Exercise	Key Techniques	Common Errors
Leg extensions ✔ Machines	• Sit on the knee extension machine with shins on the pads • Adjust the seat • Extend the knees until they are nearly straight • Return to starting position	• Throwing the weight outward • Locking the knees
Leg curls ✔ Machines	• Lie on the stomach • Make sure the pads of the machine are just below the calf muscle • Bend the knees toward the buttocks • Return to the starting position	• Arching the hips through the movement • Arching the back • Throwing the weight
Heel raises ✔ Dumbbells ✔ Barbells ✔ Machines	• Stand on the edge of raise platform • Lower the heels as far as possible • Raise heels up until you are on the toes • Weight can be held in the hands (dumbbells) or on the shoulders (barbells) • Can be completed using the leg press machine, but only working the calf muscles • Bending the knees slightly will work the soleus muscle more	

Don't Forget the Abdominals

The abdominal muscles are those that essentially link the upper and lower parts of the body. Hence, any motion that brings the upper and lower body closer together will involve a contribution from the abdominals. This means essentially that this muscle group is involved in most sports and physical activities. Unfortunately, the abdominals are often forgotten during the design of weight training programs, but, ironically, are often a prized component of the workout results. Consider just how many "ab fads" there have been that promote various machines and other apparatus that promise a transformation from flabby abs to the fabulous "six-pack" (steely stomach). Further, one only has to pick up any strength-training magazine to find at least one abdominal training article.

Sadly for the proponents of all these workout programs, six-pack abs are more a result of a certain level of body fat than a result of intensive training of the muscle groups. The washboard that is so desired by many results from having a percentage of body fat approaching 10%. The key to the abdominal six-pack then, is *not* doing thousands and thousands of sit-ups, but a quality aerobic and fat-burning exercise program.

In organizing the abdominal program, however, a teacher needs to understand the muscle group in general. The abdominal cavity consists of the abdominal muscles—the rectus abdominis, stretching between the bottom of the last rib on each side, the bottom of the sternum, and the pubis in the hip girdle; the internal and external obliques on each side of the rectus abdominis; and the transverse abdominis, which runs laterally between the pubis and the lower ribs. Further, although the rectus abdominis is one long muscle, for the purposes of training, it is often trained as though it had an upper and a lower section.

Training the Abdominals

Because of the general anatomy of the abdominals, it is valuable to train all sections of the muscle group. Different exercises will tend to involve a greater contribution from the different muscles, and, hence, variety is needed. As a general rule, the abdominal group follows these essential principles:

1. Exercises that involve keeping the feet on the floor and raising the upper body off the ground will involve the "upper" parts of the rectus abdominus.
2. Exercises where the upper body is fixed and the legs are raised toward the trunk will involve the lower parts of the muscle.
3. Exercises that cross the midline will involve the oblique muscles.

Table 7.1l shows the various exercise options available for strengthening the abdominals.

Table 7.11 Abdominal Exercises

Abdominal Area Emphasized	Exercise	Description
Upper abdominals	Crunches *Note:* Only the spine should bend; the hips should not move. If the hips move, the psoas is being moved in preference. This exercise should be done slowly to avoid using momentum to help.	• Lying on the back, put the knees up in the air so that the thighs are at a right angle to the torso, with the knees bent • Place the hands either behind the head or gently touching the sides of the head • Slowly raise the shoulders off the ground, and try to touch the breastbone to the pelvis, breathing out
	Bent-leg sit-ups	• Sit with feet anchored • Bend knees at a 90-degree angle • Position arms with the fingers touching the elbows • Raise the trunk to a vertical position, and then return to the starting position
Lower abdominals	Reverse crunches *Note:* This exercise is very similar to a hanging knee raise, but a little less intense	• This exercise can be done on the ground or on an incline sit-up board • All that is needed is something behind your head to hold • If an incline board is used, place the feet lower than the head • Lying on your back, hold a weight or a chair leg (if lying on the floor) or the foot bar (if using the sit-up board) • Keep the knees slightly bent
	Vertical lying leg thrusts *Note:* If any strain is felt on the lower back, bend the knees a little more.	• Lie on your back, with the fists under the buttocks to form a cradle • Raise the legs in the air 10–12 inches off the ground, knees slightly bent • Raise the head and shoulders off the ground slightly to help keep the abs stressed The exercise itself has four phases: 1. Raise the legs until the feet are above the pelvis; focus on contracting the abs 2. Thrust the heels to the ceiling, breathe out, and keep contracting the abs raising the pelvis out of the cradle of the fists 3. Lower out of the thrust back to the fists, leaving the feet above the pelvis 4. Lower legs back to the initial position

Table 7.11 Abdominal Exercises *(continued)*

Abdominal Area Emphasized	Exercise	Description
	Hanging knee raises *Note:* This exercise needs a chin-up bar or something to hang from.	• Grab the bar with both hands with a grip a bit wider than the shoulders, cross the ankles, and bring the knees up to your chest • The pelvis should rock slightly forward • Pause at the top of the movement for a second, and then slowly lower the knees by relaxing the abs • Don't lower the legs all the way; repeat the movement using just the abs to raise the knees
	Lying leg raises *Note:* • Students who are big and/or have long legs should probably avoid this exercise. • For people with legs that are too heavy for their lower abs' strength, this exercise pulls the lower back into an exaggerated arch, which is bad (and painful).	• Begin by lying down with the hands (palms down) placed under the buttocks • Make sure the knees are slightly bent • Raise legs about 12 inches off the floor, and hold them there • Now, trying to use just the lower abs, raise the legs by another 6 inches
Obliques	Cross knee crunches	• Like ab crunches, take the lying, bent-knee position, but crunch diagonally, trying to touch each shoulder to the opposite hip alternately • At the top position, one shoulder and one hip should be off the ground
	Side lying crunches	• Begin in a lying position, but on one side • Rotate so that the shoulders and head are in a more horizontal position • Complete the crunch movement raising the trunk vertically

Don't Forget Balance

Developing abdominal strength without similarly developing the spinal erectors (the muscles that straighten the lower back) can result in strange and possibly damaging posture. Hyperextensions in particular are good lower back exercises.

Hyperextensions are best done on a hyperextensions bench but can be done on an ordinary bench with something (or someone) holding down the ankles. To perform a hyperextension, lie face down, with the hands touching the sides of the head and the body draped over the edge of the bench. Make sure the hips are supported so the pelvis can't move. Slowly raise the torso to the horizontal position, but no higher. Keep the head, shoulders, and upper back arched through the whole movement.

Avoid the Aversive

"Doing sit-ups" is a real pain—both figuratively and literally—for many people. The exercises can hurt, we tire quickly, and muscles can stay sore for quite a while if the exercises are done without practice. In developing a sit-ups training program, teachers should begin with small goals. Also, changing the muscle targeted during a workout (i.e., upper abdominals, then lower abdominals, then obliques) can make for a less taxing experience.

An Abdominal Strength Test

For most muscle groups, the ultimate test of strength is the 1RM test, that is, the maximum amount of weight that can be lifted one time only. For the abdominal group, this is a difficult exercise, because there is a challenge. However, there is a fun seven-stage protocol that can be used. The general rules are as follows:

1. The beginning position for all stages is lying on the back, feet bent at 70 degrees with heels flat on the floor.
2. Disqualification occurs at any time the heels are raised from the ground.
3. Only one attempt at each level is given.

The seven stages are as follows:

Stage 1. Start with the hands flat against the thighs—on "go," slide your hands up your thigh until the fingers reach past the knee.

Stage 2. Start with the arms crossed, so that the hands touch the opposite elbow (one will be over, the other under)—on "go," slide your hands up your thigh until the fingers reach past the knee.

Stage 3. Start with the fingers on one hand touching the opposite shoulder— on "go," rise up so that the elbows touch the knees.

Stage 4. Start with the hands behind the head—on "go," rise up so that the elbows touch the knees.

Stage 5. Start with the hands crossed behind the head to touch the opposite shoulder—on "go," rise up so that the elbows touch the knees.

Stage 6. Repeat stage 5, holding a 5-pound weight in the hands.

Stage 7. Repeat stage 6, holding a 10-pound weight in the hands.

Stage 5 testing

Dumbbells versus Barbells—What Students Should Know

Variable resistance machines are effective tools for building strength and muscle tone and are designed to work the target muscle in isolation, without the assistance of the surrounding muscles. Free weights (barbells, dumbbells, and machines that provide the same equal resistance to a muscle) allow you not only to target a particular muscle group but also to engage other muscles that assist in the work. Once they are conditioned, these assisting muscles help you to increase the weight you use in training the target muscles in order to stimulate the most growth in muscle fibers. The assisting muscles help stabilize the body, support limbs, and maintain posture during a lift. Lifting free weights improves coordination by improving the neuromuscular pathways that connect the muscles to the central nervous system.

Safety in Lifting and in the Weight Room

Students need to be formally taught the safety rules and protocols that go with working in a weight room. Weight-training rooms by their nature are very busy, and they also involve the movement of a considerable amount of heavy equipment and, in many cases, the use of machines with bulky, heavy moving parts. Essential safety features should involve student dress. Students need to be dressed for class in such a way that they can move effectively, without being constricted, to allow them to perform all skills properly. Hats should be removed, loose-fitting clothes kept to a minimum, and enclosed shoes (i.e., not open-heeled) worn. These are all important features of tending a safe environment.

Other safety rules should address keeping drink containers out of the weight room to avoid spills; it is important to keep floors nonslippery. Students also need to be advised of rules regarding jewelry, particularly chains that might become tangled in the pulley system of machines.

Weight room protocols are important

Safety also involves dealing with equipment. Teachers should have rules about the replacement of dumbbells and barbells, as well as weight plates. Furthermore, at the end of each lesson students should be required to place all equipment on racks, and remove plates from all barbells. Students also need to be taught that if their particular exercise equipment is not immediately available, they should seek alternative lifting mechanisms (such as using dumbbells instead of a barbell, or a machine instead of a barbell).

While these seem simple and commonsense notions, there are two additional reasons why it is important to keep the weight room well presented. First, it allows for more efficiency; after one class finishes, the next class can arrive and begin work immediately. Second, and perhaps more important, it presents an image of seriousness about the work environment. Weight rooms with trash on the floor, with loose weights strewn all about the room lying on the floor does not present an image of professionalism or caring and in general suggests to students that this isn't a place for quality work.

Spotting

Students should also be taught correct spotting techniques. In the tables in this book, exercises that require spotting are indicated with an asterisk. Spotting techniques need to be formally taught, tested, and reinforced by the teacher during the time in which students participate in the weight room. As students become more skillful, spotting becomes more important. Further, when students leave your program and continue to work out in other settings, they will use these spotting techniques as part of the weight lifting culture. For more information on spotting techniques, see the excellent textbook written by Baechle and Groves (1996).

Important Issues in Teaching Weight Training

In addition to teaching the basic weight-training principles to students in a general physical education course (or an elective unit on weight training), teachers also need to address some other specific teaching issues. Teachers not only should be able to develop lessons that include all the content areas listed above, but also should teach weight room protocols, advise students how they can continue to be active outside school, and teach consumer awareness, so that students can make

Students need to learn spotting skills

informed decisions in choosing a gym and be able to evaluate information that is presented to them in magazines, on television, or on the Internet.

Weight Room Management and Protocols

To help make the weight room a manageable environment and one that fosters maximum efficacy, teachers need to put in place a number of protocols and rules. Teachers need to develop protocols concerning students' entry into the weight room. What are the students required to do on arriving? Where are they to place their school materials and book bags? Should students begin immediately to warm up, or are students formally gathered at the start of each lesson for some instruction? Should students collect their workout cards from the class file, or log into the computer to access their workout database? Should students get weighed and record their weight on entry?

It is important for teachers to develop protocols to ensure maximum efficiency and to present an air of seriousness. Teachers need to set up protocols for using and replacing equipment, as has already been mentioned, Students should also be made aware that for most muscle group exercises, dumbbells and barbells and machines are options. Students should be encouraged to seek out alternative lifting mechanisms in cases where the particular workout item they planned to use is not available.

One particularly enlightening university study suggested that all students engaged in weight-training classes fall somewhere on a continuum from "sweaters" to "slackers." That is, some students in the weight room will work consistently, will not waste time, will not take excessive breaks between exercises, and will move through their particular workout routine efficiently and will gain maximum benefit. At the other end of the continuum are those students who appear to spend more time socializing with their friends or avoiding work than achieving any fitness goal. Furthermore, these slackers are very skillful at becoming undetected by the classroom teacher because they appear to be working. They appear to be weight lifting, spotting, or waiting for a turn just as the teacher nears their area of the room. However, when one follows these students through an entire lesson, it becomes clear that their volume of work is actually quite minimal.

Designing a Personal Program

Some students may want to increase their strength but not their weight, while other students might want to increase their muscle size. It is indeed important that each student understand how best to achieve his or her own goals. The major factor here is the intensity of the work—in this case, the resistance and the speed of the movement. To gain strength without increasing body weight, a student should increase the weight lifted and reduce the number of repetitions. To increase total body mass, the student should increase the number of repetitions and reduce the speed of the movement. One chapter in Brzycki's 1995 book, *A Practical Approach to Strength Training,* is devoted to designing personal programs. The web-based reference http://www.exrx.net/Lists/WorkoutMenu.html also provides a number of workout templates.

Consumer Awareness

One of the biggest challenges to students who develop an interest in weight training is deciphering and evaluating information in the plethora of magazines that appear on the newsstands. Each one of these seems to provide a magical solution to some "problem"—"getting bigger biceps," "toning the calves," or just "getting ripped." One noted author has commented that "the appalling irony of bodybuilding and strength training is that the training methods most popular today are utterly unfit for drug-free and genetically typical people." That is, only the select few can really benefit from the training programs outlined in these magazines, and, moreover, it is unlikely that our students will have anywhere near the muscular base to begin such programs in any case. We only need to look at the photographs of these magazines to see that most youth have not achieved such physical development. Our task within weight-training programs in physical education is to help students set realistic goals and learn the basic training principles so that they can design their own programs that will give them the health benefits required.

A second area of teaching consumer awareness is to help students choose a workout site for out-of-school hours. We need to help students construct a checklist of issues they might address as they make a decision to join a facility. These might include:

- availability of reduced fees for school students
- hours of operation
- availability of individualized help during workouts
- availability of personalized workout designs
- type of equipment available
- the time commitment required by contract (i.e., number of months or years)

Including Students with Disabilities

Strength training can certainly be of benefit to students with disabilities. As it does for nondisabled students, exercising against some resistance can build strength for students with disabilities. Moreover, for these students, weight training can also help in some everyday functional skills, such as walking. For students with progressive diseases, weight training can help them maintain the strength they have and prolong function in other muscles. For those in wheelchairs, increases in muscular strength can be particularly advantageous in situations where they need to overcome their body weight, such as transferring their body from a wheelchair to a car or bed.

There will be significant differences in the way teachers approach weight training for these students. For example, some students may have muscle weakness so great that they cannot exercise a limb against even the force of gravity. For others, there may be challenges in their ability to maintain balance when working out. In all cases, however, we need to make genuine attempts to make weight training accessible for students with disabilities. We can do this in three ways:

1. understanding not only their limitations BUT also their abilities
2. providing resistance techniques that are suitable for these students, such as exercise bands, pulleys, or light hand-held weights or cuffs
3. making weight machines accessible, which is the most appropriate mode of resistance for many students with disabilities

Table 7.12 Weight-Training Considerations for Students with Disabilities

Disability Condition	Key Considerations
Wheelchair bound	• Many students have overdeveloped anterior shoulder muscles; for these students, specific attention should be given to developing the posterior shoulder and shoulder girdle muscles in order to promote muscle balance • Stretch bands are useful where free weights are not accessible
Lower extremity prosthesis	• May have postural defects because of their gait—strengthen the overstretched and weaker muscles • Stretch the shortened muscles • Important to exercise the residual limb
Cerebral palsy, head injury, and incomplete spinal cord injury	• Strengthen the muscles opposite those exhibiting spasticity to help overcome possible imbalances • Use single-joint rather than multiple-joint exercises to allow students to maintain balance and focus on technique • Exercises using light weights that work both sides of the body at the same time (bilateral exercises) may be used • Use machines rather than free weights
Hemiplegia and severe coordination/balance problems	• Because of the need for trunk stability and balance during exercise, use only unilateral exercises (i.e., those that work only one side at the time) • Stabilize the trunk during exercise) • Avoid using free weights—use machines or stretch bands
Muscular dystrophy	• *Seek the student's medical team first—weight training has questionable benefits for these students* • For students who are able to do so, mild intensity training of the unimpaired muscles may serve to preserve strength

Table 7.12 outlines specific considerations for students with various disabilities. The list is not exhaustive, and you certainly should consult with a student's medical team before beginning a training program. In all cases, your objective should be to include students with disabilities in your classes and to help them enjoy the benefits that strength training may bring.

IN-SCHOOL TASKS

The User-Friendly Weight Room

Visit a nearby high school, and ask to complete a tour of their weight room. Take note of the equipment available to students. Ask yourself and reflect on the answers to these questions:

1. What are the predominant pieces of equipment? Are these biased toward one particular way of working out? (For example, is the equipment all

devoted to developing lower body strength, or are bench press benches all that's available?)

2. Are there sufficient pieces of equipment to conduct a reasonable physical education class for *beginning* weight training?

3. Are there enough weights of appropriate poundage for beginning students and/or female students?

4. Are there blackboards or other tools to enable a teacher to conduct mini lectures on relevant topics?

5. Is there a cabinet or other retrieval system where students can access their weight-lifting records?

Weight Training Messages

Visit a nearby high school, and ask to complete a tour of their weight room. In this assignment, you focus not on the weight-training equipment itself, but on how the room is decorated. What posters, signs, charts, etc., are posted on the walls of the weight room? Ask yourself and reflect on the answers to these questions:

1. Are there indeed any materials posted on the walls of the weight room? What do these materials (or their absence) suggest about how classes are conducted?

2. What genders are depicted in any photographic posters (e.g., muscular football players, baseball players, girls doing aerobics)?

3. What is the physicality of people depicted in the posters? Is the focus on health-related fitness or on the development of muscularity?

4. Are there any positive messages about the benefits of working out, maybe in the form of teacher-designed motivational posters or commercially produced materials?

5. Are class rules and protocols the only materials posted? Are these presented in a positive or negative context?

Sweaters or Slackers?

Arrange to observe a weight training class in progress. As the students enter the room, randomly select four students (perhaps of different physique and gender) to observe throughout the lesson. Ask yourself and reflect on the answers to these questions:

1. In what overall category would you place each student you observed— "sweater" or "slacker"? What was the major factor of their involvement that led to your decision?

2. Did the students work harder on some pieces of equipment than others?

3. Did the students have any choice in the selection of the exercises they completed? How might this have affected their engagement?

4. How social was the work environment? That is, were students free to chose their partners or spotters?

5. How accountable did the teacher hold the students for their work for the day? At what level was this accountability: (a) behaving and not disturbing others, even if they were not doing any work; (b) just doing something and not standing around; (c) being engaged in activity at a solid level of intensity throughout the lesson; (d) not only being engaged, but recording their workout data into a folder or computer?

PORTFOLIO SUGGESTIONS AND ARTIFACTS

Weight-Training Videotape (S1–P1, K7)

Design a weight-training video for a specific body area (e.g., arms, or chest and shoulders, or legs). In this videotape, you should demonstrate the correct techniques of the various exercises you include, and you should verbally and visually identity the key technical cues. It would also be useful to show examples of poor form and common lifting errors.

Content Knowledge Written Assessments (S7–K2)

Design a written test that examines students' knowledge of muscle group names and/or appropriate exercises for specific muscles. Make sure you use a variety of questioning techniques in the test (true/false, multiple choice, matching, and short answer), and also make sure your test includes questions from various levels of the cognitive domain; that is, some questions may simply involve recall or comprehension, while others can require analysis or evaluation.

Positive Message Poster (S4–D1, P1)

Design a poster that portrays the benefits of strength training for youth. Include positive images of students of both sexes working out together, with knowledge about the health-related benefits associated with the activity.

STUDENT ASSESSMENT OPPORTUNITIES

In 1992, the National Association for Sport and Physical Education (NASPE) appointed the Standards and Assessment Task Force to develop content standards and assessment material based on the question "What should students know and be able to do in physical education?" Seven content standards were developed based on the definition of a physically educated person. These standards provide the key tools for assessing student performance in physical education.

Presented below (and in Chapters 6, 8, and 9) is a series of assessment examples that correspond to each of the seven standards. Each content standard is listed and described, followed by one or two techniques appropriate for assessing student achievement of the specified content standard. The assessment examples provided are not meant to be a complete listing of available assessment techniques, nor are they necessarily the best ones for all situations. Feel free to use these in your classes or develop new ones more suited to your situation.

NASPE Standard 1: Demonstrates Competency in Many Movement Forms, and Proficiency in a Few Movement Forms

1. Student poster: With the aid of a digital or disposable camera, the students may design a poster showing them perform the correct sequence of movements for three weight-training exercises.

2. Teacher observation checklist: The teacher may randomly select three or four exercises for the student to demonstrate. The teacher provides the name of the exercise, so the student must be able first to identify the matching movements and, second, to perform these correctly.

NASPE Standard 2: Applies Movement Concepts and Principles to the Learning and Development of Motor Skills

1. Exercise problem: The teacher composes an exercise problem (e.g., Sara wants to develop strength in her biceps). The student responds by demonstrating at least two exercises that will achieve that goal, while also explaining the number of repetitions and sets required for the goal.

2. Error detection: The teacher produces a videotape of four weight-training exercises, all containing one or two technique errors. The student prepares an analysis of the errors and describes the appropriate corrections.

NASPE Standard 3: Exhibits a Physically Active Lifestyle

1. Exercise log: The student keeps a current exercise log of his or her participation in the weight-training class (or community-based program). This log is submitted to the teacher each month, with an annotated account of improvement, inhibitors of improvement, and motivational facilitators or obstacles. A sample log is shown in Table 7.13.

Table 7.13 Weekly Weight Training Log

Name _____

Week # _____

Today's date _____

Your body weight _____

	SET 1		SET 2		SET	
Exercise name	**Wt**	**Reps**	**Wt.**	**Reps**	**Wt.**	**Reps**

NASPE Standard 4: Achieves and Maintains a Health-Enhancing Level of Physical Fitness

1. Self-testing data: The student participates in a relevant test of muscular strength and endurance and meets the criteria for his or her age and gender (see Tables 7.14 and 7.15).

2. Personal goals project: The student assesses his or her current fitness level through self-administration of a relevant fitness test. The student then designs a personal program with specific goals over a predetermined period. At the end of the time, the student determines the extent to which those goals have been met.

NASPE Standard 5: Demonstrates Responsible Personal and Social Behavior in Physical Activity Settings

1. Teacher checklist: The teacher observes students as they participate in class activities. Sample positive social behaviors include spotting for a classmate on request and being in compliance with class rules and protocols. A rubric of "always," "mostly," "sometimes," or "rarely" could be used to classify student achievement.

Table 7.14 Health-Related Reference Standards—Curl-Ups

Age	Fitnessgram		President's Challenge	
12	Boys	18	Boys	20
	Girls	18	Girls	20
13	Boys	21	Boys	25
	Girls	18	Girls	25
14	Boys	24	Boys	25
	Girls	18	Girls	25
15	Boys	24	Boys	30
	Girls	18	Girls	30
16	Boys	24	Boys	30
	Girls	18	Girls	30
17	Boys	24	Boys	30
	Girls	18	Girls	30

Source: Reprinted with permission from the *President's Challenge Physical Activity and Fitness Awards Program Manual*, 2001, Bloomington, IN: The Presidents Challenge. *Source:* FITNESSGRAM® data reproduced with permission, The Cooper Institute, Dallas, TX.

Table 7.15 Health-Related Reference Standards—Push-Ups

Age	Fitnessgram		President's Challenge	
12	Boys	10	Boys	9
	Girls	7	Girls	8
13	Boys	12	Boys	10
	Girls	7	Girls	7
14	Boys	14	Boys	12
	Girls	7	Girls	7
15	Boys	16	Boys	14
	Girls	7	Girls	7
16	Boys	18	Boys	16
	Girls	7	Girls	7
17	Boys	18	Boys	18
	Girls	7	Girls	7

Source: Reprinted with permission from the *President's Challenge Physical Activity and Fitness Awards Program Manual*, 2001, Bloomington, IN: The Presidents Challenge. *Source:* FITNESSGRAM® data reproduced with permission, The Cooper Institute, Dallas, TX.

NASPE Standard 6: Demonstrates Understanding and Respect for Differences among People in Physical Activity Settings

1. Teacher checklist: The teacher observes students as they participate in class activities, making note of evidence of inclusive and discriminatory behavior. For example, do students demonstrate behaviors that allow all their classmates to participate freely with equipment, or are some classmates excluded at particular stations?

2. Group project: Students form a small group to design a series of three weight-training activities that could be accessible to students with a specific physical disability.

NASPE Standard 7: Understands That Physical Activity Provides the Opportunity for Enjoyment, Challenge, Self-Expression, and Social Interaction

1. Written report: Students compose a report that requests one of their friends to participate in a weight-training program with them during after-school hours. The report should present the reasons why the friend might find participating in the program enjoyable and rewarding. The report should also foreground reasons why this friend may decline the offer and what strategies the writer may include to address these concerns.

REFLECTION TIME

Now that you have read this chapter, how confident do you feel in

- designing a weight-training program for a group of students who have never lifted before?

- designing a weight-training program for a group of students who have taken your elective class in body shaping and strength development?

- demonstrating the exercises that train the various muscles and muscle groups?

- identifying the safety features to be considered when setting up a weight-training program?

- your ability to explain to a class of 9th-grade girls that they will not become overmuscled as a result of their participation?

REFERENCES

Aaberg, E. (1999). *Resistance training instruction*. Champaign, IL: Human Kinetics.

American Alliance for Health, Physical Education, Recreation and Dance (AAHPERD). (1999). *Physical education for lifelong fitness: The Physical Best teacher's guide.* Champaign, IL: Human Kinetics.

Baechle, T. R., & Groves, B. (1996). *Steps to success: Weight training instruction*. Champaign, IL: Human Kinetics.

Brungardt, K. (1993). *The complete book of abs*. New York: Villard Books.

Brzycki, M. (1993). Strength testing: Predicting a one-rep max from a reps-to-fatigue. *Journal of Physical Education, Recreation and Dance, 64* (1), 88–90.

Brzycki, M. (1995). *A practical approach to strength training*. Grand Rapids, MI: Masters Press.

Faigenbaum, A., & Westcott, W. (2000). *Strength and power for young athletes*. Champaign, IL: Human Kinetics.

Johnson-Cane, D., Cane, J., & Glickman, J. (2000). *Complete idiot's guide to weight training*. Indianapolis, IN: Alpha Books.

Miller, P. D. (1995). *Fitness programming and physical disability*. Champaign, IL: Human Kinetics.

Nieman, D. C. (1999). *Exercise testing and prescription: A health-related approach*. Mountain View, Ca: Mayfield Publishing Company.

Shields. R. K., & Heiss. D. G. (1997). An electromyographic comparison of abdominal muscle synergies during curl and double straight leg lowering exercises with control of the pelvic position. *Spine, 22,* 1873–1879.

WEB RESOURCES

The following web link list was generated upon publication of the text; however, over time, the sites may become obsolete if an organization dissolves, discontinues online services, or relocates to a different URL. If a link listed below does not connect, please search for the organization by name.

http://www.exrx.net

ExRx is an Internet resource for the exercise professional or fitness enthusiast. ExRx offers perhaps the most comprehensive exercise instruction and structural kinesiology reference on the web. Over 300 animated weight-training exercises, 77 stretches, 12 plyometric movements, and 43 illustrated muscles are cross-referenced by joint articulation and muscle group.

http://www.drsquat.com/index.htm

Home page of Frederick C. Hatfield, Ph.D., M.S.S. (known as Doctor Squat). Contains power-lifting, weight-training, and fitness articles and advice.

http://www.strongwomen.com

Contains a number of animated exercises and detailed information about developing bone strength.

http://www.ripped-abs.com

Discusses the keys to developing specific training for the abdominals. The major message is this: "Abs are made in the kitchen, not in the gym!"

http://www.nsca-lift.org/menu.asp

Home page of the National Strength and Conditioning Association.

CHAPTER 8

Designing Quality Sporting Experiences

Scenario

It is a sunny Saturday afternoon in the fall—it's a football Saturday. All of your senses are in overdrive; there are tastes, smells, sights, and sounds all around. You're tailgating with some friends—the BBQ, the roast pork, the pies, and the drinks, all serve to enhance the ambience that is part of the tradition leading up to the contest. A group of students with faces painted in school colors walk past and holler, "War Eagle!" It's close to game time, and you make your pilgrimage to the entrance of the stadium, where the marching band makes its traditional raucous and energetic entrance. Around the crowd, people are listening to radio broadcasts of other games, watching TV, catching up with old friends, or bantering with opposing fans. The atmosphere is electric. It's fun to be part of this tradition, and it's certainly festive.

Most of you reading this book attend a college that has a football or basketball team that many students, local fans, and alumni follow. If I were to ask you to come up with as many words as you could, in two minutes, that relate to your college football or basketball experience, what words would your list contain? The list below gives one sample from a group of students:

- quarterback
- tickets
- mascot
- umpires
- advertising
- radio commentators
- linebackers
- Toomer's Corner
- champions

- coaches
- beer
- fans
- goalposts
- time clock
- hedges
- trainers
- drunkenness
- winning

- tailgating
- cheerleaders
- band
- scoreboard
- press box
- field
- Tiger Walk
- parties
- conference

- home games
- field goals
- police
- ushers
- popcorn
- marching band
- painted faces
- banners

- away games
- statistics
- ticket takers
- vendors
- laser show
- half time show
- painted chest
- bowl game

- touchdowns
- running back
- programs
- hotdogs
- groundskeepers
- orange and blue
- noisemakers
- conference championship

It is possible to place each of the words in this list into one of six categories that identify some of those features we apply to competitive sport. The categories are *seasons, affiliation, formal competition, record keeping, culminating event,* and *festivity.* Table 8.1 shows the allocation of our list of words to the various categories.

When we apply our list of terms to those that might legitimately occur within a sports unit within physical education, however, we see a significantly diminished list. Those that we could justifiably identify appear in bold, whereas those that *may* occur are italicized. Within physical education, there is an almost exclusive focus on the role of player within formal competition, but also note how informal this is as well (Table 8.2).

Typical physical education sports units nearly always involve game play and in some cases focus on the development of skills. In very few cases is there formal instruction of strategy and tactics, and in even fewer cases will the result of the games be of any consequence. Indeed, note the complete absence of any festivity or affiliation with fans and alumni. In many physical education lessons, teams are formed ad hoc, and different teams are formed each day. Where games are played under this context, the only outcome is the bragging rights of the winners of that game—a very short-lasting event. In some cases, there will be a short

Table 8.1   Categories of Sport-Related Terms

Seasons	champions, winning, conference, home games, away games
Affiliation	cheerleaders, mascot, fans, band, advertising, Tiger Walk, marching band, orange and blue, painted faces and chests, noisemakers
Formal competition	quarterback, coaches, tickets, umpires, goalposts, scoreboard, time clock, press box, radio commentators, linebackers, trainers, running backs, police, ticket takers, programs, ushers, groundskeepers
Record keeping	touchdowns, field goals, statistics, retired numbers, banners
Culminating event	laser show, bowl game, conference championship
Festivity	tailgating, beer, Toomer's Corner, drunkenness, parties, vendors, hotdogs, popcorn

Table 8.2   Sport-Related Terms Evident in Typical Physical Education Units

Seasons	*champions*, **winning**
Affiliation	
Formal competition	**quarterback**, *umpires*, *scoreboard*, **goalposts**, *time clock*, **linebackers**, **running backs**
Record keeping	*touchdowns*, *field goals*
Culminating event	
Festivity	

Terms that commonly occur in physical education units appear in boldface; those that may occur in some units appear in italics. You will note that the categories of affiliation, culminating event, and festivity seem to have no place in the common physical education experience.

tournament at the end of the unit, but even then, the consequences of such participation are minimal. Furthermore, the organization of these games still rarely resembles any of the attributes of the culminating event of interscholastic, collegiate, or professional levels.

Many fans have strong affiliation with their teams

Participation in sport can indeed help young people appreciate health, exercise, and fitness. Participation in sport can help our youth learn about themselves and about handling adversity. It can help them experience teamwork and sportsmanship. However, sports can also be a breeding ground for aggression and hostility. It can lead to significant marginalization of students. Sport within physical education can turn off many adolescents from sport as an avenue for healthy engagement in physical activity. Even for many highly skilled students, sport in physical education can be boring and frustrating. Our task is to present a sport format for youth that will be inclusive, engaging, and fun.

Sport Education—An Alternative Curriculum Model

As a response to many of the problems and difficulties in the presentation of sport within physical education, Siedentop (1994) has developed a curriculum model called *sport education*. The sport education curriculum model has as its theoretical base the notion that sport in physical education has been typically decontextualized. As Siedentop (1994, p.7) comments, this happens in several ways.

Skills are taught in isolation rather than as part of the natural context of executing strategy in game-like situations. The rituals, values, and traditions of a sport that give it meaning are seldom even mentioned, let alone taught in ways that students can experience them. The affiliation with a team or group that provides the context for personal growth and responsibility in sport is notably absent. [In summary] physical education teaches only isolated sport skills and less-than-meaningful games. Students are not educated in sport.

The sport education curriculum model was therefore designed to promote a positive sport experience for *all* students through simulating the key contextual features of authentic sport (Siedentop, 1994):

- Sport is done by seasons.
- Players are members of teams and stay on that same team for the entire season.
- Seasons are bounded by formal competition, which is interspersed with directed practice sessions.
- There is a culminating event to each season.
- There is extensive record keeping.
- There is a festive atmosphere in which the season (and particularly the culminating event) takes place.

Sport education has as its main goal "to educate students to be players in the fullest sense, and to help them develop as competent, literate and enthusiastic sportspeople" (Siedentop, 1994, p. 4). In this context, the following definitions apply:

- *a competent sportsperson:* one who has developed the skills and strategies to such a level where he or she can participate successfully in a game

- *a literate sportsperson:* one who understands and values the rules, traditions, and values of a sport and who can also distinguish between good and bad sport practices

- *an enthusiastic sportsperson:* one who plays and behaves in ways that preserve, protect, and enhance the sport culture

Below these global objectives are other performance objectives. These include sharing in the planning and administration of sport within physical education, providing responsible leadership, being able to work effectively in groups, developing and applying knowledge about officiating sport, and becoming a critical sport consumer. With respect to this last objective, we specifically want high school students to be able to identify discriminatory and exclusionary sports practices (such as greater playing time to the more skillful) and to have a voice in addressing these practices.

In sport education, units are now presented as seasons, as we try to replicate some of the key features of formal sport. Rather than teaching a few lessons of skills drills followed by a nonsequential series of meaningless games, in sport education, we replicate the training camp, the preseason scrimmages, and the competition phases of a full season. Skills and tactics are learned early, and significant time is allocated to the development of a team identity. This is followed by practice in scrimmages and, finally, participation in games that count.

Sport education is *not,* however, direct replication of collegiate or professional sport into the physical education setting. There are indeed some specific and critical differences. These include participation requirements, developmentally appropriate involvement, the taking of diverse roles, and different social expectations. Table 8.3 gives specific details of these differences.

Sport education is designed to make sport more accessible to students, and to structure a sport experience that is designed primarily for the benefit of the participants. This is not always the case in professional sport.

Sport education, therefore, entails a number of modifications. We think in terms of a *season,* rather than a unit, because like professional sports, sport education requires an extended length of time. The National Football League does not conduct itself as a 3-week unit, and even in its strike-shortened season, the National Basketball League still presented a schedule of 50 games.

Table 8.3 Specific Sport Education Requirements Differing from Competitive Sports

Participation requirements	• Full participation by all players all the time (there is no "bench" in sport education). • Large teams are inappropriate. All players need to have a substantive playing role within their team—there will be no opportunity for hiding in the outfield. • The culminating event involves all students in some form.
Developmentally appropriate involvement	• There are no full-sided games (no 6 vs. 6 volleyball, or 11 vs. 11 soccer, or 9 vs. 9 softball games). • Games themselves have modified rules to enhance activity levels (no waiting forever to get a hit). • Modify the rules to prevent domination of the action by the highest-skilled players. • Equipment is also modified to promote skill development.
Diverse roles	• Students take roles other than player (referees, some statisticians, trainers, team managers, sport board members). • Students rotate through various roles in order to become more sport literate.
Different social expectations	• Fair play and responsible personal and social behavior is foregrounded. • Competition embraces more than winning.

Sport education seasons, by their very nature, require a commitment of at least 20 lessons in order to be effective. A lot is involved in a season of sport education—there are so many more tasks we need to address, and all of these take time. We need time to help train students in the roles they will be taking. We need time to help student coaches develop their teams with sufficient skill and strategy to compete successfully. The season needs to be long enough to include team practice and competition, as well as the culminating event. Further, if we are to replicate the fundamental features of fully contextualized sport, we need to have time between games for teams to regroup, revise their plans, and practice. In contrast, physical education sports plans that have unit-ending tournaments do not allow teams to experience the highs and lows of competition as it exists throughout a lengthier season.

A Sample Sport Education Plan

Table 8.4 shows an excellent outline of a season plan for a sport education unit on soccer. It includes details of teacher and student roles, assessments, and homework, and it provides a lesson-by-lesson description of tasks to be covered. Other sample sport education season plans are provided in Appendix A.

Table 8.4   Sample Progressive Teaching Stages for a 20-Lesson Sport Education Soccer Unit for Students with Limited Experience of Soccer (Class of 30)

Lesson	Content

Stage 1—Getting Started and Early Skill, Strategy, Rule, and Role Work

1
1. Explain concept of sport education and what pupils will be doing in the unit (i.e., season, different roles, participating on a team, preseason, regular season, postseason, playoffs, etc.).
2. Explain evaluation system (process, product, cognitive, game-play).
3. Announce teams (e.g., 5 teams of 6 pupils).
4. Elect *captain* for each team (each captain to sign contract).
5. Elect *coach* for each team (each coach to sign contract).
6. Select team names (or choose countries or cities from another country), logos (cats, lions, etc.), and color.
7. Elect *board* of 5 pupils from entire class (one pupil from each team) to deal with various administrative tasks during the season. (If necessary, this board can also deal with any disciplinary problems during tournament play, such as fair play).
8. Each team to elect an *equity officer* whose job is to report inequities to the captain, coach, and teacher—for example, pupils not getting an equal chance to take on different roles and play in matches.
9. Assign homework (yes, PE homework!). Pupils complete player profile sheets (provided by teacher) and locate a shirt in the team's color.

2
1. Take team photographs (develop and post on sport education bulletin board).
2. Post team lists on bulletin board to which pupils have easy access. Also post player profiles of each team, which have been collected by each team captain.
3. Post approximate season schedule on bulletin board.
4. Provide teacher-directed lesson on basic skills (e.g., dribbling, tackling, beating a player, passing, receiving), strategies (e.g., pass and move, space-finding and denial, marking, getting "goal-side") and rules of soccer (e.g., direct and indirect free-kick offenses, goal kick, corner kick, and penalty kick). Teach through skill practices and small-sided games (no more than 3 vs. 3).
5. If countries or cities chosen for team names, PE homework is to find out more about the country or city each team represents (e.g., location, population, language, history, food, terrain). Suggest pupils use Internet or even get in touch with a tourist board. Provide pupils with worksheet and specific instructions.

3
1. Have team captains lead their team in warm-up activity supplied by the teacher (first 5 minutes of lesson only).
2. Provide teacher-directed lesson on basic skills (as in lesson 2).
3. Assign homework. Coach and captain of each team come up with an A and a B team (i.e., two teams of 3) for the next day. The captain has to be in the A team and the coach in the B team.

Stage 2—Pre-Season 3 vs. 3 Tournament

4 and 5
1. During both lessons, conduct two 3 vs. 3 round-robin tournaments (one for A teams and one for B teams). Each team in each tournament plays each other team in a 7-minute game. Pitch (approximately 20 × 10 meters) is marked by cones. Goals are the cones at end of each pitch. Score by hitting cone. No goalkeeper. Rules: Normal, except no offside. Defending players must be 2 meters away from site of free kick, corner kick, or goal kick. Penalty kick is a free shot at the cone taken from 10 meters (i.e., no oppositional interference). Pass ball in with foot instead of throw-in.

Table 8.4   Sample Progressive Teaching Stages *(continued)*

Lesson	Content
	2. Establish tournament scoring: 3 points for a win, 1 for a draw, and nothing for a loss.
	3. Post league standings for both tournaments following both lessons on bulletin board (include data on number of games played, number of wins, losses, draws, goals scored, goals conceded, total points, and goal scorers).
	4. Throughout tournaments, organize, provide skill and strategy feedback, motivate, and record results.
	5. Teacher and sport board select tournament MVPs for A and B tournaments (one for performance and one for fair play).
	6. Assign homework after lesson 5: Learn list of basic rules (e.g., corner kick, goal kick, penalty kick, free kick, throw-in) and get ready for rules test next day. Explain that pupils will need to pass rules test to be eligible to play in the regular season league play but that they will have several opportunities to pass the test (teacher to provide handout on rules).

Stage 3—Rules Tests, More Skill and Strategy Work

Lesson	Content
6	1. Give simple and quick (use multiple-choice format) 10-question rules test in first 5 minutes of class. Collect test, and grade after class. Must score 10 out of 10 to pass.
	2. Have captains lead 5-minute warm-up of teams (material provided by teacher). Teacher to assist.
	3. Provide teacher-directed lesson on skills lasting 25 minutes (e.g., heading, goalkeeping, shooting, advanced passing and receiving).
	4. End with team (3 vs. 3) scrimmage with the focus on strategy (e.g., pass-and-move offense, designated players as "attackers" and "defenders," defending and attacking at corner kicks, free kick strategy). Urge captain and coach to work with their teams on these strategies.
	5. If countries are chosen as team names, have teams learn the national anthem of their team country and translate the words. Post translation on the bulletin board.
7	1. Retest for "rules failures" in first 5 minutes of class (teacher led) while having each team's coach lead the team in 5-minute warm-up and fitness activity. Provide handout or worksheet.
	2. Provide teacher-directed lesson on skills and strategy using skill practices and small-sided games, as in lesson 6.
8	1. Hold final retest for rules failures while captains lead teams in warm-up and each team coach leads team in stretching (teacher to provide material).
	2. Have captains lead their teams through a series of skill drills on skills practiced in lessons 6 and 7. Teacher assists or backs up captains.
	3. Have each team coach organize team (3 vs. 3) scrimmage and focus on giving feedback on certain aspects of play (e.g., defense and attack in corner-kick situations). Provide each coach with material and assistance.

Stage 4—More Roles and Responsibility

Lesson	Content
9 and 10	1. Teach *scorekeeping* (hand out a scoresheet). This is a whole-class activity that is teacher led (5 minutes maximum).
	2. Teach *stat-keeping* (hand out a stat sheet). This is a whole-class activity that is teacher led (10 minutes maximum).
	3. Teach (i.e., lecture on) *refereeing* skills. Provide handout on key rules plus key points to look for in a good official (e.g., is fair, understands rules, helps play flow, is assertive but not aggressive, makes quick decisions, is confident)—5 minutes maximum.

Table 8.4   Sample Progressive Teaching Stages *(continued)*

Lesson	Content

4. Practice refereeing skills, stat-keeping, and scorekeeping by having 4 of the teams scrimmage (i.e., 6 vs. 6) on 30- × 20-meter pitches marked by cones (goal marked by two cones 5 meters apart). Fifth team referees (two pupils), keeps stats (two pupils), and keeps score (two pupils). Rotate pupils of one team in officiating roles so that all get a chance to learn all three roles. Also rotate the "officiating team" so that all teams get a chance to learn new roles.
5. Invite sport board and others (e.g., cooperating teacher) to conduct regular-season poll to rank teams. Post results of poll on bulletin board.
6. Have each team elect two *newspaper reporters* who have to interview the coach and the captain (more homework!) about the upcoming regular season and provide a written report for the bulletin board. Provide an interview guide.

Stage 5—Regular-Season League Play

11–13
1. Play regular-season round-robin tournament (5 vs. 5). Games to last 10 minutes. 2-minute half-time for captain- and coach-led team-talk. Pitch is marked by cones (approximately 30 × 20 meters). Goals are marked by two cones at ends of each pitch, 5 meters apart. Goalkeepers can handle balls only within 5 meters of their goal. Rules: Normal, except no offside. Defending players must be 5 meters away from site of free kick, corner kick, or goal kick. Regular throw-ins. Penalty kicks taken from 8 meters out. Coach or captain to substitute players when ball is "dead" (i.e., throw-in, goal kick, corner kick).
2. Establish tournament scoring: 3 points for a win, 1 for a draw, and nothing for a loss. One additional point is also available for sportsmanship at the discretion of the officials.
3. Teacher to post on bulletin board league standings for tournament following each lesson (include data on number of games played, number of wins, losses, draws, goals scored, goals conceded, total points, goal scorers).
4. Throughout tournaments, organize; provide feedback on skills, strategy, and roles; motivate; and record results.
5. Teacher and sport board select tournament MVPs (one for performance and one for fair play).
6. Have the team that is not playing referee, keep stats, and keep score. Supply stat and score sheets, whistles, and striped shirts for officials.

Stage 6—Formal Evaluation

14
1. Provide challenging cognitive test covering the rules, skills, and strategy of soccer.
2. Time permitting, have each team scrimmage or practice skills under team captain and team coach (teacher to assist).

15
1. Provide challenging product (skills) test.
2. Test one team at a time. Have teams that are not being tested practice for skills test, led by their team coach and captain (teacher to supply material).

Stage 7—Postseason Tournament Leading to "World Cup"

16–19
1. Run knock-out tournament, and base seedings on placings in regular-season league play. Have the team that is not engaged in play be the officiating team. Post as much information as possible on the bulletin board (e.g., brackets, list of goal-scorers).
2. Rules as for regular season tournament.
3. Class board to meet and decide on MVPs (for fair play and performance), MIP (most improved player), best referee, etc. Board to also name All-Class team (5 players).

Table 8.4   Sample Progressive Teaching Stages *(continued)*

Lesson	Content
	4. Following each lesson, have an elected *press officer* for each team write a brief account of the games in which his or her team played. Reports to be submitted to the *editor* and *assistant editor* (elected from class) who have the job of putting together a weekly sports newspaper. Teacher to guide press officers and editors.
20	1. Conduct awards ceremony. Pupils dress smartly. Select one or several pupils to "host" the ceremony, in the style of televised award shows. Provide light refreshments at each team's table. 2. Announce MVPs, MIP, etc. Present winners with certificates or other prizes. Announce All-Class team.
Other	*Ideas for inclement weather days, for injured or ill pupils, additional roles, and homework* • Hold a fitness circuit session indoors geared toward soccer. • Hold a quiz on the rules, skills, and strategy of soccer. Conduct in the style of TV game shows. Post the results of the contest on the bulletin board. (Have a points system in which teams compete against each other). • Prepare a sports report for school newspaper. For example, one pupil interviews others in his or her team (teacher may supply the questions) about how the season has gone so far. One pupil "draws" or takes an action photograph; another pupil produces a headline. Three pupils work as a team and write up the interview in a short report. Post reports on bulletin board. • Graph team statistics for presentation on bulletin board (i.e., supply team with raw data from stat sheets and have them graph it in a bar graph or pie chart). • Produce a team emblem (teacher to provide paper and materials). Post on bulletin board. • Produce a team song or chant. • Sport nutrition lesson. Lecture on basic principles, and then set group task (e.g., identifying good and bad elements of specific foods in terms of sports nutrition or evaluating team members' diets of last few days). Teacher to supply specific task and materials. • Practice taking statistics from video (preferably a video taken by teacher of a class game). Alternatively, watch video and take stats from a televised soccer match. • Have the captain and coach lead a team meeting (part of a lesson only). Teacher to provide outline of elements to be discussed. • Lecture on and practice basic first-aid procedures (e.g., teach pupils how to tape an ankle.) This could lead to naming a trainer for each team.

Source: Created by Dr. Matthew Curtner-Smith, University of Alabama.

Research on Sport Education—Key Findings

Research has revealed that students describe their experiences in sport education as preferable to other sport formats within physical education (Carlson & Hastie, 1997; Ennis et al., 1999; Grant, 1992). Students seem to particularly enjoy sport education seasons because of the opportunities for socializing and having fun. Many students comment how much they enjoy being with their friends (camaraderie is developed through consistent team membership) and being free to make decisions independent of the teacher.

Unlike other "fun" activities in physical education, however, sport education can accommodate the students' social agendas in such a way that encourages high levels of student investment. Often, students who are just having fun are engaging in activities that tend to divert attention away from the instructional tasks or are inventing and testing strategies to reduce involvement in tasks. In

Camaraderie develops through consistent team membership

sport education, by contrast, students have fun by playing good games and performing well as a team. This means that the students' social agendas are often consistent with the teacher's agenda for the season.

What students learn during sport education depends on their skill level, their age, and their experience with an activity. For lower-skilled students at all age groups, learning occurs in the more familiar aspects of game play, such as in developing game skills and applying the skills in game situations. These students also report increased understanding of team strategies and tactics, as well as increased knowledge of the rules. For the higher-skilled students, learning centers more on developing leadership skills, developing and promoting cooperation and teamwork, and teaching other students.

As mentioned in the introduction to this chapter, participation in sport in physical education has a history of intimidation and marginalization. Two groups of students particularly at risk are girls and lower-skilled students. Of particular interest has been the repeated evidence that these groups favor sport education as an attractive option within physical education. As Carlson (1995) has revealed, low-skilled students' response to sport education is best summarized as, "Now I think I can." These students report not only that they have improved in skill levels, but also that they now believe they can make a positive contribution to their teams. These feelings were accompanied by a sense of belonging and trust from their teammates. In other studies, girls reported that they get equal practice and playing opportunities and particularly enjoy playing on teams consisting of both boys and girls.

There seem to be three factors that help explain these positive responses. First, team size is small, so all students are important to their team's success. The more skillful players soon realize that incorporating all team members offers a better opportunity for success than neglecting them. Second, because teams remain a continuous unit throughout the entire season, they have the opportunity to build a feeling of cohesiveness. Nearly all students in all sport education studies state their preference for remaining on the same team throughout an entire season. Third, the season is of sufficient length so that teams are able to take the time to help lower-skilled players improve. Interview data with lower-skilled players from a number of sport education teams have confirmed that these players do not feel marginalized.

Students are not the only ones who benefit from sport education. From a teacher's perspective, the model offers opportunities for increased freedom from direct instruction. Where teachers are no longer the "ringmasters," they are able to attend to specific student needs, assess student work, or emphasize other curricular objectives (such as promoting positive social behaviors by correcting poor competitive attitudes during game play). The teacher is able to provide skill clinics for particular teams or players, work with the referees, or assist captains in designing their practice plans. Of particular interest is that in one study, 8th and 9th grade students reported strong preferences for student coaches over teacher instruction (Carlson & Hastie, 1997).

Sport education allows teachers to provide individual feedback

Designing a Sport Education Season

Despite the significant role of students in the conduct of sport education, the teacher is still the *architect of the model;* that is, you as the teacher are responsible for its efficiency and vitality. Good planning is essential; in particular, you need to have the entire season outline ready before the commencement of the first lesson. Sport education does not allow for "making it up as you go along." You need to prepare not only the season plan, but also administrative forms (e.g., score sheets, statistics sheets, role definitions, and captains' contracts).

As a teacher in sport education, you are still an instructor. You need to be able to teach skills *and* strategy. You need to be a good class manager, because one of the most important tasks in the beginning of the season is to develop routines and procedures. You also need to be able to explain, model, and provide practice for good sporting behavior.

Planning a Season: Some Basics for Getting Started

Because teams in sport education remain constant throughout the entire season, it is valuable to get students into their teams as early as possible. Affiliation is the key to many of the personal growth features so evident in many sport education seasons that have been reported in the literature. Once in teams, students face a number of tasks. They need to devise a team name, adopt team colors, and elect a team leader. It is often useful to have teams and their elected captains sign some form of contract prior to the beginning of the season that formalizes such an arrangement. One example of such a contract is shown in Table 8.5.

The second feature to consider in planning a season is to determine the modifications to the parent game. Recall that in sport education, students participate in small-sided teams, which require a greater contribution from each player. A

Table 8.5 Captain's Contract

I, _____, as the captain of the team _____, promise to my teammates, that I will

- work hard to help everyone improve their skill
- involve all players in practice sessions
- have my practice sessions planned before class
- be an excellent example of fair play
- perform all duties as required of me by the teacher

Signature _____   Date _____

We, the players on the team named _____, promise that we will show support for our captain by

- not arguing at his or her decisions
- working hard to improve our skills
- listening to our captain during practices and games
- performing our roles as best we can when we are game officials

Signature _____   Date _____

Signature _____   Date _____

Signature _____   Date _____

Signature _____   Date _____

Signature _____   Date _____

number of factors will enter into determining the extent of the modification. These factors include class size, facilities, equipment, and the preferred type of competition format.

There are several ways to place students into teams, and this task can be completed by the teacher, either independently of or in conjunction with the sport board. One way is to select teams prior to the commencement of the season based on the selection panel's previous knowledge of the students' skills, attitudes, and attendance history. Alternatively, the teacher or sport board can use data collected from one-minute challenges conducted during the earliest lessons to rank students and then select teams from those ranks. A novel method is to have the students elect team captains, who then, in private, select even teams. However, a key aspect of this format is that the captains themselves are assigned to teams through a lottery; that is, when the captains select the original teams, they themselves do not know which of those teams they will become a member of.

Irrespective of the selection format chosen, a number of important considerations must be taken into account. First, *all* students need to take part in selecting teams, not just the most skilled. Second, the teacher needs to establish clear criteria for team selection. Students should be asked to consider the skill and fitness requirements of the game, to balance the number of boys and girls on each team, and to consider the leadership abilities of the members of each team, as well as the possibility of personality conflicts. Finally, it is important that all panel discussions remain confidential. We are all too familiar with the humiliation and embarrassment afforded students who are chosen last in the public selection process. Likewise, there is no need to disclose the details of the private method.

Training Camp

The training camp section of sport education is similar to any regular unit of physical education where you are teaching a game or a sport. In this phase, the students learn the skills of the game, some tactical components of the game, and strategic problem solving. However, in sport education, there are other features that are crucial and need to be developed, learned, and practiced during this stage in order for the season to run as smoothly and efficiently as possible.

In professional sports teams, the coach sets the rules, standards, and protocols during training camp. Likewise, in this stage of sport education the teacher helps the students understand the need for efficiency. Teams will be given specific time to practice in this stage, independently of the teacher; students will need to learn their roles so that when they begin practice matches they don't waste time. For example, students need to learn the protocols of entry into the gym. In sport education, this means that students will most likely assemble in their team area and begin to warm up or practice skills. In sport education we do not see students enter the gym and then sit in the bleachers. We also rarely see formal roll taking; in cases where teachers are required to take roll, this can be done efficiently in team groups.

As mentioned, the training camp section of the season is where students spend significant time learning the skills of the game. In early lessons, it is the teacher who teaches skills and drills. The role of the captain is to assist the teacher in providing feedback to the players in the team or, in some cases, organizing the group for the tasks set by the teacher.

Sport education skill learning does not involve giving equipment to the captains and saying, "OK, captains, go practice." Captains are there as assistants; they may lead a warm-up, record scores for skill challenges developed by the teacher, or follow a series of task cards for leading their group in instruction. A common option for teachers during this phase of learning is to instruct the whole class in one particular skill (e.g., in softball, fielding and responding to a bunt play) and then to give the captains three task cards with drills from which the teams may choose to practice.

The teacher may need to teach a formal warm-up and in early lessons to lead instruction for the whole class. Later lessons may consist of the teams repeating or perhaps modifying these procedures. For example, the teacher may each day ask one particular team to lead the class in the warm-up.

Another form of skill practice during the training camp consists of presenting the class with a series of stations. The teacher may set out eight stations that each have one-minute skill challenges, and each student in a team completes the challenge while the captain records the score. Teams then rotate through the stations until all eight are

Captains may lead team warm-ups

completed. This format can also be modified to give students more responsibility and empowerment. For example, each group may design a one-minute skill challenge for that particular sport and present that challenge to the class. A second group then will present its challenge, followed by the rest of the groups.

During the later phases of the training camp, the teacher may introduce particular tactics. Tactics may be practiced by an *intrasquad* 3 versus 3 scrimmage. Further, the teacher may ask each team to design its own game, based on the particular tactical problem that is common for the particular sport. In one particular sport education season, student captains were required to devise a drill as part of their homework. One captain designed a task that the class enjoyed so much that it was henceforth named "the Ricky drill," and it became part of the sport culture of that particular class.

In the main, students do enjoy having student captains and, in many cases, prefer to have the captain teach them rather than the certified teacher. Peer coaches are still seen as friends rather than authorities. As one student commented, "When you've got a guy as a coach, you can joke around. You're still friends. If the teacher is the coach, it's like talking to your parents."

Nonetheless, being a coach is not always easy. When asked what was the hardest part of his job, one student coach responded, "Keeping everyone on my team happy." Furthermore, some captains and coaches have reservations about their authority:

> At first I thought it would be tough because people wouldn't actually listen to you — they'd be playing with the puck, but after a while they started to listen to you and we got together and started to do good. (from Hastie, 2000, p. 365)

The second key instructional task of the training camp is to teach the students their roles. Students need practice in performing these roles as much as any other component of sport education. The practice itself comes in the preseason, but it is during the training camp that students learn the roles and what they entail.

Students often prefer peer coaches

It is important that these roles be clearly defined. Students need to know what to do during the game and, perhaps of most consequence, what to do before and after the game. Students must also understand that they will be held accountable for their role performance. We cannot expect students to apply themselves to a role unless it counts for team and individual assessment. Table 8.6 includes the various roles that may be included.

All players also need to pass a rules test. In many sport education seasons, passing this test is a prerequisite for playing games. In some cases, the entire team will take the rules test together, pooling their answers. In order to be eligible for scrimmage, the team must score 100% on the test. Teams that fail to score 100% may still practice internally and will retake the test until they score

Table 8.6   Sample Roles and Role Definitions

Coach/captain	Statistician
• Leads warm-up	• Records pertinent performance data
• Directs skill and strategy in practice	• Compiles team data
• Makes decisions about line-ups	• Summarizes across competitions
• Turns in line-ups to teachers or managers	• Turns in to appropriate people
• Provides general leadership	**Publicist**
Referee	• Completes weekly sports sheets
• Manages contests	• Contributes to school newspaper
• Makes rule decisions	• Produces sport education newsletter
• Keeps things moving	**Manager**
Scorekeeper	• Submits relevant forms
• Records game scores	• Helps get teams to right places
• Keeps a running status of the competition	• Makes sure team members know their roles
• Compiles overall scores	**Other roles**
• Hands in scores to appropriate people	• Trainer
	• Sports council member
	• Broadcaster

100%. In giving a team-based rules test, the teacher should have all players sign off on the rules test, stating that they are in agreement with the answers given by that team.

Preseason

In the preseason, a new set of class entry procedures may need to be developed. The first task students need to adhere to on entering the gym is to check the team notice board. On that board will appear the teams that are playing, those that are officiating, and the areas in which games are scheduled. It is during this second phase of the season that time can be either significantly wasted in class management or streamlined to maximize playing time. Indeed, one school has managed to have over 100 students compete in matches within 6 minutes of their arrival at the gym (and that time also involved moving outside to the playing fields).

There are two ways in which students may move from their practice area to the playing area.

OPTION A

- As the students enter the gym, they check the notice board to determine their playing/officiating role and location (this will vary daily).
- Teams move immediately to the designated playing area, where the captain will begin a physical warm-up.
- The equipment manager, rather than going immediately to the playing area, gathers the relevant materials for the team for that day.
- If the team is officiating, the manger will collect all the game-related equipment in a box. The teacher will have included the score sheets and statistics sheets, pencils, whistles, referees' uniforms, and other playing equipment (down markers, softball bases, etc.) required for competition.
- Equipment managers of playing teams will collect whatever balls, sticks, and bats are needed from the equipment area. Some teachers even have the balls numbered so that teams always collect the same equipment. For flag football, the equipment manager will collect the flags and, for floor hockey, the appropriately colored stick.
- After a specified time for team warm-up and practice, teams will move to their designated playing area and begin competition on the signal from the teacher or field manager.

OPTION B

- Teams will enter the gym and go to their designated warm-up/practice area (it remains constant).
- The team's exercise leader will begin the warm-up.
- The captain is responsible for collecting the playing equipment and beginning skill practice.
- The assistant captain will report to the teacher to find out the playing/officiating task for the team for that day.
- The assistant will then report to that captain which team they will be playing, or what match they will be officiating, and on which field. In this case, the assistant will have collected the relevant materials from the teacher.

Whichever format is selected for the beginning class, students need to be formally taught these protocols and held accountable for them. The major agenda is to maximize playing time.

It is during the preseason that teams will play against other teams for the first time. The results of these games (just like the preseason games in the NFL or NBA) do not count on the season's scoring table and are meant to be used by teams to experiment with their playing personnel, practice playing together, dis-

cover team strengths and weaknesses, and determine what areas of skill practice they may need to
revisit before the next game.

The preseason is also the time that teams will
begin to officiate, and it is to this area that the
teacher needs to allocate his or her major attention. The teacher needs to become the "commis-
sioner of officials" with the power to intervene in
games to clarify rules interpretations, to resolve
arguments between players and officials, to help
referees to become more assertive, and to ensure
that the statisticians and scorekeepers understand
their tasks and can collect their data accurately
and report the data as required.

With regard to referees, the teacher needs to
discuss the role of a referee with the class before
play begins and to give the referees support. The
discussions focus on the purpose of the referee.
Most of us acknowledge that the best referees are
the ones who are hardly seen. They go about their

Players begin recording statistics in the
pre-season

job in a commanding way but are seldom mentioned after the contest. The role
of the referee is to ensure a fair contest in which the conditions of play are the
same for both teams. The referee is not in place to find fault with the players or
to favor one of the teams. It is quite legitimate for the teacher to stop a game, to
discuss a referee's decision, and in a nonconfrontational way to help the referee
improve. The notion here is that this, too, is a new skill for the student and that
the student is going to make mistakes—but not deliberately.

Fortunately for both teacher and referees, during this phase the results of
matches are of no consequence. It does not matter who wins or loses during the
preseason, because the games count for nothing. A refereeing error is therefore also
of no consequence. Students learning this new skill can be assured that their errors
won't count, and that from their errors they can learn to be better in the future.

Students can find this a rather challenging time. A quote from a student
named Billy:

> *It was fun being in charge, but it was annoying because you'd say one thing, like
> "tripping," and they'd be all up in your face, screaming at you. You'd say, "trav-
> eling," and they'd be upset, and if you called "three seconds," they'd say you
> can't count.*

In many sport education seasons, the teacher gives the referee (or the officiating team as a whole), the license to award fair play points at the end of each

match. These can be used in a number of ways. First, they can count toward the season's points total. (Sport education seasons do not have to have a simple win/loss league scoring system, like that of professional or collegiate sport. Points awarded daily can count toward season totals.) Second, these points can count toward an award given at the end of the season to the most sporting team. Third, fair play points can be accumulated to act as tie-breakers for postseason rankings or even to determine eligibility for the postseason. Teams that do not reach a certain fair play points target may not be eligible to compete (at least at the highest levels) of postseason play.

One of the other tasks that referees struggle with during the early stages is their ability to follow the ball up and down the court or field. Many referees remain in one place, and the teacher needs to be active in helping these students become efficient in their movement with the ball and being firm in their decisions. On one day during the preseason, the teacher may use a video, showing the relevant positions of referees to the ball. For games such as softball, where officials need to change position according to the base runners, the teacher may also show film indicating where the umpires position themselves. Still further, some teachers will invite a referee from the collegiate ranks to explain to students the most difficult challenges they face in their particular settings.

In helping students learn scoring and keeping statistics, the teacher can stop a game to check that the statisticians have recorded the appropriate response. For example, in flag football, a record will be made of the receiver and thrower of a touchdown. The teacher can develop a protocol where the scorer and thrower inform the statistician of their names; alternatively, this may be the referee's job. The teacher also needs to give statisticians the power to stop the game and clarify a point in cases where they are unsure of a decision. Particularly in the preseason, where game scores do not count, this is helpful.

A few quick words on statistics:

- First, don't make the statistics too complex, and don't have too many. Otherwise, the students will struggle to keep up with the play.
- Use the finite actions of the play as the statistics to be recorded. In invasion games, these may include interceptions, goals or touchdowns, and, in some cases, assists.
- For batting and fielding games, simple statistics may include caught fly balls, put outs for base, or assists (for the person who threw to the base to make the out).
- Batting teams can keep statistics on number of outs, bases reached, or runs batted in.

In determining what statistics are kept, teachers should take into account the history of the sport and the statistics in that sport's history that have the most meaning. Remember, teaching sport literacy is part of sport education, and we want students to understand some of the benchmark scores. Of course, in cases where the students have devised new games within their own classes or schools, these may be used to develop histories of school records.

Formal Competition Phase

The formal competition phase of the season is where the games that "count" take place. These are the games that entail a formal gathering of win/loss records, of fair points, and of other data relevant to that particular season. This is where sport education can become its most competitive.

In many cases, teams will simply play as a unit, as in a 5-a-side softball league. The five Devils will always play the five Eagles, while the five Panthers will act as the officials. Depending on the number of teams in the class, the competition format may be a round-robin, where all teams play each other once. In larger classes, where there are more teams, those teams might be allocated to conferences. In the initial rounds of competition, teams will play each of the teams in their conference, and on any remaining playing days may engage in interconference competition. In one setting, an 18-team league of Frisbee played in "north," "south," and "central" divisions. Each team played all other

---

A Word on Competition

Many students view competition from a win-at-all costs philosophy. They see competition as a concept of zero-sum—"I win; therefore, you lose." We need to spend considerable energy in helping students focus on appropriate competition, competition that means more than just winning or losing. Competition is first of all a festive coming together and celebration of play. Students need to understand that without a second team, there is no game. We need to be thankful that teams have decided to engage in competition in their pursuit of competence under a single agreed-upon set of rules. Although there is a state of rivalry, that rivalry is essentially based on each team's commitment to perform as well as it can. The challenge for students (and for many teachers) is to develop the ethic of "play hard, play fair, honor your opponent, and accept that once the game is over, it's over." Indeed, many teachers in sport education require their teams to line up and shake hands after each game.

By the time the formal season is under way, we need to have determined what the competition format is going to be. Whatever choice is made, however, in *all* cases students remain in the same team for the entire season. This is a non-negotiable component of sport education, and no student can be traded to another team.

teams in its division and then played against three teams from each of the other divisions.

A second way of conducting games is to divide a team of six into two mini-teams of three (or a team of eight into two teams of four). This is often the case for 3-a-side basketball, or 4-a-side hockey, where prior to each match the coach or captain will make decisions about the division of labor. The officiating team will provide three or four players to each game. The teacher or sport board may set desired parameters for competition among the mini-teams (e.g., must consist of both boys and girls, teams must change players each day, etc.). Often, the scores of the two matches are combined to determine the winner for the day. Teams may choose to divide into a stronger mini-team and a weaker one, although experience has shown this option to be doomed to failure. Teams are far more likely to achieve success in the long run by creating two evenly matched mini-teams, both with a chance of winning. One further advantage of the split-squad format is that it can cater for student absences. A team of eight with two mini-teams may have a stronger team of three and a second team of four on a day where one student is absent.

A split team is also an option when conducting a dual sport season within the team context. For example, in a badminton, tennis, or pickle ball season, a team of six players may have two doubles teams and two singles players, all of whom compete for their team. At the end of the day's competition, the scores from the four matches are accumulated and a winner is determined. The composition of these singles and doubles teams may also vary according to skill level. It is a common feature of collegiate tennis to have a number 1, number 2, and number 3 singles and doubles teams. This allows for students to compete against those with similar skill level. The teacher or sport board needs to decide whether players remain in their set role (e.g., remain singles players for the entire season) or whether teams are able to adjust and manipulate their line-up according to the opposition they will be facing that day. Likewise, in golf, a team of five may consist of a singles player, who plays match play or stroke format; a best-ball pair, where the players select the better ball of the two they hit and then hit again; and an alternate format, in which each player hits every second ball.

For competition in sports where players normally compete as individuals (e.g., track, weight lifting, swimming, or gymnastics), the competition format is normally arranged around weekly challenges and a final culminating event or carnival. For example, teams will practice during the week, and on Friday they will compete in one or two events. For example, the Track Burners may send three of its athletes to the long jump and a second three to the shot put. Again, the teacher or sport board will determine the criteria for this selection. Using a points scoring system, a team will accumulate points, as is common in the Grand Prix series held in professional track and field.

The culminating event in this case is the carnival, where a number of events will be held and teams will nominate different members to different events. Again, the teacher or sport board will organize the carnival so that all team members of all teams will have some officiating and competitive responsibilities.

With regard to the composition of the official's team, the question is whether students should take the same role during the season or rotate. The answer is situation specific. If some students do not wish to referee, the teacher may deem it appropriate that they at least understand the nature of that role and require them to referee only during the preseason, so that they experience what the role entails.

Culminating Event

It is the very nature of sport to find out who is the best, and the sport education model embraces this idea. The incorporation of a culminating event provides an incentive for hard work. Teams can set goals and purposefully spend their practice time working toward these goals. The culminating event is not simply a stage for determining a champion. It is meant to be a celebration of the work all contestants put in during the season. This festive nature not only enhances meaning for participants, but also adds an important social element. Consider the Olympic Games and its closing ceremony. We could hardly think of a more fitting climax to a major spectacle, and while our sport education seasons will not take on that magnitude, it is appropriate that we celebrate.

Sport by its very nature is festive

How teams qualify for the playoffs is a decision for the teacher or sport board. Notwithstanding, unlike the Super Bowl or the World Series, in sport education we make a purposeful attempt to include all teams in this culminating event. Typically, all teams will make the playoffs, although there may be different levels of playoffs. For example, in a 12-team league, we may have gold, silver, and bronze divisions of playoffs, where the teams ranked 1–4 play each other, as do 5–8 and 9–12. In this way, the final day sees six teams still playing for some formal recognition.

League Scoring Systems

Another fundamental difference between sport education and professional sports is in the nature of determining a winner or at least ranking teams. Most sports competitions involve only win/loss records as the determinant of league rankings (except for Collegiate Division 1 football, which uses a complex and very debatable computer-based rating scheme). Given that there are multiple objectives within sport education, with winning being only one of many, it is legitimate to use a league ranking system that involves more than win/loss records. Indeed, the beauty of sport education is that as a teacher, you can reinforce any particular attributes you (or the sport board) choose. Win/loss will certainly be part of this system, but a team's commitment to fair play may also factor into its rankings, as may a team's performance in its officiating duties.

Table 8.7 provides some of the dimensions of constructing a league scoring system.

Including Students with Disabilities

One of the inherent benefits of sport education is that it offers students with disabilities a legitimate contributory role in their teams. First, physically challenged students can complete many of the important nonplaying roles, such as scorekeeper and statistician, no differently from nondisabled students. Second, these students can take important roles in team leadership, such as exercise leader, team manager, and sport board representative or sports reporter. Finally, while their disabilities may prevent some students from demonstrating specific skills, these students may be completely capable of serving as team captains or coaches. The roles of captain and coach do not always require the most physically competent player. Many sports team leaders throughout history have not been the best players on their teams, but their leadership abilities have been inspiring and have led their teams to great victories.

To accommodate students with disabilities during game play, simple rule adaptations can allow for active participation. These may include reduced defen-

Table 8.7　Possible League Scoring Systems

Win/loss records	• Scores can be allocated for wins, ties, and losses (e.g., 3 points for a win, 2 for a tie, 1 for a loss by less than a certain margin, and 0 for a loss by more than a certain margin). • Straight win/loss ratios.
Fair play	• Teams can be allocated fair play points by the officiating team based on predetermined criteria. • Points can range from 1 point given for the team's reaching a set standard of fair play, to a formal judging of specific criteria. • Specific questions may be asked of the officiating team, with teams being awarded points based on the judgment of their fair play. Sample questions may include the following: 　• Did this team play by the rules and not argue with the referee? 　• Did the players on this team treat their opponents with respect (e.g., no trash talking; shaking hands at the end of the game)? 　• Did the players act appropriately and supportively when a teammate made a mistake?
Officials' performance	• As with the awarding of fair play points, the playing teams can allocate points to the officials based on how well they completed their task. • A single point may be given if the officials reached a satisfactory level, or more specific questions may be asked. For example: 　• Did this team know and enforce the rules of the game? 　• Did this team stay alert and active throughout the competition? 　• Did this team act in a neutral manner and not favor one team over the other?
Other criteria for awarding points	• Effort—did a team give a full effort throughout a game? • Organization—was a team ready and on time for a game? • Equity—did a team attempt to use all its players throughout a game?

sive pressure, elimination of time restrictions, and alternative scoring options. What is more, sport education presents a wonderful opportunity for the nondisabled students to explore ways of including those with disabilities into game play. The sport board itself may take the responsibility for outlining any rule modifications that will promote inclusion. In this way, the students not only are more likely to appreciate the special challenges facing the disabled student, but also are more apt to value and protect those rule changes. Some specific beginning examples are given in Table 8.8.

It is important to recall that sport education aims to develop competent, literate, and enthusiastic sports participants. Through the creative alteration of some rules to allow the player to be included during game play, and by acknowledging and engaging the important roles that all students can make to the success of a season, teachers and students can provide students with disabilities the means to achieve the same outcomes as abled students.

Table 8.8   Possible Game Modifications to Integrate Students with Special Needs

Modify activities to equalize competition.

- Allow a student to kick or hit a stationary ball that might otherwise be pitched.
- In volleyball, allow a student to catch the ball and throw it, and/or allow the ball to bounce.
- Allow a length of time to get to base or the goal that is commensurate with the student's abilities.
- Where indoor and outdoor venues are used concurrently, attempt to schedule the games in the gymnasium or on another smooth surface so that it is easier for the students to get around (e.g., avoid a grassy field).
- Involve the student in decision making concerning rule modifications.

Decrease distances.

- Move bases closer together.
- Allow students to be closer to the target/goal/net.
- In volleyball or badminton, allow students to serve from midcourt.

Provide more chances to score.

- 3 foul shots instead of 2; 4 strikes instead of 3; 10 arrows instead of 6; etc.

Analyze positions according to the abilities of students.

- Allow the student to be goalie or pitcher, or to hold another position that entails less movement.
- A student with a heart problem may be goalie in soccer or a pitcher in softball.
- A student with a one-leg amputation may be a pitcher or play first base.

Provide adapted equipment that makes performance easier, such as

- larger bat
- larger, lighter and/or softer ball
- larger, flat bases, goals, baskets
- larger racquet (face and shaft)

Source: Reprinted and modified with permission from Granite District Schools, Salt Lake City, Utah: http://www.granite.k12.ut.us/Special_Ed/homepage.html.

IN-SCHOOL TASKS

Sports Unit Philosophy

Visit a nearby high school, and find out how many lessons are allocated to each unit of team sports. Continue by interviewing the teacher(s) of this unit on the following issues:

1. What is the rationale behind the decision of unit length? How do the teachers justify this time allocation?

2. What determines the sports that are taught (available equipment, teacher's skills, perceived student interest)? Who makes the key decisions?

3. Reflect on these decisions. What sorts of experiences do you think these decisions will create for students in sports units?

Sports Unit Practice

Observe one lesson of a sports unit in a nearby high school.

1. How are the teams selected?

2. How many players are on each team?

3. What is the composition of the teams (both sexes, single sex)?

4. Are there any modifications to the game rules (equipment, court size)?

5. What is the teacher's role? Is there any interaction between the teacher and the students during game play? Is there any skill instruction?

6. Select one student at random. How many opportunities are there for this student to participate during the game? Give some explanation of your results.

7. Reflect on this lesson in general and the answers to the above questions in particular. What sorts of experiences do you think these decisions will create for students in sport units? What changes would you make to the design of this lesson?

Student Interviews

Interview two groups of high school students as they participate in a sports unit.

1. First, identify a group of students who you perceived as marginally interested in the selected sports unit.

2. Determine the major reasons that these students do not wish to participate. Factors might include

   - the activity
   - their perceived competence
   - peer interactions
   - teaching style

3. Repeat this exercise with a group of students who seem highly engaged in the activities of the lesson. Determine their chief motivators.

4. Reflection: What major themes run through the experiences of motivated and unmotivated students? How many of these are related to internal factors (e.g., self-efficacy, interest, physicality) or external attributions (e.g., peer interactions, teaching style)?

PORTFOLIO SUGGESTIONS AND ARTIFACTS

Rules Checklist (S7–K2)

Develop a rules checklist for one sport to be used in a sport education season. Include the modifications to the parent game. This sheet will be used as a basis for developing a knowledge test taken by the students in the class.

Practical Performance Evaluation (S7–K2, P2)

Design a peer evaluation or self-evaluation of practical performance (in game context). Include both skills and tactical dimensions of the game, and write a scoring rubric that the student or an observer could complete.

Roles Checklist (S6–K3)

Design a "roles checklist" that clearly outlines the responsibilities of all the roles involved in a sport education season. Following the development of this checklist, design and produce the various forms that will be used during the season. These might include a score sheet, a statistics sheet, and/or a referees (or fair play) report.

Sport Board Constitution (S6–D4, P2)

Define the roles and powers of a sport board that you would initiate for overseeing a sport education season. Include how students would be recruited to the sport board, the time outside class they would be required to invest, and the extent to which you as the teacher have an executive role on the board.

Season Plan (S6–K1,3: P1)

Design a 20-lesson season plan, using the following "Magic 10 questions."

1. What sport have you chosen, and what are the modifications you have made to the parent game?
2. What is the content for each of the 20 individual lessons?
3. Have you included formal descriptions of all students' roles and sample tasks those roles involve?
4. What is the process you will use for selecting teams (who picks the teams, and when is this done)?
5. What are the exact details of the makeup of the teams (how many teams are there, how many players per team)?

6. What is your description of the preseason scrimmage format?

7. What is the competition format for the formal season?

8. What scoring system will be used to determine the season champions?

9. What is the culminating event (what awards will be given)?

10. How are students to be assessed? (List the points allocation for all assessment items.)

For more sample season plans, see the appendix on p. 349.

STUDENT ASSESSMENT OPPORTUNITIES

In 1992, the National Association for Sport and Physical Education (NASPE) appointed the Standards and Assessment Task Force to develop content standards and assessment material based on the question "What should students know and be able to do in physical education?" Seven content standards were developed based on the definition of a physically educated person. These standards provide the key tools for assessing student performance in physical education.

Presented below (and in Chapters 6, 7, and 9) is a series of assessment examples that correspond to each of the seven standards. Each content standard is listed and described, followed by one or two techniques appropriate for assessing student achievement of the specified content standard. The assessment examples provided are not meant to be a complete listing of available assessment techniques, nor are they necessarily the best ones for all situations. Feel free to use these in your classes or develop new ones more suited to your situation.

NASPE Standard 1: Demonstrates Competency in Many Movement Forms, and Proficiency in a Few Movement Forms

1. Skills checklists: Teachers can devise simple skills checklists to be implemented by student coaches during scrimmages or team practices.

2. GPAI checklist: Students are trained to use the Game Performance Assessment Instrument developed by Griffin, Mitchell, and Oslin (1997). This instrument involves a checklist system that monitors a player's positioning, execution, decisions, and involvement during a game. It produces a final Game Performance Index. Students can observe a student from the playing team to derive this score.

NASPE Standard 2: Applies Movement Concepts and Principles to the Learning and Development of Motor Skills

1. Team game analysis: Students watch a videotape of one of their scrimmages. Using a checklist prepared by the teacher, the students explain the team's areas of strength and weakness from an execution context. See the following brief example from a hockey season.

	No way	Sometimes	For sure!
Our trapping skills are good.			
We can shoot accurately and with power.			
We have a competent goalie.			
Defensively, teams struggle to get past us.			

2. Rules tests: Students complete short written tests of game rules. It is important to ensure the modified rules are being measured on these tests. (See the chapter discussion concerning the requirements for game eligibility based on these tests.)

3. Individual portfolio (for sports such as weight training, swimming, or track): Students will develop a portfolio of their training/preparation for a particular event (e.g., long jump). Support for the portfolio can come from videos of performance and a technique checklist, from observational records by the teacher or team coach, and a conditioning plan.

NASPE Standard 3: Exhibits a Physically Active Lifestyle

1. Student journal: The student keeps a dairy of his or her training program for a particular sport education season. Included in the journal will be both in-class and out-of-class activities.

NASPE Standard 4: Achieves and Maintains a Health-Enhancing Level of Physical Fitness

1. Sport-specific fitness profile: Students will determine which of the Fitnessgram (or other test protocols) elements will be the most important for success during the season. Students will then test at the beginning and end of the season to determine whether they have met the criteria established for their age and gender.

NASPE Standard 5: Demonstrates Responsible Personal and Social Behavior in Physical Activity Settings

1. Referee checklist: During one selected match, the players from each team will complete a referee checklist on the official for that game. The referee will be responsible for collating the data and completing a reflection task based on the players' perceptions tests (see checklist in Table 8.9).

Table 8.9   Referee Assessment Report

Grade the referee from today's game according to his or her performance.
Circle one of the five options for each category.

Active and dynamic	Always
Keeps up with the play	Mostly
Is consistent in enforcing the rules	Sometimes
Knows the rules	Rarely
Uses the whistle effectively or gives good signals	Never
Passive	Always
Watches the play but does not move much	Mostly
Makes occasional rulings, but more a spectator	Sometimes
Knows most of the rules	Rarely
Is not assertive in using the whistle or gives wishy-washy signals	Never
Distracted	Always
Seems more interested in the other games going on	Mostly
Misses some calls because of inattention	Sometimes
	Rarely
	Never
Out to lunch	Always
Does not watch or follow the play at all	Mostly
Rarely makes a rule decision	Sometimes
Engages in other activities (e.g., talking to friends) that are detrimental to refereeing performance	Rarely
	Never

Source: Adapted, by permission, from P. A. Hastie, 1996, Student role involvement during a unit of sport education, *JTPE, 16* (Champaign, IL: Human Kinetics), 94.

2. Postmatch self-evaluation form: Students will complete a series of personal evaluations over the course of the preseason scrimmages and the formal competition. They will then collate the data from these sheets and examine their progress during the season. The students are responsible for submitting a summary statistics graph and their reflection (see checklist in Table 8.10).

Table 8.10 Personal Post-Competition Reflection Form

Date _____   Season phase _____

Circle the best option for your play in this game.

I argued with the ref.	Never	Sometimes	Mostly	Always
I gave my best effort in the game.	Never	Sometimes	Mostly	Always
I played within the rules.	Never	Sometimes	Mostly	Always
I encouraged my teammates.	Never	Sometimes	Mostly	Always
I was too aggressive during play.	Never	Sometimes	Mostly	Always
I competed in the true ethic of competition.	Never	Sometimes	Mostly	Always

Circle the best word or phrase to describe your level in this game.

Angry	Under control	Just playing	Hustling	Helping

Source: Modified from P. A.Hastie and A. M. Buchanan, 2000, "Teaching Responsibility through Sport Education: Prospects of a Coalition," *Research Quarterly for Exercise and Sport, 71*, 25–35.

NASPE Standard 6: Demonstrates Understanding of and Respect for Differences among People in Physical Activity Settings

1. Participation on the class equity board: The student takes an active part on the equity committee of the sport board. This committee is responsible for monitoring the accessibility of students to various roles and playing opportunities during the season.

2. Inclusion self-check: Students develop a personal self-check list to determine the extent of their engagement with potentially marginalized students within their teams. A daily check can be made on a simple yes/no criterion-based assessment on three basic questions:

   ■ Did I make a positive comment about *(student's name)* effort today?

   ■ Did I make an active effort to include *(student's name)* in our practice/game today?

   ■ Did I avoid expressing overt levels of frustration when *(student's name)* made an error today?

NASPE Standard 7: Understands That Physical Activity Provides the Opportunity for Enjoyment, Challenge, Self-Expression, and Social Interaction

1. Youth/rec league critique: Students visit a youth league or recreation league game of sport in their local area. They are to identify in a report those factors that promote or inhibit the enjoyment of the participants. Particularly, the report should focus on the in-game factors (rules, substitutions, coach conduct) and out-of-game factors (parents, other fans) that could enhance or inhibit the enjoyment of the players.

2. Sport education season journal: Students record in a journal their experiences and thoughts as they participate throughout the season. They should identify those factors that promote their enjoyment and success.

REFLECTION TIME

Now that you have read this chapter, how confident do you feel in

- defending why sports units need to be longer (e.g., more than 20 lessons) than those customarily presented in physical education?

- taking a typical sport and reshaping its rules to present a quality, developmentally appropriate modified game?

- designing a 20-lesson season around the modifications of a particular game?

- listing and defending various ways of selecting teams?

REFERENCES

Carlson, T. B. (1995). "Now I think I can": The reaction of eight low-skilled students to sport education. *ACHPER Healthy Lifestyles Journal, 42* (4), 6–8.

Carlson, T. B., & Hastie, P. A. (1997). The student social system within a unit of sport education. *Journal of Teaching in Physical Education, 16,* 243–257.

Ennis, C. D., Solmon, M. A., Satina, B., Loftus, S. J., Mensch, J., & McCauley, M. T. (1999). Creating a sense of community in urban schools using the "Sport for Peace" Curriculum. *Research Quarterly for Exercise and Sport, 70,* 273–285.

Grant, B. C. (1992). Integrating sport into the physical education curriculum in New Zealand secondary schools. *Quest, 44,* 304–316.

Griffin, L., Mitchell, S., & Oslin. J. (1997). *Teaching sport concepts and skills: A tactical games approach.* Champaign, IL: Human Kinetics.

Hanrahan, S., & Carlson, T. (2000). *GameSkills: A fun approach to learning sport skills.* Champaign, IL: Human Kinetics.

Hastie, P. A. (1996). Student role involvement during a unit of sport education. *Journal of Teaching in Physical Education, 16,* 88–103.

Hastie, P. A. (1998). Skill and tactical development during a sport education season. *Research Quarterly for Exercise and Sport, 69,* 368–379.

Hastie, P. A., & Buchanan, A. M. (2000). Teaching responsibility through sport education: Prospects of a coalition. *Research Quarterly for Exercise and Sport, 71,* 25–35.

Metzler, M. W. (2000). The Sport Education model. In *Instructional models for physical education* (Chapter 10). Needham Heights, MA: Allyn & Bacon.

Siedentop, D. (1981, August). Must competition be zero-sum game? *The School Administrator, 38,* 11.

Siedentop, D. (1994). *Sport education: Quality PE through positive sport experiences.* Champaign, IL: Human Kinetics.

Tannehill, D. (Ed.). (1998, May and June). Sport education. Two-part feature presented in the *Journal of Teaching in Physical Education, Recreation and Dance, 69* (4) and (5).

WEB RESOURCES

The following web link list was generated upon publication of the text; however, over time, the sites may become obsolete if an organization dissolves, discontinues online services, or relocates to a different URL. If a link listed below does not connect, please search for the organization by name.

http://www.yahooligans.com/Sports_and_Recreation/
Provides multiple links for all sports, where you may find details about history, rules, and national federations, along with some skill tips pages.

http://www.pelinks4u.org/links/sportgamesactivities.htm
Provides links to a number of international sports federation home pages.

http://www.hillarysport.org.nz/
New Zealand's Hillary Commission for Sport Fitness and Leisure.

http://www.onslow.org.nz/nzcoac26.htm
Provides some modified soccer games and skill drills.

CHAPTER 9

Designing Outdoor Recreation and Adventure Programs

Scenario

"C'mon Katie, it's cool—you're doing great."

Not to Katie, it's not! She is frozen with fright at the top of the climbing wall, taking her first tentative steps as she begins her descent.

It is the second lesson of the day, and several students dangling from ropes and harnesses are rappelling down a 40-foot-high wall. A second group of students is climbing a wall of rocks, while others are kayaking in the indoor swimming pool. Indeed, these classes are so popular that students compete in a lottery to get in.

Introduction

As physical educators search for ways to present meaningful experiences to their students, many turn to outdoor adventure activities. These activities provide a number of learning experiences valued by educators but not always available within the mainstream fitness and sport content areas. In addition to the psychomotor and cognitive skills developed through activities such as canoeing or rock-climbing, proponents of adventure education seem particularly attracted to the unique contributions that can be made in the affective domain.

Adventure-based programs are highly valued because they offer experiences in which participants develop trust, teamwork, leadership, and strategic planning skills. Research over the past two decades has demonstrated the value of using outdoor adventure activities and outdoor settings to increase participants' self-esteem, alter their locus of control, reduce antisocial behavior, and improve problem-solving abilities.

Adventure education emphasizes the value of the process of participating in an activity, such as climbing, and deemphasizes the outcome of the activity.

As Rohnke (1986) notes, at the center of this "do-it-yourself-with-guidance approach to learning" is the concept of *challenge*. Furthermore, a value-added advantage of adventure experiences is that many students who are particularly successful or skillful in sports are not always the ones who shine. Indeed, adventure programs offer each student an opportunity to experience activities that challenge, motivate, and assist his or her self-actualization of the learning process. The main reason is that the activity is essentially one of problem solving rather than competitive dominance.

Challenge also has a group dimension. In most cases, students are required to work as a team to solve a particular task, and even in smaller cases where students are working individually (e.g., rock climbing), students still rely on the skills and success of others for their health and well-being. In rock climbing, the climber relies on those involved in belaying. Herdman (1994) refers to this trust when he describes most activities as "group dependent." Further, he notes that during these activities, students have to step out of the comfort of isolation and interact with their peers. It is this trust that makes adventure programs particularly attractive.

In addition to the significant personal and social development that adventure education can provide, participation can also significantly enhance health. As brief examples, rock climbing involves considerable muscular strength and endurance, while kayaking, snowshoeing, and hiking provide significant cardiovascular benefits. Table 9.1 provides a summary of the potential education benefits of a number of recreation and adventure activities. These benefits can be categorized as

Many adventure activities are "group dependent"

Table 9.1 Outcomes Achieved through Participation in Outdoor
Recreation and Adventure Programs

Psychological	Social	Physical
Self-concept	Compassion	Skills
Confidence	Group cooperation	Muscular strength
Self-efficacy	Respect for others	Muscular endurance
Well-being	Communication	Coordination
Personal testing	Friendship and belonging	Balance

psychological, social, or physical. They are all legitimate outcomes of a quality physical education program and clearly fit within the global outcome goals for a physical education person, as stated in the standards developed by NASPE.

Factors to Consider When Designing an Adventure Program

When designing an adventure experience, we need to be aware that we are trying to create an environment for students that is "intellectually challenging, personally stimulating, and emotionally rewarding" (Manning, 1986, p. 40). It is therefore important to understand the nature of learning outcomes that can be achieved from various activities.

Differences between Outdoor Recreation and Outdoor Adventure

The activities listed in this chapter will belong to one of two categories—outdoor recreation activities or outdoor adventure education. Although both can be justified within the context of physical education, they serve different participants with different needs, expectations, and motivations. Whereas outdoor recreation involves only fun, with no deliberate seeking of risk, outdoor adventure education is a structured outdoor experience that deliberately seeks to take its participants outside their own zones of comfort.

The Concept of Risk

Ewert (1989) writes of the Chinese term "wei-jan," which translates to "opportunity through danger," which is essentially the true essence of adventure. Outdoor adventure education, then, involves an interaction with the natural environment, and this interaction requires an element of risk leading to a sense of uncertainty of the outcome.

To Ewert, risk taking is the sine qua non of adventure. However, he quickly adds that this is not a risk dictated solely by chance or fate; although the outcome is uncertain and not completely controllable, it can be influenced by the participant. Because adventure is a state of mind, it is therefore possible for a student to experience adventure in an environment of apparent rather than real danger (consider Katie in this chapter's beginning scenario). "As long as he feels the situation is dangerous, in the sense that a mistake or lack of effort on his part could lead to some sort of physical harm or unpleasant situation, then he may experience adventure in the fullest sense of the word" (Ewert, 1989, p. 5).

To this end, we can classify activities in terms of their potential risk. Low-risk activities include hiking, in-line skating, cycling, and ice skating. Medium-risk activities include horseback riding, cross-country skiing, and snorkeling. Rock climbing, caving, white-water rafting, and SCUBA diving would classify as high-risk activities.

Role of the Teacher

When students are learning new skills and applying these to new situations, considerable anxiety and doubt are to be expected. Nevertheless, as confidence builds and the challenge is mastered, pride, satisfaction, and an expanded sense of self-efficacy are the result.

Ewert notes that it is particularly important for the teacher to help students attribute success to their own ability and not to some external force. The role of the teacher, then, is to take students somewhere they haven't been before; to advise and direct them and to serve as a model (Ewert, 1989, p.45). Ewert calls this teaching style "leading from behind." The following excerpt from a student's diary (Herdman, 1994) demonstrates clearly this supportive, but nondirective, teaching role.

> *Before we went rock climbing I had been so confident of myself. I was looking forward to starting climbing. When we were ready to go up I said, "I want to be first." I started my climb and at the same time said to myself, "This is the easiest thing I have ever seen."*

> *I was having fun until I got stuck. It was a place where there were no holds. It was all flat like the floor. I told myself, "It is impossible to go up." I looked down on Paul [the teacher] to see if he could give me direction. But he himself did not know how I could go on. I looked up and was near the top. I looked down once*

again to Paul and yelled at him that I was going to bail out. He said, "No, you can do it. I want you to think real hard." I was getting real angry at him and upset with myself.

Then I thought to myself it would be better if I could calm down as Paul said and follow instructions. That is where the poem that we read in the classroom went into my mind. I remember that there was this person in the poem that could not move because of a wall which represented a problem, but at the end he climbed the wall. I thought of all the problems that I had in my life and how I have to climb my way out of the walls. So, I could not let this wall beat me, this small wall could not be the first wall to conquer me, I was not going to let this wall take the best of me. So I started up real fast, real smooth, just as I said I would in the classroom.

Students' Contributions

Whereas the teacher has a significant role in the outdoors learning experience, demands are also placed on students. First, they need to develop adequate fitness and stamina in order to carry out various technical skills they develop. Second, they need to develop an ability to deal with stress and uncertainty and a willingness to invest time, commitment, and energy. Both these objectives take time, and therefore it is inappropriate to attempt to deliver an outdoor recreation or adventure experience in a short 10-lesson unit.

Of even more consequence for students are attributes that may take even longer to develop: a willingness to accept and acknowledge professional instruction and leadership and to develop and maintain a strong communal bond. Herdman (1994) relates an experience in New York in which "students often spoke in Spanish when they didn't want us to understand. Basically, they were typical 9th and 10th grade urban students, but unlike some, they still had hope that they could make it. On our first rock climbing trip they were distant and mistrustful, but by the end of the semester they were a unit."

The Structure of This Chapter

This chapter will present a number of outdoor activities ranging in degree of adventure risk. For each activity, a potential skill learning sequence is outlined. However, it is *not* the purpose of this chapter to make the reader an expert in any one particular activity; rather this chapter aims to lay the groundwork that will enable future physical educators to recognize the positive outcomes that can be achieved by including outdoor leisure and adventure activities within their programs. With this in mind, each section will follow a template that includes an introduction, expected learning outcomes, a possible content progression, safety/liability issues, as well as resources and references.

Challenge Ropes Courses

A challenge ropes course is a series of individual and group physical challenges that require a combination of teamwork skills and individual commitment in order to solve a movement problem, usually the successful negotiation of an obstacle. A ropes course is constructed of cables and ropes and makes extensive use of safety equipment to keep participants from danger. Working with people's natural discomfort with heights, but using safety equipment to reduce real risk, participants face a sense of "perceived" risk.

When groups or individuals go up on a ropes course, they have a great opportunity to learn about risk taking, their own perceived limits, how they take risks or perform under pressure, how they can give or receive support from other people in taking "appropriate" risk, and how working with others can help them achieve more then they thought they could accomplish.

Expected Learning Outcomes

Psychological	Social	Physical
Problem solving	Communication	Balance
Overcoming fear (self-efficacy)	Group membership	Coordination
Belonging	Trust	Agility
		Strength

Types of Courses

There are several different ropes courses available. The *static belay maze* course allows the whole group or a portion of the group to experience the ropes course together. A single maze course consists of a number of elements linked together. In *dynamic belay course*, only one participant at a time completes the activity. These courses can be a single element or a series of elements linked together.

Trees or Poles?

Ropes courses can be built in trees or on utility poles, or a combination of the two. Many companies will provide construction either indoors or outdoors, and each type of course has advantages and disadvantages (Table 9.2).

Table 9.2 Advantages and Disadvantages of Ropes Course Structures

	Advantages	Disadvantages
Trees	• Trees are aesthetically pleasing, and the course will have a feeling of being a part part of nature. • The initial cost of a tree course can be significantly less.	• As a part of the ecosystem, tress can be damaged by natural forces or die. • Because the tree is living and growing, any costs saved in initial construction may need to be spent on maintenance and repair over time. • The layout of the course is confined to the trees on site and may require removal of some trees. • Not all tree species are appropriate for ropes course construction.
Utility poles	• Poles are treated and remain constant for a long period of time. • The course layout can be designed in any configuration. • Course location can be chosen and put on sites without natural resources. • Pole courses generally require less maintenance.	• Poles are not as aesthetically pleasing, and the course will be more artificial. • Poles add to the initial cost of course construction.

Source: Reprinted with permission from Experiential Systems, Inc.: http://www.experientialsystems.com/pages/ropes.html.

The Learning Sequence

Most ropes courses consist of elements with differing degrees of difficulty. As students gain mastery on one task, they can progress to one that is more challenging. Table 9.3 gives examples of a number of activities of varying difficulty.

Table 9.3 Sample Ropes Course Elements

Novice	Intermediate Difficulty	Advanced Difficulty
Pole climb	Multilane traverse	Bosun chairs
Ladder climb	Balance beam	Burma loops
2-line bridge	Burma bridge loops	Commando crawl
Burma bridge	Pirates crossing	Space loops
	Tension traverse	
	Zip zap	
	Horizontal ladder	

For a more complete experience, however, teachers should follow a learning sequence that incorporates considerable discussion, reflection, and team building. Used extensively in corporate business workshops, that sequence is listed below. Full details of each level are provided in Table 9.4.

- Level 1: Goal setting
- Level 2: Awareness
- Level 3: Trust
- Level 4: Cooperative activities
- Level 5: Group challenge
- Level 6: Extended challenge
- Level 7: Application

The professional team building company Experienced Based Learning Inc. (http://www.ebl.org) comments that "group learning and development follows a sequential process and the effectiveness and mastery at one level contributes to each subsequent level. Each level can be viewed as both an outcome and a phase of group development."

Safety

Ropes courses should be inspected each time before they are used. Ropes or cables that are showing any sign of damage or dry rot should be replaced. Ropes courses should also not be used in wet weather.

The instructor should always supervise students as they are using a ropes course. The students should also be trained in belaying techniques.

Ropes courses buid trust

Table 9.4   The Teamwork Learning Sequence

Level 1: *Goal setting*

Goal setting is a critical component of the program because it provides a way to measure achievement. Goals should be set prior to the group's arrival or very shortly after the beginning of the program. The goals should be understood by every individual and be measurable so that action plans may be devised. These goals provide for a benchmark that can allow for further advancement during future programs.

Level 2: *Awareness*

Awareness activities are designed to help participants feel more comfortable in their group environment and appreciate the relationship between peers and co-workers. Discussion pertaining to the scope of issues can be brought up before the group. The defining of the issues is directly tied to the goals and the measurement components of the program.

Level 3: *Trust*

Trust is an element of a successful team. Activities focus on fostering trust between individuals and among the group. The purpose of some activities is to support other group members; other activities are designed to develop belief in oneself.

Level 4: *Cooperation*

The activities at this level are designed to give the participants a sense of accomplishment through cooperation and to develop group cohesion. Groups work together in accomplishing activity goals.

Level 5: *Group challenge*

Activities are geared to problem solving and tie the experience to the work setting. Groups have to work together in order to find a solution. Efficiency, quality, and speed are achieved through the group's ability to interact and use each group member's skills. Cooperation, communication, group decision making, conflict management, trust, and leadership are benefits attained at this level.

Level 6: *Extended challenge*

Challenge is defined differently by members of a group. For this reason, individual needs must be met to provide meaningful challenge experiences. These activities encourage participants to stretch themselves beyond their limits by facing challenge in a perceived risk environment, typically through the high ropes course. Participants experience an increased sense of competence, risk-taking ability, leadership behavior, and the value of group support.

Level 7: *Application*

Structuring and implementing a follow-up phase after a group's experience is an important step to obtain ongoing results. As an automobile requires maintenance, so does a team. We initiate the follow-up program at closure of the on-site experience, through a final process session. Reflection, evaluation, and goal review become critical for the learning process. Many times, groups will choose to reschedule a follow-up experience, thus tying the lessons to a larger time scale. This broader scope facilitates the implementation of positive experiences and helps limit the amount of "bounce back" (old habits and ways of doing things).

Training

Illinois-based Experiential Based Learning (http://www.ebl.org/tech_train.html) is a company that offers technical training workshops for ropes courses. These workshops range from 2 to 5 days (16 hours–40 hours), depending on the participant's skill levels. Topics include introduction to high ropes courses; elements and selection; course operation, design, and element sequence; ropes, harness, and safety hardware inspection; knots; belay practices; and course inspection practices.

Resources and References for Ropes Courses

Priest, S., & Rohnke, K. (1999). *101 of the best corporate team-building activities we know*. Dubuque, IA: Kendall/Hunt.

Rohnke, K., Tait, C. M., & Wall, J. B. (1997). *The complete ropes course manual*. Dubuque, IA: Kendall/Hunt.

Ropes Online. http://www.ropesonline.org/

Ropes Online is devoted to the development and marketing of ropes/challenge course programs. The purpose of Ropes Online is to provide a free source of information to ropes/challenge course owners, facilitators, users, and students.

Rock Climbing

Rock climbing has the potential to be an adventure of the greatest magnitude. The climber competes with himself or herself and the elements. In many cases, that competition can be self-determined, because different climbing sites offer routes of varying difficulty. As students become more skillful and confident, they select sites that present greater levels of difficulty. The beauty of rock climbing is that each climb is a new experience, even if it involves the same course.

Expected Learning Outcomes

Psychological	Social	Physical
Self-efficacy	Trust	Muscular strength
Personal testing	Communication	Muscular endurance
Confidence	Group cooperation	Balance
Sensation seeking		Coordination
		Agility
		Flexibility

The Learning Sequence

A beginning course in rock climbing will focus on two main skills: belaying and climbing techniques. In most cases, top-rope climbing is the system followed: A climber and belayer are tied to the respective ends of a rope that runs from the climber though a carabiner attached to a fixed anchor and down to the belayer. Where lessons can be conducted outdoors, rappelling is a further activity that may be introduced. A list of activities suitable for use in rock climbing units is presented in Table 9.5.

Table 9.5   Suggested Learning Experiences for Rock Climbing

Getting started	• Planning a trip • Equipment care

Equipment	*Clothing*
	  • Footwear
	  • Clothing
	  • Helmets
	
	Technical equipment (use and care)
	  • Ropes
	  • Slings/harnesses
	  • Carabiners

Knots
(www.climbing.ie/knots.html)
	Uses of knots
	  • Joining ends of ropes
	  • Anchoring a rope to a fixed object
	  • Tying loops
	  • Securing an end person
	
	Types of knots
	  • Bowline (on a bight or a coil)
	  • Figure-eight
	  • Fisherman's' knot
	  • Water knot
	  • Prusik

Belay techniques	• Dynamic and static belays • Anchors • Hip belay • Belay communications and signals

Climbing techniques	• Body position
	• Three points of contact
	• Climbing holds (hands and feet)
	
	Special holds
	  • Lay back
	  • Chimney
	  • Undercling
	  • Jam series

Rappelling	• Breaking system • Rappel techniques • Belaying

Safety

According to Steffen and Stiehl (1998), the two most important factors in climbing safety are the condition of the climbing face and the equipment that is being used. Teachers should select climbs that are appropriate for the level of the students' skills. Equipment should be checked for wear and/or damage, and on artificial walls, the strength of materials and fastenings should receive regular inspection. Further, matting or soft cushioning should be placed at the base of artificial climbing walls where they are used.

Safety skills are important for any climb

Students should be well trained in the safety systems put in place for protecting climbers; knowledge of safety equipment, mastery of basic climbing skills, and the ability to belay. Students should also learn and master the skills of climbing communication.

In all cases of climbing and rappelling, supervision is critical. Supervision begins before any climb takes place, with the checking of harness buckles, knots, and clothing and verifying that the climber is tied to the harness correctly. During a climb, the instructor needs to provide active supervision to *both* climber *and* belayer. Some examples of such active supervision include the following (Steffen & Stiehl, 1998):

- ensuring that the belayer's hand is on the brake and that the belayer is using the delay device correctly
- ensuring that the belayer is maintaining a secure stance
- ensuring that the belayer is managing the rope correctly
- alerting the climber to keep the rope on the correct side of his or her leg
- providing cues to climbers as to possible hand and footholds

Resources and References for Rock Climbing

Long, J. (2000). *How to rock climb*. Helena, MT: Chockstone Press.

Luebben, C. (2000). *How to rappel*. Helena, MT: Falcon Publishing Company.

Lewis, S. P., & Cauthorn, D. (2000). *Climbing: From gym to crag*. Seattle, WA: Mountaineers Books.

Steffen, J., & Stiehl, J. (1998). Rock and wall climbing and rappelling. In N. J. Dougherty (Ed.), *Outdoor recreation safety*. Champaign, IL: Human Kinetics.

Thomas, R. (1995) *Building your own indoor climbing wall*. Helena, MT: Chockstone Press.

Great Outdoor Recreation Pages. http://www.gorp.com/gorp/activity/climb.htm

GORP's climbing page with advice for beginners, and details sections on learning skills, where to climb, a gear guide, photo galleries, and web links

Rock and Ice magazine. http://www.rockandice.com/

Online version of *Rock and Ice* magazine, with sections concerning gear, events, and guides, as well as some useful links for instruction.

Hiking and Backpacking

Hiking and backpacking are health-enhancing activities that are suitable for people of all ages. Aside from the exercise benefit (with the potential to burn over 4,000 calories a day), hiking and backpacking offer significant psychological benefits—particularly in stress reduction. Karen Berger of GORP (Great Outdoor Recreation Pages, www.gorp.com) provides an amusing "Top 15 Reasons to Hike." Those that are relevant to teenage youth are presented below:

- You can eat all you want and still lose weight.
- Your boss (mother/teacher) doesn't come with you.
- You can honestly say, "No I didn't get your message—there was no cell phone reception in Dead Horse Gulch."
- It gives you a good excuse to sleep for 10 hours straight: You're exhausted, and besides, it's dark out.
- Everything tastes better after you've walked 10 miles.
- You can actually find something to do with that Swiss army knife with the scissors, nail file, sawing blade, and power screwdriver.

- Nobody will think you're dressed stupid, even if you wear shorts over your long underwear.
- You will remember what air smells like when it doesn't come packaged with exhaust fumes.
- You will remember what silence sounds like.
- And birds.
- You will feel a sense of real satisfaction when you realize that you can live without hot showers, running water, a soft bed, and with so little stuff that you can carry it around on your back.
- When you return back home, you will feel a sense of real satisfaction that you have hot showers, running water, a soft bed, and so much stuff that you couldn't possibly carry it all around on your back.

Expected Learning Outcomes

Psychological	Social	Physical
Actualization	Friendship	Cardiovascular endurance
Catharsis	Sense of community	
Stress relief	Belonging	

Enjoying the sound of silence

The Learning Sequence

A course in hiking and backpacking contains eight main areas. The extent of learning and instruction in each of these areas depends on the extent to which the class will be completing off-campus hikes. Overnight backpacking trips will obviously involve more preparation and longer units of instruction. Table 9.6 gives an outline of topics that might be covered within each of these areas.

Safety

It is recommended that at least two, and preferably all, members of a wilderness expedition understand first aid and medical rescue, including mouth-to-mouth breathing, cardiopulmonary resuscitation (CPR), bandaging, and splinting. In addition, survival equipment, such as maps, compass, waterproof matches, a knife, nonperishable food, a flashlight, and adequate first-aid supplies, should accompany any trip.

Table 9.6   Suggested Learning Experiences for Hiking and Backpacking

Getting started	• Planning a trip • Where are you going? • How much time do you have? • What kind of shape are you in?
Trip preparation	• Basic preparations every hiker needs to make before hitting the trail
Gear	• What you need and how to use it, from packs to water filters • Selecting a backpack • Packing a backpack • Lightening the load
What to wear	• Separating fact from fashion • Understanding fabrics and layers • Learning to layer
Boots and blisters	• Selecting hiking boots • Blister prevention and treatment
Route finding	• Finding your way • Getting *un*lost • Using a GPS
Extreme environments	• Winter hiking • High country hiking • Desert hiking
Trail skills	• Using hiking sticks • Crossing creeks and streams • Preserving the ecology of trails

Resources and References for
Hiking and Backpacking

Curtis, R. (1998). *The backpacker's field manual: A comprehensive guide to mastering backcountry skills.* New York: Three Rivers Press.

Logue, V. (2000). *Backpacking: Essential skills to advanced techniques.* Birmingham, AL: Menasha Ridge Press.

Randall, G. (2000). *The outward bound backpacker's handbook.* New York: Lyon Press.

Great Outdoors Recreation Pages.
http://www.gorp.com/gorp/activity/hiking.htm

GORP's hiking and backpacking page. Includes sections on know-how, what to use, where to go, and finding a trail. This is an extensive site.

Camping

Camping continues to grow as a popular activity among Americans, as the American Camping Association reports:

- It is estimated that more than 9 million youth attend summer camp at an estimated 8,500 to 10,000 camps nationwide. Of those camps, 75% are run by nonprofit organizations, and 45% serve children with physical or mental challenges.

- An estimated 3,000 day camps exist in the United States.

- In the past 10 years, the number of accredited camps has increased 154%, with the YMCA reporting that family camps have increased more than 500% in the past 12 years.

- Approximately 900,000 camp jobs are filled each summer by college students, teachers, doctors, and nurses.

- Since 1992, summer camp enrollment has risen 8% to 10% every year.

Within physical education programs, camping units can be completed in conjunction with units on backpacking/hiking, or they can stand alone as independent entities. Certainly, there is sufficient content within the realm of camping to justify it as a separate course of study. In addition, hiking is not necessarily the mode of transport to a campsite. Many camping trips are water, cycle, or even horse based.

Expected Learning Outcomes

Psychological	Social	Physical
Actualization	Group cooperation	Depends on the type of camp and the activities selected
Self-efficacy	Respect for others	
	Communication	
	Friendship	
	Belonging	

The Learning Sequence

The components of a camping unit are based on the objectives of the course. A unit whose culminating event is to complete a wilderness survival camp would include certain skills that might not be covered if the final objective were to camp in more "civilized" settings. For example, a section on camp toilets and disposal of rubbish may not be a priority if students are traveling to a permanent camping site. Further, students may stay at the same campsite for the duration, or split their time between two different sites.

Table 9.7, while not exhaustive, provides a number of topics that might be included across a gamut of camping units. Some skills are more specific to primitive camping, whereas others are more general.

Planning a Class Camping Trip

Among the factors to be considered in deciding on the type of trip to take are the following:

- characteristics of group members, such as age, special needs, and special skills
- purpose for which the camping trip is to be made
- length of time the trip will last, including traveling time
- distance to be traveled, mode of transportation, and destination
- activities anticipated and support tasks to be performed
- season of the year

In all cases, however, camping trips can serve as a wonderful component of an integrated project. Students may participate in the following learning experi-

Table 9.7   Suggested Learning Experiences for Camping Units

Planning a camp	• Different types of camp • How long should the trip be? • Choosing a site • Determining camp supplies • Getting there
Tents and shelters	• Types of tents and shelters • Site selection • Pitching tents • Constructing a primitive shelter
Camp hygiene	• Camp toilets • Disposal of rubbish
Cooking on camp	• Menu planning • Food preparation and storage • Camp ovens • Safety with gas
Fire building and safety	• Woodpiles and chopping areas • Safety with saws and axes • Emergency fire procedures
Basic first aid and emergency procedures	• Environmental hazards • Special environments
Basic ecology	• Minimum-impact camping • Environmental protection
Post-camp duties	• Drying wet materials • Storing camping equipment • Restocking supplies (e.g., batteries)

ences during a camping trip. Consider the possibilities of coalitions with botany or geology classes (observe, identify, and/or collect specimens of leaves and flowers, or rocks and soils), with geography classes (viewing natural sites, landscapes, and various topographies), or with history classes (visiting historical sites). Of course, the physical education components of these trips may include the development of a number of camping skills (e.g., fire building and camp cooking), or participating in outdoor adventure activities (e.g., canoeing or rock climbing and rappelling).

Selecting a Camping Site

While numerous sites are available for camping trips, the major consideration is the objective of the camp. As such, location will be the key. If the camp is auxiliary to field trip application of classroom studies, the site will need to be near the desired beach, lake, historical site, or gem field that students will attend during the day.

Campsites vary significantly

The next consideration is the type of camping environment. Many sorts of sites can be suitable for camping trips. These include areas administered by government agencies, such as the national or state parks services, the Corps of Engineers, the Bureau of Land Management, and the National Forest Service. In addition, there are multitudes of privately owned campgrounds. Even further, camping may be available on private properties.

Of course, facilities will vary according to location and purpose. In some cases, the campsite will be essentially primitive, with few or no amenities. Others may offer conveniences such as picnic tables, grills, firewood, tent pads, restrooms, showers, drinkable water, and electricity. Most camping guides provide descriptions of all amenities and facilities, as well as their availability. Many camping sites provide web pages featuring pictures of their facilities. Direct bookings may also be made online.

Resources and References for Camping

Hodgson, M. (2000). *Camping For Dummies*. Foster City, CA: IDG Books.

McPherson. J., & McPherson, G. (1993). *Primitive wilderness living & survival skills: Naked into the wilderness*. Randolph, KS: Prairie Wolf.

Scoutbase. http://www.scoutbase.org.uk/activity/outdoor/camping/

This is the Camping Skills page of Scoutbase, the official web site of the Scout Association (UK). The site provides resources for many aspects of camping.

American Camping Association. http://www.acacamps.org/

Home page of the American Camping Association, a community of camp professionals dedicated to enriching the lives of children and adults through the camp experience.

Mountain Biking

Mountain biking is an increasingly popular activity, particularly because it is so versatile. One can ride purely for enjoyment in the woods or engage in highly challenging and intense competition. In nearly all cases, participants are able to determine their level of daring while obtaining an excellent exercise workout.

Expected Learning Outcomes

Psychological	Social	Physical
Personal testing	Respect for others	Balance
Self-confidence		Coordination
Sensation seeking		Cardiovascular endurance
		Muscular endurance
		Riding skills

The Learning Sequence

A course in mountain biking contains four main areas: the bike and other equipment, riding skills, safety and fitness issues, and trip planning. Table 9.8 gives an outline of topics that might be covered within each of these areas.

Safety

Safety in mountain biking begins, of course, with rider skill. Students who can control the bike and negotiate hazards will be considerably less likely to suffer from injury as a result of falls or collisions. However, once the student rides outside the school training setting, the environment becomes more unpredictable. To this end, the International Mountain Biking Association lists a number of trail rules that relate directly to safety. These are described below, with additional annotations from a group called ROMP (Responsible Organized Mountain Pedalers: www.romp.org).

1. *Ride on open trails only.* Respect trail and road closures (ask if you're not sure), avoid possible trespass on private land, and obtain permits and authorizations that may be required. Federal and state wilderness areas, as well as with many regional open space lands, are closed to cycling.

Table 9.8 Suggested Learning Experiences for Mountain Biking

Riding equipment	*Bike*
	• What is a mountain bike?
	• Bike parts
	• Which bike is for you?
	• Extra gear
	• The right fit
	• Perfecting the fit
	Riding gear
	• Helmet
	• Clothing
	• Bags
	• Pumps
	• Water bottles
Riding skills	• Where to start
	• The riding position
	• Braking and shifting
	• Cornering
	• Climbing up and riding down hill
	• Obstacles
	• Rocks, roots, logs, mud, and more!
	• Extreme stuff—steep hills and dropping off
	• Getting vertical
Healthy and safe riding	• How ready is your body?
	• Improving your mountain biking fitness
	• Maintaining your bike for safe riding
	• Crossing water
	• Carrying your bike
	• Cautions for safe riding
Planning and completing a riding trip	• Planning a ride
	• Trail etiquette
	• The tool kit
	• What to pack
	• Pre-ride checks
	• Repairs on the trail
	• Post-ride cleaning

2. *Leave no trace.* Be sensitive to the trail beneath you. Cyclist can cause significant trail damage when they skid their tires and when the trails are muddy.

3. *Control your bicycle!* Inattention for even a second can cause problems. Obey all speed laws.

4. *Always yield the trail.* Make known your approach well in advance. Show your respect when passing others by slowing to a walk or even stopping. Anticipate that other trail users may be around corners or in blind spots.

5. *Never spook animals.* An unannounced approach, a sudden movement, or a loud noise startles animals. Give animals extra room and time to adjust to you.

6. *Plan ahead.* Know your equipment, your ability, and the area in which you are riding, and prepare accordingly.

Resources and References for Mountain Biking

Davis, D., & Carter, C. (1994). *Mountain biking.* Champaign, IL: Human Kinetics.

Overend, N., & Pavelka, E. (1999). *Mountain bike like a champion.* Emmaus, PA: Rodale Press.

Pavelka, E. (2000). *Bicycling magazine's mountain biking skills: Tactics, tips, and techniques to master any terrain.* Emmaus, PA: Rodale Press.

Cyber Cycle. http://library.thinkquest.org/10333/index.html

Home of Cyber Cycle, a web site with links to many areas of biking

Responsible Organized Mountain Pedalers.
http://www.romp.org/rides/beginnerguide.html

Beginner's mountain bike information guide, containing information about etiquette, and safety, techniques, equipment, repair, and maintenance.

In-Line Skating

In-line skating is a recreational activity that has witnessed explosive growth over the past decade. According to the International Inline Skating Association (IISA), the reason for this growth is that the activity appeals to many different interests. As IISA notes,

> . . . inline skating isn't one-dimensional; it does not require the skater to conform to a particular style or even to one particular sport. It can be taken up by nearly anyone regardless of athletic ability, age, gender, or fitness level. Clearly, the many benefits associated with inline skating go a long way toward explaining its tremendous popularity. Inline skating is easily accessible to nearly anyone; it is inexpensive, versatile, healthy, safe, and most importantly, fun.

Expected Learning Outcomes

Psychological	Social	Physical
Personal testing	Friendship	Balance
Self-confidence	Belonging	Coordination
Sensation seeking		Cardiovascular endurance
		Skating skills

The Learning Sequence

Once the student has become familiar with the skates and understands and values the need for protective gear, the challenge is to spend sufficient time on the skates to become confident. One suggested learning sequence is to progress from skating forward and stopping, to turning, skating backward, and negotiating novel and more unpredictable terrain. A list of activities in these areas is presented in Table 9.9.

Safety

The key to safety in in-line skating is the correct use of the protective equipment. The teacher needs to ensure that all participating students have well-fitting

Table 9.9   Suggested Learning Experiences for In-Line Skating

Skating equipment	• Skate anatomy and maintenance • Protective equipment—helmet; wrist, elbow, and knee pads
Skating forward	• Swizzles • Stride 1—basic forward motion and natural starting point if you are new to the sport • Stride 2—uses a healthy knee bend to create stronger strides and longer glides • Stride 3—aggressive stride used mostly by racers and speed skaters
Skating backward	• Backward swizzle • Backward stroke • Front-to-back pivot • Back-to-front pivot
Turning	• A-frame • Parallel • Slalom • Forward crossovers • Backward crossovers • Lunge
Braking	• Standard heel stop • Cuff-activated heel stop • Grass stop • Spin stop • T-stop • Lunge stop • Backward power slide • Forward power slide • Parallel stop
Handling terrain	• Curbs • Stopovers • Side step (going up hills) • herringbone (steep hills)

and comfortable safety gear. In addition, students must not be placed in risky situations (e.g., near heavy traffic) until they develop their control skills.

Resources and References for In-Line Skating

Nealy, W. (1998). *Inline: A manual for beginning to intermediate inline skating.* Birmingham, AL: Menasha Ridge Press.

Powell, M., & Svensson, J. (1998). *In-line skating.* Champaign, IL: Human Kinetics.

My Sports Guru. http://www.mysportsguru.com/

Provides animated in-line skating lessons on the in-line skating link from this home page. Outstanding resource for learning skills; includes technical cues as well as practice drills.

International Inline Skating Association. http://www.iisa.org/

Canoeing and Kayaking

Canoeing and kayaking have become very popular recreational and adventure activities. There is a boat and a body of water suitable for just about everybody, regardless of age, ability, or interest. Be it a leisurely paddle across a flatwater lake or navigation down a river of churning rapids, water-based activities deliver the promise of a peak experience.

Expected Learning Outcomes

Psychological	Social	Physical
Self-efficacy	Respect for others	Muscular strength
Self-concept	Communication	Muscular endurance
Sensation seeking	Trust	Cardiovascular endurance
Personal testing		

The Learning Sequence

Irrespective of the crafts that are being used in a unit of study, students will need to know a common core of skills. These will include transporting and launching, paddling skills relevant to the boat, rescue and capsize drills, as well as the ability to perform some of the skills unique to each discipline. Table 9.10 provides a list of the general and specific skills that could be included in canoeing and/or kayaking units.

Table 9.10 Suggested Learning Experiences for Canoe and Kayak Units

Anatomy of a canoe/kayak	Parts of the craft
	• Different accessories
	    • Helmets
	    • Paddles
	    • PFD
	    • Spray skirt

Transporting and launching a kayak	• How to lift and carry various canoes and kayaks • Getting into a canoe or kayak successfully (from land and from in the water) • Launching from a dock • Beach entry

Basic strokes for different craft	*Canoe*
	    • J-stroke
	    • Stern pry
	    • Canadian stroke
	    • Pitch stroke
	    • Indian stroke
	
	Kayak
	    • Forward stroke
	    • Back stroke
	    • Sweeps
	    • Sculling
	    • The draw

Rolls	• Eskimo roll • Screw roll • Hand roll
Rescue techniques and capsize drills	• Capsize drills • Emptying a swamped canoe or kayak • Throwing a rescue rope
Surf skills for sea kayaks	• Beach entry and exit • Wave dynamics, lulls and sets • Surf landings and launchings • Surf rescues • Getting on and off a wave • Surfing etiquette

Safety

It has been said that training, preparedness, and common sense are the three most important things you can take on a river trip. They don't weigh anything, they are easy to pack in your boat, and they don't smell bad after an overnight river trip. With this in mind, there are a number of "givens" when it comes to watercraft safety. First, personal flotation devices (PFDs) must be worn at all times; they are lifesavers. Where whitewater is involved, helmets are also mandatory. Footgear also needs to be worn. The main rationale here is that a paddler may be required to assist in a river evacuation, where bare feet are indeed a hindrance. All students should learn and be competent in self-rescue techniques. They should also be skillful with a throw rope.

In designing paddling units, lessons should first take place in safe water. This serves to give the student confidence, making it easier to deal with a real emergency if one develops. Finally, all students should be competent swimmers. Competent swimmers are more confident and relaxed in moving water, a critical issue in rescue situations.

To present a safety message in a humorous way, the Oregon Kayak and Canoe Club has developed the "Axioms to Paddle By":

1. Don't go into the field unless you are dressed to play.
2. The river is always the boss!
3. Q: How strong is the river? A: Stronger than me.
4. Mother Nature plays dirty.
5. The river gives the test, *then* teaches the lesson.
6. Having rapids named after you is generally a bad thing.
7. Cold, tired, hungry, stressed-out paddlers tend to make bad decisions— even if they are your friends.
8. Don't paddle it if you can't swim it.
9. Portaging is much easier than CPR . . . so is scouting.
10. All bleeding stops . . . eventually.
11. If it's cold, get it warm. If it's wet, get it dry.
12. When in doubt, dress for immersion.
13. Improper use of rope on the river can kill you. Proper use can save your life.
14. No on-the-job training at a real rescue.
15. It is much more important to feel good than to look good. (Unless you're a rodeo paddler or a raft guide.)
16. Fear is God's way of letting you know he wants you to stay alive. Pain is God's way of letting you know you are alive.
17. Pain is temporary. Embarrassment is forever.

Resources and References for Canoeing and Kayaking

Bennett, J. (1996). *The complete whitewater rafter*. Camden, ME: Ragged Mountain Press.

Davidson, J. W., & Rugge, J. (1983). *The complete wilderness paddler*. New York: Knopf.

Grant, G. (1997). *Canoeing: A trailside guide*. New York: W.W. Norton.

Paddling.net. http://www.paddling.net

Information on canoes and kayaks, outfitters and schools, upcoming events, as well as news and views.

Canoe and Kayak magazine. http://www.canoekayak.com/

Home page for *Canoe and Kayak* magazine. Contains articles, links, an events calendar, and paddling resources.

Snorkeling

Snorkeling is an activity with significant potential for lifetime involvement. Given that it does not require a considerable level of fitness, there is virtually no age barrier to participation. It is truly one of the few all-family activities. Snorkeling is not expensive, nor does it require equipment that is difficult to transport (no kayaks, mountain bikes, or camping gear). Snorkeling is also an activity that can be taught in the school's swimming pool.

Expected Learning Outcomes

Psychological	Social	Physical
Confidence	Respect for others	Cardiovascular endurance
Self-efficacy	Friendship	
Sensation seeking		

The Learning Sequence

A snorkeling unit includes lessons on selecting equipment, wearing the equipment, and specific on-water and underwater swimming skills. These are summarized in Table 9.11. Early lessons are most suited to a swimming pool, but students need to experience natural water conditions as well.

Safety

Every snorkeling location, whether a lake, river, pond, or ocean, will have a unique safety concern. These concerns include water temperature, current, rapids or falls, and plant and animal life. The main safety precaution is an evaluation of

Table 9.11 Suggested Learning Experiences for Snorkeling Units

Snorkel equipment	• The mask—the single most important piece of equipment • The snorkel • The fins
Wearing equipment	• Clearing the snorkel • Clearing the snorkel mask • Donning the fins • Defogging the mask • Testing for leaks
Swimming skills	• Swim training for snorkeling—the flutter kick • Correctly entering the water (from different situations) • Snorkel breathing and clearing the snorkel • Surface dives and surfacing • Pressure equalizing

the location prior to an excursion. Where the temperature is likely to be cold, it may be necessary to spend less time in the water. In all cases, but particularly those where the current is strong, it is recommended to set specific snorkeling boundaries. In addition, the exit point for the snorkelers should be made clear, so that they can move toward it before the end of their swim, when they are most likely to be tired. It can become stressful to have to fight a current to return to a boat or exit point.

The second significant safety concern with snorkeling is active supervision. Each swimmer should have a buddy, and buddies are expected to be responsible for one another's welfare. Buddies should remain together throughout a snorkel trip and should adhere to the "one up, one down" rule; that is, if one swimmer wishes to submerge to get a closer look at something under the water, the buddy should remain on the surface. Students should also be instructed in the various hand signals, particularly those that relate to direction and safety (e.g., the OK sign and distress signals). Students should also be encouraged to give regular signals to the land-based supervisor of the snorkel trip.

Resources and References for Snorkeling

French, B. (1995). *Snorkeling . . . here's how*. Houston, TX: Pisces Books.

Newman, J. (1999). *Scuba diving and snorkeling for dummies*. Foster City, CA: IDG Books.

British Sub-Aqua Club. http://www.bsac.com/snorkel/

Home page to the British Sub-Aqua Club, a snorkeling and diving training agency and the United Kingdom's governing body for underwater swimming.

Cross-Country Skiing

Lauded as "the world's best aerobic workout," together with its quick learning curve and low injury rate, cross-country skiing is one of the great outdoor winter activities. Given its natural motions, cross-country skiing allows people of all ages, fitness levels, and interests to enjoy the rhythmic, low-impact feeling of gliding across snow. Because of its versatility, you can cross-country ski just about anywhere there is snow. Furthermore, you can match the terrain to suit your fitness level and interests.

Expected Learning Outcomes

Psychological	Social	Physical
Well-being	Friendship	Cardiovascular endurance
Catharsis	Respect for others	

The Learning Sequence

One of the advantages of cross-country skiing is that it has a rather easy learning curve. It does not take too many lessons before students are able to travel at least on a groomed trail and on relatively flat terrain. However, for maximum enjoyment, a unit of skiing will need to address the skills of turning, stopping, and

Cross country skiing has an easy learning curve

traveling up and down slopes. One series of learning experiences is presented in Table 9.12.

Safety

As in most winter activities, a major concern in cross-country skiing is hypothermia. One can become quite sweaty during cross-country skiing, so it is important for students to dress in layers. Students should be taught the signs and methods of preventing drops in body temperature, and instructors should be vigilant in identifying students who appear to be struggling.

A second safety consideration lies in the trails themselves. Trails that involve the crossing of streams, bridges or roads deserve particular caution and provide unique challenges.

Resources and References for Cross-Country Skiing

Cazeneuve, B. (1995). *Cross-country skiing: A complete guide*. New York: W.W. Norton.

Gaskill, S. (1998). *Fitness cross-country skiing*. Champaign, IL: Human Kinetics.

Lovett, R., Petersen, P., & Morton, J. (1990). *The essential cross-country skier: A step-by-step guide*. Camden, ME: McGraw-Hill.

American Cross-Country Skiers. http://www.xcskiworld.com/

This site includes details on training, technique, equipment, and waxing, as well as an education library and links.

Great Outdoors Recreation Pages.
http://www.gorp.com/gorp/activity/skiing/ski_cros.htm

GORP regional cross-country skiing guide.

Table 9.12 Suggested Learning Experiences for Cross-Country Skiing Units

Ski equipment	• Boots • Poles • SkiS • Differences between cross-country and alpine skiing
Skiing skills	• Diagonal stride • Skating technique • Turning • Stopping • Recovering from a fall • Skiing over mixed terrain
To wax or not to wax	• Advantages and disadvantages of waxless and waxable skis • Wax charts (temperature and snow conditions)

Cross-Country Skier magazine. http://www.crosscountryskier.com/
Includes details on travel, equipment, and instruction, as well as links to other relevant sites.

Snowshoeing

Most people think of snowshoeing as something akin to strapping a couple of tennis rackets to your feet and plodding off into the snow. Well, it actually is—but try doing it without snowshoes, and see how far you get before you disappear up to your knees. Snowshoes were first developed to allow for effective winter hunting and transportation in arctic conditions, but now they provide a means of hiking in places that are inaccessible on skis or snowmobiles. As a result, snowshoeing is particularly popular with people who wish to explore nature in quiet scenic areas. You can see many animal tracks in the snow, bear claw marks on tree trunks, and sometimes animal dens, all while getting a good cardiovascular workout.

Expected Learning Outcomes

Psychological	Social	Physical
Actualization	Friendship	Cardiovascular endurance
Catharsis	Sense of community	
Stress relief	Belonging	

The Learning Sequence

A course in snowshoeing will involve not only the skills of walking with something similar to tennis rackets on your feet, but also instruction in equipment, clothing, and backcountry safety. Further, snowshoeing has exciting prospects for integration with other subject areas. Table 9.13 gives examples of a number of activities that would be included in a snowshoeing unit.

Safety

The main areas of concern for showshoers are avalanches and cold weather exposure. Before attempting any excursion into the backcountry, students need some basic understanding of these hazards.

Avalanches occur most frequently on slopes of between 20 and 60 degrees. Slides are most likely to occur from 30 to 45 degrees, usually within 24 hours of a snowfall. As a result, hikers should wait a day after a major snowfall for the snow to settle before attempting a walk on sloped ground. In particular, the main

Table 9.13 Suggested Learning Experiences for Snowshoeing Units

Equipment	• Parts of the snowshoe • Selecting and wearing a snowshoe • Clothing for snow hiking
Climbing	• To ascend a slope, kick the front of your snowshoe into the snow and press down to compact it into a step. Make sure that each new step is sufficiently above the last one to avoid collapse.
Descending	• Heel cleats are the key to an easy descent. Keep your knees slightly bent, lean back, and keep your weight on the heel cleats to maintain control.
Edging	• The best way to traverse a slope. Kick the side of the snowshoe into the hillside, engaging the cleats. Swing your heel hard toward the uphill slope, and then stomp down, securing the snowshoe edge in the slope. Poles are also helpful.
Breaking trail	• When snowshoeing in a group, walk in a single line behind the leader, who Is breaking the trail. When it's your turn to lead, take consistent, even steps that are easy for everyone to follow.

danger areas are snow-covered convex slopes, lee (sheltered) slopes where snow has accumulated, and deep, snow-filled gullies.

Timing is also important. Before noon, travel only in shaded areas, because the heat of the sun on snow can cause avalanches. Likewise, in the afternoon, travel only on those slopes that have been exposed to sunshine, avoiding the ones that are now in the sun for the first time. The Avalanche Center (www.csac.org) is an excellent site for avalanche education.

The other main concern when snowshoeing is exposure to cold weather. Frostbite, snow blindness, and hypothermia are potential hazards, but some basic safety measures can help prevent serious problems. The main precautions include avoiding tight clothing that will reduce circulation, keeping clothes dry, always wearing gloves and keeping those gloves dry, and never touching metal with bare hands.

Resources and References for Snowshoeing

Edwards, S., & McKenzie, M. (1995). *Snowshoeing*. Champaign, IL: Human Kinetics.

Prater, G., & Felkley, D. (1997). *Snowshoeing*. Seattle, WA: Mountaineers Books.

Snowshoe Central. http://www.svidaho.com/snowshoeing/

Contains details about snowshoeing technique, equipment, history, safety and first aid, and places to snowshoe. Has an extensive link and reference list.

Including Students with Disabilities

Given the potential of outdoor adventure and recreational activities to provide wonderful learning experiences beyond just developing skills and fitness, it behooves us to find creative ways to include students with disabilities. Although it is beyond the scope of this book to provide examples of inclusion for each of the content areas mentioned, other resources are available. For example, Wendy Ellmo and Jill Graser's book *Adapted Adventure Activities: A Rehabilitation Model for Adventure Pprogramming and Group Initiatives* provides extensive discussion on adapting outdoor activities for special populations.

IN-SCHOOL TASKS

Adventure Philosophy

Visit a nearby high school and inquire about their inclusion of outdoor recreation and/or adventure units within their curriculum. Do an inventory of the activities that are included and the rationale. If the school does not have any such activities, try to determine the reasons. Make a reflective comment on the possible reasons for the inclusion or exclusion of an adventure component of the curriculum.

IN-CLASS DEBATE

You may find participation in this debate a fruitful exercise in examining the role of adventure-based programs within physical education. Prepare a case either for or against the following proposition: "There is no point trying to do all this outdoors stuff within physical education. It's too expensive, none of the teachers are trained, and besides, it's not going to be part of the lifestyle of kids in this community anyhow."

PORTFOLIO SUGGESTIONS AND ARTIFACTS

Adventure Inventory (S8–D1)

Make a list of all the outdoor recreation or adventure activities you have completed. What was your role in these? Were you simply a participant, or did you have some leadership position? From this listing, provide some reflection concerning how you enjoyed the activity and the potential you see for including some activity like this within a physical education program.

Adventure Mastery Skills (S1–P1, K7)

Make a list of any certifications, awards, or other experiences you have in outdoor recreation or adventure. Where appropriate, provide documentation that supports your skills in these areas.

STUDENT ASSESSMENT OPPORTUNITIES

In 1992, the National Association for Sport and Physical Education (NASPE) appointed the Standards and Assessment Task Force to develop content standards and assessment material based on the question "What should students know and be able to do in physical education?" Seven content standards were developed based on the definition of a physically educated person. These standards provide the key tools for assessing student performance in physical education.

Presented below (and in Chapters 6, 7, and 8) is a series of assessment examples that correspond to each of the seven standards. Each content standard is listed and described, followed by one or two techniques appropriate for assessing student achievement of the specified content standard. The assessment examples provided are not meant to be a complete listing of available assessment techniques, nor are they necessarily the best ones for all situations. Feel free to use these in your classes or develop new ones more suited to your situation.

NASPE Standard 1: Demonstrates Competency in Many Movement Forms, and Proficiency in a Few Movement Forms

1. Teacher observation checklist: Design a checklist for the skills and other competencies that students will develop as a result of participation in your outdoor unit. Provide a rubric for the level of mastery of these skills.

NASPE Standard 2: Applies Movement Concepts and Principles to the Learning and Development of Motor Skills

1. Video analysis: The students watch a video of themselves performing the skills of a particular adventure activity. They are able to correctly identify performance errors, explain the reason for the errors, and identify some remediation task. Students should also be able to identify correct technique, with an explanation of the key point relating to successful performance.

NASPE Standard 3: Exhibits a Physically Active Lifestyle

1. Activity log: The student keeps a current log of his or her participation in an adventure or outdoor recreation activity. This log is submitted to the teacher each week, with an annotated account of improvement, inhibitors of improvement, and motivational facilitators or obstacles.

NASPE Standard 4: Achieves and Maintains a Health-Enhancing Level of Physical Fitness

1. Personal goals project: The student assesses his or her current fitness level through self-administration of a relevant fitness test. The student then determines what improvements may be made through participation in any outdoor recreation or adventure program. The student then sets specific improvement goals over a predetermined period. At the end of the time, the student examines the extent to which those goals have been met.

NASPE Standard 5: Demonstrates Responsible Personal and Social Behavior in Physical Activity Settings

1. Self-report: Students complete a report concerning their development of personal and social responsibility in the outdoors setting under study. Students are asked to respond to the following statements: (a) "I have acted in a way that ensures the safe achievement of adventure goals for a classmate (family member or friend)"; (b) "I have initiated (or soon will initiate) an action plan within my family to help us participate in an outdoor recreational or adventure activity in the next month."

NASPE Standard 6: Demonstrates Understanding and Respect for Differences among People in Physical Activity Settings

1. Group project: Students form a small group to design a series of activities for a particular adventure sport that would facilitate the participation of a classmate with a physical disability.

2. Assignment: Students identify adventure activities associated with various minority groups (e.g., Native Alaskans, Plains Indians) or with other national groups (e.g., Norwegians, New Zealanders),

NASPE Standard 7: Understands That Physical Activity Provides the Opportunity for Enjoyment, Challenge, Self-Expression, and Social Interaction

1. Written report: Students compose a report that requests family members to accompany them on a class-based adventure excursion. The report will outline the benefits of participation in the activity and their opinions of how this will promote family ties.

2. Trip planning: Students plan an actual adventure trip relating to one of the skill areas discussed in this chapter (e.g., a down-river canoeing trip or a camping trip).

REFLECTION TIME

Now that you have read this chapter, how confident do you feel in

- being able to perform a variety of outdoor recreation or adventure skills?
- your ability to design a sequence of lessons that would comprise a safe, meaningful, and exciting adventure experience for students?
- your ability to find local expertise in various areas of outdoor recreation?
- your ability to convince fellow physical educators that including outdoor recreation or adventure activities within their physical education curriculum holds particularly worthwhile outcome potential?
- your ability to convince a school administrator that funding your attendance at an adventure training workshop would be a good investment for the school?

REFERENCES

Darst, P. W., & Armstrong. G. P. (1980). *Outdoor adventure activities for school and recreation programs.* Minneapolis, MN: Burgess Publishing Co.

Ellmo, W., & Graser, J. (1995). *Adapted adventure activities: A rehabilitation model for adventure programming and group initiatives.* Dubuque, IA: Kendall/Hunt.

Ewert, A. W. (1989). *Outdoor adventure pursuits: Foundations, models, and theories.* Columbus, OH: Horizons Publishers.

Gass, M., & Williamson, J. (1995). Accreditation for adventure programs. *Journal of Physical Education, Recreation, and Dance, 66* (1), 22–28.

Henton, M. (1996). *Adventure in the classroom: Using adventure to create a community of lifelong learners.* Dubuque, IA: Kendall Hunt.

Herdman, P. (1994). When the wilderness becomes a classroom. *Educational Leadership, 52* (3), 15–20.

Manning, R. (1986). *Studies in outdoor recreation*. Corvallis, OR: Oregon State University Press.

Rohnke, K. (1986). Project adventure: A widely used generic product. *Journal of Physical Education, Recreation, and Dance, 57*, 68–70.

Steffen, J., & Stiehl, J. (1998). Rock and wall climbing and rappelling. In N. J. Dougherty (Ed.), *Outdoor recreation safety*. Champaign, IL: Human Kinetics.

WEB RESOURCES

The following web link list was generated upon publication of the text; however, over time, the sites may become obsolete if an organization dissolves, discontinues online services, or relocates to a different URL. If a link listed below does not connect, please search for the organization by name.

http://www.gorp.com/

Great Outdoors Recreation Pages (GORP) describes itself as a site for outdoor recreation and adventure travel. The site provides expert advice on numerous activities (such as hiking, biking, paddling, climbing, and wintersports), advice on purchasing gear, and an extensive listing of books and maps.

http://www.adventuresports.com/

Welcome to Adventure Sports Online provides access to outfitters and tour guides, event calendars, and beginner's tips. They also have extensive lists of outdoor gear and products.

http://www.pa.org/

Project Adventure is a company offering custom training and consulting, challenge course design and installation, leading-edge adventure equipment, and the latest in adventure-based books and publications.

http://www.usoutdoors.net/

U.S. Outdoors.Net is a web site that allows you to search for outdoor activities by state and by the activity that you want to engage in, including camping, hunting, fishing, rafting, skiing, and other winter sports.

http://www.nols.edu/NOLSHome.html

The National Outdoor Leadership offers courses in outdoor skills and leadership ranging from 10 days to full semesters in the world's most spectacular wilderness classrooms.

http://www.hiddentrails.com/usa/index.htm

Lists over 100 horseback riding destinations in 21 states. The site is searchable by state and includes other horse-related activities (e.g., cattle drives and working ranches).

http://www.castle-rock.org/

The Castle Rock Institute is an educational community devoted to balancing academic work in the humanities and outdoor adventure. It sponsors an off-campus study program for college students that combines a semester of coursework in religion, philosophy, literature, and art with backpacking, climbing, biking, and paddling.

CHAPTER 10

Block Scheduling and Project-Based Learning

Scenario

Hand me the wrench, will you?
Sure, but I'll trade you for the grease rag.
You didn't do it again, *did you?*
Yeah, the stupid thing keeps slipping, and I can't get the chain back on.

* * * *

This dialogue is between two students who are preparing to ride in a five-day "Ride for Cancer." They are among a group of 15 other students in this elective physical education class who decided they needed to raise funds because one of their classmates recently underwent chemotherapy for leukemia.

These students are enrolled in a school that adopts the block-scheduling format, so they are able to spend extended periods of time each day to work on their bikes, complete aerobic training, and communicate with potential sponsors of their trip. As part of this project-based learning curriculum, these students have invited schoolmates from outside their physical education class to join them. Indeed, one science teacher has also signed up.

Introduction

In 1994, the National Education Commission on Time and Learning made a statement that "time is learning's warden" (U.S. Department of Education, 1994). What this particular commission was critical of was the degree to which the dynamics of clock and calendar control today's American school. The commission suggested that the rigidity of time schedules in public schools was not founded on findings from educational research, but was rather a pragmatic

231

tradition. Furthermore, the commission suggested that the time allocated within schools governs how material is presented to students and the opportunities they have to comprehend and master that material.

The commission made a number of recommendations:

- Schools should focus more on learning than time.
- Schools should redesign education so that time is allocated to support learning rather than to limit it.
- Teachers should be provided with the time and opportunities they need to prepare quality curricula and instruction.

One of the consequences of this report was a revisiting of the block-scheduling reform movement. Typically, schools had operated on six, seven, or eight daily periods of somewhere between 40 and 60 minutes in length. Block scheduling arose out of specific criticisms of these schedules. Some of the criticisms suggest that multiple single periods contribute to an impersonal high school climate (where teachers present mostly by lecture), that they may exacerbate discipline problems (particularly in the transitions from class to class), that they do not permit flexible time for teaching and learning, and that they consequently limit teachers' ability to teach.

The block schedule involves breaking up the day into larger segments. The periods within block scheduling are typically twice as long (but may be even longer) than the traditional 45- to 50-minute lesson. While the time in each class is increased, the number of classroom periods is correspondingly decreased, so the overall length of the school day is approximately the same.

Block scheduling is designed to reduce the number of class changes and movement from class to class as well as to reduce the number of courses teachers must prepare. Through having fewer classes and substantially longer lessons, teachers are provided with blocks of time that allow and encourage the use of active teaching strategies, as well as extensive practical and laboratory work. The physical education unit described in the opening scenario to this chapter is but one example of the possible uses of this extended time.

According to the proponents of block scheduling, a number of benefits can accrue. However, there are also strong advocacy groups that oppose block scheduling. The American Federation of Teachers has listed the pros and cons of the issue. These are provided in Table 10.1.

Block Scheduling Formats

There are several models of block scheduling, and they all have a common goal: allowing schools to adopt a flexible program that responds to the needs of the

Table 10.1   Pros and Cons of Block Scheduling

Pros

• Students can study and learn subject matter in greater depth.

• Instruction is less fragmented, with greater time for serious discussions, cooperative activities, labs, group work, and projects.

• It allows for extended and variable instruction for students who may need additional support or have difficulty learning in short "sound bites."

• If structured correctly, teachers work with fewer students at a time, allowing for more personalized instruction and an improved school atmosphere.

• The usual 50-minute teacher preparation period is almost doubled to 90 minutes, allowing for honing of lessons, more collaboration with colleagues. and more time to work in one-on-one sessions with students.

• Fewer class changes mean fewer times when thousands of teenagers are released into narrow hallways. The result in a reduction in discipline problems, noise, and stress.

Cons

• Cognitive science shows that regular review, spaced out over a long period of time, fosters long-term retention of subject matter. Block scheduling diminishes opportunities for review, especially where yearlong courses are compressed into a single semester. Thus, the practice may actually serve to diminish student performance.

• Ninety minutes is a long time to hold students' attention, and few teachers or other instructional staff have been trained in how to use this period of time effectively.

• Student transfers to and from schools with block schedules can be highly troublesome; in some subjects, an entire year's curriculum is lost through a mid-year transfer.

• Missing one day of school under block scheduling can be like missing almost a week under traditional scheduling. For students who miss a week due to illness or other problems, catching up may be almost impossible.

• Some block schedules actually result in less instructional time. A 55-minute class that meets five times a week gives the instructor 550 minutes every two weeks, for example, whereas a 90-minute meeting on alternating days for two weeks (five days) gives the instructor 450 minutes.

Source: American Federation of Teachers, Washington, DC.

schools and students. Some of the most common formats (and some that are even more creative) are described below.

4 × 4 Semester Block Schedule

The 4 × 4 format is one of the most common structures of intensive scheduling. In this model, standard yearlong courses are converted into half year (semester) courses of typically 90-minute classes. Students take two courses in the morning and two more in the afternoon. Teachers will teach three classes per day, with a 90-minute break (or a 45-minute planning period and other school tasks). At mid-year, a new schedule is produced for all teachers and students. Table 10.2 shows an example of this arrangement.

Table 10.2   Sample 4 x 4 Block Schedule

Block / Time	Semester 1	Semester 2
1. 8:00–9:35	Biology 1	English
2. 9:40–1:10	Algebra	Earth science
3. 11:55–1:25	**Physical education**	Health
4. 1:30–3:00	World geography	Elective

The stated advantages for students in semester block are that they have fewer classes and, as a result, fewer quizzes, tests, and homework assignment, on any one day. Moreover, a student who fails a course can repeat it in the next semester. Although classroom instruction time will remain the same, or increase in some cases, teachers will have fewer total students and fewer preparations. They also don't have to keep as many grades.

Acceleration through the curriculum is also another exciting possibility. For example, students taking algebra in the first semester of the 9th grade can then take geometry in the second semester. In this way, they are able to catch up on a track that many other students begin in the 8th grade. However, although block scheduling may facilitate acceleration, it also may hinder acceleration. For example, a student might complete one math course at the beginning of the 9th grade but not take the next course until the second semester of 10th grade. This is considered by many educators to be particularly troubling. Another disadvantage of block scheduling is that taking a course over one semester rather than the entire year makes for less continuous development of skills.

Alternating Block Plan—The AB Schedule

The alternating block plan is also called an AB plan. It is similar to the 4 × 4, except that students will take four classes on one day and four different classes the next. In this way, the students will carry eight classes for the entire year, even though they meet every other day. This form of scheduling is perhaps the most conservative of the block models. It does not reduce the teacher-student workload because the teachers will see up to 150 students and will need to prepare for twice as many classes (except in cases where they teach multiple sections of the same course).

It has been suggested that the alternate day plan offers greatest advantage in the case of vocational schools and schools for gifted and talented students. In the

Block scheduling works well in vocational schools

vocational schools, for example, students on AB plans can meet for a full day in the vocational school on day 1, and on day 2, attend their regular school. This allows students to maximize the time they spend on tasks such as mechanical work and bricklaying. In cases where school districts share vocational technology centers, schools can send students on alternate days. This can ease crowding and eliminate daily travel between the technical center and the regular school.

Table 10.3   Sample Alternating (AB) Plan

Block / Time	Day 1	Day 2
1. 8:00–9:35	English	Algebra
2. 9:40–1:10	U.S. history	Technology
3. 11:55–1:25	**Physical education**	Health
4. 1:30–3:00	World geography	Elective

The 75-75-30 Plan

Another block scheduling format consists of two 75-day semesters followed by one 30-day session. These 30-day sessions present a number of possibilities. First, they can be used for remediation or to repeat a failed course. Alternatively, they can be used by other students to accelerate in a discipline, such as math. They may be used for enrichment courses, electives, or out-of-school experiences, such as community service or internships. Indeed, the prospects are quite thrilling, especially for creative teachers of physical activity (Table 10.4).

Table 10.4   Sample 75-75-30 Plan

First 75-Day Session	Second 75-Day Session	30-Day Session
English	Algebra II	English enrichment
Driver's education	Biology	History mini course
Physical education	Health	**Kayaking**
Spanish 1	Elective	

Trimester Plans

Some schools favor a trimester model. In this structure, students still participate in a four-period day, but the entire block lasts 12 weeks. Only two courses are taken, however, with each lasting half a day. In this plan a student has just two classes per day—each for 180 minutes. The course is accelerated and completed in just 60 school days. This method enables students to concentrate on just two classes at a time. Every 30 days, the schedule for every teacher and student changes.

In less intensive iterations of this plan, a yearlong course can take two sets of 12 weeks to complete, while a one-semester course is completed in one set of 12 weeks. All courses meet four times per week for 70 minutes, and once a week for 2 hours. In these cases, classes during the long day will take either all morning or all afternoon. The half days are designed for field trips, the pursuit of major projects, or the completion of ambitious laboratory work. Typically, a quarter will involve three academic classes and one practical (e.g., art or physical education) or off-campus project. An example is shown in Table 10.5.

Table 10.5   Sample Trimester Plan with Two-Day Extended Sessions

Monday	Tueday	Wednesday	Thursday	Friday
English II	English II	English II		English II
U.S. government	U.S. government		U.S. government	U.S. government
Applied chemistry	Applied chemistry	Applied chemistry		Applied chemistry
Physical education	**Physical education**		**Physical education**	**Physical education**

In another variation of the trimester plan, students take two core courses for the 60-day period and repeat other courses throughout the entire school year (Table 10.6).

Table 10.6 Sample Trimester Plan with Two Core Courses and Yearlong Courses

Period	First 60 Days	Period	Second 60 Days	Period	Third 60 Days
1	English	1	**P.E.**	1	Accounting
2		2	Art	2	
3	Science	3	Choral	3	**P.E.**
4		4	Algebra	4	Art
5	**P.E.**	5		5	Choral
6	Art	6	World history	6	Economics
7	Choral	7		7	

Prospects for Physical Education within Block Scheduling

When a school makes a commitment to block scheduling, there are certainly some implications for physical education. In the initial stage, these will be determined by the state requirement for physical education for graduation. If the requirement is simply one year (or one Carnegie unit), then it is possible that the physical education experience in high schools will be one required semester during grades 9 through 12. In different structural formats, of course, that one year may be a class taken through the entire year (on the AB format). In a modified trimester series, classes may meet for the regular 45-minute periods throughout the entire year, in which case there may not be any change in practice. We need, however, to consider the likely prospect that physical education will consist of classes lasting 90–120 minutes.

While a state may require only one course in physical education for graduation, this does not eliminate the possibilities of offering a number of elective courses in addition to the required program. The extent to which this happens depends on the reputation of the existing program in a school. Claxton and Bryant note that "if physical education is regarded as a class which meets no worthwhile objectives, the transition to block scheduling may be a convenient time to eliminate it altogether. If it is seen as a vital part of the school curriculum, however, it has a good chance of assuming an equal role with other subjects" (1996, p. 49).

One particular advantage of the block schedule for physical education is that it allows time for the achievement of objectives in a number of domains. In some cases, for example, where students take only one semester of activity, it is increasingly important to achieve a number of cognitive objectives. Indeed, several states with a one-unit/semester requirement for physical education adopt a "fitness for life" focus. Students having such short exposure to physical education need to be taught about appropriate levels of activity for health and fitness, and they need to learn ways in which they can engage in activity outside class and outside school. One significant result is that students may have only one experience with physical education in four years. You will recall from Chapter 4 that the predictor of continued activity in youth is not simply knowing the health benefits, but knowing *how* to become active.

Block lessons allow not only for more time in the development of cognitive objectives, but also for extended periods of time in cardiovascular and muscular endurance activities from a fitness perspective. Indeed, these may be alternated so that students spend three days per week in aerobic conditioning and two days in strength training, or split a 90- to 120-minute time frame to achieve both activities in one lesson.

The extended lesson time also allows for allocating more time to skill development. Students can participate in team practices (e.g., in sport education seasons—see Chapter 8). Teachers can work with select groups of students; for example, they may hold a goalkeeper seminar during a hockey season, bringing in a local professional player. These lessons allow time for extended game play as well.

Another advantage of the extended period is the increased access to off-campus facilities. Classes can take place at the bowling alley or the golf course, the swimming pool or the skating rink. Whereas travel time in the shorter (e.g., 55-minute) periods precludes many of these options, block formats that allocate an entire half day to an activity (see Table 10.5) allow for significant off-campus opportunities. This is particularly advantageous for including activities that entail significant preparation time, such as climbing walls (getting into harnesses, etc., and the fact that only one student can work at a time) or putting together riggings in windsurfing. Nonetheless, despite the advantages offered by block scheduling, in each and every school, the standing of physical education will determine whether it becomes a casualty of education reform and eliminated completely, remains in a status quo, or takes a prominent place within the school curriculum.

Feedback from Teachers Currently Using Block Schedules in Physical Education

Although only few studies have examined the perceptions of teachers currently using block schedules, the results are quite consistent. Hynes-Dusel (2001) found in her interviews with eight physical educators that they all preferred block formats over traditional scheduling, principally because they had more time to measure skill development. Bukowski and D'Antonio Stinson (2000) also found that teachers perceive block scheduling as less stressful. The common theme expressed in these teachers' responses was that block scheduling made "things run more smoothly" by reducing the normal hassles of attendance and locker room procedures and making the class climate more manageable. Teachers cited other positive outcomes; increases in team teaching, more time for interacting with students, and more time for teacher planning. Indeed, one participant in that study stated that "going to school was fun again."

Despite these positive responses, teachers in Bukowski and D'Antonio Stinson's study also called attention to some of the mechanical problems of block scheduling. The most commonly voiced problem was that block scheduling denies students access to the entire "physical education curriculum experience"; that is, students having long periods of time in high school without any exposure to physical education. Although this is a valid concern, one wonders whether these teachers were perhaps not creative enough to offer attractive electives or did not have enough political savvy in their schools to gain greater physical education requirements. As a result, when students had completed their one-semester requirement, they saw no need for nor were motivated to continue participation.

Teachers also commented that student absences were more costly and that transfer students were at a disadvantage. Additionally, they also remarked that *teacher* absences were costly, noting that substitute teachers frequently struggled with the larger blocks of time.

Block scheduling allows more time for student-teacher interaction

These teachers have also suggested that their days are "more relaxed" and "take a less hectic pace." However, it is important to note that quantitative data analysis of block schedules reveals that classes spend significant time waiting for turns and *less* time in activity than teachers might believe. In particular, teachers also allow more transition time than they imagine, resulting in student response rates that are also low. Indeed, activity time is often 50% less than estimated, whereas management and transition time is 20% higher than believed (Rikard, et al., 2001).

While teachers on block schedules may indeed be negotiating time with students for cooperation for the full 90 minutes, they still need to be aware of setting levels of accountability for work and activity that are no different from the regular classes. Although a less frantic pace is positive, it also holds considerable potential for increasing nonproductive time in classes.

Teaching on the Block Schedule

It would make sense that teaching on a block schedule should look substantially different from teaching in a single-period lesson. Indeed, many teachers do struggle when attempting to provide a full 90 minutes of meaningful activity, particularly in cases where there is no staff development prior to adoption of the block model. Note, too, the comments from physical education teachers that substitute teachers especially seem to experience a number of difficulties in making productive use of class time.

Teaching on the block is not as simple as completing two lessons back-to-back within the one time block. For example, a fitness lesson that may occupy an entire 45-minute lesson could not be stretched for the full 90 minutes unless those students were highly trained—and we have little evidence that American youth are indeed trained. Even so, this would not be pedagogically appropriate.

To help teachers prepare for the block, nearly all texts and reports strongly reinforce the requirement for staff development before the block schedule is implemented. Furthermore, as Bukowski and D'Antonio Stinson propose, educators must also address this growing trend by encouraging novice teachers to look at blocks of learning in alternative ways and to consider different divisions of that learning.

Given the extended periods of time in contact with students, a number of subject areas have devised strategies for teaching meaningful lessons. The most common is the three-part lesson, in which teachers progress through a sequence of *explanation, application,* and *synthesis.* Explanation is the lecture process of a class and is essentially teacher directed. Occupying between 25 and 40 minutes, the explanation phase is where the teacher presents the objectives of the lesson and explains what students are to learn. During the application phase (a period of roughly 40 minutes), students become more active learners in this "hands-on" segment of the lesson. The lesson is concluded with the synthesis phase. Taking between 15 and 20 minutes, the teacher will involve the students in connecting the beginning two parts of the lesson. This is a time for review and reflection, but also in some instances for reteaching or additional explanations.

Two examples of the three-part lesson from English and math are provided in Table 10.7.

Table 10.7   Sample Lesson Outlines for 90-Minute Classes in English and Math

English	Mathematics
1. Homework review	1. Homework review
2. Whole-class reading of Act III, Scenes 1 and 2 of *Macbeth*	2. Mini-lecture—"exponential growth"
3. Small group brainstorming on two separate characters	3. Lab—recording bacteria growth (daily task over one week)
4. Whole-class discussion	4. Related problems—practice
5. Writing workshop—*invent a new character*	5. Review and learning log
6. Closure and goal setting	

In addition to cognitive objectives, however, physical education addresses psychomotor, affective, and organic (fitness) goals. As a result, block scheduling is ideally suited for allocating time to all these domains within the same lessons. However, it is clear that the benefits of a block schedule are determined by the effectiveness of the teachers using the schedule, because there are several ways to fill 90 minutes. As Claxton and Bryant (1996) so emphatically state: "To simply take the material that currently occupies 35 minutes and stretch it to fill 75 minutes would be as unacceptable as it would be to add more objectives to the curriculum and do a poor job of meeting them" (p. 49).

Four examples of teaching in the block are described below, along with a lesson from four different content areas: (1) the three-transition model, (2) the classroom lab/activity model, (3) the repeated activity model, and (4) the extended activity model

Three-Transition Model: Warm-up–Fitness–Sport Activity

The three-transition model is perhaps the predominant model used in the block system. In this scheme, students participate in 20–30 minutes of physical fitness activities and then spend the remaining class time in practical pursuits (both class work and applications). One detailed example is provided in Table 10.8.

Table 10.8   Lesson Plan for Three-Transition Warm-Up–Fitness–Sport Activity (Block Model)

Time	Activity
8:00–8:05	Dress out and roll call
8:05–8:10	General warm up—followed by stretching
8:10–8:30	Cardiovascular or strength fitness routine
8:30–8:40	Formal lesson instruction—teacher directed (from the following) • Fitness concepts • Game rules and strategies • Ethical considerations
8:40–9:10	Applied activity (from the following) • Skill practice • Skill testing • Scrimmage • Game
9:10–9:20	Wrap-up/debriefing • What did you learn? • What key skill elements do you remember? • Did you and your classmates work and play fairly?
9:20–9:30	Dress for next class

Source: Modified from Claxton and Bryant (1996).

Classroom Lab/Activity Model

A second way of dividing lessons is to include a classroom laboratory, in which 25–30 minutes of a lesson is spent investigating a particular wellness concept. As for the three-transition model, the remaining 50 minutes is spent engaged in some physical activity and 10 minutes in reflection. In cases where a number of teachers are scheduled to teach in the same block, students elect to move from the classroom to an activity of their choice (e.g., Frisbee, aerobics, weight training). In the one block lesson then, students may be taught by different teachers, depending on their interests. Table 10.9 provides an outline of a lesson on this block, and Table 10.10 gives a few examples of potential lecture/lab topics.

Table 10.9   Lesson Plan for Classroom Lab—Activity Block Model

Time	Activity
8:00–8:05	Dress
8:05–8:30	Classroom lecture/lab: Target heart rate
8:30–9:10	Applied concept activity: Choose either from Frisbee, mini-soccer, or step aerobics
9:10–9:20	Review: What did you learn? Assessment: Measurement of the health-fitness component
9:20–9:30	Dress for next class

Table 10.10 Sample Lab Topics

Topic	Suggested Activities
The exercise and physical activity pyramid	• Provide copies of the pyramid to students.[1] • Discuss the progressive nature of the activities. • Identify the extent to which students engage in the various part of the pyramid. • Identify activities in each student's life corresponding to a section of the pyramid.
Determining heart rate training zone	• Explain the concept and value of tracking resting heart rate. • Explain the concept of training heart rate. • Using the appropriate formula (220–age × .55 or 220–age × .90), have students calculate their zone ranges. • Complete a stair-stepping exercise, stopping to calculate real heart rate and comparing it with the calculated heart rate at times when the student feels the exercise is (a) moderately intense, and then (b) very hard.
Flexibility and stretching	• Discuss the need for flexibility and the concepts of stretching (i.e., passive stretching and PNF stretching). • Perform a sit-and-reach test for each student after passive stretching. • Repeat with half the class completing proprioceptive neuromuscular facilitation (PNF) stretching while the other completes more passive stretching. • Retest and compare the results.
Body mass index (BMI)	• Discuss the concept of BMI and its uses. • Have students calculate their own BMI. • Use the tables presented in Chapter 4 to determine results.
Cardiovascular disease risk	• Discuss fatness as a cardiovascular disease risk. • Have students measure circumferences at waist level (halfway between the navel and the lowest part of the sternum), and at the hip level (largest circumference of the buttocks/hips). • Determine the ratio of waist/hips, noting that for males, a healthy range is under 1.00, whereas for females, a score of less than 0.80 is recommended.
Food Guide Pyramid	• Present and explain the Food Guide Pyramid.[2] • Have students identify their compliance with the pyramid over the past day. • Have students identify foods they enjoy eating from the base levels of the pyramid. • Involve students in goal setting.
Food labeling	• Have students bring at least one food label to class. • Explain the key components of food labels. • Have students compare their labels and identify foods high in fats or sugars. *Note.* Soda cans are a real eye-opener.

[1]Available from Metropolitan Life Insurance Company.

[2]Available from the U.S. Department of Agriculture and the U.S. Department of Health and Human Services.

Repeated Activity Model

One model that contains a high emphasis on conditioning offers two different fitness labs across the entire 90 minutes. The first may offer aerobic conditioning options, while the second focuses more on muscular strength and endurance. Hence, during one block students may complete two sessions (Table 10.11).

Table 10.11 Content Options for Two Fitness Sessions

First-Half Options (Aerobic Conditioning)	Second-Half Options (Muscular Strength)
Jogging for fitness	Weight training
Frisbee	Stretch and tone
Cardio karate	Yoga

Indeed, these offerings could rotate through a week—and suggestions certainly may be contributed by the student physical activity advisory committee based on in-school polls.

Extended Activity Model

The fourth option is to devote the entire class time to one activity, such as bowling, rock climbing, or kayaking. This model is particularly advantageous for offsite activities that entail travel to another venue. Many sport education seasons can easily accommodate the 90-minute schedule, with time allocated for team practice, games, team reflection, and further practice, and a second series of games (Table 10.12).

Weight training adapts well to block scheduling

Table 10.12 Lesson Plan for Extended Activity Block Model

Time	Activity
8:00–8:15	Dress out, team meeting and administration
8:15–8:25	General warm-up—followed by stretching and game preparation
8:25–8:40	Game 1
8:40–8:55	Transition—team reflection and review
8:55–9:10	Game 2
9:10–9:20	Class debriefing—announcements from sports board
9:20–9:30	Dress for next class

Project-Based Learning

One of the wonderful advantages of the block-scheduling format is the opportunity it offers for *project-based learning* within physical education. Project-based learning is a comprehensive instructional approach to engage students in sustained, collaborative investigation (Bransford & Stein, 1993). During project learning, students are placed in situations that are anchored in a real-world problem and ideally use multiple content areas. As part of the process of project-based learning, the students plan and work on complex tasks, as well as assess their performance and progress. A critical feature of project-based learning is that projects originate from students as opposed to being extrinsically assigned teacher- or school-created tasks. A project is designed around issues, questions, or needs *identified by the students*. Furthermore, the project culminates with a consequential task in which students' thinking is made both *visible* and *public*. The main purpose of this culminating event is not only to disseminate new knowledge, but also to help develop a learning community.

Early Stages of a Project

Before students begin their projects, they must write a plan and have it approved. The plans communicate the importance of thinking through the project in its entirety before actually beginning work. The plan should include topic questions that the students want to answer, possible resources, how they will show what they've learned, when their research will begin and end, and when they will present their finished project to the class. After completing their projects, students must also write a self-evaluation (see Wolk, 1994).

The Instructional Sequence in Project-Based Learning

There are two essential components of projects: the "driving question" and the "culminating product." A driving question serves to organize and direct activities that, taken as a whole, amount to a meaningful project. The culminating product(s) is in effect a series of artifacts or some consequential task that meaningfully addresses the driving question (Brown & Campione, 1994).

As part of the driving question, students will work through a series of problems. To address these problems, they will develop cooperative teams in which individual expertise will be acquired as groups begin to solve the problems posed and categorized. In many cases, personnel external to the class will be enlisted as part of a cooperative team. From this point, and after sustained study into the problem itself, the distribution of individual expertise is completed.

Blumenfeld et al. (1991) suggest that students seek solutions to problems by engaging in the following practices:

- asking and refining questions
- debating ideas
- making predictions
- designing plans and/or experiments
- collecting and analyzing data
- drawing conclusions
- communicating their ideas and findings to others
- asking new questions
- creating artifacts

It is important to give students freedom to generate their own artifacts, because it is through this process that they construct their own knowledge. Because artifacts are concrete and explicit (e.g., a model, report, consequential task, videotape, or film) they can be shared and critiqued. This allows others to provide feedback, makes the activity authentic, and permits students to reflect on and extend their knowledge and, in turn, to revise their artifacts.

The Role of the Teacher

Barron et al. (1998) comment that implementing project-based curricula requires simultaneous changes in curriculum, instruction, and assessment practices. They suggest that four design principles appear to be important for maximum student learning: (1) defining learning-appropriate goals, (2) providing scaffolds, (3) ensuring multiple opportunities for formative self-assessment, and (4) developing social structures.

Sample Projects

Three sample projects are presented below. The first is a real-life science project involving students engaged in environmental conservation. The second and third examples are from physical education.

Environmental Science

As part of the division of wildlife's River Watch program, students at Logan School for Creative Learning in Denver had been monitoring water in South Boulder Creek. When they discovered that something was polluting the creek, the young environmentalists decided to do something about it. They searched and found the source of the pollution in groundwater near the old mine. Students then wrote a grant proposal and received seed money to work on the innovative wetlands technology created by Thomas Wildeman from the Colorado School of Mines.

About once a month, the class goes up to the Perigo mine area 3 miles south of Rollinsville in northern Gilpin County to take water and chemical samples, and to maintain four wetlands they built to purify runoff that goes into nearby Gamble Gulch.

By monitoring water downstream, they can tell how well the wetlands are working. The students have been able to significantly reduce the acidity level in the water. The project is actually a pilot program, that if successful, the Colorado Division of Wildlife may implement on a larger scale.

Previous classes built four wetlands areas, made up of rock, manure and compost that act as natural filters that encourage bacteria growth. The bacteria, in turn, reduce the acidity in the water.

The work can sometimes be difficult. In winter, for instance, students must snowshoe into the mine area and work in frigid cold. "Whatever comes up, we have to deal with it," said Kate Aid, 13, adding that the snow is sometimes 3 feet deep at the site.

The students are also developing a Web page on the Internet to educate others about mine contamination. And once the pilot project is complete, the students will have another problem to solve: how to clean up their artificial wetlands, now inundated with heavy metal waste. (Modified, with permission, from an article in *The Denver Post*, September 13, 1997, p. A-01.)

Physical Education—Open-Water Kayak Touring

A physical education class has decided it wants to extend its kayaking unit to involve some substantive culminating event. It is their last semester in high school, the last time this group will be together. Their school is located on a bay that has a number of nearby islands, many of which have camping facilities, some of which are uninhabited mangrove colonies.

In their previous kayaking unit in the 11th grade, these students developed competence in basic paddling skills—they believed they were ready for a significant challenge. Their determined challenge was to (1) construct their own kayaks, (2) paddle across the bay to one of the islands, and (3) camp out for the weekend and return on Sunday.

The numerous problems facing these students included, among others: (1) raising funds to construct their craft (their teacher had expertise in building kayaks); (2) developing sufficient aerobic and muscular endurance to complete the open-water paddle; (3) investigating tide times, water conditions, and maritime regulations; (4) booking camping facilities on an island; (5) transporting their cargo to the island; and (6) developing contingencies in case of poor weather or conditions on their planned return.

In addition to these logistical issues, the students also needed to develop ways in which to document their learning and experiences and make a formal presentation to share their new knowledge.

Physical Education—School Walking Trail

One of the key learning outcomes in a beginning physical education wellness course for students of Jackson High was to provide opportunities for all members of the community to engage in physical activity. Taking a sociological view of health and wellness, their teacher had described how access to fitness had become increasingly privatized; that is, people with the funds available had easier access to health clubs.

Many of these students lived in neighborhoods that consisted of a number of low-income families. Their school did, however, border on some semi-open bush land. The students decided on a project to construct a walking trail that would be accessible to all members of the community. They also made plans to actively promote its use.

Some of the concerns facing these students included (1) determining a safe, but scenic, route for the walking trail; (2) deciding how to mark its course; (3) figuring out how to get local government authority to clear the nearby vacant land; (4) figuring out how to get their message about the trail to others in the school as well as those in the community; (5) figuring

A student-maintained walking trail

out how to maintain the trail, including enlisting local council support; and (as in all cases of project-based learning) (6) deciding what artifacts to collect to demonstrate their learning and how to present these in a public forum—particularly because the students wanted to make a videotape. Finally, the students needed to decide how they would present the results of this project to the school and local communities.

IN-SCHOOL TASKS

Teaching on the Block—Teacher Attitudes

Interview teachers at a local high school about their beliefs and attitudes concerning block scheduling. If they already conduct classes using the block format, get their reactions to this organization: What do they find to be the most challenging features, and how do they respond to these? Using their responses, reflect upon how you would consider conducting your physical education classes in that particular school.

Teaching on the Block—Teacher Actions

Visit a school that uses a block-scheduling format, and arrange to observe at least one physical education lesson. Complete the following tasks during this visit:

1. Record a timeline of activities as they occur during the class. Include time for dressing, roll taking, the introductory activity, the time in each consequent practical activity, and closure and dressing at the end of the lesson.

2. Make notes within these timelines of what you believe to be the major objective for that segment (i.e., cognitive, affective, psychomotor).

3. Make note of the time within the given lesson during which students are *actively engaged*; that is, to what extent do they have the opportunity to work toward active health objectives?

4. What (if any) work is required for submission from these students? Are they responsible for *producing* anything during class (e.g., completing a worksheet, submitting score sheets, writing a reflective report, recording their fitness work)?

5. Are the students given any homework? If so, describe it.

Reflect on your findings. What sorts of perceptions do you think that students will have about physical education as a legitimate, meaningful, substantive, and engaging subject in the context of their schooling?

Student Vigor During a Block Lesson

Select three students for observation during a block physical education lesson. Watch one student for 2 minutes, and code his or her actions every 10 seconds; that is, watch for 10 seconds, then take 10 seconds to record your decision. After 2 minutes, switch to another student. After the third student, revert to the first. Take account of the times that students spend in the following activities, using the codes listed:

- dressing out (D)
- engaged in other management tasks (roll call, homework collection) (M)
- seated and listening to the teacher concerning cognitive work (e.g., rules, fitness concepts) (L)
- actively engaged in cognitive work (e.g., completing worksheets, participating in a lab) (C)
- actively engaged in physical activity (beyond walking pace) (A)
- waiting for a turn or otherwise not engaged in an activity (W)
- engaged in off-task or noncompliant behavior (O)

Analyze your data using a pie chart, showing the relative percentages of each of these components. Second, make a four-quartile chart, one that shows the relative percentages for your lesson over four equal time periods (e.g., first, second, third, and fourth periods of 22 minutes in a 90-minute lesson)

Comment on these results—in particular, on the allocation of overall time, as well as any time trends you find in your data.

In-Class Debate

You may find participation in this debate a fruitful exercise in examining the issue of project-based learning. Prepare a case either for or against this comment: "Project-based learning is all well and good, but there is no way you can complete all those tasks given the climate of litigation and the whole issue of safety in schools."

Portfolio Suggestions and Artifacts

A Position Statement on Block Scheduling (S6–K3)

Within your philosophy section, present a position statement outlining your attitudes and beliefs concerning block scheduling. Provide also some specific examples of how you would construct a lesson (or unit/season) using the block format.

A Position Statement on Project-Based Learning (S8–D2)

Similar to the exercise above, present as part of your philosophy a position statement outlining your attitudes and beliefs concerning project-based learning. Provide any examples of projects you have seen used in schools (even if they come from areas other than physical education).

Sample Projects (S4–D4, K3, P5, 6)

While acknowledging that project-based learning topics are student initiated, develop templates for two projects that you would like to undertake in a school setting. Take yourself though the process of developing a driving question and a culminating product. What artifacts would you want to see students collect? How would you like to see them documenting their learning? Recall that your role in project-based learning is to provide some scaffolds for student task development, not to to abandon them altogether.

REFLECTION TIME

Now that you have read this chapter, how confident do you feel in

- designing lessons that would actively engage students in meaningful learning experiences over an extended period of time using block scheduling?

- being able to conduct an extended lesson without reducing the demand for quality student work throughout the entire lesson length?

- designing units that involve taking students off campus for activities such as golf, tennis, or rock climbing?

- being able to negotiate with a private activity agency (e.g., an aquatic center) for offering reduced rates to students from your school?

- giving students a choice in developing their own movement projects—can you "let go" from having to be the central authority in content selection?

- supporting students engaged in project-based learning experiences?

REFERENCES

Barron, B. J., Schwartz, D. L., Vye, N. J., Moore, A., Petrosino, A., Zech, L., Bransford, J. D. (1998). Doing with understanding: Lessons from research on problem- and project-based learning. *Journal of Learning Sciences, 7,* 271–311.

Blumenfeld, P. C., Soloway, E., Marx, R. W., Krajcik, J. S., Guzdial, M., & Palincsar, A. (1991). Motivating project-based learning: Sustaining the doing, supporting the learning. *Educational Psychologist, 26* (3 & 4), 369–398.

Bransford, J. D., & Stein, B. S. (1993). *The IDEAL problem solver* (2nd ed.). New York: Freeman.

Brown, A. L., & Campione, J. C. (1994). Guided discovery in a community of learners. In K. McGilly (Ed.), *Classroom lessons: Integrating cognitive theory and classroom practice* (pp. 229–272). Cambridge, MA: MIT Press.

Bukowski, B. J., & D'Antonio Stinson, A. (2000). Physical educators' perceptions of block scheduling in secondary physical education. *Journal of Physical Education, Recreation & Dance, 71* (1), 53–57.

Claxton, D. B., & Bryant, J. G. (1996). Block scheduling: What does it mean for physical education? *Journal of Physical Education, Recreation & Dance, 67* (3), 48–50.

Hynes-Dusel, J. M. (2001). Block scheduling: A catalyst for change in middle and high school physical education. *Research Quarterly for Exercise and Sport, 72,* A–67.

Illescas, C. (1997). Students do science in the field. *The Denver Post*, September 13, 1997. p. A-01.

Rikard, C. L., Banville, D., & Marks, M. (2001). The impact of block scheduling on teaching physical education. Paper presented at the Annual Meeting of the American Educational Research Association. Seattle, WA.

U.S. Department of Education. (1994). *Prisoners of time: Report of the National Education Commission on Time and Learning.* Washington, DC: Author.

Wolk, S. (1994). Project-based learning: Pursuit with a purpose. *Educational Leadership, 52* (3), 42–45.

WEB RESOURCES

The following web link list was generated upon publication of the text; however, over time, the sites may become obsolete if an organization dissolves, discontinues online services, or relocates to a different URL. If a link listed below does not connect, please search for the organization by name.

http://carei.coled.umn.edu/BlockScheduling/BSMain.htm

Includes question-and-answer section, a Listserv, a research report and literature review, as well as links to web sites, ERIC abstracts, how-to guides, and other reference materials.

http://killeenroos.com/link/block.htm

An extensive list of links to block-scheduling issues.

http://college.hmco.com/education/pbl/

This site is designed to allow its visitors to do sustained inquiry on extended problems and projects, get background knowledge on its theory and use in classrooms, and revisit generic teaching concepts.

http://www.iearn-canada.org/guideontheside.html

"The Guide on the Side": An extensive list of project-based learning resources from Canada.

CHAPTER 11

The School-Based Fitness and Sports Club

Scenario

"All right! Let me see it," senior Tayla Bolling shouted to classmates spread out across Belmont High's basketball court.

And, 12 pairs of legs got busy creating rhythmic thunder. Bodies moved forward, back, across, around. Feet pounded out beats and hands slapped chests, thighs, and the floor, sounding like exclamation marks.

Welcome to step. Not as in high-impact aerobics a la Jane Fonda and thong leotards, but as in the attitude-driven formation dancing popular among African-American sororities and fraternities—and the newest version of physical education at Belmont High where workin' it counts as working out.

Hoping to get students to develop lifelong fitness habits, the school allows the after school funky footwork to count as physical education. It's the latest addition to other forms of exercise that also can fulfill the physical education requirement: Tae Kwan Do, Tae-Bo, and modern dance.[1]

Many reading this scenario may consider it to be the beginning of the apocalypse for physical education as we know it, and, indeed, many professionals in the field question whether such activity is as challenging and structured as traditional physical education curriculum offered during school hours. More alarming to these people is the implied answer to this question: If lots of kids opt out of the program what will ultimately happen to the existing physical education in the schools?

Let us put a different spin on this case. As we have explored before, physical education as it currently exists in the schools is dysfunctional! What will ultimately happen *is* a function of the current situation—that many students do not

---

[1]Reprinted courtesy of the *Boston Globe*, May 8, 2000, p. B1.

find physical education inviting, challenging, or structured. The *Boston Globe* article continues:

> *Bolling, who has run track in the past, said she didn't create Belmont's step squad as a way to get out of PE class. But, she said she gets more out of her step work than she ever did from traditional physical education.*
>
> *"I brought it to the athletic director and he said we could do it if we had enough practice time," Bolling said. "So, we tallied the time and found that we practice an hour more a week than regular physical education."* (Reprinted courtesy of the *Boston Globe*, May 8, 2000, p. B1)

One of the key issues that we confront here is the purpose of physical education. As we have read in the earlier chapters of this book, physical education in its present form is often elitist and exclusionary. We will also recall the argument from Tinning and Fitzclarence (1992) that many students are very active during their out-of-school hours but find physical education irrelevant and boring. Somewhere we are missing the link. The students in the step group are motivated, engaged, and indeed empowered. The activity has meaning for them. Consider how effectively this step setting embraces the social bonding, cultural appreciation, challenge, tension release, fitness development, and self-expression that defines meaning for high school students (see Chen, 1998).

A Radical (?) Alternative

This chapter presents the notion of a radical (but not so far-fetched) concept of abandoning the common idea of formalized physical education as we see it and replacing it with a school fitness and sports club. Instead of having regularly scheduled courses, which typically focus on team sports units, we assume the role of resident activity expert and make that expertise available to the school community in the provision of a number of activity options—just as would be offered at the local Y or private health club.

Let us first examine some of the features that seem to make health clubs attractive for their members and compare these features with what we typically see in the school setting. We will focus on the notions of "inviting" and "engaging" as our themes as we explore the community health club setting.

Dress—Getting Ready to Be Active

Westcott (1992) asks us to consider the following question about dressing for activity: "Is it essential to the educational process and the activity experiences of high school students to wear look-alike uniforms?" Participants in health clubs wear clothing that is functional and comfortable. Certainly, different activities require different clothing—whereas it is not appropriate to wear baggy pants, chains, and other loose clothing in rock climbing, for many activities dress is of no consequence. In the school setting, we tend to spend inordinate amounts of time being concerned with students' dress. Is it perhaps that we miss the point and should be more concerned with what we are asking them to do *after* they have dressed? Westcott has also noted that when youth do attend commercial fitness programs, they indeed do wear appropriate attire for activity.

Facility for Changing—Prior to and in Recovery from Exercise

Health clubs provide facilities that are attractive and secure. They provide privacy and allow people to get back to normal in a pleasant environment, with hot showers, hair dryers, and well-lighted mirrors. Health clubs also do not put a time limit on how long it takes to shower and change.

Given that appearance is a key issue in youth, it seems counterproductive to offer students facilities for dressing that they find uninviting and even unhygienic. Although it is acknowledged that in a 45-minute period excessive time cannot be allocated for dress and recovery, we often exacerbate the problem by continually hassling students to "get wet, get dry, and get out." Schools that offer block scheduling are less likely to suffer from "dress stress," but students' responses to dressing and showering are not going to change unless the environment is respectable. We should at the very least provide some privacy for students in the form of curtains.

Choice of Activity

One of the great attractions of fitness clubs is that most of them offer a variety of equipment related to muscular strength and cardiovascular endurance. They also offer a number of activity options—including aerobics classes in various forms, pool-based activities, and rock climbing walls. Tables 11.1 and 11.2 provide examples from one health club that show the potential diversity of activity offerings. The underlying feature of these sessions is that while they all have an activity focus, there is enough diversity to suit different consumers.

Choice of Time

One can see from Tables 11.1 and 11.2 that different activities are scheduled around the customers' work schedules. However, people (and teenagers, too) choose to be active at certain periods of the day, depending on what precedes and follows exercise. With an extended time format and repeated opportunities, such

Table 11.1   Schedule for the Group Fitness Room

	Monday	Tuesday	Wednesday	Thursday	Friday
6:00 A.M.	Step		Kickboxing		Step/Hi-lo combo
9:10 A.M.	Step and tone		Body toning		Variation step
10:30 A.M.		Yoga basics		Yoga basics	
2:20 P.M.	Step, butts and guts				
5:30 P.M.	Body toning	Kickboxing	Step	Step and tone	Body toning
6:30 P.M.	Funk for ALL	Variation step	Yoga/Pilates	Beginners' aerobics	

Table 11.2   Schedule for the Aqua Exercise Pool

	Monday	Tuesday	Wednesday	Thursday	Friday
8:00 A.M.	Tone and stretch		Low intensity circuits		Combo class
9:30 A.M.		Low intensity		Cardio and toning	
10:30 A.M.	Low intensity		Tone and stretch		Aqua circuits
1:00 P.M.	Senior water		Senior water		Senior water
4:30 P.M.		Shallow water fun		Advanced circuits	
5:30 P.M.	Advanced circuits	Advanced water	Instructor's choice	Water variations	

as offering two aerobics classes a day, students may miss one and come to the other. Giving students different schedule options can only enhance their potential for involvement.

Participation Focus

Health clubs emphasize elective participation—most of the time spent in a health club is spent in exercise. In physical education (although some class man-

Fitness clubs offer a wide variety of activities

agement is necessary to provide a safe learning environment) considerable time is often wasted. Indeed, few school programs reach the Surgeon General's recommendation to spend 50% of lesson time in moderate to vigorous levels of physical activity.

Choice of Instructor

Fitness clubs typically employ a number of professionals within the same area. Participants often prefer one style of exercise leader to another and attend sessions accordingly. Although that option is less feasible in a school with fewer teachers, repeated sessions with different teachers is something to be considered.

The Structure of the School Fitness and Sports Club—What Does It Look Like?

Table 11.3 provides the schedule for one week at Tiger High Fitness and Sports Club (FSC). As can be seen from this table, there are several differences from the typical physical education schedule.

Extended Time—It's Not Open Only During School Time

The school FSC is not just open during school hours; it starts before other classes and extends its hours after regular classes end. This schedule not only makes the FSC more accessible to more students, but also allows for attendance by other faculty and workers in the school.

Given this arrangement, there may be a time during the day when no activity is scheduled, but still some areas of the FSC may be available for self-directed activities such as jogging or pick-up basketball (see open gym and the walking club in Table 11.3).

The teacher's workday is also affected by this schedule. Given that the FSC is open longer than the regular school, one teacher may work the early morning shift and finish by 1 P.M. (see, for example, Ms. Smith's schedule in Table 11.3). Likewise, another teacher may not arrive at school until 11 A.M., but will be on site until 5 P.M. These teachers may also change their schedules according to other aspects of their employment—such as coaching duties. A teacher involved with football during the fall semester may work the early schedule during August through December and be finished by lunch. In this way, the teacher has the afternoon to prepare for practice, scout, and do other coaching-related tasks. Likewise, this same teacher in the spring may work only the afternoon sessions.

Opportunity for Other School Community Members to Participate

The FSC is open by its nature to other members beyond students. Among the biggest factors affecting high school physical education during the 1980s and 1990s were continued job cuts and reductions in time requirements. The extended opening hours and the voluntary nature of the FSC's membership allows physical activity to take a prominent place in the school's mission—by catering for all students all the time.

The school FSC with an active membership of teachers and students can only promote the status of the physical education staff as experts and can only serve to promote activity participation. Recall the significant drop in participation as students progress in age through their teen years; the FSC offers many attractive participation options.

Accommodating Required Physical Education Courses

The FSC concept does not preclude requiring students to complete a formal course for graduation credit. Indeed, the fitness club embraces this idea. The required course is but one of a number of offerings during a given day. The required course may actually act as a prerequisite for further courses or activities. For example, students may be required to have a passing grade in the required course before they are eligible to use the weight room as a self-directed activity.

Table 11.3   Weekly Schedule for Fitness and Sports Club

Time	Monday	Tuesday	Wednesday	Thursday	Friday
7:00	Aerobics—SM	Kickboxing—BR	Aerobics—SM	Kickboxing—BR	Aerobics—SM
7:30	↓	↓	↓	↓	↓
8:00	Wellness—SM	Wellness—SM	Wellness—SM	Wellness—SM	Wellness—SM
8:30					
9:00	↓	↓	↓	↓	↓
9:30	Sv. Learn—SM	Sv. Learn—SM	Sv. Learn—SM	Sv. Learn—SM	Sv. Learn—SM
10:00					
10:30	↓	↓	↓	↓	↓
11:00	Open Gym—GR Open wgts—BR	Open Gym—GR Open wgts—BR	Open Gym—GR Open wgts—BR	Open Gym—GR Open wgts—BR	Open Gym—GR Open wgts—BR
11:30	Golf unit—GR Open wgts—BR	Golf unit—GR Open wgts—BR	Golf unit—GR Open wgts—BR	Golf unit—GR Open wgts—BR	Golf unit—GR Open wgts—BR
12:00					
12:30	↓	Walking club—SM	Walking club—SM	Walking club—SM	Walking club—SM
1:00	Walking club—SM	Walking club—SM	Walking club—SM	Walking club—SM	Walking club—SM
1:30	Wellness—BR	Wellness—BR	Wellness—BR	Wellness—BR	Wellness—BR
2:00					
2:30	↓	↓	↓	↓	↓
3:00	Open wgts—BR	Open wgts—BR	Open wgts—BR	Open wgts—BR	Open wgts—BR
3:30	Open wgts—BR	Open wgts—BR	Open wgts—BR	Open wgts—BR	Open wgts—BR
4:00	Intramurals—GR	Intramurals—GR	Intramurals—GR	Open gym—GR	Open gym—GR
4:30	Intramurals—GR	Intramurals—GR	Intramurals—GR	Open gym—GR	Open gym—GR

BR = Mr. Brown; GR = Ms. Green; SM = Ms. Smith; Sv. Learn = Service learning PE program

What Is Offered?

The activities that are offered in the FSC are limited only by the human and physical resources available in a school, as well as the creativity of the physical education staff in their scheduling. The beauty of the structure of the FSC is that it allows for scheduling a number of options. These include not only required physical education classes, but also elective physical education classes, volitional fitness activities, and self-directed options. Within these combinations, we can divide the offerings into four main areas. Table 11.4 provides some examples of these categories.

Underpinning all of these options, however, are ongoing opportunities for testing and self-testing. Recall that our agenda is to create fitness-educated and independent learners and get them to a level where they can solve their own activity and fitness problems.

Outside Opportunities

It should not be expected that teachers within one school be competent in all areas of health and fitness content. As a result, the offerings at a school FSC will most likely be those with which teachers have good content knowledge. Nevertheless, this condition does not necessarily eliminate all other activity options. Teachers in a school may also investigate links with health clubs outside school, allowing students to attend classes in which the physical education department lacks either facilities (e.g., spin cycling or water aerobics) or content knowledge

Table 11.4   Activity Offerings in a Sports and Fitness Club

Course Focus	Sample Activities	Most Likely Offering Type
Knowledge-based courses	Lifetime physical activity education	Required course for state graduation
Health-focus courses	CPR and first aid Nutrition and weight control	Elective classes
Fitness activities	Aerobics Weight training In-line skating	Elective courses Voluntary Self-directed
Sport activities	Frisbee Volleyball Golf Badminton Basketball	Elective courses Voluntary Intramurals
Adventure programs	Rope course Rock climbing Kayaking Camping and hiking	Elective courses

The cardio theater may motivate students to use fitness equipment

(e.g., kickboxing). It should also be noted that the committed teacher *would* be motivated to seek out opportunities for professional development so that he or she may introduce these new activities into the school-based program.

In the cases where students participate in outside agencies, the main concern is that students gain a worthwhile learning experience. In addition, there is a need for accountability. Students who wish to include outside components need to provide evidence of their learning and improvement in activity and skill levels. In these cases, a useful method is to develop a learning contract—not a new concept in education. These learning contracts can indeed be quite rigorous and would include the following items:

- a rationale and justification for this outside activity
- a list of formal knowledge and skill goals for the experience
- an activity log of all dates and exercise sessions
- testing dates with validated test records
- interviews with the instructor(s)—to learn more about how they became an expert in the area

Students who take this route should also make a formal presentation of their learning. Consider the step group that we read about in the opening scenario—what better way for them to present evidence of not only their skill learning, but also of their fitness development than through a formal presentation?

Each month, a presentation day may be scheduled at the FSC, when students who complete outside projects (not just those taking off-campus fitness courses, but all students involved in project-based learning) present their materials and data. Students scheduled for formal physical education classes, as well as administrators and other school faculty who may be interested, attend these presentations.

Accountability

So, how do we hold students accountable for their participation in an FSC? Accountability can be defined as an exchange of rewards or grades for performance. If students' attendance and participation in the FSC is purely volitional and not for grade, then there is no accountability. All one is doing is offering a service for continued activity options that promote healthy lifestyles. If students choose to take up that opportunity, they will experience health-enhancing physical activity. To require students to attend defeats the entire purpose.

If, however, students are participating as part of a required or elective course, then we need to involve authentic assessment instruments as part of their program. Several assessment tasks are included in the content chapters of this book (Chapters 6–9) that suggest numerous ways to gather assessment data on students.

There are, however, examples of accountability in some of the voluntary activity offerings. For example, students may be required to reach eligibility standards in order to participate in field trips and excursions. For instance, a student (or a member of the school's faculty) would not be able to attend a field-based rock-climbing trip without completing a certain number of hours on the school's climbing wall and demonstrating ability to perform a series of belaying skills. Likewise, students would not be permitted to participate in a snorkeling trip unless they have demonstrated certain competence in the school swimming pool. Students are held accountable to reach desired standards. Although it may be possible for them to attend some sessions but not others, they are the ones who choose how far they wish to participate in an activity. This is strongly aligned with our notion of giving students choices and empowering them.

The School-Based Walking Club

Walking has become very popular in recent times as a health-enhancing activity. Indeed, according to the National Sporting Goods Association, exercise walking is the most popular sports or recreational activity among Americans aged 7 and older. By 2000, over 77 million participated in walking, a figure that represented a 25% increase over the decade of the 1990s.

It is not difficult to imagine why walking is so popular. Location is usually no barrier (you can walk almost anywhere that it is safe), it is cheap (the only cost is a comfortable pair of shoes), and it requires no formal training. Further, and perhaps this is a significant attraction of walking, it can be a significant social experience. Friends and couples will frequently walk together in a daily combination of camaraderie and exercise.

The boom in exercise walking came about in the early 1990s, when many people found jogging and other more intense aerobic exercise to be aversive. The discovery that a 150-pound person walking at 3.5 miles per hour on flat ground burns about 300 calories an hour (or 350 calories an hour at a 4-mph pace) meant that walking came to be considered a significant and legitimate health-enhancing exercise. Further, walking has so many natural modifications that it allows total flexibility for the participants. Either walking faster or using the upper body in a more active way can easily increase intensity. Walking up hills can also help increase the number of calories burned.

As noted, although walking can be a self-directed activity, one of its major attractions is the social element. The increase in the popularity of walking as a form of exercise has led to concurrent growth in the popularity of walking clubs. Many of these are simply informal groups of people who get together to walk, but there are also more organized groups who have regular meetings, attend walking events, and even give out certificates or awards for attaining mileage marks or other goals. For example, the American Volkssport Association (www.ava.org) is a nonprofit organization of walking clubs whose specific mission is to promote health, fun, and fellowship through noncompetitive walking and other sporting events for everyone. Clubs host weekend events, with the members selecting interesting trails and walking routes for everyone to enjoy.

It makes sense, then, to align a school fitness and sports club with a school-based walking club. Promoting a walking club as part of the school setting offers an appealing option for students and faculty who may not be attracted to the more intense aerobic activities, such as step or aerobic dance classes. Again, the social component cannot be underestimated.

Developing the Walking Club

In setting up the school walking club, the first thing you need is a venue for walking. Obviously, having a series of walking tracks with different pathways, routes, and distances helps to increase the variety and therefore the attraction to the club. Some tracks may be more uphill, or at least undulating, while others may be more level.

If only a school track is available, it is still possible to provide some variety. In this case, you provide an intensity system with, perhaps, color codes for different lap speeds. The red circuit may involve a lap time of 4.5 minutes, while the green level may be quicker at 4 minutes per lap. The blue circuit may be quickest of all, with a walking speed of 3.75 minutes per lap.

Other features that need to be considered when developing a walking club include variety, regularity, affiliation, record keeping, incentive programs, and annual school walking events.

Variety

When designing a series of walking tracks, you should vary not only the pathways, routes, times, and distances, but also the intensity of the walks. Walkers should be encouraged to vary the days of high-intensity work with days of lower-intensity work to help prevent boredom and lead to faster improvements in fitness and health.

Regularity

A walking club must have regular meetings. People are more likely to walk if there is a consistent time in their day that they can allocate to walking.

Affiliation

It is critical for the success of any walking club for its members to feel some common purpose. Indeed, perhaps the greatest attraction offered by formal walking clubs throughout the world is the chance to meet other walkers and build some support system for walking. Further, many walking clubs align some post-walk activity into their exercise program. These can range from breakfast after a morning walk, to picnic lunches after walks in a forest or park. Some walking clubs also develop a specific identity. Most have names, and many produce identity articles, such as hats or T-shirts.

Walking clubs provide the opportunity to build support systems

Records

Perhaps fewer than half the people who walk for exercise keep formal records of their activity. Nevertheless, one feature of walking clubs is that they put into place a habit of goal setting and monitoring of performance. Improvement will tend to plateau if the walker maintains the same walking distance and cadence, but formal record keeping will help accelerate improvement. The record data need not be extensive but should provide a stimulus for the walker to become more knowledgeable about potential health gains. A sample weekly walking log is provided in Table 11.5.

Table 11.5   Weekly Walking Log

Week of: _____

Sunday (Target) mi/km: time: speed: notes:	**Monday** (Target) mi/km: time: speed: notes:
Tuesday (Target) mi/km: time: speed: notes:	**Wednesday** (Target) mi/km: time: speed: notes:
Thursday (Target) mi/km: time: speed: notes:	**Friday** (Target) mi/km: time: speed: notes:
Saturday (Target) mi/km: time: speed: notes:	**Week Total** mi/km: time: speed: notes:

Goals:

Progress made:

Ideas for next week:

Incentive Program

Keeping formal walking records also allows for the development of an incentive program. Walkers can strive to earn certificates or awards for attaining mileage marks or achieving other goals. These goals may include milestones such as walking for 10, 20, or 30 consecutive days or reaching distance targets (e.g., 50 or 100 miles).

Annual School Walking Event

A school-based walking club may choose to organize and host a walking event. This event may be a simple heart-health awareness event, a fund-raiser, or a charity event. Although the main objective of the walk is to promote walking as a health-enhancing activity, a well-conducted event can also promote the entire physical education program.

If it is not possible for the members of a walking club to host an event, other possibilities include acting as volunteers for major walks sponsored by other organizations, such as the March of Dimes, Walk America, or the American Heart Walk.

In-School Tasks

Site Visit

Arrange to visit a nearby high school and take a walk around its facilities. Consider places within the school grounds and in the immediate neighborhood where you could develop a walking trail. What factors would you need to include, particularly as they relate to

- accessibility—how easy is it to get to the walking trail?
- safety—are you near busy roads or areas of potential crime?
- variety—are there woods, already established pathways, or other geographical features you could include?
- aesthetics—how visually pleasing is the route you have chosen; would it be a pleasant walk?
- distance—how long would your route be?

PORTFOLIO SUGGESTIONS AND ARTIFACTS

As the physical educator in a high school, you are considered to be the resident health fitness expert. As a service to the students, staff, and faculty, you and your colleagues have decided to make your expertise available in a fun and motivating way—by starting a fitness club for your school. There are no dues and no membership requirements other than having a school ID.

Fitness Club Promotional Materials (S5–P3: S9–P1)

Design a flyer announcing, describing, and promoting your new fitness club for faculty, staff, and students. Include details of

- a catchy name for your club
- objectives—who is this club meant to service?
- opening times
- classes or activities available
- facilities (don't forget to include outdoor areas, pools, weight rooms)
- existing equipment
- your role, service and credentials

You may also want to produce a PowerPoint slide show that could be presented to the board of education, administrators, faculty, and parents outlining your new club.

A Fitness Club Schedule (S4–P4)

Design a sample outline showing how you would schedule activities in a school-based fitness center for one month. In your schedule, provide full details of the following:

- teacher-directed activities (e.g., aerobics, weight training, rock wall)
- self-directed activities (e.g., jogging, 3-on-3 basketball)
- courses available for school credit (e.g., 9th grade required or elective course in golf)

A Fitness Club Budget (S6–P4)

You and your colleagues applied for and have been awarded a $2,500 grant by the American College of Sports Medicine and Healthy People 2010 to outfit your new school fitness club. Exactly how would you spend this $2,500? Include details and a justification for the purchase of each item.

REFLECTION TIME

Now that you have read this chapter, how confident do you feel in

- being able to sell the concept of a fitness club to school administrators?
- your ability to design a workable timetable for the running of a sport and fitness club?
- your ability to market a sport and fitness club concept to students who have already achieved their physical education required credit?
- your ability to design, promote, and administer a school walking club?

REFERENCES

Chen, A. (1998). Meaningfulness in physical education: A description of high school students' conceptions. *Journal of Teaching in Physical Education, 17*, 285–306.

Iknoian, T. (1995). *Fitness walking.* Champaign, IL: Human Kinetics.

Jacobson, J. (1999). *Healthwalk to fitness.* Levittown, NY: HeartFit Books.

Tinning, R., & Fitzclarence, L. (1992). Postmodern youth culture and the crisis in Australian secondary school physical education. *Quest, 44*, 287–303.

Westcott, W. (1992). High school physical education: A fitness professional's perspective. *Quest, 44*, 342–351.

WEB RESOURCES

The following web link list was generated upon publication of the text; however, over time, the sites may become obsolete if an organization dissolves, discontinues online services, or relocates to a different URL. If a link listed below does not connect, please search for the organization by name.

http://www.global-fitness.com/

An online guide to healthy living and optimal fitness. Particularly useful is an extensive listing (by state) of more than 16,000 health clubs in the United States. Also included are tips on how to choose a health club that can meet your needs.

http://walking.about.com/

A comprehensive site with links to many issues about walking, including a beginner's guide, selecting shoes, weather tips, and walking off weight. It even has a link to an ultrasonic dog repellent!

CHAPTER 12

The Place of Technology in Physical Education

Scenario

Mr. Jensen's 11th grade physical education class is planning a weekend canoeing trip. They will be paddling to an island that lies in the middle of a nearby lake and camping for two nights. An accomplished craftsman, Mr. Jensen is enlisting the help of four students in helping him build three new canoes. These students are part of the construction team for that class. Meanwhile, four other students are making a video on how to put up the tents the students will be using during the trip. Another team is completing a student-assisted learning package on the Internet that teaches wilderness first aid. These students are from the medical team of the class. Four more students, who comprise the reporting and promotions team, are designing a web page and taking digital photographs of the events leading up to the trip. Finally, the fitness team is using a set of heart rate monitors to design a canoe training program that all students complete three times per week as part of this course project.

We can all recall some use of technology in our schooling. For me, that started in the 1st grade, with a slate and chalk pencil that we used instead of a paper notebook. I guess this could be called technology, because we could instantly erase any errors, just as we now hit the delete button on the computer. That progressed to the use of color television by the time I had reached high school, and the advent of video (although none of us had them in our homes) was quite exciting. When I began teaching I taught a 9th grade gymnastics class in which I used reel-to-reel videotape. Each Friday students would perform their skills on a selected apparatus. After the routines were all recorded, we went to the library and completed peer evaluations.

With the technological innovations that have occurred in the last five years, we would probably be safe in suggesting that the biggest change in education in the past decade has been the use of technology in schools. Indeed, early in the

1990s the United States Department of Education projected that the centerpiece of education by the year 2000 would be interactive video.

When investigating technology sites from vendors and software producers, we see a plethora of materials available for science and social studies, but in this mix physical education is not forgotten. Indeed, there is now significant interest in the use of technology in our subject area, and we now have specialist books and conferences dedicated to the use of technology in physical education.

The purpose of this chapter is to provide some ideas about how technology can become part of the arsenal of tools available to the physical education teacher. It is not the purpose of this chapter to provide you with the skills to be able to use the technology. Nevertheless, at the end of this chapter are listed several resources, both electronic and paper, that you can consult for assistance.

Rather than describe each of the pieces of technology and how they can be used in physical education, this chapter will examine the uses of technology in the life of the physical educator. The following topics will be examined:

- managing teachers' roles—using technology in noninstructional contexts to save time, organize tasks, and enhance prospects for professional development

- enhancing students' cognitive learning—how technology is used in many areas of school to promote students' understanding of content and concepts and to promote problem solving

- enhancing students' skill learning—how the use of videotape and other forms of feedback can help students become more skillful in a number of games, sports, and activities

- enhancing students' health and fitness levels—how technology allows students to better monitor their performance, set more appropriate goals, and improve their fitness

- showcasing students' learning—how many high school students have used technology to work on projects and to make substantive presentation of their work

Managing Teachers' Roles

The world of the physical educator does not begin and end in the classroom or the gym. Indeed, many of the tasks that occupy a lot of a teacher's day are related to administration, such as keeping records and attending meetings. In addition, teachers in exemplary programs also spend considerable time promoting physical education within their school and community and acting as advocates for their subject. Many teachers are also engaged in professional learning—by taking courses at universities or by correspondence, attending and presenting at meetings, or reading professional literature.

Technology can assist these teachers in two ways. First, many of the mundane tasks that take up a teacher's time can be made less arduous through the use of various technologies. Second, software applications can help launch messages from teachers to the wider community. In this section, we will examine some tasks teachers need to perform and how technologies can help.

Attendance

Irrespective of the mechanisms through which teachers take roll, whether through the formal calling of names or gathering reports from student leaders, attendance data need to be recorded. Most frequently a paper grade book is used, so that at the end of a particular period teachers can tally an individual's absences and tardiness. However, through the use of a simple spreadsheet, a teacher need only record those who are absent and then write a formula that will tally the number of absences. In this way, the computer can collate and sort the data according to date, student name, or by the number of absences.

An even more sophisticated means of recording attendance is through the use of a personal digital assistant (PDA). A PDA can provide a choice of options from preprogrammed software, recording, for example, an absence (the computer will also record the data from its internal clock) or student lateness (recording the time the student arrived and, depending on the teacher's programming skills, the number of minutes late). These data can then be downloaded into a desktop computer or printed from the PDA.

Heads Up—What Is a PDA?

A PDA is a personal digital assistant: a small hand-held device for personal information management that extends the functionalities of a desktop computer to a mobile environment. A PDA can be connected to a desktop computer, and the information between the two can be exchanged.

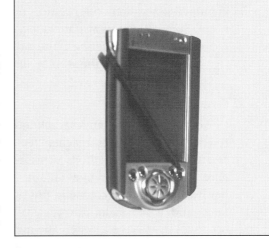

Given that these data are quickly retrieved, teachers may also use word-processing programs that have "form fields" to send messages to parents concerning student attendance. One simply scripts a letter with the regular fields (e.g., name and address) and enters the appropriate number of absences.

All of these formats streamline the administrative tasks for teachers. Likewise, depending on school policy, a teacher may compile a monthly file of attendance and e-mail that to the administrative center of the school or perhaps to a school counselor.

Locker Administration

In schools that allocate lockers to students, particularly those that are shared, teachers need to keep accurate records of the students and their respective form of locker security. It is not difficult to produce a spreadsheet with records of student names, locker number, combination, and issue and return dates. These data can be sorted from these spreadsheets, allowing teachers to easily retrieve information at the end of a specific period, when lockers need to be reallocated. As with attendance, simple form letters containing the students' names and locker numbers can be prepared, and print copies can be sent to students reminding them of their responsibilities.

Calendars

As part of good planning, many teachers keep calendars of events in paper form. Important dates may relate to grading periods, holidays, testing dates, and meetings. Electronic calendars allow not only for the recording of these important dates, but also for the placement of icons onto specific dates to act as visual reminders. The calendars can be searched for particular events and can be programmed to send reminder notices perhaps two or three days before a particular event. Some calendars also include a daily planner, in which teachers can schedule appointments, meetings, and other tasks. Many sites on the Internet offer free calendar software that can be directly downloaded.

Grading

One of the major challenges teachers of physical education face is grading. Unfortunately in many cases, teachers feel that grading "takes too long" and teachers resort to simplistic methods of assessment that merely reflect attendance and effort. Neither of these gives an authentic account of what the student knows or has learned during a course in physical education. If we value authentic assessment and if we adopt the idea of following the NASPE standards, then it behooves us to have a systematic method of collecting data on students' performance and of recording the results of those performances.

Computerized grading sheets are a beginning point for recording data from students' assessments. Furthermore, through the formula function within a spreadsheet, all data can be recorded (whether they are formative or summative) in raw score terms. In this case, the teacher does not have to manually convert tests with different weights, but simply writes a formula that recognizes various weightings and calculates a student's score.

Teachers can have separate files for different classes, using the spreadsheet formula for summary statistics (e.g., assignment averages or class averages). Through the use of other formulas, teachers can identify the number of students that reached a specific competency standard or a particular set of objectives (skill, cognitive, or affective). These can provide an indication of the relative success of the program.

Technology can be used not only for recording grades but also during assessments themselves. The use of PDAs allows a teacher to record a level of performance according to a particular rubric for each student in the class. For example, to assess student performance in refereeing during a basketball game, the teacher may have identified four characteristics a student official should be able to demonstrate: knowledge of the rules, effective use of the whistle with clear and accurate signals, attention to the game, and moving to the correct position on the floor. A simple rubric of (1) *always*, (2) *mostly*, (3) *sometimes*, (4) *rarely*, and (5) *never* can be developed to score these criteria. The teacher then selects the student's level of achievement and records this on the software. These data are then available to download or read directly from the screen.

In a more formative assessment context, the teacher may set up a computer work station where students can enter the results of peer evaluations of classmates performing skills as player or official. From here, the data are saved, and the students rotate through roles. The summary information is then available for students to retrieve and examine.

PDAs allow teachers to collect multiple data

Physical Education Advocacy

As mentioned, one characteristic of good teachers in quality physical education programs is the extent to which they become advocates of physical activity in general and physical education within the school. In this role, teachers may use desktop publishing software to generate newsletters, advertisements for upcoming elective courses, or other promotional materials. They may also create invitations to open days, such as the finals of a sport education season, or to presentations of student portfolios from project-based learning units.

> ### Heads Up— Public Domain
>
> Most commercial software is copyrighted, so it is illegal to make copies. Public domain software, however, is usually created by someone with a particular interest in a topic. That programmer then donates the software to the public. In this case, copying and sharing are legal.

Given the easy access to public domain clip art and various presentation software, teachers can easily distribute materials in a professionally presented format. There is an abundance of sites offering free clip art on the World Wide Web.

For promotions within school, teachers may create videotapes of students' work for broadcast on a school television network. One creative teacher in Ohio, for example, has produced a weekly Sportscenter, where he edits "plays of the week" from the various sport education seasons that are being conducted during physical education. These features are televised through the school on its in-house broadcasting system.

For a more extensive way of marketing a program, teachers can develop a web page. Images can be collected with either digital cameras or by scanning processed photographs and then uploaded to the school or district server. In this way, the latest news can be presented to the wider community, messages can be distributed, and other positive features of the physical education curriculum can be showcased.

> ### Heads Up—Listservs
>
> A listserv is an e-mail announcement and discussion forum where people post and respond to messages on an electronic community bulletin board. The other function of a listserv is to distribute information regarding meetings, conferences, and presentations.

With the advent of the Internet, and particularly the development of a number of listservs, teachers now have a more immediate and convenient access to materials, ideas, and resources they can use for their own professional development. Any teacher with access to electronic mail can become part of a listserv.

The Internet can also foster professional development. Several colleges and universities around the United States offer advanced degrees through distance learning. Other organizations, such as the Cooper Institute, offer continuing education units electronically. Furthermore, the Internet provides an extensive source of information regarding numerous topics that relate specifically to the physical education teacher: health, wellness, fitness, and various sports.

Lesson Planning

Technology can also help teachers in their lesson planning. First, there are several Internet sources that provide ideas and tips; two especially useful sites are PE Central and PE Links4U. Second, desktop publishing programs can help teachers organize their lesson plans and print them in easily usable form.

> ### *Heads Up—HyperStudio*
>
> HyperStudio is a multimedia authoring program allowing users to create their own multimedia projects and presentations. The authoring system offers the ability to bring together text, sound, graphics, and video.

A more sophisticated approach is to have these lesson plans tagged as part of a database where they may be retrieved through a particular search term. Of course, this requires the teacher to have skills in such software technologies as HyperStudio.

Enhancing Student Cognitive Learning

One of the biggest challenges for teachers of any subject area is to promote students' cognitive learning. Of course there are many exciting and innovative ways to do so that do not use technology, but technology has allowed the delivery of instruction to be particularly stimulating. Further, with advances in computer software technology, more and more students are accessing interactive applications either from commercially packaged programs or those available on the Internet.

Videotape and DVD

One of the most popular forms of information presentation technology is the videotape. There are many commercially available (albeit expensive) videos that

> ### *Heads Up—Using Video Successfully*
>
> - Preview programs and applications for suitability.
> - Have materials ready to start at the appropriate place.
> - Show only the sections relevant to instructional topic.
> - Use projection systems for large classes.

teachers can use to present information to students. These videos offer content that is more lifelike and animated. When applied to the cognitive dimensions of physical education, most of us would think of various aspects of physiology that can be presented using videos. However, videos can also be used to introduce new concepts of games, learning how to referee a particular sport, learning some strategy from a game, or observing high-level performance.

Of course, the teacher does not have to rely on commercially prepared videos to get value from this technology. Provided that copyright laws are followed, and depending on the protocols, procedures, and expectations of one's school and administrative authorities, materials recorded directly from television can provide other sources of learning resources. Video not only depicts live action, but also allows the teacher to pause and rewind the tapes to highlight specific points.

Of course, teachers can also produce their own videotapes.

A more recent innovation in audiovisual presentation is the DVD (digital versatile disc). The resolution of these CD-ROM discs is particularly high quality and material can be searched more easily and accessed more quickly. In addition, DVDs can be played through a computer that has a DVD drive installed.

Heads Up—What Is DVD?

DVD is a new medium that is an advancement on the audio CD. DVD allows for digital images to be recorded, so that the CD-ROM can be used to view movies or other educational programs.

Computer-Assisted Instruction

One of the major innovations in recent years has been the development of computer-assisted instruction. With advances in technology, computer-assisted instruction has progressed from simply clicking yes or no buttons to highly interactive, student driven sequences of learning materials. A particular benefit of computer-assisted instruction is that it provides for unlimited practice, review, and remediation.

The basis of computer-assisted instruction is to provide feedback to questions immediately after the student gives an answer. Again, with the increased sophistication of computer-assisted instruction, that response has progressed from providing a simple "correct" or "incorrect" response to providing a demonstration and maybe even an explanation of why the student's answer was incorrect in the first place. The more sophisticated computer-assisted instruction programs also allow the student to navigate and search various editions of the program. Further, they allow the student to enter the information stream at a variety of points, rather than having to follow a predetermined path.

In addition to the extensive availability of computer-assisted instruction programs for health, wellness, and other physiology topics, there is also an increasing number of programs relating to the skills and concepts of sport. For example, one program shows students how to score ten-pin bowling (see http://www.pesoftware.com/fitware/software/bowl.html).

Internet Projects

In the past, students have gone to the library to search books, encyclopedias, dictionaries, and other reference materials as part of their project work. Nowadays, much of this can be done from computer terminals. The advent of the Internet and the World Wide Web has significantly increased students' access to information and promoted their capacity to learn new skills. The following scenario provides one example of the power of this resource.

Three 9th grade students are studying a section on heart health as part of their wellness project. At one web site from a renowned medical school, they are watching a video of a working heart and even creating their own specific heart problems. The students are seeing a working heart with a dynamic chart that illustrates heart efficiency. By clicking on a fat-blocked heart, they watch the heart's efficiency drop dramatically. Intently engaged in the process now, the three decide to click on the aorta to see an enlarged view of a healthy and a fat-clogged aorta. Next they click on the clogged aorta and receive a written description of how the heart got this way and its potential impact on the owner. The students take notes and copy the picture into the notebook that is written into the program. When they are done, the students download and print the notes. (McLean, 1996)

Students using the Internet

Despite its clear appeal, the World Wide Web also presents the challenge of validating the information garnered from it. Teachers do need to spend time helping their students identify reliable sources of information and to critique the information they get from the Internet.

Teachers may also spend time helping students design their searches, a process that can be frustrating given the vast array of information on the web. Indeed, while the Internet has been described as "bringing the world into the classroom," searching for relevant sites can be particularly time-consuming. In fact, a text has been published that aims specifically to give teachers ideas to help students maximize their efficiency in using the World Wide Web (see Hall & Leigh, 2000). In addition, several university libraries have begun to create web pages of links to Internet resources for physical education.

Enhancing Student Skill Learning

When learning a new physical skill, one first needs to understand what a skillful performance looks like. Of particular advantage is to have an idea of the mechanics and of the sequence of skill segments. In many cases, a teacher is able to demonstrate a skill at a level that students can then copy and practice. In other cases, the teacher may enlist a student in the class who is competent enough to demonstrate a skill. Technology allows us to take visual presentation of skills to a new level.

Using Video to Model Performance

The advent of video has been a boon to many teachers as they help students learn new skills. For example, students can watch a game they have never played before in order to get an idea of how the game is organized, what roles players take, and what skills are involved. Indeed, there are many professionally produced instructional videotapes for a number of sports. Several publishing companies have developed instructional videos that demonstrate skills, highlight key technical points, and give examples of common errors.

The advantage of the video over a live demonstration is that it can be rewound and reviewed a number of times, and the pause button and slow motion features allow for more detailed analysis. If professionally produced videotapes for a particular sport are not available (or are too expensive), there still exists the possibility of recording games from television. Although these clips will not provide commentary about how to achieve skills, they at least provide models of performance available for analysis. Nevertheless, this advantage is metered by the content knowledge of the teacher and his or her ability to identify key learning cues in the first instance.

Providing Feedback

Once students start practicing, they need feedback concerning their own performance in order to improve. Given the remarkable drop in price of video cameras and camcorders, the potential of using this technology to help students improve their performance is significant.

When using video as a form of feedback, teachers can choose from several methods. Table 12.1 provides examples of the different arrangements teachers can use to implement videotaping.

A newer piece of technology is the digital camera. Although these cameras provide only still images, they allow very convenient and immediate feedback to students. The digital camera enables the teacher to take a photograph and almost instantly show a student his or her performance on a particular skill. Provided that the teacher focuses on a specific cue as part of the critique, this form of feedback can be invaluable.

Students can use videotape as a form of feedback

One further advantage of the digital camera is that the images can be either discarded or stored electronically for later reference (i.e., for use in student projects or for formative assessments). More expensive digital cameras have large

Table 12.1   Organizational Options for Incorporating Video as Feedback

Option	Videotaping	Feedback
1	Teacher videotapes selected students.	Whole class watches the tape as the teacher reviews performances.
2	Teacher videotapes selected students.	Students watch the tape and complete their own analysis using a checklist or an assessment rubric.
3	A group of students is allocated the camera, which they use to videotape themselves on a teacher-determined skill.	Students view the tape at a workstation, and the teacher provides specific feedback.
4	A group of students is allocated the camera, which they use to videotape themselves on a self-selected skill.	Students complete peer or self-evaluations.

LCD screens and can store images on a $3\frac{1}{2}$- inch floppy disk. Here, students can record their own disk of pictures and return the camera to the teacher without spending time downloading those images to a desktop computer.

Showcasing Student Work

An underlying theme of this book is that we need to make a radical move away from the idea that assessment in physical education is based on attendance and participation. We have been provided with national benchmarks and expectations for student performance, but even more, we need to give students the opportunity to showcase their work and to become advocates of physical activity for themselves. We also want students to accommodate the notion that physical education can be a subject with significant credibility in secondary education. To that end, where we have asked students to demonstrate their competence, this has typically been done through written reports and tests. This section provides ways in which students can showcase their work beyond a paper or poster format.

Student-Designed Web Pages

In addition to revolutionizing the spread of information to promote student learning, the beauty of the World Wide Web is that it allows people to present their own work. The World Wide Web is not a private domain where only those who are selected or privileged can publish their efforts. Moreover, as a learning tool in physical education, web pages do not have to be uploaded onto the Internet. They can exist simply as a file on a floppy disk like any other software file (e.g., word-processing document or a spreadsheet). Further, because the World Wide Web is so universal, many students can complete their projects at home or in local libraries.

In the high school context, students' web pages are most likely to contain text and images. However, the key is that students who are unable to demonstrate their competence or their understanding will not be able to produce a web page because they will have no artifacts to include. For example, a student who is unable to perform a particular skill will not be able to include a photograph of that skill as evidence of mastery.

> ### Heads Up—VHS or 8-mm Camcorder?
>
> - VHS camcorders are cheaper.
> - VHS camcorders are bulkier and heavier.
> - 8-mm camcorders are more compact.
> - 8-mm can record for longer times.
> - 8-mm has superior audio to VHS.
> - 8-mm cannot play in a VHS video recorder.

Another advantage of web pages as tools for displaying work is that the technology (i.e., software) required to write them is very accessible. For example, the Netscape browser is accompanied by a software application called Composer. Composer is essentially a sophisticated word-processing application, but it also allows for the inclusion of links, e-mail, and other media.

Student-Produced Videos

Even if a school does not have the hardware or the time to convert videotape scenes into digital movies, students can still produce videos to showcase their learning, particularly to demonstrate extended times of practical performance. For example, students can produce their own videos to show complete aerobics routines or any other skill mastery projects.

As noted, video cameras now are not very expensive (some are less than $300), and videotapes are relatively easy to edit. Furthermore, dubbing videotapes with sound or music is a task that most high school students will find easy and motivating.

Other Nonlinear Presentation Forms

Students who do not have all the skills to create web pages can use other forms of nonlinear presentation to demonstrate their work. Both Corel and Microsoft have applications that allow for the presentation of text, sound, and images. These software programs also allow for linking content to other documents or even to the Internet.

Enhancing Health and Fitness Levels

We only need to enter a modern health club to see an abundance of hi-tech exercise machines. The contemporary health club has numerous electronic apparatus, such as treadmills, exercise bikes, and stair steppers, all of which have built-in computer applications that the users can preprogram to design their own workout. Indeed, in the past few years these machines have become increasingly sophisticated through their interface with computers that take records of workout duration and intensity. For example, many aerobic exercise machines now have hand-held pulse meters connected to their internal computers that provide a reading of exercise heart rate.

In the secondary school, however, the increase in fitness technology has most often been represented by the increasing use of heart monitors. As we know, one of the major challenges in aerobic fitness is to remain in the heart rate training zone. For teens, this zone may be as high as 150 beats per minute, and these high rates are often difficult to record manually.

Pulse meters and heart monitors record heart rate, thereby allowing students to concentrate on their workout while receiving constant updates on their exercise intensity. Indeed, some monitors are programmed so that if the user moves out of the target zone, a beep will alert the exerciser user that he or she is going too fast or slow.

Essentially, there are two types of heart monitors. The first are the pulse meters, which work by detecting blood flow from the pulse of the blood through the capillaries. The second group of monitors includes those that monitor the heart rate itself. They involve a transmitter that detects the heart rate and sends a signal to a receiver. This receiver is most often a watch worn on the wrist.

Pulse meters are typically worn on the index finger or ear lobe. However, heart "wands" are a recent innovation that resemble bicycle handlebars. A student will grasp the wand for a few seconds before a digital display shows the current heart rate.

Purchasing a monitor for use in a physical education program is going to be determined by budget and also by the teacher's objectives for recording heart rate. If a teacher simply wants a reasonably accurate record of heart rate, then the bottom-of-the-line monitors (pulse meters and wands) are most acceptable. If however, the teacher wants to gather more information, then the top-of-the-line models (e.g., heart monitors with transmitters) provide extra advantages. They can store heart rate data, and if one purchases an interface, the data can be transferred from the monitor to a computer. The software in the computer can provide graphs and summary data from a workout. This creates an advantage for student learning and provides data sources for ongoing personal fitness problem solving. Kirkpatrick and Birnbaum (1997) have published a book called *Lessons from the Heart,* which contains 38 practical lessons, all of which use heart rate monitors in some form.

There are also many devices on the market that measure body fat. Digital skinfold calipers can be purchased for under $50; body fat analyzers, which use bioelectrical impedance technology, are closer to the $100 price range.

In addition to the numerous pieces of hardware that are available for enhancing fitness, there are also software packages that can be used to monitor fitness and activity levels. The Fitnessgram kit, for example, provides an extensive software program outlining details on health-

Downloading heart rate data

related fitness levels and suggested exercise options. In addition to the Fitness-gram, the Activitygram assessment allows students to enter their predominant activity for each 30-minute interval during the day. The computer then integrates the information and provides a detailed report of the student's activity level.

Summary of Technology

Having read the preceding sections of this chapter, you will have noticed that many technologies are useful for a number of purposes. For example, video cameras can be used to film student presentations that can be shown over a school network, but can also be used to provide feedback to students as they learn a new skill. In similar fashion, a PDA can be used by a teacher to first take roll and then collect data on student game play during a volleyball lesson. Table 12.2 provides a summary of some of the potential uses of the technologies mentioned earlier in this chapter.

Getting the Biggest "Bang" for Your "Buck"

One's budget for physical education is going to determine in a significant way the extent to which technologies can be incorporated in a program. Whereas some items are relatively cheap (such as disposable cameras that might be used to take snapshots of a student project), other items, such as sophisticated treadmills, can cost in excess of $1,000.

Table 12.3 provides a progressive pricing scale for various technologies. This list is not definitive, and there will always be price fluctuations and "bargains" that become available. However, this list will give *some* idea of how far the dollar will stretch.

At this point, however, a critical word of caution is necessary—*purchase before planning invites waste and confusion.* It is essential to take stock of your objectives for using technology, your skill in using and maintaining it, and reflecting critically on all the hype that comes from its corporate origin.

Locke (1997) also warns about the hidden costs involved in purchasing technology. In addition to the item cost, there is a need to estimate the costs of teacher training, hardware maintenance, software purchase, system management, upgrading, replacement, and evaluation.

It is important to recognize, however, that your budget for physical education need not be the only source of funds for purchasing technology. The grants administration office within your school system should be able to provide details about entitlement grants and block grants. Furthermore, many local businesses may donate funds or equipment to your program. The article by Greenberg (1998) provides good ideas about writing grants for technology.

Table 12.2   Uses of Various Technologies

Technology Item	Uses in Physical Education
Desktop computer	• Administrative tasks • Creating lesson plans • Creating promotional materials (banners, certificates) • Creating web pages and presentations
Laptop computer	• A mobile version of the desktop computer
PDA	• Real-time data collection of administrative tasks (e.g., attendance) • Real-time recording uses for authentic assessment tasks
Scanner	• Conversion of paper photographs to electronic images for use in lesson plans, promotional materials, and web pages
Digital camera	• Recording class activities for promotional use • Providing immediate feedback to students during skill learning
Video camera	• Creation of promotional materials • A feedback tool during student skill learning • An assessment tool for recording student skill performance for later, more detailed evaluation • Used by students in creating presentations or records of their work
CD burner	• Used by students and/or teachers to showcase their work, using photographs, video, and sound
VCR	• Showing instructional videotapes for either cognitive or skill learning • Replaying student performances for summative assessment
DVD player	• Showing audiovisual instructional materials
Video capture devices	• Converting videotape movies to electronic forms, which can then be used in multimedia presentations or placed on web pages
Electronic mail	• Communication with colleagues in other schools
World Wide Web	• Searching for lesson and other teaching ideas • Resource tool for student research
Listserv and discussion groups	• Professional development • Ideas for lesson planning • Notification of professional development opportunities
Heart rate monitors	• Aids in student learning concerning aerobic fitness • Goal-setting tools

What Are Your Skills?

Recognizing the potential of technology for improving practice in physical education is not enough; teachers must also be confident in their skills to implement technology. In game play, if a student is limited in skill, so too are his or her

Table 12.3   Technology Price List

Price Range	Items
$0–$50	• 100 MB Zip disks (often in packets of three) • Digital pedometer—displays mileage and calories burned • Digital skinfold calipers
$50–$100	• Webcams (computer-mounted digital cameras) • Polar Beat heart rate monitors (nonrecording—output only) • FitSmart High School Edition software and manual • Body fat analyzers
$100–$200	• Color deskjet printer (basic) • Flatbed scanner (price increased with dpi resolution) • External ZIP drive (for storing graphics and MP3 files) • MovieWorks and Dazzle video digital creators (both used to create multimedia electronic movies) • PDA—organizers (e.g., address and date book, memo pad, calculator) • FITNESSGRAM 6.0 software and manual • Polar interface—a communication device that connects the heart rate monitor to a personal computer
$200–$500	• Color deskjet printer (more dpi per print as well as faster) • Digital camera (price increases with increased resolution) • PDA—with expansion slots and more sophisticated software • Microsoft Office software (price increases with the number of productivity tools) • Polar programmable heart rate monitor
$500–$1,000	• Desktop computer—64 MB RAM and 10–20 GB HDD (no monitor) • Digital camcorder (price increases with zoom capacity, LCD monitor size, and memory mode)
$1,000–$2,000	• Desktop computer—128–256 MB RAM and 15–20 GB HDD (no monitor) • Laptop computer (5–7 GB hard drive) • Exercise bikes with preprogrammed workouts and heart rate control
over $2,000	• Laptop computer (10+ GB hard drive, 128+ RAM) • Digital projectors

options to use tactics in competition. Likewise, a teacher who has limited technological skill and experience is perhaps less likely to take advantage of the many opportunities technology presents.

Many state departments of education are now requiring some technology competencies from graduates of teacher education programs. Concurrently, many colleges of education are providing coursework for students in instructional media. Table 12.4 lists a number of computer technologies the beginning teacher should have. Check this list and see how you fare.

Table 12.4   Technology Skills Checklist

Technology Task	Related Competencies
Computer operation skills	• Boot and shut down computer system and peripherals • Identify and use icons, windows, menus
Setup, maintenance, and troubleshooting	• Make backup copies of files, disks, and drives • Protect against viruses • Identify local technical support
Word processing	• Copy, edit, and manipulate blocks of text • Add tables and columns • Add clip art and other graphics • Check spelling and grammar
Spreadsheet/graphing	• Create spreadsheets with column and row headings • Perform calculations within spreadsheets • Create graphs from spreadsheet data • Insert graphs into word-processing documents
Databases	• Create a database with multiple fields and records • Sort a database by specific fields, add and delete record • Create reports
Telecommunications	• Use electronic mail • Access and join listservs • Access and use resources on the Internet and the World Wide Web
Desktop publishing and presentations	• Use software packages to create posters, banners, and awards • Produce electronic slides using PowerPoint
Hypermedia presentations	• Understand and use HTML to create web pages • Create presentations using HyperStudio

IN-SCHOOL TASKS

Technology Inventory

Take stock of the technology used in a local school's physical education department. First, list the hardware and software to which students have direct access. Determine when and how these are used in classes, and try to get some idea of the extent to which they are used.

Following this, investigate how the teachers use technology in their daily roles as physical educators. Do they have computers on their desks? Are they linked to the Internet? How often do they use software to record grades, attendance, or other administrative tasks?

On gathering these data, reflect on the attitudes and values that this department places on the use of technology. What would be your technology goals if you were to work in this setting?

Portfolio Suggestions and Artifacts

Your Technology Philosophy (S6–D2)

You might care to add a section to your philosophy statement that deals directly with your viewpoint concerning the use of technology in physical education.

Your Technology Skills (S6–K4: S5–K4)

What technology skills do you have? How sophisticated is your ability not only to use technology hardware and software, but also to design resources specifically for use in instruction, assessment, or as organizational/management strategies?

Do you have samples of your technological productions, such as web pages, posters, or videos, that you could use to demonstrate your competencies?

Technology Budget (S6–P4)

You have been awarded $2,000 to spend on technology. Provide a list of the materials you will buy, their potential use, and a rationale for why you chose these items over others that you chose not to purchase. Also, list the vendors and the model names of the materials you will purchase.

Reflection Time

Now that you have read this chapter, how confident do you feel in

- using a number of software packages, for even basic tasks such as word processing, spreadsheets, and linear presentations (e.g., PowerPoint)?

- your ability to create a web page that could be used to promote your physical education program, or at least be a resource for students?

- your ability to argue for and justify a specific technology budget for physical education?

- being able to help students showcase their learning in physical education through the production of multimedia presentations?

- convincing your future colleagues of the need for strengthening their commitment to using technology for instruction and assessment?

References

Greenberg, J. (1998). Writing a grant proposal for technology. *Teaching Elementary Physical Education, 9* (3), 26–27.

Hall, A., & Leigh, J. (2000). *Using the Internet—physical education*. Cambridge, England: Pearson Publishing Co.

Kirkpatrick, B., & Birnbaum, B. (1997). *Lessons from the heart: Individualizing physical education with heart rate monitors*. Champaign, IL: Human Kinetics.

Locke, L. F. (1997). Minutes of the Commodore Club: Even Luddites chat on the Internet. *Quest, 49*, 270–279.

Mendon, K., & Van Blom, J. (1999). Using technology to enhance fitness. *Teaching Elementary Physical Education, 10* (3), 20–30.

McLean, D. D. (1996). Use of computer-based technology in health, physical education, recreation, and dance. *ERIC Digest*, ED390874. Washington, DC: Eric Clearinghouse on Teaching and Teacher Education.

Mills, B. D., & Mitchell, C. A. (1997). *Jumpstart with weblinks: A guidebook for sport education and activities 97/98*. Englewood, CO: Morton Publishing Company.

Mitchell, D. L., & Hunt, D. (1997). Multimedia lesson plans—help for preservice teachers. *Journal of Physical Education, Recreation & Dance, 68* (2), 17–20.

Mohnsen, B. (1999). Using heart monitors for curriculum integration. *Teaching Elementary Physical Education, 10* (1), 34–35.

Mohnsen, B. (2001). *Using technology in physical education* (3rd ed.). Cerritos, CA: Bonnie's Fitware.

Mohnsen, B., & Thompson, C. (1997). Using video technology in physical education. *Strategies, 10* (6), 8–11.

Mohnsen, B., Thompson, C., & Mendon, K. (1996). Effective ways to use technology: Innovative new devices and programs are revolutionizing PE. *Teaching Secondary Physical Education, 2* (1), 14–17.

Stratton, G. (1999). Physical education and technology teachers: The PETTs of the new millennium. *Bulletin of Physical Education, 35* (2), 124–137.

WEB RESOURCES

The following web link list was generated upon publication of the text; however, over time, the sites may become obsolete if an organization dissolves, discontinues online services, or relocates to a different URL. If a link listed below does not connect, please search for the organization by name.

http://www.pesoftware.com/Technews/news.html

The purpose of this newsletter is to keep K–12 physical educators abreast of current trends in using technology in physical education. The newsletter is published monthly (except July and January).

http://www.mediabuilder.com/

Provides a number of font tools, image creating tools, and access to image libraries, all of which can enhance electronic presentations and web pages.

http://www.polarelectro.com/

Home page of the Polar Heart Rate Monitor Company.

http://education.adam.com/

CD-ROM and online interactive products relating to heath and medical information (e.g., Adam Online anatomy and IP interactive physiology web).

http://transition.alaska.edu/www/portfolios.html

How to create your own electronic portfolio based on the "5-by-5 model" of electronic portfolio development.

http://www2.ncsu.edu/ncsu/cep/tap/

Many states now require students seeking initial licensure to have a technology portfolio that demonstrates the technology competencies required by that state. This site provides Internet resources for the technology competencies as well as practice quizzes for each competency.

CHAPTER 13

Teaching Physical Education in Diverse Settings

Scenario

Un niño hispanico y su hermana están sentados en los asientos de su clase de educación física. Mientras, algunos de los otros estudiantes de la clase juegan baloncesto. Muchos de estos estudiantes de las escuelas urbanas no toleran a los otros que no son tan habiles como ellos. Además, José y su hermana, Maria, no saben cuanto tiempo van a estar en esta escuela ya que sus padres seguramente se tendrán que mudar de sitio muy pronto en búsqueda de un nuevo sitio donde empieza una nueva safra de frutas. Como un profesór de educación física, si puedes leer este escenario es muy posible que estes mucho mejor preparado para trabajar con este tipo de estudiante. Si no, te puedes encontrar con una desventaja particular.

Introduction

Students who enter teacher education programs in physical education have remarkably similar backgrounds. Research tells us that they are mostly Caucasians (over 90%) who played high school athletics (almost 100%) and wish to continue in the coaching area as well as teach (nearly 80%). They recall their own physical education programs as ones that focused on traditional team sports, games, and fitness programs, with less emphasis on individual sports and expressive or noncompetitive activities. Further, almost two-thirds of recruits have attended high schools in which varsity athletes were excused from regular physical education classes (see Placek et al., 1995).

Placek and colleagues' study also asked future physical educators to describe the main purposes of the subject. Learning skills/activities and the development of fitness were listed as clearly the most important goals. Although this is not surprising, the goal of "valuing physical activity" was infrequently mentioned, and cognitive knowledge also was not considered particularly important. Further, *none* included any mention of *social reconstruction* as a goal of the subject; that is, none of these teaching recruits discussed the potential for physical education in developing social responsibility goals or those of global citizenship.

But does it really matter that most physical educators have similar backgrounds? Well, go back and read the scenario—can you translate it? If you can't, what if you take a job where more than half the students in the class have Latino origins?

There are numerous schools in the United States situated in other than white middle-class settings, and these schools exhibit vastly different ecologies from the suburban white school. Further, these schools present specific contextual features that can pose problems in the presentation of physical education. Many recruits into physical education have great difficulty envisioning any possible curriculum model for physical education other than one consisting of sport and games, and in settings of mostly white middle-class schools. Consequently, many physical education teachers run the risk of essentially being unaware of their personal biases, their own cultures, and, more important, the biases and cultures of their students.

> ## Take a Closer Look at Social Reconstruction
>
> Social reconstruction is an orientation toward education in which teachers accept a role in making school curricula vehicles for creating a better society. Students are made aware of social inequalities and taught strategies to prevent or alleviate injustices.

The term *culturally responsive pedagogy* has been used to describe a process of teaching that deliberately responds to the cultural identities of the learners in the class. This means that teachers have a moral responsibility to design curricular programs that are responsive to the educational needs of learning from diverse cultural backgrounds. Culturally responsive content recognizes the influence of culture, language, race, gender, or other characteristics that mark children as different from the majority (see Sparks, 1994).

The purpose of this chapter is to outline the prospects for, and challenges associated with, presenting an engaging and relevant physical education in two particular settings: the inner-city school and the Native American reservation. For each setting, the context will be described, followed by the thoughts of students and teachers who study and work in those settings.

The structure of the chapter will be in the form of dialogues between the author and teachers and student in schools. Although these dialogues are fictional, the questions and answers are based on research conducted on physical education. To that end, text boxes, that encourage you to "take a closer look," refer to these dialogues. In these text boxes, we examine the educational literature associated with the issue being discussed. In particular, this chapter focuses on successful strategies. By the time you complete this chapter, you should have at least some idea of how you may begin to achieve some success in such a setting—rather than simply survive.

Urban Schools

The Youth of the Inner City

In many urban settings in large American cities, children attend schools located in settings surrounded by disempowering social circumstances. Consider the case of Cabrini-Green, a housing project on the near north side of Chicago. Constructed in the 1960s, Cabrini once housed 20,000 people. It became the symbol of everything that was misguided about public housing. It was the scene of concentrated poverty, poorly maintained buildings, unemployment, family disintegration, crime, and drugs. The case of Cabrini-Green is not limited to Chicago. Across the nation, many students in urban schools, through no fault of their own, must negotiate their daily lives within a toxic environment, limited social services, poverty, crime, drugs, and inadequate educational resources.

Several states are also showing substantial increases in the segregation of minority children over the past 20 years. For example, the typical Latino student attends a school that is only 25% white. Schools segregated by race also tend to be segregated by poverty, and, in fact, a predominantly African American or Latino school is up to 16 times more likely to be poor than a mostly white school (Hacker, 1999).

The Schools of the Inner City

Working conditions in inner-city schools have been found to be inferior when compared to schools outside the city, and such conditions have a direct impact on teachers' effectiveness, morale, attitudes, behaviors, and ability to do their job (see Velez Arias, 1999). To compound a lack of morale, *Newsweek* reports that problem schools serving the poorest children had fewer credentialed and experienced teachers. *Education Week* has reported that schools in urban districts are twice as likely to hire teachers who have no license or only an emergency or temporary license. The result is that the percentage of unlicensed and underlicensed teachers can reach as high as 31%. As Van Horn (1999) notes, the education profession has great difficulty recruiting qualified teachers to work in the nation's inner cities and has just as much trouble keeping them there.

Haberman (2000) suggests that urban schools have a particular primacy on classroom management and minimal focus on learning substantive work. He notes that many teachers have a custodial orientation, in which they expend most of their energy on classroom management and discipline. Describing these schools more as day camps, Haberman comments that because students' "studies" are pursued as time fillers and place no demands on students, there is little expectation anything will be learned systematically or pursued to any great depth.

Teachers, too, are faced with a number of tasks beyond simply instruction. Haberman (2000) suggests that successful teaching in the urban school extends well beyond the knowledge of the curriculum:

> *The knowledge bases that can inform the personal-experience base currently used by successful urban teachers include a great variety of studies. Urban teachers have sophisticated craft knowledge that enables them to de-escalate violence, deal with a wide range of handicapping conditions in the same class, cooperate with other human service and health professionals, communicate in the informal codes and languages of their diverse students, survive and function in the bureaucratic chaos of their districts, learn from parents and caregivers who are raising children and youths under extremely debilitating conditions, recognize the symptoms and uses of pharmaceuticals and street drugs, interact with teenage mothers in realistic ways, use computers and information systems for academic purposes and for securing services and opportunities for students, understand how religious participation is affecting the behaviors of their students, and deal realistically with the impact of peer groups on the lives of their students.* (Haberman, 2000)

Urban Students Speak about Physical Education

Q: Tell me about your physical education experiences.

A: For me, I think sometimes I would rather fail PE than actually participate, and that's mainly because it can be tough out there.

A: Yeah, I mean, it's scary sometimes. The boys just want to play rough; they dominate games, and if you are not very good, they couldn't care less and never let you play.

A: But if you do play and mess up, people are all in your face and fuss and yell at you, and that's not fun. It really is embarrassing for us to go out there and really try.

Take a Closer Look

- Participants report a sense of fear and alienation in physical education (Ennis et al., 1997). For many, it is not a fun place to be.
- Few students in urban schools are likely to share the values, beliefs, and norms emphasized in the traditional curriculum (Chen, 1999). There seems to be an "official knowledge" that requires students to inherit an ideological property of the dominant culture that they are denied access to in their lives outside physical education.

A: It's more than that—it's boring. One of the things is that the activities—they are not worth our time. When are we going to do this stuff outside school? We can't even go to the park—it's not safe, and they are trying to teach us. Some of us can't even go outside in our neighborhood, and they tell us to go out and be active. . . . And it's not just violent outside school—in some of our classes, people are picking fights when they play games.

Q: So, what *is* important in physical education?

A: For a start, it needs to be fun—what we are doing.

A: The best part of PE is being with your friends. You can't do that the rest of the day—you can't talk to them in other classes, or the teachers get mad. In PE you can hang out with them, and they can help you out.

Take a Closer Look . . .

- Friends are information sources, emotional and cognitive resources, and keys to the successful social dimension of physical education (Cothran & Ennis, 1998).

- Teachers who ignore this powerful dimension run a risk of alienating students.

———————————

Q: What about your *teachers*?

A: Well, some of them are more worried about whether we are dressing out than whether we are learning anything. They seem totally concerned with controlling the class. You know, they seem to be always focusing on stuff that we are doing wrong—and it's all our fault.

A: I think some of them have given up. They let us do what we want so long as we don't give them any problems—and they seem to be happy with that. They never ask what *we* like to do in PE. We never have any chance to have any input into what's happening in our classes. They all think we have bad attitudes and that we are lazy.

Take a Closer Look . . .

- Many physical educators emphasize a curriculum discourse of control based on a belief of dual responsibility. In this way, education seems to be spilt between teachers, who are responsible for control, and students, who are responsible for learning (Chen, 1999). Mention of partnerships is almost absent from any discussion.

———————————

Q: What about your *good* teachers?

A: Well, first, they show us they care, and they talk to us, you know, and they try to understand where we are coming from—rather than blaming us.

A: And the stuff they have us do, it means that everyone can be successful—because we don't have to just try to survive in class, but it's a positive place to be.

A: The good teachers let you learn with your friends, too.

Take a Closer Look . . .

- Students often report that many of their physical education and school experiences fail to promote a sense of membership.

- Likewise, the lack of, or possibilities for, social connection among themselves and with their teachers either reduces or enhances their willingness to participate in class activities (see Cothran & Ennis, 2000).

- The bottom line: We have to come up with ways to increase the teens' attachment with school and one another, and we need to get better at learning how to communicate and to develop skills that foster personal relationships with students.

Urban Teachers Speak about Physical Education

Q: So, how do teachers cope with these difficult work conditions?

A: A lot of teachers change their goals to just entertainment. We send the message to kids that "we will keep you busy or at least not ask you to do too much, and you will not give us trouble."

A: There are also lots of teachers who really focus on what's wrong with the students' lives. They see the gang involvement, the substance abuse, and the dysfunctional families, and the first thing they do is to tighten security: to provide *less* choice and opportunity for students to come to grips with these issues.

Take a Closer Look . . .

Waxman, Huang, and Padron (1995) use the term "pedagogy of poverty" to describe a pedagogy that emphasizes controlling student behaviors rather than teaching appropriate content. Nonparticipation leads to failure, which leads students to withdraw from learning.

Q: How do you respond in your situations—ones where you have had some success?

A: One of the things we are finding here is that somehow you have to try to connect with these students.

A: Lots of teachers are also now focusing on social responsibility issues—trying to work on cooperation and teamwork. Many of these kids do not have those skills. They are coming from circumstances where they are not given a lot of leadership in their lives. The main social affiliation they get is often through gangs—and one of the things we try to work on here is this whole notion of membership.

A: What we have found is that there are certain curriculum models that we can put in place that really do a better job than most of the traditional stuff that teachers serve up. Take sport education for example, where we give students a choice, and give them some responsibility and help them feel important and take ownership of their learning.

A: But it's more than that, we have offered them with different ways and more opportunities to be successful.

Urban Teachers Speak about Successful Physical Education

Q: What programs have shown particular promise?

A: As we have said, sport education seasons seem particularly attractive, but we have modified this model to come up with a new version—called "Sport for Peace." Many kids who come to school figure the only way they can solve their problems is through fear and intimidation—and that's scary for lots of students.

Take a Closer Look . . .

Sport for Peace was created by Ennis and colleagues (1999) to address particular concerns in an urban school district regarding student violence, fighting, profanity, and physical and sexual harassment, which had been identified as particularly troublesome.

A: We have also put in place an emphasis on conflict negotiation, as well as care and concern for others. There is a requirement that all students play during every class, and rules require students to rotate through every position and responsibility (except coach). Students practice the techniques for collaborative negotiation, mediation, and consensus building during the preseason using role-playing, problem solving, conflict analysis, and game simulations.

Take a Closer Look . . .

- Of greatest difficulty for the teachers is understanding when and how to incorporate conflict negotiation in their classes. The greatest challenge for teachers is knowing when to intervene and when to permit teams to work out the problem on their own.

- Teachers are often eager to intervene immediately to resolve the problem themselves. They are inclined to restructure the class proactively to avoid conflicts rather than use them as teachable moments (Ennis et al., 1999).

———————

A: Sport for Peace is designed specifically to disrupt the behaviors of dominant, aggressive players. Because all students are required to play in the games and the tournament, coaches are motivated to help low-skilled players learn and feel confident in their performance and then encourage others to support them and work productively with them in games.

A: The highly skilled students are unable to gain respect through dominant play. Instead, they have to earn respect through thoughtful decision making, effectual teaching, and positive support for every player. They earn respect by solving problems and responding to their players' criticisms and settling disputes.

Take a Closer Look . . .

- Sport for Peace creates a safe place for both high- and low-skilled girls and boys in the physical education curriculum.

- Safe places are those in which students can affiliate with others and know that their emotions and sense of self will be protected.

- Curricula with this purpose promote a feeling of belonging that many adolescents seek in urban schools (Ennis et al., 1999).

- Sport for Peace aims to overcome the more common situations that, according to Haberman (2000), arise in schools where students come to expect preventive segregation and, thus, do not try to improve communication with rivals or to practice peaceful coexistence. They have learned well the street values of power and control.

———————

A: This whole idea of community, too, is critical.

A: What is critical is that the kids see a sense of belonging—to be treated with respect.

Take a Closer Look . . .

- Bayonne (New Jersey) High School is an urban four-year, comprehensive high school with 2,100 students from diverse ethnic and socioeconomic backgrounds. The school is divided into six houses and features small physical education classes stressing teamwork and adventure activities (Wanko, 1997).

- Kallusky (2000) reminds us that kids don't care very much how you classify them (e.g., at-risk, problem), as long as you treat them with dignity.

Native Americans

The Context

The number of people identifying themselves as Native Americans (American Indians) or Alaska Natives in 2000 increased to 2.5 million and if these groups are included with new mixed-race categories, grew to 4.1 million overall. The Native American population in South Dakota alone rose to 62,283, a 23% increase during the 1990s. Native Americans, the state's largest minority group, now make up more than 8.2% of South Dakota's total population.

Although this number shows an increase in those who wish to identify themselves as members of Sovereign Nations, there is still no doubt that Native Americans represent one of the most forgotten minorities. Even though they have been romanticized through images of fierce warriors and significant bravery by sporting icons, the true facts reveal that Native Americans have some of the worst health care and highest death rates from alcoholism, diabetes, accidents, and suicide in the nation. Further, many tribal programs that must rely on federal funding are frequently shortchanged. As noted by Native American youth workers, "There are limited opportunities on the reservation, especially those in rural areas . . . and given that and the history of alcoholism and poverty, I think it all plays into students getting depressed and frustrated—and in certain serious cases, violent" (see Kelley, 2000).

The Native American Student at School

"Today, American Indians who don't go to special schools are faced with different challenges. Those living in cities are likely to go to public schools where their cultural heritage is rarely dealt with, if at all. Those on reservations may attend schools operated by the Bureau of Indian Affairs, but the vast majority of teachers are not Indian" (Martinez, 1999, p. 3). Further, the dropout rate among Native Americans is the highest among all racial and ethnic groups.

Many teachers of Native American students, then, may not be aware of the belief systems, social trends, languages, and customs of their students. In particular, family attributes and child-rearing practices are significantly different from Anglo styles. When working with Native American students, physical educators must educate themselves about the cultural similarities and differences associated with these groups. Lake (1990) provides as an example a letter from one parent urging teachers not to engage in "victim blaming," but to respect the unique contributions his son can make in the school setting:

> He is not culturally "disadvantaged" but he is culturally different! . . . He is caught between two worlds, torn by two distinct cultural systems. . . . I want my child to succeed in school and in life. I don't want him to be a dropout or juvenile delinquent or to end up on drugs or alcohol because of discrimination. I want him to be proud of his rich heritage and culture, and I would like him to develop the necessary capabilities to adapt to, and succeed in, both cultures. But I need your help. What you say and what you do in the classroom, what you teach and how you teach it will have a significant effect on the potential success or failure of my child. . . . All I ask is that you work with me, not against me, to help educate my child in the best way. My son, Wind-Wolf, is not an empty glass coming to your class to be filled. He is a full basket coming into a different environment and society to share. Please let him share his knowledge, heritage, and culture with you and his peers. (Lake, 1990, pp. 51–52)

Nichols (1994) presents three situational categories to help teachers understand some of the key features of Native American life. Knowledge of family, education, and social dimensions provides at least a template of understanding of some of the differences between Native American and Anglo cultures (Table 13.1).

Indian Students Speak about Physical Education

Q: Tell me about your physical education experiences.

A: Teachers and non-Indian students do not understand that we don't change clothes in public, so we get in trouble when we don't dress out.

A: Don't ask us to demonstrate skills when we are no good at them, and don't get us to comment on the work of our fellow students.

Take a Closer Look . . .

- For Native Americans, exposing one's bodily sacredness to the indiscriminate view of others violates the holiness of the being

Table 13.1   Characteristics of Native American Culture

Family Life

• Extended family includes all relatives.

• Family members look to elders for advice.

• In disciplining children, many parents believe in talking quietly to the child rather than scolding and helping children understand the consequences of the behavior, after which the child decides whether or not to continue the behavior.

Education

• Education is based on observation of the environment.

• Listening and observing are expected skills.

• Hurrying is disharmonious with nature, so clock time isn't important.

Social/Cultural

• Children are taught not to invade others' privacy, so they may not like teachers or others touching them.

• Bravery is expected, and one is responsible for supporting friends.

• Patience is important, as is sharing with others.

• Children see an important connection between humans and their environment.

• Children have a rich oral history and enjoy storytelling.

Source: Adapted from Sutliff (1996).

(Locust, 1988).

■ In the Anglo culture, learning through public mistakes and getting credit for trying are an acceptable way of learning. In Native American cultures, however, it is not respectful to perform publicly before competence is achieved. Native American students prefer methods of repeated observation and self-testing in private (Reyhner, 1992).

Q: So, what about your *teachers* in physical education?

A: Demonstrate, don't talk. We learn by watching and doing.

A: Also, don't get all angry and loud at us if we get in trouble. You just might find that we simply get up and walk away. That's not a threat, but we will often just leave a place of disharmony.

Take a Closer Look . . .

■ Traditional education for Native American youth is not linear and frequently not verbal. Native American children learn by watching their elders: by having grandparents identify for them the whole of the task, the complete circle, the perfection of completion. The whole is then marked into meaningful parts (Locust, 1988, p. 327).

- Native American parents, in contrast to the Anglo ethic of swift punishment, will mostly counsel children in their home in a positive manner. In the school context, therefore, the first response of a student being disciplined is to physically remove himself or herself from disharmony. If this is not possible, then the student may choose to protect his or her spirit by removing it through spirit travel—resulting in a situation perceived by non–Native Americans as rude inattention or "spacing out" (Locust, 1988).

Q: So, what about the *activities* you do in physical education?

A: Team sports activities and group challenges are the most fun.

A: We are not a people whose aim it is to look better than each other.

Take a Closer Look . . .

- Many Native American students avoid competition when they view it as unfair (Dumont, 1972).

- Native American children also tend to avoid individual competition, especially when it makes one individual appear to be better than another (or, as noted, when they may be exposed as inadequate). Individual humility is something to be respected and preserved (Rehyner, 1992).

- Competitive tasks in group settings, which require cooperation (e.g., basketball or team sports) will encourage more ready participation (Rehyner, 1992).

Q: What else should we know about physical education activities?

A: Boys and girls infrequently dance together in our culture.

A: Even at the pow-wows, men and women have mostly separate dances.

A: We like activities where the whole group has to be successful.

Take a Closer Look . . .

- Many Native American groups hold fast to a standard of achievement that all students can meet. Hence, high-ability students will often not display their true competence (Reyhner, 1992). Activities in PE that allow for all students, irrespective of ability, to contribute to a team goal will be well accepted.

Teachers of Native American Children
Speak about Instruction

Q: What are some instructional key factors to consider when you work with Native American youth?

A: You need to provide lots of individual, nonpublic practice in noncompetitive settings.

A: It's not part of Indian culture to look you in the eye—so all those eye contact strategies won't be appropriate.

A: Native students will *not* ask for your help, so you need to recognize when you need to offer it. They *will*, however, take your advice, since being respectful of one's elders is a strong cultural component.

Teachers of Native American Children
Speak about Curriculum

Q: What would be your advice about designing a curriculum?

A: Most teachers don't know how to integrate Native American culture into their lessons. Often, teachers who make any mention of Indian people at all do so in a stereotypical way.

A: If [the curriculum] never mentions who you are and where you come from, kids will make the connection that this isn't important.

Take a Closer Look . . .

- Schools are now presenting curricula that mix a classic curriculum with Native American culture, closely integrating the two. For example, math and English are learned alongside ancient songs and native languages (Martinez, 1999).

- Native American imagery in school athletics, as it has been perpetuated by school districts and communities, reflects the Anglo culture's ignorance of Native American culture. Moreover, it has been noted that these images contribute not only to a hostile culture and classroom climate for Native Americans but also miseducate Americans in general about their shared history (Staurowsky, 1999).

———————

Teachers preparing to work with Indian students must begin by asking challenging questions, such as, How can one culture's teachers educate another culture's children without obliterating a precious heritage? How can teachers plan instruction that is informed by culturally based learning strengths rather than perceived weaknesses? How can teachers in K–12 schools support language restoration efforts (see Diefenderfer, 1997)?

Below are some specific hints in response to these questions:

1. Be a learner yourself. It is *critical* to make attempts to learn the culture of the particular group you are working with. Learn at least some basic vocabulary and make an effort to *respect* the belief systems of the Native American group you are working with.

2. Encourage family participation in physical education. In particular, grandparents are valuable sources of knowledge, language, and skills that can be brought into the class.

3. Don't try to assimilate students into an Anglo culture. Your task as an educator is to enhance both cultures, not supplant the existing Native American culture.

4. Don't be afraid to ask questions about appropriate practices—you are unlikely to be told without asking. Once you ask, however, advice is clearly given.

Take a Closer Look . . .

- Many students enjoy writing in their personal journals about physical education. This allows them a private way to communicate with the teacher. This is particularly important because students are unlikely to raise their hands in class.

Teachers Speak about Successful Physical Education for Indian Students

Q: What programs or practices have shown particular promise?

A: Group cooperative tasks and challenges are particularly successful, as are team sports.

A: Student-designed games are well appreciated and developed enthusiastically.

A: When working on fitness activities (e.g., aerobics), allow students to have their own space, design their own sequence, and avoid public correction.

A: Allow students to use their language in your classes.

Take a Closer Look . . .

NOTE! Be particularly sensitive when engaging in outdoor adventure activities. Items in nature often have specific symbolic meaning. For example, a certain mountain may be sacred, whereas a flowing river may be evil. Moreover, there will be significant tribal differences in the meaning of some items. For example, eagle feathers have different levels of taboo between Plains Indians and the Cheyenne (see Littlebear, 1992).

A Final Word

Teaching Native American students can be a particularly rewarding and fascinating experience, and you will probably learn more from the students than you can teach them. The caveat is not to try to assimilate the students into your culture, but rather to enhance both cultures. Littlebear (1992) offers some splendid recommendations (Table 13.2).

Table 13.2   Recommendations for Teachers of Native Americans

1. Teachers from the dominant society should be aware of their own ethnic and cultural origins so that they can better understand Native American cultural differences.

2. Teachers need to become aware of tribally specific differences.

3. Teachers must learn about their students' tribes, including their histories and the aspirations of parents and the local community.

4. Teachers should not rely on preconceived stereotypes and popular misconceptions of Native Americans—there is no generic Indian.

5. Teachers need to make modern American education more acceptable to Native Americans—ask parents to come in and share their experiences, for example.

6. Teachers should be aware of linguistic differences and influences on their students.

7. Teacher should keep their expectations high.

8. Teachers must remember that many students are not sophisticated in their own culture and that certain information about their beliefs is not to be told to outsiders.

9. Teachers should be very careful of what they say—a good rule is not to say anything about a person away from him or her that you would not say about that person in his or her hearing.

10. Teachers should be aware of the factors that enhance the self-perception of Native American students, such as instruction on Native American contributions to the country.

11. Teachers should not deliberately shame a student.

12. Teachers should not have a "savior" complex—the Native American student does not need saving (except from people with a savior complex!).

13. Teachers should try to grow while they are in Native American reservations—and particularly should become acquainted with the local elders and community people.

Source: Littlebear (1992, p. 107-109).

Teaching Successfully in Diverse Settings

By now, it should be clear to you that some contexts in which physical education takes place are significantly different from those of white middle-class settings. Moreover, it is not just that physical education practice is different, the entire histories and biographies of these schools and their students are poles apart from their suburban counterparts. As a result, to reach these students and have activity become a meaningful part of their lives requires a different approach to teaching and learning. Unfortunately, that approach has no clear template.

To help guide us through that process, imagine two sets of travelers to a distant and foreign land, say, Zimbabwe. The first group (the tourists) travels in air-conditioned buses, gets delivered right to the gates of Victoria Falls (instead of making the mile walk from downtown past refugees, hawkers, and beggars), and eats and stays in fine hotels. These tourists also take their wild animal safaris in large enclosed vehicles. The second group (*National Geographic* freelance writers) travels in old four-wheel drive jeeps, camps out or stays with families in rural villages, and eats food purchased from local people at their markets. When these travelers seek out native animals, they trek on foot and in open vehicles off the beaten path with local guides. Furthermore, the writers will visit places considered too dangerous for the comfortable tourist.

The tourists and the writers will have different experiences and will learn different lessons during their time in Africa. When we translate this analogy to teaching in diverse settings, the "tourist" teacher seems to have an invisible barrier between himself and his students. There is a distance, and there are clearly marked borders that neither group will cross—a pedagogical no-man's-land. The "tourist" teachers do not fully know or understand their students, except for the day-to-day interactions of their classrooms—much like the glimpse the tourists have of the native dance troop that performs at a fancy dinner. The "writer" teacher, in contrast, seeks to know *and* understand the lives and worlds of the local people, their customs, their beliefs, and their language.

Teachers who take on the "writer" role spend considerable time attempting to find a *connectedness* with their students. They make significant attempts to learn about the students' world outside physical education. They share stories about their lives outside school, trading music or poetry (see Kallusky, 2000), and report that such endeavors bring a new respect between teachers and students.

It is this broad notion of *respecting students* that is critical for developing such a connectedness. In these cases, respect ranges from simply not yelling at students, to more complex actions such as giving students voice and responsibility. The teacher is also put in situations of having to respect students (and their caregivers) even when it is difficult for the teacher to do so (consider the journalist who witnesses tribal customs that make him uncomfortable). Your students' lifestyles, beliefs, attitudes, and behaviors may be significantly different from your norms. However, to discount these is a certain route to losing the potential to have a significant influence on these students' lives.

It's Messy

To teach in these diverse settings is not the easiest path. In the travel analogy, having to rely on local buses is problematic, as is learning local customs and language. Camping is sometimes primitive, usually rough, and sometimes dangerous. Gaining entry into people's homes is not simple, and a degree of trust has to be developed. So, too, is designing a curriculum that is relevant and engaging for students in urban schools or on reservations. Gaining trust is critical.

A key factor in both the cases of the journalist and the teacher counterpart is *persistence*. Urban and reservation schools are replete with challenges that take time to adopt to, including students who attend school either armed or stoned, teachers who are unwilling to support your innovations, or belief/peer systems that seem to inhibit the potential of the most talented students. What is critical, however, is not to give in. Each day brings a new lesson: not the brief viewing of the giraffe and elephant from the bus, which will be all the tourist sees, but a new understanding of the habits and protective strategies of the elephant; not a lesson on Frisbee in which most students opted to not participate, but an understanding of why the Frisbee game as planned might not have been the most attractive activity option for the students.

Taking the more difficult road in one's approach to teaching in diverse settings always requires a preparedness to be vulnerable, to engage and listen to students, and to give up the need to be in control all the time. This is a significant challenge for many teachers and may indeed explain why so few really derive some feeling of self-worth in these settings.

Remember Your Role

To return once more to our travel analogy, it is critical to note that the magazine writers are *not* taking on the role of missionaries. Likewise, as teachers, our task is not to *save* students in these difficult contexts, but rather to empower and value them. We need to develop a climate within physical education that gives students a sense of belonging. To do this, you need to be prepared to follow the notion of "teaching kids, not the content." Be in a position where you, too, see yourself as a learner. By engaging students in the subject matter of physical activity, you will help them develop a sense of belonging in your classes. They will see that they are being treated differently. At first, many will not know how to react with some of the freedoms and choices you provide for them, but with time, many will come to appreciate your efforts and persistence. As Kallusky (2000, p. 114) reminds us, "Perseverance is necessary. However, the rewards gained through establishing trusting relationships with the students is well worth the effort."

We conclude this chapter with a quote from Martinek:

Taking up the challenge of making a difference in kids' lives will require an understanding of the culture of kids and their values. Understanding their view of schooling and school, their neighborhood, adults, and life in general are all part of the agenda. Without this backdrop, efforts to connect with youngsters and provide worthwhile experiences will fall short. And yes, it helps to have peer, faculty, and institutional support. But the most important ingredients for success are your commitment, your preparation, and your persistence. (Martinek, 2000, p. 248)

IN-SCHOOL TASKS

Movie Reflection

Watch the movie *Harlem Diary*. What are the most striking features of this setting for you? Does sport or physical activity feature in these teens' lives? What lessons might you learn from this movie in terms of teaching successfully in an urban setting?

Local Native Americans

Locate the site of your nearest tribal leader and/or Bureau of Indian Affairs (BIA) representative. Arrange for the chief, chairperson, governor, or president of the tribe to visit your class and discuss that tribe's perspective on physical activity for children and what opportunities you may have to learn more about their culture.

IN-CLASS DISCUSSION

You may find discussing the following article a useful way to clarify your understanding of Native American culture. Read the accompanying box concerning graduation dress. What is your position?

Indians Seek OK to Wear Native Dress at Graduation

In Albuquerque, New Mexico, a number of Native American students sought permission to wear traditional Indian dress for graduation instead of the usual cap and gown. The students said their native dress symbolizes cultural pride, but they don't have much hope of being able to wear it at commencement ceremonies. The superintendent of public schools, acting on feedback from principals, is insisting on the wearing of caps and gowns; to wear anything else would not represent what school is all about. Quoting that any deviation for one specific group would lead to others expecting similar treatment, the board rejected the Native American students' request.

PORTFOLIO SUGGESTIONS AND ARTIFACTS

Your Diversity Position Statement (S3–D1-4)

Teachers must understand their personal biases, their own cultures, and the biases and cultures of their students to help students develop the sensitivities to function in a diverse world. (Chepyator-Thompson, 1994)

Write a position statement concerning your teaching in a multicultural classroom. Further, include a detailed statement of the specific interpersonal skills you believe you possess that could contribute to mutual understanding and acceptance.

REFLECTION TIME

Now that you have read this chapter, how confident do you feel in being able to envision a program of physical education that is substantially different from the ones experienced by most white, middle- and upper-class students?

REFERENCES

Castill, A. (1994). We would like you to know. In L. M. Carlson (Ed.), *Cool salsa: Bilingual poems on growing up Latino in the United States*. New York: Henry Holt.

Chen, A. (1999). The impact of social change on inner-city high school physical education: An analysis of a teacher's experiential account. *Journal of Teaching in Physical Education, 18,* 312–335.

Chepyator-Thompson, J.R. (1994). Multicultural education: Culturally responsive teaching. *Journal of Physical Education, Recreation, and Dance, 65* (9), 31–32.

Cothran, D. J., & Ennis, C. D. (1998). Curricula of mutual worth: Comparisons of students' and teachers' curricular goals. *Journal of Teaching in Physical Education, 17,* 307–326.

Cothran, D. J., & Ennis, C. D. (1999). Alone in a crowd: Meeting students' needs for relevance and connection in urban high school physical education. *Journal of Teaching in Physical Education, 18,* 234–247.

Cothran, D. J., & Ennis, C. D. (2000). Building bridges to student engagement: Communicating respect and care for students in urban high schools. *Journal of Research & Development in Education, 33,* 106–117.

Diefenderfer, H. (1997, April 25). Evergreen State College adds degree program designed to fix failures in American Indian public education. *Indian Country Today.*

Dumont, R. V. (1972). Learning English and how to be silent: Students in Sioux and Cherokee classroom. In C. Cazden, V. John & D. Hymes (Eds.), *Function of language in the classroom.* New York: Teachers College.

Ennis, C. D., Cothran, D. J., Davidson, K. S., Loftus, S. J., Owens, L., Swanson, L., & Hopsicker, P. (1997). Implementing curriculum within a context of fear and disengagement. *Journal of Teaching in Physical Education, 17,* 52–71.

Ennis, C. D., Solmon, M. A., Satina, B., Loftus, S. J., Mensch, J., & McCauley, M. T. (1999). Creating a sense of family in urban schools using the "Sport for Peace" curriculum. *Research Quarterly for Exercise and Sport, 70,* 273–285.

Haberman, M. (2000). Urban schools—Day camps or custodial centers? *Phi Delta Kappan, 82,* 203–208.

Hacker, H. K. (1999, January 10). Racial gap widens. *Ventura County Star.*

Kallusky, J. (2000). In-school programs. In D. Hellison, N. Cutforth, J. Kallusky, T. Martinek, M. Parker & J. Stiehl (Eds.), *Youth development and physical activity: Linking universities and communities* (pp. 87–114). Champaign, IL: Human Kinetics.

Kelley, M. (2000, July 13). American Indian youth crime rises. The Associated Press News Service.

Lake, E. (1990). An Indian father's plea. *Teacher, 2* (1), 49–52.

Littlebear, D. (1992). Getting teachers and parents to work together. In J. Reyhner (Ed.), *Teaching American Indian students.* Norman, OK: University of Oklahoma Press.

Locust, C. (1988). Wounding the spirit: Discrimination and traditional American Indian belief systems. *Harvard Educational Review, 58,* 315–330.

Martinek, T. (2000). Challenges. In D. Hellison, N. Cutforth, J. Kallusky, T. Martinek, M. Parker & J. Stiehl (Eds.), *Youth development and physical activity: Linking universities and communities* (pp. 245–248). Champaign, IL: Human Kinetics.

Martinez, P. (1999, May 9). Arizona antidote to Indian dropout rates: Tucson charter school mixes a classic curriculum with Native American. *Christian Science Monitor,* p. 3.

Nichols, B. (1994). *Moving and learning: The elementary physical education experience* (3rd ed.). St. Louis: Mosby.

Placek, J. H., Doolittle, S. A., Ratliffe, T. A., Dodds, P., Portman, P. A., & Pinkham, K. M. (1995). Teaching recruits' physical education backgrounds and beliefs about purposes for their subject matter. *Journal of Teaching in Physical Education, 14,* 246–261.

Reyhner, J. (1992). *Teaching American Indian students.* Norman, OK: University of Oklahoma Press.

Sparks, W. G. (1994). Culturally responsive pedagogy: A framework for addressing multicultural issues. *Journal of Physical Education, Recreation, and Dance, 65* (9), 33–36; 61.

Staurowsky, E. J. (1999). American Indian imagery and the miseducation of America. *Quest, 51,* 382–392.

Sutliff, M. (1996). Multicultural education for Native American students in physical education. *Physical Educator, 53* (3), 157–163.

Van Horn, R. (1999). Inner-city schools: A multiple-variable discussion. *Phi Delta Kappan, 81,* 291–298.

Velez Arias, H. O. (1999). A multi-case study of physical education teachers and working conditions in inner-city schools. *Dissertation Abstracts International, 59* (7–A), 2422.

Wanko, M. (1997). Managing diversity at a large urban high school. *High School Magazine, 5* (2), 26–29.

Waxman, H. D., Huang, S. L., & Padron, Y. N. (1995). Investigating the pedagogy of poverty in inner city middle level schools. *Research in Middle Level Education, 18,* 1–22.

WEB RESOURCES

The following web link list was generated upon publication of the text; however, over time, the sites may become obsolete if an organization dissolves, discontinues online services, or relocates to a different URL. If a link listed below does not connect, please search for the organization by name.

http://www.search-institute.org/

Search Institute, a nonprofit, independent research organization based in Minneapolis, Minnesota, has identified 40 concrete, positive experiences and qualities—developmental assets—that have a tremendous influence on young people's lives and choices. These include family support and adult role models, equality and social justice, and sense of purpose. The bad news is that the vast majority of young people in the United States—regardless of race, ethnicity, age, gender, cultural background, religion, or income level—experience too few of the assets. Indeed, on average, young people report experiencing just 18 of the 40 assets. This web site is filled with research and other information about the developmental assets and how individuals, organizations, and communities can—and are—working to ensure that all children and youth throughout the community experience more of these developmental assets.

http://www.indiancountry.com/

Indian Country is the nation's leading Native American news source. The paper examines current issues and provides editorials and other information relevant to the Sovereign Nations.

http://www.public.iastate.edu/~savega/amer_ind.htm

This list of Native American web sites includes selected Native American web resources useful for academic research and information purposes.

CHAPTER 14

Helping Students Change—
Keys to Motivation

Scenario

Tara and Billy have always been overweight. They sit in the bleachers dreading their turn to be called out to complete the sit-ups test. Testing is not the only area of physical education where their weight has been a disadvantage. Because they are not very dynamic athletically, both Tara and Billy are rarely included in the game play components of their lessons—not that they mind. The gym is small, and not everyone can play at one time. Besides, they hate having to struggle with activities that look so easy for the slimmer and more athletic individuals. Both Tara and Billy know that changing their exercise and dietary habits would help lessen their obesity problems; they just can't find anything about PE that motivates them.

Introduction

It is doubtful that we could find a single teacher who has not had students in class who could be described as unmotivated or who seem not to value physical activity. Of course, this is not a situation specific to physical education. Each of you reading this book probably had one or two courses in high school or university that were not immediately attractive or may indeed have even been boring. Although most students will persist with a particularly boring course in high school or college in order to "do enough work to pass," those of us in physical education are concerned with more long-term goals. We are hoping to motivate students to embrace a lifetime of physical activity—to motivate them to adopt physical activity as a significantly meaningful component of their lifestyle.

We are hoping to produce through physical education some form of *behavior change* in many of our students. That change, of course, is one from inactivity or limited activity, to an embracing of activity as a positive component of their lifestyle.

Our main concern regarding behavior change is that we help students become self-motivated (intrinsically motivated). We know that although we can have some control over students' work in the school setting, we have no control over their lives either outside school or when they leave school. We have spent time in earlier chapters discussing how we can help students become independent in designing their own fitness programs; this chapter outlines how we can help them become independent behavior change agents.

So What Do We Know?

Ferrer-Caja and Weiss (2000) write that the strongest predictors of intrinsic motivation, effort, and persistence are task goal orientation, perceived competence, and the learning climate. Vlachopoulos and Biddle (1997) also suggest that task orientation and perceived competence are needed for adolescents to derive positive affective experiences from physical education. Perceived competence refers to individuals' conception of how much ability they have, while having a task orientation includes a belief that effort and outcomes are correlated (i.e., effort will lead to personal progress and mastery).

These components of physical education settings seem to have some impact on post-school activity levels. Duncan (1993) reports that higher levels of perceived success, personally controllable attributions, companionship, and esteem support have been found to influence positively adolescents' motivation toward

We participate in activities in which we perceive we have competence

activity. This in turn influences their future expectancies for success and enjoyment in physical activity outside school. That is, students who were put in situations where they could be successful and where they had some control over their subject matter were more likely to continue to be active. The activities and curriculum projects described in this book are designed to promote student success and empowerment.

Understanding Behavioral Change

In devising a physical education program that will help students to adopt more active lifestyles, we first need to teach formally the strategies necessary for behavior change. People rarely wake up one morning and suddenly change their behavior. Whether they want to go from being a smoker to a nonsmoker, or from living a sedentary lifestyle to an active one, people are more likely to go through a change process that involves various stages.

Prochaska (1984) has identified five stages of change that people move through in a sequential manner as they attempt to modify their behavior. Describing the "transtheoretical model of behavior change," Prochaska identified five progressive stages (Figure 14.1).

Precontemplation is characterized by a person's lack of intention to change his or her behavior in the foreseeable future. This may be due to the fact he or she is uninformed of the long-term consequences of current behavior or is discouraged about past attempts to change.

When the individual acknowledges that he or she is seriously thinking about making some change but has not taken any specific action, the person is said to be in the *contemplation* stage. We have all experienced this stage—maybe even in completing some of the assignments in this book!—and we often spend considerable time in this stage telling ourselves that we will (eventually) get around to it.

The *preparation* stage involves making a formal plan to take action. It is one stage that people move out of very quickly as they either move into action or slip back into simply contemplating some future action.

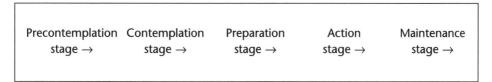

Precontemplation stage →	Contemplation stage →	Preparation stage →	Action stage →	Maintenance stage →

Figure 14.1 Five progressive stages of behavior change.

Source: Concept from Prochaska (1984).

The *action* stage sees specific attempts by individuals to modify their behavior. They may begin to exercise, may go without cigarettes, or may choose to resist high-fat foods. Prochaska and Marcus (1994) suggest that this stage is quite "unstable" and has a high risk of relapse.

When an individual consistently adheres to the new behavior, he or she is said to be in the *maintenance* phase. Although many experts state that a person must have sustained the new behavior (or kept to a new schedule) for at least 21 days before it can be called a habit, others argue that maintenance is attained only after at least 6 months in the action stage.

The diagram presented in Figure 14.1 suggests that behavior change is a linear process. However, Prochaska (1984) argues that behavior change has a circular nature. To this end, he provides a "revolving-door" schema to better describe the typical pattern of change behavior (Figure 14.2).

As can be seen in the figure, there is a potential for "relapse" as well as "points of exit" from the cycle; that is, people will progress to a certain point in the change cycle, but they always must reenter at the point of contemplation.

Let us examine each of the stages of change from the position of helping students learn about themselves and become more motivated to become or remain active. For each stage, we will examine the typical characteristics of a person in

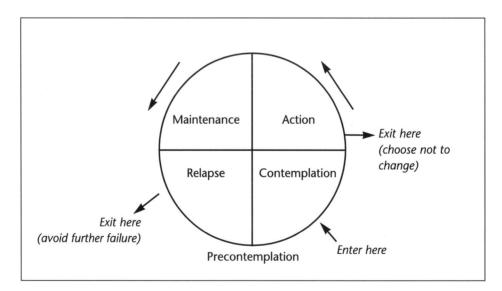

Figure 14.2 Revolving-door schema of change behavior.

Source: Prochaska (1984).

that stage, the processes that are occurring during that stage, and what form of helping relationship we as teachers can provide during these stages.

Precontemplation

Characteristics

The following list describe the attributes of someone who has not yet contemplated becoming active (or more active), together with quotes you may hear from them:

- Denial—"I don't need to be active, besides, I do enough already."

- Defensive—"That's easy for you to say; you don't understand."

- Deny responsibility—"Well, the teachers never make us do anything."

- Rationalize—"There is nowhere that I can go and exercise, anyway."

- Resistance to change—"I don't like getting all hot and sweaty."

- Apathetic—"It's just too much bother to go through to do all that stuff."

Processes

Two processes at this stage can help move the person to at least think about the potential for becoming active. These include *consciousness-raising* and *social liberation*. Consciousness-raising involves helping the person become conscious of the self-defeating defenses that get in the way of change. It is a time when teachers can provide students with opportunities to examine their lifestyles and to discover the parts of their thinking that seem to preclude them accepting the prospects of change.

The other key area of consciousness-raising lies in gaining information. In order to perceive problems clearly, the individual needs access to accurate information about ways to exercise, the need for only moderate to vigorous physical activity (MVPA) rather than strenuous work in order to gain a health benefit, and all the different activities that the person can engage in.

At this stage of consciousness-raising, teachers can post activity bulletin boards in their weight rooms or gyms, providing information and activity cues that serve to heighten awareness. Students should be made aware not only of the health benefits of exercise, but also of the psychological and other affective advantages that can be gained. Further, the message that exercise can be thought of as additive (you accumulate minutes per day) and that it need not be aversive should also be foregrounded.

Consider for example, one consciousness-raising exercise—the concept of "The Power of 5" (see the accompanying box).

The Power of Five

The next five minutes will pass. It will pass quickly. You can use it for fitness or lose that time forever.

- In just five minutes you can go from being a couch potato to taking an invigorating walk.
- In just five minutes you can do a complete body stretch and loosen up those stressed, tight muscles.
- In just five minutes you can stop eating a junk food snack.
- In just five minutes you can move your body around and burn 20 calories.
- In just five minutes you can make a different choice about exercise.

Source: Reprinted with permission from Lynn Kennedy: http://www.fitnessmotivation.com/

The second process involves creating more alternatives for students who have not thought about change. Defined as social liberation, we need to offer choices for individuals and public support for those who want to change; that is, we need to provide at least a safe environment in which our students can be active. It is also critical to make this environment attractive through the presentation of relevant and engaging activities that stimulate students' desire for change.

Helping Relationship

During the precontemplation stage, your teaching role is to help break the defenses of those students who have not considered the prospects of becoming active. It is a sort of "getting out of the darkness" problem. Your task is *not* to nag, push, or enable. Your challenge is to help students become aware of the defenses they are building and to help them recognize that you are there to help them.

Contemplation

Characteristics

The contemplation stage is accompanied by both positive and negative characteristics. On the one hand, the person is now more aware and open to change. But on the other hand, he or she also may be in a state of procrastination. As people mull over changing their behavior, they may be engaging either a fear of failure or perhaps ambivalence toward changing.

Processes

Students at this stage should be encouraged to conduct a form of *self-reevaluation*. This reevaluation is an emotional and cognitive appraisal of the problem behavior and the self—it follows naturally from consciousness raising. The students should evaluate both the present (negative or nonengaging behaviors) with the positive future possibilities, with the end result being an altering of perception about the effects of a particular behavior on one's lifestyle.

The contemplation stage is also a time for *emotional arousal*; that is, while keeping in mind that there are no quick solutions, the person should call on their emotions to bolster the resolve to change.

Helping Relationship

The role of the helper during the contemplation stage is to empathize, listen, and provide a form of caring about the person that is not accompanied by the imposition of "conditions." For example, statements such as, "I know you will do the best you can," should be offered as support for those who are considering the effort to change.

Preparation

Characteristics

During the preparation phase, the student is in a position to "go public"; that is, the student is not only planning to commence exercising (which includes developing a plan of action), but also making some level of commitment. Going public is a process of making formal the plan to change some behavior, be it to oneself, to a teacher, or to a friend or group of supporters.

Making a plan is part of the "I can do it!" strategy for enhancing the prospects of remaining on track to become active. Some specific techniques for this plan include the following:

- Set goals—be specific, and aim for a goal that is doable and measurable. For example: "Monday, Wednesday, and Friday, I will spend 20 minutes of my lunch break walking."
- Put it in writing—write down goals that are realistic, fun, and small.
- Get comfortable—find an exercise form that is fun to do and that you can look forward to.
- Plan for rewards—there is no need to postpone gratification until the final goal is reached. Appreciate the day-to-day benefits that come from exercise, and plan for small rewards for participation and persistence.

- Prepare for the unexpected—things do not always work out with a written plan, so it is useful to plan for setbacks. In that way, you will be in a better position to handle them.

Processes

Self-reevaluation is also a process engaged during this preparation stage. The major difference between this stage and that of contemplation is that now is the time for making change a priority, rather than a possibility. This is the beginning of the point at which the person will begin to turn away from the old behavior. The preparation phase is future oriented—it involves a *commitment*, a willingness to act. Further, preparation must be accompanied by the belief in one's ability to indeed change.

Helping Relationship

When students are in the preparation phase, it is very important for the teacher to help them set realistic goals. It is a time for the teacher to be assertive and proactive—to tell students how proud you are of them, and to offer help in cases where they might feel overwhelmed. Again, however, it is critically important not to nag. For example, asking, "When are you going to get started?" may serve to decrease the students' belief in their ability to change, especially if they sense that you (by nagging) are giving the impression that they cannot do it.

Action

Characteristics

The action phase is characterized by progress, accompanied by assertive and motivated behavior. The student is now completing some exercise, or if he or she has already been active, making further progression toward a higher goal.

During this stage, the student is also able to counter some of his or her previous problem behaviors (e.g., playing many hours of video games) by engaging in the planned behavior (e.g., spending 30 minutes each afternoon walking the dog on the neighborhood golf course).

Processes

Numerous processes are taking place during the action stage. First is a *commitment*, characterized by a willingness to act and a belief in one's ability to change. As noted in the planning phase, a *reward* process should accompany this commitment. Rewards may be as simple as self-congratulation but are perhaps more effective when they are formalized and planned for. They act as an incentive.

A second process that takes place during the action stage is *countering*. Countering is the process of substituting healthy responses for problem behaviors. This can include active diversions (such as going for a walk when one is tempted to play "just one more game" on the playstation), or it can be in the form of counter-thinking—replacing negative thoughts with more positive ones. For example, "I know I will feel really good about myself if I go work out for just 20 minutes" replaces the original thought of "Mary can't do it with me today, and I don't feel really energetic."

The third process that is put in place during the action phase is *environmental control*. Here, the person is active in changing the situation, either through avoidance (e.g., not even turning on the computer game), through the use of reminders (e.g., notes, calendars, or clocks), or through recognizing the cues that trigger one's problem behavior. In the case of exercise, these cues are often in the form of distractions or excuses. For example, one can learn to recognize that thoughts such as "I really should go to the video store and see if that new DVD is in yet," is often just self-talk for "I don't really want to go work out." Having the capacity not to succumb to these negative self-suggestions is a skill that can be learned but must be practiced. Teachers can help students practice this cue exposure.

Helping Relationship

Apart from helping students recognize the self-defeating temptations they may experience, teachers should be particularly positive to students who are taking action. They should boast to them about their progress and remind them not to forget to neglect the rewards that were planned.

Apart from this reactive helping role to student engagement, perhaps the teacher's greatest contribution to the action stage is to provide an environment that is both inviting and safe, both physically and affectively. The teacher can, for example, ensure that the weight room has equipment that is appropriate for use by all students, not just the strong and gifted. Likewise, the teacher can provide an instructional climate that focuses on effort and mastery, rather than surpassing normative-based standards.

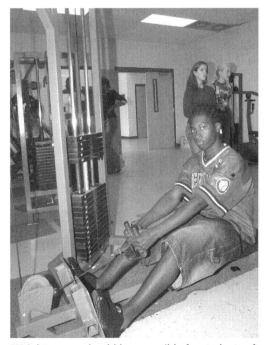

Weight rooms should be accessible for students of all fitness levels

Maintenance

Characteristics

On reaching the maintenance stage, the person has successfully revised his or her lifestyle. The person has in some way controlled his or her environment so that countering and active diversion are now not so much tactics to be employed, but rather natural processes. Short-term goals have been achieved, and the person now is working toward more long-term objectives.

Nevertheless, there is the potential for relapse (see Figure 14.2). Overconfidence and disproportionate expectations are two factors that can lead to relapse. Likewise, some other problem behavior not previously encountered (e.g., a change in class or work schedule or the recent unavailability of a facility) may change the environment sufficiently that the person does not maintain the positive behavior.

Processes

As noted, those who are successfully maintaining their changed behavior not only are *committed*, but also are successfully *countering* problem behaviors and focusing their energy on positive outcomes.

Helping Relationship

The teacher still has a role to play during this stage. Students may need assistance in revising their contracts, expanding their initial efforts, or setting new goals. In addition, these students can be encouraged to help someone else who might be in the earlier stages of precontemplation, contemplation, or preparation.

Those who have reached a maintenance stage but then experience a relapse often blame themselves for this condition. The teacher in this case can provide a helping relationship by not letting students be too hard on themselves and helping them to set new goals.

Setting a Class Climate Conducive to the Development of Behavior Change

There is no point in teaching the specific strategies for behavioral change if we continue to present a physical education curriculum that fails to be relevant or engaging to students. We as teachers, then, also need to change. We need to present a climate for students that gives them the freedom to make decisions, to make mistakes, and to learn to fix them. We need to provide them the opportunities to become self-motivated.

Research has shown that a mastery motivational climate has important effects on motivation and achievement in physical activity. Several studies have examined students' perceptions of class climate and have determined that those who viewed the climate as mastery oriented were more task involved, believed success was due to effort, experienced greater satisfaction and less boredom, and rated their improvement higher (see Carpenter and Morgan, 1999).

Spray (2000) also found that students who continued to be active after leaving school had recalled their physical education programs as having a prevailing mastery climate. In his study of high school graduates, Chen (1998) noted that the learning approach could also have implications for students' perceptions of boredom; students become bored in situations where they have little control over their learning (e.g., in a performance-oriented climate). Further, this boredom often represents itself in resistance to participate.

Ames (1992) has designed an intervention to foster a motivational climate based on six dimensions of the classroom structure. Known as TARGET, the keys to implementation revolve around the concepts of task, authority, recognition, grouping, evaluation, and time structure.

Task

According to Ames (1992), interest in learning associated with a mastery orientation is more likely to occur when the tasks involve variety, novelty, diversity, challenge, and short-term goals. Also, students are more likely to approach and engage in learning consistently when they perceive meaningful reasons to engage in the activity. Features of the

A mastery-oriented climate should include novel and challenging tasks

task that help to achieve desirable mastery motivational climate include (1) discovery or problem-solving structure, (2) variety of tasks, (3) level of difficulty that fits individual or small group needs, (4) individual realistic goals, and (5) short-term goals. Inclusion of these factors should result in the adoption of a mastery goal orientation, which in turn enhances motivation.

Reflect on the content sections presented in this book as they relate to these features. Table 14.1 presents a summary of the relationships.

Table 14.1   Relationship between Task Features for Mastery Motivational Climate and the Content Presented in This Book

Task Feature	Component of Content Accommodating This Feature
Problem solving	• Weight training and aerobic conditioning—students determine what areas of their fitness need improving and design programs to take effect. • Sports courses—students solve problems concerning maximizing team resources during sport education seasons, design team practice sessions, and solve strategic problems as they relate to their own team's strengths and weakness. • Adventure education programs are essentially problem based—students are placed in numerous positions where the task provides inherent challenges.
Variety	• Weight training and aerobic conditioning—students are able to choose from a variety of exercise programs to meet their goals; teaching a variety of fitness solutions helps students make personal choices. • Sports courses—students are able to take differing roles in different sport seasons; the nature of the games and scrimmages provides for frequent changes in opponents. • Adventure education—by its very nature, no one adventure problem remains the same; even the climbing wall has different routes to success.
Appropriate level of difficulty	• Weight training and aerobic conditioning—students work at intensity levels that match their goals and current fitness status. • Sports courses—students are given voice in determining the rules of games; some seasons allow for the division of teams into mini-squads where players compete against opponents of their similar ability level. • Adventure education programs allow for a specific matching between perceived ability and risk. Students can take different routes up a climbing wall or can modify their level of "extreme" on a mountain biking course.
Realistic and short-term goals	• Weight training and aerobic conditioning—students are encouraged to set personal goals relating to progress and improvement. • Sports courses—students devise practice sessions to achieve goals of team improvement and success in competition. • Adventure education programs—students can set individual goals concerning their level of challenge.

Authority

Ames (1992) suggested that involving students in decision-making situations enhances intrinsic motivation toward learning. Motivation is also increased when teachers support student autonomy by allowing students to pace their learning, to establish priorities, and to develop self-management and self-regulatory strategies.

Authority is also associated with the notion of control. Lepper and Hodell (1989) suggested that one potential source of intrinsic motivation involves providing students with a sense of control. They state that

> *empowering, and hence intrinsically motivating, learning environments will be those in which the student's outcomes may vary greatly and as a direct function of his or her own responses. Activities and environments that undermine a learner's sense of control, by contrast will have detrimental effects on subsequent motivation and interest.* (Lepper & Hodell, 1989, p. 92)

Table 14.2 provides examples of opportunities for authority that students can be afforded in the activities proposed in this book.

Table 14.2   Relationship between Opportunities for Authority and Autonomy and the Content Presented in This Book

Content Area	Opportunities for Authority and Autonomy
Weight training and aerobic conditioning	• Students are able to work on the exercises of their choice. • Students can choose to use free weights or machines to complete weights exercises. • Students can elect either walking courses, step aerobics, or cardio karate classes to achieve aerobic fitness goals.
Sports-based courses	• Students become members of a sport board that determines many of the operating functions of the sport season. • Teams are afforded independent practice sessions under the direction of a student-coach. • Teams are free to create their own identities.
Adventure education	• Students are able to choose their own solutions to adventure problems (e.g., in team challenges or at an individual level on a climbing wall). • All adventure education operates through a concept of challenge by choice.

Recognition

Recognition is concerned with the use of rewards (both formal and informal), incentives, and praise. Epstein (1988) suggests that maintaining or enhancing students' motivation to learn can be achieved by (1) recognizing and rewarding individual progress and improvements, (2) creating opportunity for rewards, (3) giving recognition and rewards in ways that do not derive their values at the expense of others, and (4) focusing on self-worth.

The key component as it relates to the development of a mastery climate is that recognition and rewards must be carefully planned to avoid social comparison. Although certain components of sport education do indeed salute the victorious team(s), it should be noted that (1) success in sport education comes from more than just winning games and (2) students are encouraged to become part of the recognition process. That is, rather than the teacher being the source of rewards, the sport board sets policy regarding the types of rewards and the criteria for earning them. Table 14.3 shows the implications of recognition as they relate to the content presented in this book.

Grouping

Teachers can enhance students' motivation toward a mastery orientation by providing flexible and heterogeneous grouping arrangements and allowing students

Table 14.3 Implications for Recognition and Reward and the Content Presented in This Book

Content Area	Implications for Recognition and Reward
Weight training and aerobic conditioning	• Recognition should be for individual progress and improvement, rather than comparison among class members. • Students should be involved in designing their own rewards for reaching specific fitness targets. • Fitness test awards should be based on criterion-referenced standards rather than norm-referenced standards.
Sports-based courses	• Awards for "hustle," "effort," and "teamwork" can be included alongside awards for the most successful teams. • Students can have a significant role in the process of awarding recognition. • Teams are encouraged to recognize progress by individuals within their ranks.
Adventure education	• Rewards for successful completion of challenge tasks are essentially intrinsic. • Because challenge is individually determined, teachers should avoid public comparison of achievements (e.g., "Students who have achieved the gold level climbs are [list of names]"). A simple task for one student might be Mount Everest for another.

multiple grouping opportunities (Epstein, 1988). In weight training and aerobic conditioning classes, this means that students should be able to choose their own workout partners. In team-building problem tasks in adventure settings, groups should contain students across gender, race, and skill dimensions. Teams in sport education should also be diverse.

Evaluation

Nicholls (1989) asserts that when students are evaluated publicly, many may become concerned about the adequacy of their ability. This in turn increases the student's tendency to evaluate himself or herself in terms of "ability as capacity"; that is, instead of focusing on how much effort is needed to achieve a goal, the student tends to focus on his or her ability as a limiting factor. Levine (1983) has also found that where teachers focus on social comparison (how one compares with relevant others), the students are continually overwhelmed with information about their peers' performance, and their own interest in learning subsequently decreases.

Where evaluation is based on comparing one's present level with one's prior achievements (that is, improvement), ability as capacity is deemphasized. When students perceive that effort is valued, they view mistakes as part of learning; when the focus is on self-improvement, they are more likely to seek new challenges and new opportunities.

Epstein (1988) lists four evaluation strategies that encourage students' mastery orientation. These include (1) using criteria of individual progress, improve-

Providing feedback encourages mastery

ment, and mastery; (2) providing evaluative feedback; (3) involving students in self-evaluation; and (4) creating a reasonable opportunity for students to experience success from their efforts. Table 14.4 provides examples of how these strategies can be applied to the content of this book.

Time

In this context, time deals with the appropriateness of the workload, the pace of instruction, and the amount of time allocated to completing learning tasks (Ames, 1992). To promote a mastery orientation, teachers should incorporate a flexible schedule for students of all abilities by providing enough instructional time for students to learn the skills and complete coursework.

Developing a Mastery Climate in the Fitness/Sports Club and Project-Based Learning

You will recall from Chapters 10 and 11 that the fitness and sports club and project-based learning approaches to secondary school physical education both adopt many of the features common to mastery climate settings. Table 14.5 provides a summary of the accommodation of TARGET strategies in these two settings.

Table 14.4 Evaluation Strategies Promoting a Mastery Climate and the Relationship to the Content Presented in This Book

Evaluation Strategy	Component of Content Accommodating This Feature
Individual progress, improvement, and mastery	• Testing in weight training and aerobic conditioning classes focuses on fitness gains, rather than peer comparisons. • Checklists in sport education seasons provide details of students' mastery on selected skill and game play components. • Adventure programs are evaluated on student mastery of specific outdoor skills.
Providing evaluative feedback	• Criterion-referenced fitness data are provided to students following testing. • Peer and teacher checklists of game skills are provided to students. • Most adventure programs have built-in feedback mechanisms as part of their tasks.
Involving students in self-evaluation	• Students in fitness courses can self-test according to self-selected fitness goals. • Sport education seasons use checklists for self-evaluation and reflection. • Students can write reflective accounts of their effort and mastery of many adventure skills.

Table 14.5   Accommodation of TARGET Strategies Afforded by a
Fitness and Sports Club and through Project-Based Learning

TARGET Strategy	Fitness and Sports Club (FSC) and Project-Based Learning (PBL) Accommodations
Task	FSC—variety of tasks to suit students' motivations; multiple opportunities for active participation
	PBL—students actually design the learning tasks themselves
Authority	FSC—flexibility in choice of activity; drop-in/drop-out capacity of the health club; opportunities to include activities from settings outside the school
	PBL—opportunities for students to participate in decision making of the project; opportunities for leadership roles; freedom to choose learning activities
Recognition	FSC—student workout logs include individual recognition of accomplishment
	PBL—students present their materials at a forum that can include other students, teachers, administrators, and parents
Grouping	FSC—students can choose to work out with a partner or join a class
	PBL—students determine their own project groups
Evaluation	FSC—private consultations between the teacher and student regarding progress
	PBL—students design their own assessment structure for the project
Time	FSC—students are all on individual, independent time schedules
	PBL—given that these projects typically occur during extended lessons (block scheduling), significant blocks of time are available to work toward project goals

IN-SCHOOL TASKS

Measuring the Mastery Climate

Visit a nearby high school and ask to observe one or two physical education lessons. Using the TARGET checklist provided in Table 14.6, describe the prevailing motivational climate of these lessons. In your report, give specific examples to demonstrate the aspect of the climate you witnessed. Include, too, some reflective comments concerning how this climate seemed to affect student motivation.

Measuring Motivation

During one of your field experiences, have the students in a class complete the "Exercise Motivations Inventory" [http://www.bangor.ac.uk/~pes004/exercise_motivation/scales.htm]. Have the students score the tests and examine

Table 14. 6 Checklist of TARGET Strategies for Mastery and Command Climates

TARGET Strategy	Mastery Climate	Command Climate
Task	• Variety of tasks for each skill • Active participation during the entire lesson	• Less variety of tasks for each skill • Less participation during the lesson
Authority	• Opportunities for students to participate in decision making • Opportunities for leadership roles • Freedom to choose activities	• All class decisions are presented to the students (i.e., no student input) • No opportunities for leadership roles • No freedom to choose activities
Recognition	• Recognition of student effort, accomplishment, or improvement	• No recognition of student effort, accomplishment, or improvement
Grouping	• Heterogeneous, flexible grouping of students	• Students grouped according to ability or gender
Evaluation	• Knowledge of performance and results provided during the execution of activities • Evaluation based on effort	• Knowledge of performance and results provided • Evaluation based upon peer comparison
Time	• Variable amount of practice time for each skill	• Same amount of practice time for all students

which scales are strongest for them. From these data, reflect on the content they are currently receiving in physical education, and judge whether it is meeting these students' motivational needs.

PORTFOLIO SUGGESTIONS AND ARTIFACTS

Consciousness-Raising Bulletin Board (S4–D2, P1: S5–P2)

Design a template of a bulletin board that you could place in your gym, locker rooms, or weight room that would serve as a stimulus for those who have not adopted exercise as a potential lifestyle component. What materials would you include on this bulletin board? What messages would you include to create awareness about the health, affective, and social benefits of exercise?

Show on your template the layout of your materials, including space for students to make contributions to the bulletin board.

REFLECTION TIME

Now that you have read this chapter, how confident do you feel in

- teaching students the specific processes of the transtheoretical model for behavior change?
- taking the role of "helper" during the change process for your students?
- creating and adopting a mastery motivational climate in your physical education lessons?
- giving students authority in your classes for various levels of decision making?

REFERENCES

Ames, C. (1992). Classroom: Goals, structures, and student motivation. *Journal of Educational Psychology, 84*, 409–414.

Carpenter, P. J., & Morgan, K. (1999). Motivational climate, personal goal perspectives, and cognitive and affective responses in physical education classes. *European Journal of Physical Education, 4*, 31–44.

Chen, A. (1998). Perception of boredom: Students' resistance to a secondary physical education curriculum. *Research in Middle Level Education Quarterly, 21* (2), 1–20.

Duncan, S. C. (1993). The role of cognitive appraisal and friendship provisions in adolescents' affect and motivation toward activity in physical education. *Research Quarterly for Exercise and Sport, 64*, 314–323.

Epstein, J. (1988). Effective schools or effective students? Dealing with diversity. In R. Hawkins & B. MacRae (Eds.), *Policies for America's public schools* (pp. 89–126). Norwood, NJ: Ablex.

Ferrer-Caja, E., & Weiss, M. R. (2000). Predictors of intrinsic motivation among adolescent students in physical education. *Research Quarterly for Exercise and Sport, 71*, 267–279.

Lepper, M. R., & Hodell, M. (1989). Intrinsic motivation in the classroom. In R. Ames & C. Ames (Eds.), *Research on motivation in education: Vol. 3* (pp. 73–105). New York: Academic Press.

Levine, J. (1983). Social comparison and education. In J. Levine & M.Wang (Eds.), *Teachers and students perceptions: Implications for learning* (pp.111–134). Hillsdale, NJ: Erlbaum.

Nicholls, J. G. (1989). *The competitive ethos and democratic education*. Cambridge, MA: Harvard University Press.

Prochaska, J. O. (1984). *Systems of psychotherapy: A transtheoretical analysis*. Homewood, IL: Dorsey Press.

Prochaska, J. O., & Marcus, B. H. (1994). The transtheoretical model: Applications to exercise. In R. K. Dishman (Ed.), *Advances in exercise adherence*. Champaign, IL: Human Kinetics.

Spray, C. M. (2000). Predicting participation in noncompulsory physical education: Do goal perspectives matter? *Perceptual & Motor Skills, 2000*, 1207–1215.

Vlachopoulos, S., & Biddle, S. J. H. (1997). Modeling the relation of goal orientations to achievement-related affect in physical education: Does perceived ability matter? *Journal of Sport and Exercise Psychology, 19*, 169–187.

WEB RESOURCES

The following web link list was generated upon publication of the text; however, over time, the sites may become obsolete if an organization dissolves, discontinues online services, or relocates to a different URL. If a link listed below does not connect, please search for the organization by name.

http://www.bangor.ac.uk/~pes004/exercise_motivation/scales.htm

The Measurement of Exercise Motivation Site contains a number of exercise motivation tests that you or your students can complete. The tests also come with scoring systems. Two of the tests are the Exercise Motivations Inventory, a measure of participation motives or reasons for exercising, and the Behavioral Regulation in Exercise Questionnaire, which measures degrees of self-determination for exercise.

CHAPTER 15

Understanding and Working with the Micropolitics of Physical Education

Scenario

School A: The art teacher shaved his head and let the kids paint on it.
    (He was out the next year.)
School B: The art teacher shaved his head and let the kids paint on it.
    (He won the school's teacher of the year.)
School C: The physical education teacher proposed a plan for a climbing
    wall in the gym.
    (She was told this would be disruptive for the fans during basketball games.)
School D: The physical education teacher proposed a plan for a climbing
    wall in the gym.
    (She was funded by the principal to complete a certification course in lead climbing, and the art teacher offered to paint the wall in a mountainscape after it was built.)

Introduction

As you can see from the scenarios above, there are no set "rules" that govern all teachers' behavior. What is acceptable or even applauded in one context is frowned upon in another. Further, it seems like these "rules" are often not made explicit to beginning teachers, but rather are learned over time. Indeed, some of the role demands of teachers in schools are simply assumed. What is of significant consequence, however, is that a teacher who fails to meet implicit (or unclear) demands adequately will usually see his or her status fall within the school or academic department (see Schempp, Sparkes & Templin, 1993).

As a beginning teacher, then, one of your first tasks is to attempt to understand the micropolitics of the school culture. "It is through micropolitics that newcomers learn the traditions and trademarks of the culture that give meaning to established practices and patterns of daily school life (Schempp et al., 1993, p. 461). More simply, your challenge is to determine the vantage points from which power is exercised, to learn who has the capacity to make decisions, and to understand the consequences of those decisions. Usually, this power is central to the administration of the school, but in the case of physical education, there may also be a pernicious influence from athletic directors. Consider for example, a school where on rainy days, students in physical education cannot use the gymnasium because it is basketball season and the floor might get messed up (true story!).

Those wielding power within a school can also be friends of physical education. It is not always necessary that they be foes. Rovegno and Bandhauer (1997) comment that in schools with outstanding physical education programs, the administration trusted their teachers; encouraged professional development; supported teachers' decisions, programs, and special projects; and also provided adequate funding. Davis and Wilson (2000) also found significant relationships between a principal's empowering behaviors and teacher motivation. The more principals participate in actions that share responsibility with teachers, the greater the impact teachers feel they are able to make by fulfilling work-related tasks, and the more likely they are to see that they have choices in selecting actions that will lead toward positive outcomes.

This chapter will address two concerns of beginning teachers—(1) gaining a position as a beginning teacher, and (2) being able to gain acceptance and status within the workplace. Specific strategies will be proposed in both cases that should help make the transition from university student to professional educator somewhat more satisfactory than if one were to take blindly the first available job.

I feel at this point, however, that I must present a personal but relevant caveat. If your first priority is to seek a particularly attractive coaching position within a school, without regard to your role as a physical educator, then it is perhaps a chance for you to closely examine whether or not sports coaching can rest comfortably with the task of providing an outstanding physical education program. I speak for most in the physical education teacher education (PETE) professorate that few of us have seen examples where this is indeed the case.

Getting Your First Job (or Changing to Another)

One of the biggest challenges for beginning teachers is to make their voices heard, to be treated seriously and with respect, and to be able to put in place a curriculum envisioned as engaging and relevant for students. Macdonald (1995) has described two possible scenarios of the workplace. Teachers who find their work valued and challenging, and their work contexts professional and supportive, describe a strong sense of belonging to their school and a moral obligation to help their students. Macdonald (1995) notes that the nature and contexts of those teachers' work reflected aspects of *professionalization*, such as autonomy, authority and responsibility, and a sense of intellectual and social commitment. Dissatisfied teachers spoke of many ways in which their work was out of their control, where they lacked authority and autonomy, where they were consumed with administration and concerns that were peripheral to the task of teaching, where they felt unrewarded, and where they felt manipulated by bureaucracies and the school communities. When teachers lose control over the administrative decisions as well as the social and intellectual goals of their work, it can be interpreted as indicative of *proletarianization*, a condition described as the escalation of disempowering work (see Densmore, 1987). Teachers who become disempowered will often leave the profession or may simply burn out and become apathetic. With regard to teacher motivation, the situations described above (a sense of autonomy and control) do not seem very different from the motivational climate described in Chapter 14, which has been shown to promote student learning!

It is particularly valuable then, for a prospective teacher to spend time visiting a school, speaking with its administration and teachers, and watching classes in action before choosing to take employment. This scenario, however, is not always possible. School may not be in session when a position becomes available, and in some cases, job interviews are conducted with the school board, the superintendent, and/or others now removed from the workforce that the demands for the position entail.

One of the challenges of selecting a place of work is in determining the quality of a physical education program within a school. Although many teachers *believe* they have a quality program, there are certain markers that can be used as "sighters of quality." The process of identifying these markers can be thought of as "Deception Detection"— yes, it can be a harsh way to explain the process, but it is accurate nonetheless.

To activate Deception Detection, one simply has to ask teachers in schools or a school's principal four key questions. These questions, together with an explanation of their relevance and interpretation, are presented below. The questions are presented in two forms (1) what you actually *do* ask, and (2) what you *really* want to know (known hereafter as WYRWTK).

Visiting with a school's administrators will help you choose the right employment

Deception Detection: Phase 1

Your question	*"Can you show me a copy of your work program and key activity/testing dates?"*
WYRWTK	Have you seriously considered a program of study based on the current state course of study, the national physical education standards, and the needs/voices of students in your school?
Deception detection	1. Does the teacher actually *have* a written work program?
	2. Can the teacher find the program and access it quickly?
	3. Does the program look like it is used and followed, or does it appear more like a document that was written once as some required task and then shelved as a "well, that's done" task?
	4. Are there identifiable dates for testing, presentations, field trips, or other notable events listed in the work program? Are the dates from this year?

If the answer to any of these questions listed above is no, then "buyer beware"—deception as been detected. It would seem clear that this program is a series of ad hoc units of instruction banded together to take up time, or worse, a series of "roll out the ball" experiences that serve little purpose beyond trading-off marginal compliance from students for minimal levels of active participation in class.

However, having a quality work program on paper is not sufficient condition for having a quality physical education program. Evidence of active conduct of a work program is provided through the documentation of the work it produces. See Deception Detection, phase 2.

Deception Detection: Phase 2

Your question	*"Can you show me any samples of student work (e.g., tests, assignments, portfolios, or videos)?"*
WYRWTK	Do you assess student performance at any level beyond dressing out, attendance, and some level of participation?
Deception detection	1. Can the teacher show you any work samples?
	2. Can the teacher find these samples and access them quickly?
	3. Is there a video in the office?

These questions will at best require teachers to explain their assessment and evaluation systems, and their verbal responses will give you a strong insight into their philosophies about assessment. Teachers who can indeed show you samples of student work (particularly if it is clearly catalogued and easily retrieved) would seem to have a sense of responsibility not only to student learning, but also to other pedagogical and professional functions.

Artifacts of student work can be used to provide examples to current students about the standard required for the present work. Students should be assisted in developing high-quality work if they can see specific samples from their peers. Documenting and collecting student work samples does not only serve as an aid to other students. Teachers can use students' work to validate their own program goals and to showcase their physical education program within the teachers' own professional portfolios.

Failure to collect and store students' assessment artifacts shows that assessment is seen as frivolous and as a superficial component of a physical education program. This failure to collect artifacts may also suggest a lack of teacher pride, given that most of us enjoy showing off outstanding examples of student work.

Deception Detection: Phase 3

Your question	*"Can you tell me of or show me ways in which you have showcased the physical education program within this school?"*
WYRWTK	What level of advocacy do you have for physical activity/education beyond your group?
Deception detection	1. Can the teacher show you any examples? 2. Can the teacher tell you of any in-school activities?

When we enter almost any elementary school, we almost need a machete to clear a path through the forest of student work decorating the walls, ceilings, and classrooms. Everywhere we turn we see samples of student projects, of their writing, and also of other learning/teaching aids. Add these to the fish tanks, the miniature forest, and the ongoing science experiments, and we can all recall the days when our own classes were dynamic sites of teaching and learning.

There are numerous opportunities for teachers of high school physical education to showcase students' work and promote physical education within the school. The simplest is through the development of a bulletin board. Although this may occupy space only within the gym, there are also other groups who use this facility. Where students are involved in project-based learning settings, opportunities should be taken to invite students, faculty, and administrators to any formal presentations by students.

Where videotape films have been made of physical education projects, these may be shown throughout the school in high-traffic areas (e.g., the lunch room). Remember the teacher from Ohio who makes a weekly ESPN SportsCenter version of "Plays of the Week?" He documents scenes from various sport education seasons and telecasts these throughout the school each Friday.

While Deception Detection, phase 3 is not a prerequisite for debunking claims of a quality program, one will get some perspective about the extent to which the physical education faculty holds its program in sufficiently high esteem to showcase it to the rest of the school. Furthermore, is highlighting physical education activities any different from a coach wanting to provide publicity and garner support for a school athletic team?

Deception Detection: Phase 4

Your question	*"Can you show me or tell me about ways in which you promote physical activity in general, or physical education specifically, to the community outside the school?"*
WYRWTK	Does it even come to pass that parents' perceptions of physical education are often, at best, ones that trivialize the subject and see it as secondary to the more important mission of schooling?
Deception detection	1. Are there regular newsletters that go home (either independent of other school documents or as part of a school newsletter)? 2. Is there a physical education web page that people can access to learn about and be kept current regarding the program?

The teacher's response to this question will be a continuation of the response from phase 3. If they have in-school promotions, they will probably extend that opportunity to tell you of a web page. In any case, teachers with a strong level of efficacy about their programs are often active in publishing theirs and students' work to wider audiences. The National Association of Sport and Physical Education (NASPE) has produced an advocacy kit that can assist in presenting one's physical education program in a good light. Nonetheless, the existence of a web site is not conclusive proof of a quality program; some web pages may just be "window dressing" for programs that do not deliver what they claim.

The Micropolitics of Teacher Induction (Now That You Have a Job)

Schempp et al. (1993) make a number of particularly relevant and important comments about beginning teachers. First and foremost, they note that simply by becoming a new faculty member (even before you do anything), you have changed the complexion and social balance of your work group. Further, your acceptance within that group depends on your being seen as a positive addition. You as a newcomer must prove your nerve in the workplace, but you also need to understand that this must be achieved within the conventions of acceptable practice for that school setting (like, for example, the practices of elementary school art teachers referred to earlier). If you are able to achieve this, then you are usually accorded full-member status. The greater your status, the greater your capacity to alter the thoughts and actions of the group. Let us hear from Ed, a beginning teacher, about his challenge of learning all the expectations.

> *The most difficult thing for me as I adjust to this school are all of the policies and procedures of the school itself. Things such as procedures for sending progress reports, how to set up special testing conditions for my special education students, what paperwork is involved in giving a detention, etc. . . . The real world of teaching has had so many more things than I would have thought I'd be doing. . . . I feel like there are so many things that are job- and school-specific that you have to take on and that the physical education part is not the total package.* (from Curtner-Smith, 2001, p. 91)

Your beliefs about teaching will also be challenged as you attempt to meet the demands and expectations presented to you by schools. You will be coming fresh out of college, excited that you have all this new knowledge, wanting to put in place all those things you have learned. Unfortunately for many newcomers, this level of great enthusiasm comes across as arrogance to many teachers who have been in the profession for a long time. These veteran teachers have established traditions and perceptions, which you as a beginning teacher must be able to reject, accept, modify, or accommodate while walking a thin line between alienating them and injecting your own brand of pedagogy. This challenge will be exacerbated in the cases where veteran teachers believe that all of their learning is from experience and not from going to college. You as a new teacher face the prospect that these teachers believe you need to be "trained in the ways of the real world."

Take time to understand the various role demands you face

Your challenge, then, is to examine the micropolitical components that govern the school and the physical education department and to understand the various role demands placed on you. In many cases, for you to be accepted, your primary task is to be able to demonstrate that you can discipline a class. Your survival will hinge on your being able to gain control over students. Failure to meet this demand certainly will result in lower status. Unfortunately, the concept of giving students voice and choice (indeed, the whole notion of empowering students—see Chapter 5) may run counter to the traditions and perceptions of many teachers.

For some beginning teachers, then, the strategy of survival becomes one of staying silent and accepting the situation within which one is working. Schempp et al. (1993) call this the "society of the silent." The teacher does all the "right" things, does not make waves, and does not offer opinion. Unfortunately, the silent teacher can have little impact on school change.

As noted, one of the first challenges is to find a school that you believe, even before you take a position, is one whose norms are bound in trust and encouragement. Gaining employment in such a setting should pose fewer problems in terms of your fitting in. Even so, Rovegno and Bandhauer (1997) list a number of strategies through which a teacher can gain status and, with it, the capacity to influence thoughts and actions. These include the following:

- participating in formal school committees and projects
- initiating voluntary projects and acquiring funds and space to support the physical education program

- attending to school politics (paying attention to the issues and concerns of others and the impact of school organization structures)
- telling motivational stories in day-to-day interactions with colleagues

The Notion of Collegiality

Collegiality is significantly important to beginning teachers in influencing their attitudes toward work. Where colleagues provide an environment of encouragement, support, and even humor, beginning teachers find it easier to cope with their work. As Macdonald (1995) notes, however, certain staff-room cultures can be damaging to the beginning teacher's outlook on the profession. She comments that the most difficult working environments are those in which the senior member of the physical education staff fails to respond when beginning teachers, particularly the females, are harassed or exploited, or when the staff-room culture is unmotivating.

In discussing collegiality, we must be aware that it is rather a broad term. Little (1990) presents four dimensions of collegiality to help us understand the differences. These include a progression from storytelling and scanning for ideas, to the provision of aid and assistance, to sharing, and finally, to joint work. Table 15.1 provides some examples of these forms of collegiality within physical education.

Essentially, as one moves from storytelling to joint work, teachers become more and more *inter*dependent. There is an increase not only in the frequency and intensity of the teachers' interactions but also in the prospects for conflict and the probability of collective judgment. As one moves more and more to joint work with colleagues, the individual teacher loses a degree of autonomy. Little (1990, p. 512) notes that "with each shift, the inherited traditions of noninterference and equal status are brought more into tension with the prospect of teacher-to-teacher initiative on matters of curriculum and instruction." This loss of privacy and noninterference may be one explanation as to why more teachers do not move beyond the level of scanning for ideas (often about student behavior rather than substantive curriculum matters) and providing some assistance. Let us hear again from Ed, as he describes this situation in his school.

> We almost never meet as a group to plan the use of facilities, or discuss issues, or exchange ideas. . . . Our department is very much a group of individuals rather than a team. There is not much professional interaction or exchange of ideas as a group. . . . Primarily, our interactions are short conversations in the hallways between classes but we sometimes go days without much interaction at all. (Curtner-Smith, 2001. p. 92)

A beginning teacher, then, who wants to initiate major innovations that require the work of more than one teacher (e.g., project-based learning or the development of a fitness and sports club) has to move through a process. The first step is to establish credibility within the academic department; the second is to convince colleagues (and oneself)

Table 15.1   Levels of Collegiality and Applications to Physical Education

Level	Characteristics	Examples in Action in Physical Education
Storytelling and scanning for ideas	• Teachers are nearly totally independent. • Contacts are opportunistic ("I need something"). • Contacts are sporadic and informal. • Teachers gain information and assurance in the quick exchange. of stories.	✔ "Watch out for that class in the 6th period—they are pretty wild in the locker room." ✔ "Have you noticed how most of the girls stick to the arms and calves in the the weight-training classes, while the boys all do the 'beach muscles'?"
Aid and assistance	• Mutual aid is readily available. • Help and advice are given *when asked for.* • There is a boundary between offering advice when asked and interfering. • Questions are rarely concerned with substantive issues about the business of teaching.	✔ Offers of assistance in explaining rules and protocols to a beginning teacher. ✔ Help in ordering equipment for physical education lessons.
Sharing	• Materials and methods are shared; there is open exchange of ideas and opinions. • Teachers may reveal much or little of their thinking or practice in the materials and ideas they share. • Sharing appears to depend on the extent to which teachers value the dual concepts of noninterference or a collective commitment to experimentation and mutual support.	✔ Providing ideas about successful ways to introduce aerobics lessons to boys. ✔ Sharing written tests of knowledge for a weight-training unit. ✔ Lending a series of task cards that another teacher can use during a water aerobics circuit.
Joint work	• Encounters among teachers rest on shared responsibility for the work of teaching. • Joint work involves collective action, that is, teachers' decision to pursue a single course of action in partnership. • Teachers jointly decide on a set of basic priorities that in turn guide the independent choices of individual teachers. • Teachers are motivated to participate with one another to the degree that they require each other's contributions in order to succeed in their own work.	✔ Teachers from physical education, English, and biology form an interdisciplinary team to design a weeklong activity-based excursion to an upstate trout river. Students will be canoeing on the river and tagging fish as part of a conservation project. ✔ Teachers from math, chemistry, and physical education share a concern about conducting lab classes in the block schedule. They meet daily over lunch to discuss what they are finding from different action research projects in their classrooms. ✔ Members of a physical education department decide on criteria and procedures for evaluating students' participation in out-of-school activity that counts toward credit for a wellness unit.

Source: Modified and reproduced with permission of Blackwell Publishing, Malden, MA.

Collegiality is important as new teachers begin their careers

to move into a more public domain of curriculum construction—a domain wherein teachers cannot hide. In Ed's case, he formed friendships with a group of five male classroom teachers from other subject areas. In their mid-to-late 20s and described as "committed professionals," these colleagues taught math, history, and economics. Ed would often eat lunch with this group and talk about serious issues relating to politics and schooling. For Ed, these teachers were a major source of professional support (Curtner-Smith, 2001).

So You Want Others to Work with You?

In your attempts to put in place some forms of innovation (even if this innovation is just your own teaching style and its accompanying accountability system), you may find several forms of resistance. That resistance can come from multiple sources. Fellow teachers may present challenges and obstacles, including the following:

1. We've always done it this way.
2. The students will get bored in a long unit.
3. We don't have the facilities to do that.
4. We can't use the gym (or weight room) at those times; the sports teams are using them.

To garner the support of other teachers in helping you achieve major teaching projects, you need first to understand the nature of teacher's work. As Little (1990, p. 530) comments:

Schoolteaching has endured largely as an assemblage of entrepreneurial individuals whose autonomy is grounded in norms of privacy and noninterference and is sustained by the very organization of teaching work. Teachers are now being pressed, invited, and cajoled into ventures in collaboration, but the organization of their daily work often gives them scant reason for doing so. Longstanding occupational and organizational traditions, too, supply few precedents; rather, they buttress teaching as a private endeavor. Finally, there are high transaction costs to participatory work—most prominently in time (an opportunity cost) and the risk of conflict (a cost to organizational cohesion).

Your challenge, then, is to help teachers believe that their contribution will not come at an extensive time loss to them and that you are willing to work alongside them and value their input. In some cases, *you have to do all the work and suck up the criticism!* As you saw in the scenarios at the beginning of this chapter, with innovation comes uncertainty, particularly if it involves group work. As Little (1990, p. 530) notes

Group settings more readily reveal the uncertainties of the classroom. Although the promise of praise and recognition is greater, so too is teachers' exposure to criticism and conflict. Will more collective involvement reduce the uncertainties of the classroom—or only serve to expose them?

Working together can be challenging but greatly rewarding

Students can also provide obstacles for the new teacher. Despite the exhortations of community groups who suggest students want higher standards and harder work, a teacher will quickly discover that any new program (read: new program with higher levels of accountability) provides immediate obstacles. Where a new, different, or more exacting program either threatens students' ability to socialize and have fun during class or presents barriers to passing physical education with a minimum of work, students will quickly invent strategies to enhance socializing and resist taxing work. For a new teacher (or any teacher initiating a more rigorous program of action), the first challenge is to market to the students that their social agendas need not be compromised and, indeed, in many cases will be enhanced.

Certainly, none of the innovations presented in this book present a pedagogy that could not be seen as engaging or accommodating the students' social agenda. However, from a pragmatic stance, it may perhaps be better to market the positive social agenda for students in the first instance and gradually elaborate on the increased academic work that accompanies these innovations.

IN-SCHOOL TASKS

Program Sophistication

Arrange to visit a nearby high school and speak with the head of the physical education department. The purpose of this exercise is to examine the extent to which this program is demonstrating practices that would suggest a high or low status of physical education within the school.

Consider in your discussion the following four issues: program goals, assessment, school-home links, and advocacy. The answers you get should provide you with deep insight into the role and place of physical education within the school.

1. "Could you show me your overall curriculum plan?"
   - Can they?
   - Does the document look up to date?
   - Are there *specific* dates listed in the document for testing, reporting, reviewing?
   - Does the document look as though it has been recently reviewed?
   - Could the teacher instantly *locate* the document?
2. "How do you assess students, and can you show me some examples of student work?"
   - How *do* they grade? By dressing and attendance? By attitude and effort? Where does fitness testing fit in? Are skills assessed, and how?

- Can they show you any samples of student work—such as workbooks, computer printouts of exercise programs, photographs of projects, videos of skillful performance, or student portfolios?
- How accessible are the assessment artifacts? Does the teacher have to search for them, or are they readily filed and retrieved?

3. "Could you show me any communications you make between school and home, such as newsletters, a physical education web page, or other notices?"
   - Can they?
   - What format do these take?
   - Does the teacher make any contribution to school newsletters?
   - How does this teacher feel about school-community links?

4. "What interactions do you have with the rest of the school?" How do you market physical education to the faculty and students?"
   - Are there ever any public displays of physical education student work—such as field days or open house days, or presentation of projects?
   - Do you involve teachers from other disciplines (e.g., science or computing) in any PE programs?
   - How accessible is the physical education facility to students and to teachers who are not involved directly in physical education (e.g., is the weight room open before or after class hours?)
   - Do you run an intramural program?

Reflection

- To what extent do you think this program is complying with or resisting current practices of "the same old–same old" physical education? What evidence did you see or hear to support your assertions?
- Does this program act, look, or feel "tired"? Is there an air of dynamic excitement, in which vigorous attempts are being made to provide a relevant and engaging pedagogy to students—or does the program seem to be one that maintains the status quo?
- Which of the four answers surprised you the most? Which were the most predictable?
- Would you like to work in this school? Why or why not?

PORTFOLIO SUGGESTIONS AND ARTIFACTS

Designing an Interdisciplinary Unit (S9–D1, P6)

Select a unit of work you may choose as part of an "introduction to wellness" course. In what ways could you use the resources of teachers in other subject areas to enhance learning and instruction in this unit? What would be some of the micropolitical issues involved in setting up this collaboration (e.g., use of lab space, instructional commitments by the other teachers)?

Writing a Résumé (S8–D1, P3)

Now that you are ready to enter the job world, one of the most important tasks is to secure an interview with a potential employer. The most common practice for this is to create a résumé. A useful web site is listed at the end of this chapter to provide assistance in creating a résumé.

REFLECTION TIME

Now that you have read this chapter, how confident do you feel in

- being able confidently to ask "tough" questions in a job interview?
- being able to get a solid understanding of the professionalism of a physical education department on visiting them?
- your commitment to teaching a quality program, even in conditions that are not truly supportive?
- being able to become politically active within a school setting?

REFERENCES

Curtner-Smith, M. D. (2001). The occupational socialization of a first-year physical education teacher with a teaching orientation. *Sport, Education and Society, 6,* 81–105.

Davis, J., & Wilson. S. M. (2000). Principals' efforts to empower teachers: Effects on teacher motivation and job satisfaction. *The Clearing House, 73,* 349–354.

Densmore, K. (1987). Professionalism, proletarianism, and teacher work. In T. Popkewitz (Ed.), *Critical studies in teacher education: Its folklore, theory, and practice* (pp. 130–160). Lewes, England: Falmer Press.

Little, J. (1990). The persistence of privacy: Autonomy and initiative in teachers' professional relations. *Teachers College Record, 91,* 509–536.

Macdonald, D. (1995). The role of proletarianization in physical education teacher attrition. *Research Quarterly for Exercise and Sport, 66*, 129–141.

NASPE (1999). *Sport and physical education advocacy kit* (SPEAK II). Reston, VA: American Alliance for Health, Physical Education, Research & Dance.

Rovegno, I., & Bandhauer, D. (1997). Norms of the school culture that facilitated teacher adoption and learning of a constructivist approach to physical education. *Journal of Teaching in Physical Education, 16*, 401–425.

Schempp, P. G., Sparkes, A. C., & Templin, T. J. (1993). The micropolitics of teacher induction. *American Educational Research Journal, 30*, 447–472.

WEB RESOURCES

The following web link list was generated upon publication of the text; however, over time, the sites may become obsolete if an organization dissolves, discontinues online services, or relocates to a different URL. If a link listed below does not connect, please search for the organization by name.

http://www.jobweb.com/Resumes_Interviews/default.htm

Includes details about successful interviewing (including nine sure-fire ways to blow an interview), building great résumés, writing expert cover letters, and computer-friendly résumé tips.

Sample Season Plans

Sample Season Plan: Aerobics

Background Details

- 20 lessons (50-minute lessons)
- 36 students
- 6 teams of 6

Objectives

- develop cardiovascular fitness
- learn and improve aerobic dance skills
- develop choreography skills
- develop skill in designing an aerobics routine that includes recommended elements

Team Roles

Captain

- leads practice
- assists students with skill development

Choreographers (2)

- collate ideas for team sequence and develop the formal routine
- prepare music tape/CD for the final routine

Judges (2)

- make rule decisions concerning the inclusion of all required elements in the final routine
- award points for (a) skill, (b) synchronicity, and (c) choreography during final routine

Scorekeeper
- records team scores on the endurance challenges
- calculates personal health standards using the selected fitness test

Table A.1   Season Outline

Lesson	Activity	Description
1	Selection of activities Introduction to the concept	Discussion of season format: i.e., teams, competition, designing their own routines, etc.
2	Aerobic endurance testing	Teach students to measure pulse. Complete aerobic test: 12-minute run/walk or 1-mile run.
3	Team selection Election of captains	Teacher announces teams (minimum of 6). Students select captains (discuss qualities of captains). Teams develop names and are allocated home areas in the gym. Teacher announces season plan.
4	Concept of warm-up	Teach warm-up principles. Teams develop their own warm-up (points awarded for various categories being covered).
5–9	Movement skills	Teacher directs class on aerobics movements. Teacher allocates 10 minutes at the end of each lesson for team practice and routine preparation.
10	Introduction to judging and competition format	Students learn judging techniques. Students elect judges/timekeepers/scorers from their teams.
11	Endurance competition team challenge	Each team will perform the preset routine provided in lesson 5. This is an 8-minute routine where points are earned for continuous performance with correct technique.
12–14	Step skills	Teacher introduces step aerobic movements.
15	Routine judging and criteria development	Students and teacher collaborate on the rules of routine design.
16–18	Routine design and preparation	Teams begin routine design and practice.
19	Routine competition	Teams present their final routines. Formal judging by a student panel. Optional: videotape the routines.
20	Run-walk competition	Repeat the activity from lesson 2. Awards ceremony for individuals/teams with significant improvement.

Possible Awards

- Endurance competition winners
- Most improved endurance scores
- "Healthy Heart" awards for all students exceeding the age-related health criteria from Fitnessgram or President's Challenge
- Best overall final routine
- Most synchronized final routine
- Most outstanding choreography

Sample Season Plan: Basketball— Moderate Skill Level

Background Details

- 20 lessons (50-minute lessons)
- 36 students
- 6 teams of 6 (split-squad 2 × 3)—each team has an A and B team

Objectives

- develop skills of the game of basketball
- improve shooting and rebounding skills
- improve defensive skills
- develop faking and passing tactics
- learn the rules and protocols of basketball
- increase awareness and compliance with the concepts of fair play
- achieve competence in nonplaying roles
- increase personal responsibility

Team Roles

Captain

- leads practice
- determine the team's line-ups

Team manager

- completes prematch score sheets with line-ups from the captain
- collects team uniforms and equipment prior to practices and matches

Referees (2)

- manage contests in terms of starting time
- make rule decisions

Scorekeepers (2)

- record ongoing scores
- compile final scores for each game
- update the tournament table
- also act as game timekeepers

Statisticians (2)

- record shots on goal and goals scored
- record rebounds
- record interceptions
- update own team's records with data sheets from other statisticians

Table A.2   Season Outline

Lesson	Activity	Description
1	Introduction ** Season plan ** Elect sports board	Explain rules. Conduct a skills challenge—(shooting and dribbling). The data will be used by the sport board to select even teams.
2	Training camp ** Announce teams	*Dribbling skills:* • 1 on 1 vs. defender • Use of both hands • Initial teacher instruction followed by independent team practice time • Student designed game—"design an authentic dribbling circuit to promote the use of both hands"
3	Training camp ** Team names	*Passing skills:* • Lead passes • 2 vs.1 cut and pass • Initial teacher instruction followed by independent team practice • Student-designed game—"design a 3 vs. 3 keep-away game focusing on lead passes"
4	Training camp ** Team roles	*Shooting skills:* • Outside and inside shooting • Shooting free throws • Shooting against a defender • Initial teacher instruction followed by independent team practice

Table A.2   Season Outline *(continued)*

Lesson	Activity	Description
5	Training camp ** Rules test	*Line-up options:* • Offensive and defensive positions • Practice using formations in pick-up games (intrasquad scrimmages)
6	Training camp	*Rebounding skills:* • 1 on 1 box out • Basic positioning • Initial instruction followed by independent team practice time • Student-designed game—"design a 3-on-3 game where scoring is by rebounding"
7	Preseason ** Presentation of game management protocols	*Outline of scrimmage process:* • Team practices
8–11	Preseason ** 3 vs 3 scrimmages	10 minutes before games for team warm-up/practice 15-minute games with 5-minute change-over Game 1—A v B (C) Game 2—A v C (B) Game 3—B v C (A)
12–17	Formal competition ** 3 vs 3 games	2 x 10-minute halves 2-minute team line-up changes at half time if required
18–20	Play-off rounds and championship	

Rules

- 3-a-side games.
- Teams develop an A and B side.
- On transition, teams need to take the ball beyond the 3-point arc.
- All players must contact the ball once on each possession (does not include offensive rebounds).
- All jump ball decisions take place at the free throw line.
- All fouls are awarded 1 free throw.
- All other basketball rules apply.

Table A.3 Referee's Report

Team Name		Team Name
Fair play points (circle one)		*Fair play points (circle one)*
3 = excellent		3 = excellent
2 = minor challenges		2 = minor challenges
1 = major challenges		1 = major challenges
0 = complete lack of respect		0 = complete lack of respect
MVP from this team		MVP from this team
Player with the best effort/hustle		Player with the best effort/hustle
Best sporting attitude		Best sporting attitude

Scorekeeper's Report

The winning team was _____

They defeated _____

by a score of [   ] to [   ]

Chart A.1 Statistics Sheet

Team	Shooting 0 = made shot X = missed shot	Rebounds O = offensive D = defensive	Fouls
Name			
Name			

Sample Season Plan: Golf—on a Block Schedule

Background Details

- 25 lessons (90-minute lessons)
- 30 students
- 6 teams of 5

Table A.4 Season Outline

Lesson	Activity	Description
1	Introduction	Discuss the unit. Conduct a preliminary round.
2	Stance, body position, and swing	Teacher demonstration and student practice.
3	Driving	Class practice of driving. Incorporate long irons.
4	Driving	Continue driving practice. Discuss rules of the course and the game.
5	Hit the course	Review rules and regulations. Divide into groups of 3 and play as many holes as possible in 75 minutes.
6	Chipping	Pitch, bump, and run. Practice.
7	Chipping	Continue from lesson 6.
8	Sand shots	Bunker play, rules, and practice.
9	Team selection	Explain scoring procedures. Foursomes play.
10	Rehit the course	Continue first playing round.
11–14	Team and individual practice	These sessions allocated to team practice.
15	Match play	Teams of 5 play 9 holes. Best 4 scores are turned in.
16–19	Team and individual practice	These sessions allocated to team practice.
20	Match play competition	Teams of 5 play 9 holes—best 4 scores are turned in.
21–24	Team and individual practice	Continue team skills practice.
25	Full round and awards ceremony	18-hole shootout. Six groups of 5: #1s or captains all play together, #2s play next, etc. Final awards presented.

Roles

Captain

- lead practice
- develop line-ups

Scorekeepers

- pause after every hole to record all 5 scores
- ensure all players sign their cards
- turn in cards to statistician

Statistician

- keeps record of team and individual scores
- keeps log of team best scores, best individual round, pars and birdies

Course referee

- makes decisions about rules pertaining to competition

Statistics/Awards

All scores will be kept by the cardholder for the duration of the 9 or 18 holes. All scores must be recorded following the completion of each hole. Immediately following the match, the scores are submitted to the statistician. Remember to count all strokes, including penalties.

Include the following categories:

- Most improved: from rounds 1 and 2 to the final day
- Best score for the final day from each team
- Top scorer in all five divisions
- Coach's award

Event Procedures

As you arrive at the course on the day of a match, find your team on either the driving range or the putting green. When all of your team members are present, you will receive instructions regarding which hole to begin with.

Use proper etiquette in every aspect of the game. Also remember the course management skills while playing. Your team will be playing fivesome, so remember to respect faster groups.

All scores are kept, but the best 4 count for team competition points.

Practice rounds are played over 9 holes; final rounds are played over 18 holes.

The following season plan can work for a golf unit that has fewer lessons (20) and shorter lesson times.

Table A.5 Season Outline

Lesson	Activity	Description
1	Team selection, student roles	Assign sports council to assist in team selection. Explain student roles. Have students sign fair play agreement. Explain the event for preseason and for formal competitions. Introduce the game of golf. Explain the differences in golf clubs and selection as far as distance. Explain and practice the golf grip for driving and putting.
2	Putting	Have sports council observe and evaluate individual groups practicing. Explain stance, putter, slope of the green, and its effects on putting. Teach the skill of putting. Practice from various distances. Explain ball marking, putting order, and repairing ball marks.
3	Chipping	Sports council continues to observe. Stance, alignment, and clubface relating to the ball. Teach chipping skills, out-of-bounds rules, taking a drop, and repairing divots.
4	Driving	Explain stance, alignment, and clubface relating to ball position. Practice with various clubs.
5	Putting	Assign teams and individual roles. Review putting. Uphill and downhill putting.
6	Putting: practice and statistics roles	Practice putting and tee drills. Review and practice the roles of referee and statistician for putting.
7	Chipping	Teach and practice club track drill and chip bucket drill. Practice chipping from edge of the green with wedge or 7-iron from various distances to targets.
8	Review and practice club tracking drill	Practice chipping from 30–60 yards to green.
9	Distance chipping	Practice from 60–120 yards to green. Review and practice referee and statistician role for chipping.
10	Driving	Practice driving at various distances to targets with 5- and 7-irons. Review stance, alignment, and clubface. Explain causes of hook and slice.
11	Driving: long irons and woods	Driving the ball to various distances with 3-irons and 5-wood.
12	Driving: long woods	Continue driving skills with 1- and 3-woods. Take oral test of all roles practiced and discussed.
13	Putting: intersquad scrimmage	Intersquad scrimmage of putting G1 v G2—hole 1; G3 v G4—hole 4
14	Chipping: intersquad scrimmage	Intersquad scrimmage of chipping G1 v G3—hole 5; G2 v G4—hole 7
15	Driving: intersquad scrimmage	Intersquad scrimmage of driving G1 v G4—hole 11; G2 v G3—hole 14
16	Putting competition	Each individual on teams is assigned a position on the green at various distances (2–12 feet from hole). Two teams compete at different greens while statisticians from other teams take scores. Each player has 6 balls.

(continued)

Table A.5   Season Outline *(continued)*

Lesson	Activity	Description
17	Chipping competition	Two teams compete from different fairways 30–60 yards from the green. Each player has 6 balls; the best ball out of the 6 counts. Scoring is to a target zone in 2-feet intervals (and 5-feet intervals) around the hole. Statisticians from other teams take scores.
18	Driving competition	Two teams compete from different tee boxes that vary from 130 to 160 yards. Each player gets 2 balls. The better of the 2 balls counts (design a target zone for skill level of students).
19–20	Team competition: 6-player scramble	Each team will compete at the same time from different holes ranging from 150 to 375 yards, playing from the red tees. The object is to get the ball in the hole in 6 tries. Each player on the team has one shot. The captain decides who takes which shot.

Roles

Captain
- informs team of daily competition area, leads practice and warm-up
- determines playing order for final competitions

Team manager
- distributes golf equipment in the area that is designated for practice
- fills out checklist for return of all equipment

Statistician
- fills out statistical forms during competition (lessons 16–18) and for own team during lessons 19–20
- measures distances within scoring areas for each team's points
- calculates individual scores for each player following competition

Referee
- receives stats sheets from the teacher
- distributes stats sheets to the statisticians
- checks that teams are properly represented
- begins competitions

Sample Season Plan: Floor Hockey

Background Details

- 20 lessons (30-minute lessons)
- 72 students
- 9 teams of 8 (split squad 2 × 4)
- 3 divisions of 3 teams in each division

Objectives

- develop skills of the game of floor hockey
- improve striking skills
- improve trapping skills
- develop faking and passing tactics
- learn the rules and protocols of floor hockey
- increase awareness and compliance with the concepts of fair play
- achieve competence in nonplaying roles
- increase personal responsibility

Team Roles

Captain

- prepares teams for matches
- determines team line-ups
- conducts beginning class warm-up
- sets leadership tone for the team

Referees (2)

- make decision about the rules and award free hits and goals
- judge out-of-bounds play
- refrain from showing favorites
- rate teams on fair play following each match

Scorekeepers (2)
- keep a running score of the match
- record the goal totals of each team
- nominate MVP and MFP (most fair player) in conjunction with referee

Statisticians (2)
- keep a record of shots on goal, goals, and fouls
- submit tally sheet after each match

Scout
- analyzes skills and weaknesses of future opponents
- assists captain in match preparation

Table A.6   Season Outline

Lesson	Activity	Description
1	Introduction	Explain the season plan. Announce rules. Complete a demonstration game.
2–5	Skills stations: pass, shoot, dribble	Class divided into 3 sets of 3 teams. 3 teams rotate through 3 stations—passing, shooting, and dribbling. 10 minutes at each station.
6	Preseason ** 2 × 8-minutes halves ** (X) = duty team	Courts 1 & 2: Team 1 vs. 2 (3) Courts 3 & 4: Team 4 vs. 5 (6) Courts 5 & 6: Team 7 vs. 8 (9)
7–8	Preseason	Complete internal round-robin with teams from day 6. Teams complete team analysis sheet following their 3rd game.
9–11	Preseason	Complete a second round-robin with one team from each of the previous groups (e.g., 1, 4, and 7). Teams prepare scouting reports on the teams in their division of the formal competition.
12–17	Formal competition ** 2 x 10-minute halves	3 conferences of 3 teams in each. Repeat preseason format, but with longer games.
18–20	Playoffs ** 2 x 10-minute halves	Gold, silver, and bronze division playoffs: • Top-ranked team from each division enters the gold division—play a round-robin format. • Second-ranked teams enter the silver division. • Third-ranked teams enter the bronze division.

Rules

- 4-a-side (minimum of one player of the opposite gender on each team).
- Sticks cannot be swung above the knee.
- No tripping or pushing.
- If ball is hit out by A, B gets a free push.
- You cannot score directly from an out-of-bounds push.
- A goal is scored when a player pushes the ball into the goal.
- You cannot kick the ball into the goal to score.
- After each goal, teams line up on the end line, ball rolled to nonscorers.
- Trapping allowed with sticks and feet—no hands (except goalie).
- A ball stopped by the goalie with the hands results in a face-off.
- Goalies cannot lie down in the crease.

Chart A.2 Referee's Report

Team Name	YES	NO	Team Name	YES	NO
Did this team play by the rules and not argue with the ref?			Did this team play by the rules and not argue with the ref?		
Did the players on this team encourage each other?			Did the players on this team encourage each other?		
Did the players on this team avoid getting angry when a teammate made a mistake?			Did the players on this team avoid getting angry when a teammate made a mistake?		

Scorekeeper's Report

The winning team was _____

They defeated _____

by a score of [   ]   to   [   ]

Chart A.3   Statistics Sheet

Team	Goals	Saves	Fouls
Name			
Name			
Name			
Name			

Scouting Report Card

Goaltender: Name _____

Right-handed or left-handed?

Strong side—right or left?

1 2 3 Rating

Defense: Who plays back? _____

Do they stay in position?   YES / NO

Are they quick movers?   YES / NO

Have they got good trapping skills?   YES / NO

Do they sometimes go up and try to score?   YES / NO

Forwards: Who are they? _____

Right- or left-handed?

Stick handling—can they shoot both sides?

Who is the main scorer? _____

Overall most dangerous player? _____

What tactics to stop this team? _____

Sample Season Plan: 5-a-Side Softball

Background Details

- 25 lessons (50-minute lessons)
- 30 students

Team Roles

Captain

- leads practice
- develops line-ups

Equipment manager

- is responsible for equipment
- reports equipment damage
- takes coolers with ice to dugouts

Umpires (2)

- manage contests
- one at home plate
- one at second base
- place bases out before play

Statisticians (2)

- keep book on all performance data
- summarize data across games for own team's records
- forward relevant data to sports reporter

Sports reporter

- takes team and game pictures
- writes post-match summaries
- submits material to class editor

Rules

- 5-a-side games.
- 3 bases—home, first, and second in a triangle.
- Batting team pitches to its own players (no restriction on where this pitch is made from).

- Ball must be in fair territory within two swings, or the batter is out (includes air swings).
- Ball must hit the ground *before* passing the imaginary (or chalked) line linking first and second base.
  - Following the 3rd inning, one player per team each inning is exempt from this rule.
  - Following the 6th inning, a second player is exempt.
  - In the 9th inning, all players are exempt.
- All other softball rules apply (e.g., force/tag plays, fly ball tagging up).

Table A.7   Season Outline

Lesson	Activity	Description
1	Introduction	Overview of unit coordination (team selection, etc). Sport board meets and captains are chosen.
2	Basics of fielding and catching	Students wear a number attached to shirts—captains rate performance of skills.
3	Basics of batting	Repeat #2 while students bat.
4	Scrimmage	Captains observe all players apply skills in a game context.
5	Explanation of rules and roles; meeting of Sport board and captains	Team selection. Other students learn rules and roles from the teacher.
6	Team announcement	Teams announced; roles determined in teams.
7	Place hitting	Review basic hitting; learn strategies of place hitting; practice in teams.
8	Student-directed within-team practice Rules test	Preparation for practice games—defensive and offensive practice.
9	3-inning practice games	A vs. B (Duty by C) . . . rotate. D vs. E (Duty by F) . . . rotate.
10	Team practice	Fielding—taking ground balls—throwing.
11	Bunting	Learn bunting skills; within-team bunting practice.
12	3-inning practice games	Supply a new playing schedule.
13	Base running	Learn base running strategies with team practice.
14	Student-directed within-team practice	Preparation for practice games—emphasis on base running skills.
15	3-inning practice game	Supply a new player schedule.

Table A.7   Season Outline *(continued)*

Lesson	Activity	Description
16	Throwing ahead of the runner Cut-offs	Throwing ahead of the lead runner. Cut-offs: when to use, where to throw. Team practice.
17	Student-directed within-team practice	Preparation for final games.
18	Double play and base coverage 20-minute practice games	Responsibilities of infield play; team practice.
19	1st day of competition (6-inning game minimum)	Have two games prepared on the schedule.
20	2nd day of competition (6-inning game minimum)	Have two games prepared on the schedule.
21	3rd day of competition (6-inning game minimum)	Have two games prepared on the schedule.
22	4th day of competition (6-inning game minimum)	Have two games prepared on the schedule.
23	5th day of competition (6-inning game minimum)	Have two games prepared on the schedule.
24	Semifinal playoffs	1 vs. 4 (6) 2 vs. 3 (5)
25	Consolation final Championship game Awards ceremony	6 vs. 5 2 winners from previous day MVP, Most Improved, Best Umpire, Best Sports, Statistical leaders

Statistics—Fielding

- Assists—where a player throws the ball to a person on base, who then makes an out.
- Out—the player making the out (receiving a throw on pass, making a tag, catching a fly ball).
- Error—a mishandling error or errant throw that prevents an out being made or allows a batter to advance a base.

Statistics—batting

- Bases—simply record the base that the batter *ends on* prior to the next batter (this is irrespective of opposition errors, fielders' choice).
- Scores will be either 1, 2, or 3.
- When a batter is safe at home, circle that batter's initial base record.

5-a-side Statistics Sheet: Fielding

Team Name Eagles	Assists	Outs	Errors
1. Player name *Jackie*	A A A A A 5	O O O 3	
2. Player name *Brandon*	A A A A 4	O O O O O 5	E 1
3. Player name *Teesha*	A A A A 4	O O O 3	
4. Player name *Demarcus*	A A A A A 5	O O O 3	E E 2
5. Player name *Tai*	A 1	O O O O O O O 7	

5-a-side Statistics Sheet: Batting

Team		Total bases	Total runs 4
1. Player name *Jackie*	0 ① 2 0 0	3	1
2. Player name *Brandon*	0 2 2 1 0	5	0
3. Player name *Teesha*	1 0 2 0 0	3	0
4. Player name *Demarcus*	③ ① 0	4	2
5. Player name *Tai*	0 1 ②	3	1

PHOTO AND ILLUSTRATION CREDITS

Photos
Chapter 1: pp. 4 and 6, Peter Hastie; p. 8, Jeffrey Lee; p. 9, Peter Hastie. **Chapter 2:** p. 16, Peter Hastie; p. 18, Michael Dickey; pp. 25 and 29, Peter Hastie; p. 30, Mug Shots/CORBIS. **Chapter 3:** p. 36, Michael Dickey; pp. 39 and 40, Peter Hastie; p. 41, Michael Dickey; p. 45, Steve Prezant/CORBIS. **Chapter 4:** p. 51, Michael Dickey; p. 54, Peter Hastie; p. 58, Michael Dickey; p. 62 (left and right), Peter Hastie; p. 64, Jeffrey Lee; pp. 66 and 70, Michael Dickey; p. 76, Peter Hastie. **Chapter 5:** pp. 82, 84, 88, 90, and 92, Peter Hastie. **Chapter 6:** pp. 105, 107, 109, 112, and 118, Michael Dickey; p. 119, Peter Hastie. **Chapter 7:** p. 130, Peter Hastie; pp. 134, 135 (left and right), 145, 146, and 147, Michael Dickey. **Chapter 8:** p. 161, Auburn University Photographic Services; pp. 169, 170, 173, 174, and 177, Peter Hastie; p. 181, Jeffrey Lee. **Chapter 9:** pp. 194, 200, 204, 206, 211, and 221, Peter Hastie. **Chapter 10:** pp. 234, 239, 244, and 248, Peter Hastie. **Chapter 11:** p. 257, Michael Dickey; pp. 261 and 264, Peter Hastie. **Chapter 12:** pp. 271 and 273, Michael Dickey; p. 277, CORBIS; p. 279, Michael Dickey; p. 282, Peter Hastie. **Chapter 14:** p. 314, Peter Hastie; p. 321, Michael Dickey; pp. 323 and 327, Peter Hastie. **Chapter 15:** p. 333, Melvin Smith; p. 338, Michael Dickey; and pp. 341 and 342, Peter Hastie.

Illustrations
Chapter 3: p. 44, Auburn University Student Counseling Services. **Chapter 4:** p. 53, Marian Hartsough; pp. 56 and 57, Centers for Disease Control; pp. 63 and 69, Marian Hartsough. **Chapter 5:** pp. 87 and 89, Marian Hartsough. **Chapter 6:** pp. 102 and 123, Marian Hartsough.